THE IMMORTAL LOVERS
Elizabeth Barrett and Robert Browning

ELIZABETH BARRETT BROWNING

From the portraits by
Lowes Dickinson, 1850

ROBERT BROWNING

The
IMMORTAL LOVERS

Elizabeth Barrett and
Robert Browning

A Biography by
Frances Winwar

But love me for love's sake, that evermore
Thou mayst love on through love's eternity.
E. B. B.

Harper *&* Brothers *Publishers*
New York

TO FRANCIS, MY HUSBAND

Where the heart lies, let the brain lie also . . . .

                                        R. B.

CONTENTS

Part One
PARALLEL LIVES

Chapter I: Mr. Barrett and His Young Genius

MR. BARRETT was pleased, as pleased as his rigorous nature would permit without doing violence to moralistic strictures against pride and vainglory. Yet he had good reason to be both proud and vainglorious as he held in his hand a little book hardly more than a pamphlet, bearing in bold print across the title page the words, THE BATTLE OF MARATHON. Then followed two verse quotations—a tribute to the Muses by Akenside, and Byron's famous apostrophe to "Ancient of Days! August Athena." Below appeared the name of the author, E. B. Barrett, in letters not too large for modesty yet not so small as to be self-effacing. Last of all one learned that the poem had been printed in London for W. Lindsell, of 87 Wimpole Street, in the year 1820.

Who was E. B. Barrett? The initials belonged equally to Mr. Edward Moulton-Barrett, to his son Edward, and to his firstborn, his daughter Elizabeth, in 1820 a girl of fourteen. The dedication of the four-canto epic cleared the mystery while gratifying the feelings of a stern, fanatical but devoted father. It read: "To him to whom 'I owe the most' and whose admonitions have guided my youthful Muse even to her earliest infancy, to the father, whose never-failing kindness, whose unwearied affection I never can repay, I offer these pages, as a small testimony of the gratitude of his affectionate child, Elizabeth B. Barrett. Hope End: 1819."

There were some members of the family who though still infants were yet sufficiently experienced to dread Mr. Barrett's admonitions, especially when accompanied by the resounding thunder of his wrath. For them his never-failing kindness and unwearied affection remained still to be proved. As for Mrs. Barrett, she had early made a virtue of self-withdrawal. With more than her share of meekness for a woman she bore her husband's children—twelve of them in unfailing succession—and otherwise lived a life of uncomplaining domesticity, not allowing her sweet and gentle spirit to be so soured by marital oppression as to affect her duties toward her family. In that household everyone knew who was lord and master and what

3

tributes he exacted. If sometimes flattery and dissimulation mingled with obedience, it was only to be expected. They are after all the adjuncts of tyranny.

Mr. Barrett, however, like all tyrants benevolent or otherwise, demanded obedience first, no matter what followed after. The impressions of a childhood in Jamaica where he was born had helped to form the mature mind. His own literal interpretation of the Old Testament on the relation of parents and children lent authority to his autocratic demands. As for his wife, she was his to love, honor, and obey him—with an emphasis on the last. Like his children she was as much his chattel as the black slaves had been to the wealthy plantation owners in Jamaica, as they still were to him, the heir to the estate. If the members of his family did not have iron bands round their necks proving his ownership, they felt nonetheless the invisible yet painful stranglehold of his possessiveness, all justified by divine authority mingled with a touch of eighteenth century rationalism. For Mr. Barrett's library did not exclude the writings of French and English philosophers and reformers. Indeed, he considered himself a liberal and a social reformer as well. Often, in the village of Ledbury near Hope End he would hold forth before the embarrassed yet grateful folk who, awed that the rich man should deign to instruct them, would listen in silence as he made suggestions for civic betterment or expounded texts for the improvement of their souls. His daughter Elizabeth rather than his son Edward accompanied him on these philanthropic excursions.

Perhaps because his own education had been incomplete he respected learning. He was taken to England as a child after his father's death and became the ward of Chief Baron Lord Abinger who sent him in due time to Harrow. The boy did not remain there long. The English school system of fagging gave him too unpleasant a taste of the brutality of which boys are capable and he, the son of slave owners, would not put up with it. So great was the pressure brought to bear by his wealth that the culprit was expelled and young Barrett himself taken out of school. He was later sent to Cambridge where he fell under the influence of the Greek classicist Richard Porson. But the youth was too impatient for life. At twenty he met Mary Graham-Clarke, daughter of a prosperous owner of spinning mills and glass works in the neighborhood of Newcastle-on-Tyne as well as of slaves in Jamaica, and decided to marry her. It was the first time love had entered his life. It was also the last.

Mary Graham-Clarke was gentle and malleable, qualities that Edward Barrett Moulton desired more than beauty, though she possessed it also. She was six years older than himself, and the fact that he had been able to attract a mature woman flattered his masculine self-esteem. At any rate he gave Lord Abinger no peace until he had won his consent to the marriage. It is said that after meeting Miss Graham-Clarke the guardian exclaimed: "I hold out no longer. She is far too good for him!"

On the 20th of May, 1805, the young man, still under age, entered earnestly into adult life, conferring upon his bride the redundant title of Mrs. Edward Barrett Moulton-Barrett. The second Barrett was added to the name when Edward and his younger brother Samuel became heirs to their vast Jamaican interests.

Edward Moulton-Barrett took his bride to Coxhoe Hall, Durham. There his mother, Mrs. Elizabeth Barrett Moulton, widow of Charles, lived with a companion and ward of her own age, a colorful and vivacious Creole, Mary Trepsack, called Treppy, and her other son Samuel. The house was huge and highly ornate in the Italian fashion with woodcarvings on mantels and stairs. It was set on an eminence, overlooking "the view" which was the aesthetic discovery of the moment when the mansion was built.

It was here that Mrs. Barrett bore her first child, on the 6th of March 1806. The little girl was given the name of Elizabeth after her grandmother, although she was not baptized until two years later when, together with Edward, the brother who came after her, she was taken to the font in Kelloe Church. Elizabeth had the distinction of being the first child of the West Indian plantation owning Barretts to see the light in England in more than a hundred years.

The family grew steadily. By the time Mrs. Barrett ceased bearing she had given her husband four daughters and eight sons. One of the girls, called Mary after the mother, died at the age of three. Henrietta and Arabel received names common in the Barrett family. The boys who followed Edward were duly baptized Samuel, Charles —always called Stormie for arriving into the world during a violent thunderstorm—George, Henry and Alfred. After that Mr. Barrett's list of Christian names seems to have been exhausted, so he called the two youngest in order of their arrival, Septimus and Octavius. The Latin sorted well with his classical leanings and added an impressive dignity to Barrett Moulton-Barrett.

It was his daughter Elizabeth, however, on whom he chose to fix his affection. Edward too, of course, was important as the legitimate heir and perpetuator of his name. The rest of his children, though cherished possessively in his fashion, formed merely the retinue of himself as the king and Elizabeth and Edward as the favored princess and prince. In the background Mrs. Barrett, insubstantial as a symbol, led her secluded life.

As an established paterfamilias of twenty-four Mr. Barrett thought it time to have a house of his own, no mere English manor but an impressive castle in the oriental fashion made popular by such romantic eccentrics as William Beckford whose holdings in Jamaica a Barrett relative had handled. So he bought Hope End in Herefordshire. The castle raised its domes and minarets crowded with spires and crescents amid a four-hundred acre stretch of English landscape circled by gentle hills and made stately by a grove of oaks. It had its formal gardens, but it had what was more important, limb room and spirit room wherein the children as they grew could exercise body and imagination. One of them certainly did both, with an ardor that glowed through her small, delicate frame.

Perhaps because he saw this physical fragility in Elizabeth Mr. Barrett sought to compensate it by inculcating spiritual strength. The methods were all his own. He would lift the little girl bodily and set her up on the chimney piece. "Stand up straight! Like a hero!" he commanded.

As she endeavored to obey him, standing as straight as the height and the insecure footing would allow, she felt, as she said, the walls growing alive behind her and extending two stony hands to push her down on the rug where the old dog, Havannah, lay in danger of being killed by her fall. But through her fear the indomitable voice rang out, "Straight—like a hero!"

She took her father's injunctions so much to heart that when, after her first reading of Homer she was given a flowerbed to plant, she cut the turf into the shape of a Trojan hero, a Hector of gigantic size, with gentianella eyes, a gilliflower nose, locks of flowing grasses, a helmet of daffodils and a breastplate of daisies. But then she would have selected her Hector whether or not Mr. Barrett had wanted to make a hero of her. She had begun to drink of the Pierian spring and the thirst was never to leave her.

If Mr. Barrett was a despot in his little kingdom he still knew when to relax his authority and become the playmate of his growing brood. Then there would be merry sport on the ample acres, cricket matches, running games, gallops on the horses and ponies with which the stables were furnished. The children had no lack of expensive toys, nor of delicacies from the West Indies, tamarind preserves and other exotic sweets. He also took care that both boys and girls had the advantages of their station. He bought a piano for Henrietta, the musical one of the family, and in a grand gesture also installed an organ in the Hope End hall. He had played the violin as a youth, but he seldom took it out of its case after his marriage. Making music was one of the childish things he had put away when he became a man.

Often "Granny" Moulton, accompanied by the lively Treppy whom the children adored, would come to visit, either from Coxhoe Hall or from her London house on Baker Street. Uncle Samuel was also a welcome visitor whenever the rum and sugar business did not demand his presence in Jamaica. The three made much of the Barrett children but Elizabeth very early took precedence over the rest as their favorite.

She was an endearing child in whom the good looks of her father softened to fragile beauty, gained further from the earnestness of a face that suddenly lighted into gaiety. In that household where the children learned to read almost as soon as they were able to speak, she astounded them all by her rhymed verses. By the time she was six she was the recognized Poet-Laureate of Hope End, an honor conferred upon her with a ten-shilling piece by the proud Mr. Barrett who marveled that so small a child could have rhymed to such purpose on the subject of Virtue.

Elizabeth's closest playmate was her brother Edward—Bro, as she called him. To him and to the whole family, she was Ba—short for Baby—the pet name he had given her. They were constantly together. Whether galloping in the fields or bending over a book, their hands clasped, their dark curls mingling, they doubled their joy in sharing it. Sam and Henrietta often joined them in their play, but it was understood that in such a close alliance they were participants by courtesy.

Mr. Barrett took greatly to heart his responsibility as a father. He had seen enough of the evils of lax living, even as a child, to direct himself sternly to follow the paths of that Virtue which his small daughter had learned so early to celebrate. Certainly, if not in Jamaica, he learned later of the illegitimate half-brothers and sisters

with which his father had provided him through the three separate
native households that he established. Indeed, this had been only
one of the reasons for his mother's leaving Charles Moulton to return to her own family. Hence, though Mr. Barrett played with his
children, allowing them to call him by absurd childish names—he
was Sweet Puppy to Elizabeth—he demanded unquestioning acceptance of the dictum that whatever he did was right. Elizabeth and
Edward, like favorites at the foot of the throne, learned early that
when the monarch could not be swayed by endearments he would
be influenced by diplomacy, and they dealt with him accordingly.

The time came when Edward was placed with a tutor for the study
of Greek and Latin necessary to the university career of Mr. Barrett's
heir. As a girl Elizabeth did not require such instruction. It meant,
however, that for hours she and Edward would be parted. Besides,
she was more eager to learn Greek than he was. Together they drew
up a petition that Elizabeth be allowed to share in the classical
studies and humbly submitted it to their father. Mr. Barrett mag-
nanimously acquiesced.

With her entering into that antique world it was as if Elizabeth
found the home of her imagination. Greece became nearer to her
than England and Athens than Hope End. Rome, too, she adopted,
learning Latin with marvelous facility, but for her the limpid radiance
of Greece was always to shine as the light of her spirit. Her response,
however, was of the emotions rather than of the intellect. In that
she paralleled another child, just two years older than herself, the
French Aurore Dupin, later to become George Sand. At the very
time that Aurore was erecting secret pagan altars in her grandmother's
garden and creating gods, half Christian, half Greek, for her worship,
Elizabeth Barrett, with her pinafore full of sticks and a match from
the housemaid's cupboard would steal out of Hope End and sacrifice
to Minerva, her chosen goddess—"because she cared for Athens."
Like Aurore she too had made rhymes and spun stories over her
bread and milk. Also like her she had had her period of skepticism
during which she confounded her divine allegiance, first reconciling
Apollo, Zeus and the other gods to Christianity and then doubting
altogether the existence of deity. But for that her indiscriminate
reading was responsible.

Mr. Barrett had a good library which he wisely did not keep from
his children. However, he felt obliged to exercise a certain caution in
turning Elizabeth loose in those literary pastures. "Don't read

Gibbon's history," he warned her. "It's not a proper book. Obediently Elizabeth let Gibbon alone. "Don't read *Tom Jones*." Elizabeth dutifully avoided the novel without asking the reason for the prohibition. "And none of the books on *this* side, mind!"

The books on *this* side, therefore, she did not dream of touching, but she left scarcely anything unread on the permitted shelves. Tom Paine's *Age of Reason* engaged the mind of the young rationalist confirming her further in her skepticism. Then came Voltaire's *Philosophical Dictionary*—Aurore Dupin had devoured it too—and Hume's *Essays*, and Rousseau's *Confessions* and the feminist writings of Mary Wollstonecraft. The literature of reason and emancipation, combined with her reading of the Greeks and her vague but growing doubts, colored her behavior. Night and morning as her father required, she would say the Lord's Prayer, following it with, "Bless all my kind friends." But she closed her devotions with a supplication that would have delighted Voltaire. "O God, if there is a God, save my soul if I have a soul."

Had Mr. Barrett known he would probably have taken out heavier insurance to protect his house against the wrath of the elements. Only the other day a chimney had fallen.

In the fool's paradise of his ignorance, however, he could afford to let paternal pride bask in the wonder of the budding genius under his roof. He had watched Elizabeth outgrow her "house under the sideboard" where she used to compose soliloquies for the tragedies, French and English, that would later be enacted in the nursery, and seek out the solitude of her room for the poems she would later show him—poems written in a minute hand in little clasped books. (He did not know that for her those books were objects to be thanked and kissed and laid away tenderly for the happiness they gave her.)

Perhaps he traced the influence of Byron and Coleridge in her childhood effusions. Certainly there was no denying the presence of Pope in the grand epic of the battle of Marathon which had so overwhelmed Mr. Barrett that he took it to the printer and paid for the fifty copies which purchased it a fraction of futurity. The dedication told him he had been justified. The poem was an extraordinary production for a thirteen-year-old girl, and he was the extraordinary father of this phenomenal child.

A less partial critic would have detected the immaturity of the poet through the skillful imitation, so skillful that the epic might have been mistaken for an early trial of Pope's still unfledged wings. His accent rang in the lines, slightly distorted, however, like an echo. The famous mannerisms were there aped to perfection, but they were the mimicking shadow to his substance. Obviously Miss Barrett's interests lay in ancient Greece, but her passion and emotion suffered in the transit to Hope End. Like Pope's *Homer*, Miss Barrett's *Battle of Marathon*, though written in English, was also a translation. The grand manner, however, she captured to perfection, from the opening invocation to the orotund periods of Cynaegirus' death at the close.

> They lop his limb; then Pallas fires his frame
> With scorn of death, and hope of future fame . . .
> The fainting Greek by loss of blood opprest
> Still feels the patriot rise within his breast . . .
> But strength decaying, fate supprest his breath,
> And o'er his brow expand the dews of death.
> The Elysium plains his generous spirit trod,
> "He lived a Hero and he died a God."

Every one of the family circle who read the epic was impressed except for Granny Moulton who grumbled about all this reading and writing. "I would rather see Elizabeth's hemming more carefully finished off than hear all this Greek," she declared, to which Treppy would add her own trenchant comment.

But the Greek continued, more and more of it, as the young scholar's love of it grew to a passion. Soon she had outstripped Edward and gone beyond their tutor, Mr. MacSwiney. It was a reckless rush through her chosen learning, a joyous plunge into the vivifying spring of poetry. Her Italian master, whose English gave him trouble, shook his head at her impetuosity and said there was an unpronounceable word in her language that described her exactly. *"Testa lunga,"* he called her in Italian, which she jocularly translated into *headlong*.

Headlong she was and headlong she remained, "precipitously rushing through all manner of nettles and briars, instead of keeping the path, guessing at the meaning of unknown words instead of looking into the dictionary—tearing open letters and never untying a string, and expecting everything to be done in a minute, and the thunder to be as quick as the lightning."

That impetuosity on one occasion nearly killed her. She wanted to go out riding one day and because no one was about she tried to saddle her pony Moses by herself. In the field the pony stumbled. The saddle fell upon her injuring her spine so badly that for a long time she had to keep to her room, lying flat on her back. The spinal injury, however, was not so serious as the lung affection that now manifested itself.

The period of invalidism was not without its rewards to the fifteen-year-old girl. She loved the gardens, her early morning saunters when she stole out before anyone was awake to surprise a spray of bursting blossoms and to listen to the sleepy cries of the birds. She loved the walks with Papa who had a Rousseauistic regard for nature as the foster mother of genius and accordingly exposed his nursling to her beneficent influences. (Indeed, in his love of trees he expelled the deer from the park in which he took inordinate pride.) She loved the gay exploits with Edward when they ran over the countryside for the very pleasure of the exercise or in search of little wild creatures to keep as pets. But she loved most of all the green seclusion of the room at the top of the house where she could be alone.

It was studiedly romantic, the bower in which Mr. Barrett kept his singing bird. The stained-glass panes that mellowed the daylight were festooned with honeysuckle vines. A green carpet covered the floor and green curtains carried the illusion of growing things into the room. A writing table stood near the bed, also an armchair. The window seat allowed one to stretch out and look up at the sky. She read omnivorously and filled her little clasped books with the poems she thought worthy of being copied from the scraps of paper on which she wrote them. When she left her bed she did not use her writing table but sat curled up on the window seat or on the floor, resting her book on her knees and fancying herself a Lollard.

She fancied herself many things in the long hours when her insatiable novel reading mingled with the rumors of life that reached her tower room. Lord Byron's adventures as well as his works were then on everybody's tongue. Fired by his poetry to an admiration that amounted to worship—after all, they had Athens in common!—the young girl dreamed of running away and disguising herself as a page to enter his service. What romance would be there! (And what anxiety for Mr. Barrett had he had the least inkling of his daughter's vagaries!) But that dream had to be put away with many another as she grew older and life and circumstances established a pattern which only a miracle could finally break.

Meanwhile that "creature of impetuous breath" resigned herself

not too unwillingly to her mode of living. It gave her freedom, it gave
her solitude, it gave her leisure for the intellectual life that for a
long time comprised her sole happiness, indeed, was the source of
her chief joys. She was asked years later whether she liked to write.
"It is life for me," she answered. "Why, what is to live? . . . To feel
the life in you down all the fibres of being, passionately and joyfully."

She had the capacity for both passion and joy to a degree that was
to be matched only by another, like herself early dedicated to poetry.
But at that time Robert Browning was still a child, beginning to
acquire a love and knowledge of that antiquity which was also to
release his imagination. His father, by avocation a scholar and a
collector of curious knowledge, had always in his hand some impressive tome.

"What do you read about?" his five-year-old son asked him one day.

"The siege of Troy."

"What is a siege and what is Troy?"

Mr. Browning believed in making his only son's grades toward
Parnassus as pleasurable as possible and at once set about turning the
explanation into a game.

> He piled up chairs and tables for a town,
> Set me atop for Priam, called our cat
> —Helen, enticed away from home (he said)
> By wicked Paris, who couched somewhere close
> Under the footstool, being cowardly,
> But whom—since she was worth the pains, poor puss—
> Towzer and Tray,—our dogs, the Atreidai,—sought
> By taking Troy to get possession of. . . .

The portrait of the quaint, lovable elder Browning is painted there,
just as Mr. Barrett is limned in all his dourness as he bids his
daughter, terrified on her precarious perch, to stand straight like a
hero. The two men, however, shared a common pride and aim.
Both gloried in being the parents of unusual children, and both
wished them to be poets.

In time Elizabeth Barrett's health improved. Again she was able
to go out and resume her pastimes with her brothers and sisters.
Edward was still her companion on woodland walks, the sharer of her
adolescent secrets, the only one in that overpopulated house with
whom she felt the double kinship of blood and spirit. They no
longer studied together under their Scottish tutor. Elizabeth needed

a guide of wider learning. She was eventually to find him in the blind scholar Hugh Stuart Boyd who lived close by in Great Malvern, with his wife and daughter.

Mr. Boyd had lost his sight so long ago that he scarcely remembered ever having had it. Nevertheless he possessed a knowledge of Greek classical literature that made him a fount of inexhaustible wonder to the eager Miss Barrett. He was never really her teacher. From the first the visionary girl and the sightless scholar, bridging over the years between them, established a friendship which had a tender filial gaiety on one side and a protective affection on the other. Her feminine intuitiveness—and she was wholly feminine— told her of the loneliness of the man, and her heart went out to him as well as her mind. His affliction sued for her love while it brought closer her beloved Homer who had also been blind.

She would visit Mr. Boyd in Malvern and together, with their folios spread before them, in the long mornings they would sit by the window to read. Rather, she read in her low shy voice, making sure to give the proper values to the Greek vowels, and looking up now and then toward the mountain landscape changing with the shifting of sun and cloud. Sometimes the tinkle of sheep-bells lent its pastoral music to the reading, but most often it was Mr. Boyd's voice that broke in upon hers in explanation and instruction. Aeschylus and Euripides and Plato were their guests on those golden mornings. But gradually less familiar but no less welcome visitants, not pagan but touched with the light of Christianity, made their appearance—men whose names were like solemn canticles—Chrysostom, Synesius, Heliodorus, and Nazianzen, names that made a music of their own and spoke new thoughts to her spirit.

. . . . You were older,

she was to write in tribute to her friend in "Wine of Cyprus,"

> And more learned, and a man;
> Yet that shadow, the infolder
> Of your quiet eyelids, ran
> Both our spirits to one level;
> And I turned from hill and lea,
> And the summer sun's green revel,
> To your eyes that could not see.

In the parity of their minds, however, there was room too for humor. He would not, for example, consent to call her by her pet name Ba. "It wants euphony," complained the man whom "nothing could induce to desecrate organs accustomed to Attic harmonies." He preferred Elibet. It had more than one syllable and it was rhythmic.

Mr. Boyd was also a critic of Miss Barrett's poetry. "Oh, the indisposition of your trochees!" he would moan aloud.

He execrated the corrupt taste of the modern poets and took it upon himself to give her sound advice. "That dreadful system of running lines into one another! It ruins everything. Follow Pope. Yes, follow Pope and you will wear the crown of poetry."

As it was, even before Mr. Boyd could give her such advice, Miss Barrett had stuck closer to the heels of Pope in her poem, *An Essay on Mind*, than she had in her Marathon epic. Its title betrayed her subservience, while her use again of the heroic couplet, Pope's jogging Pegasus, made it still more obvious. The opening struck the keynote and exposed at the same time the chief flaws in her ambitious venture.

> Since Spirit first inspir'd, pervaded all,
> And Mind met Matter at th'Eternal call—
> Since dust weigh'd Genius down, or Genius gave
> Th'immortal halo to the mortal's grave;
> Th'ambitious soul her essence hath defin'd,
> And Mind hath eulogiz'd the pow'rs of Mind.

Capitalized abstraction ran riot through the verses like an animated ghost. Nothing of the life about her, the life of which she was aware through every delicately heightened sense was permitted into the poem. But the library, every volume she had read, every folio she had discussed, pervaded all with a lamp-tainted air. No man of achievement failed to file into that literary pantheon. Plato trod on the toga of the Syracusan, while "beloved Shakespeare," "divinest Newton," Cato, Condillac, Byron, Pope himself and innumerable others elbowed their way past Freedom, Fancy, Memory, Poesy, Matter and Mind to their designated niche. Only the inoffensive letter e suffered discrimination and like a persistent and importunate beggar was repeatedly cast out.

Still, here and there the discerning reader of 1826—for this time the poem went out to the general public—could have caught glimpses of the poet that was to be. As yet she was simply Mind eulogizing the powers of Mind in a literary exercise that had more to do with the will to write than with the urgency of inspiration. There was much more of herself in her stanzas on the death of Lord Byron wherein her heart as well as her literary admiration spoke. The only reviewer who noticed the *Essay* commented in dismay, "This young lady imitates Darwin."

Mr. Barrett's possessiveness increased as his treasure continued to prove its worth. By this time he showed such partiality toward Ba, that the rest of the family would use her as an intercessor to his austere highness. Arabel who was skilled in drawing once made a portrait of her sister, to please him. In spite of its amateurishness the sketch caught something of Elizabeth's quality in the great spiritual eyes and the powerful brow, while the mouth in its lifted corners captured the gaiety which so far had not appeared in her writing. Mr. Barrett, however, liked best the portrait of his daughter, painted while she was still very young, in the character of a fugitive angel.

Chapter II: The Poet-Boy

IT WAS not till 1833 that Robert Browning, superior clerk in the Bank of England and, after hours, indomitable ranger over the culture of the world experienced the pleasure that Mr. Edward Barrett Moulton-Barrett had known as early as 1820. Not that Robert Browning, junior, had been less precocious than Miss Barrett in his attempts to scale Parnassus. A manuscript of his, a collection of poems modestly called *Incondita*, written when he had scarcely entered his teens, had so impressed his parents that they had made serious efforts to find a publisher. But no commercial house was willing to take the risk, poetry then as well as later suffering "a flat time" according to Henry Taylor, since "publishers would have nothing to say to poets, regarding them as unprofitable people." So *Incondita* was put aside and later destroyed but for copies of the poems kept by Eliza Flower, the young poet's friend and admirer.[1] However, the publication of *Pauline* in March of 1833 made up for the earlier disappointment, at least in the satisfaction a writer feels on seeing the creatures of his imagination set down in black upon white.

The name of Robert Browning did not appear upon the title page, nor did the publishers Saunders and Otley of Conduit Street, London, know his identity. The expenses of publication, thirty pounds, had been met by Christiana Silverthorne, Browning's aunt. At first only she and Sarianna, the poet's sister, had been let in on the secret. But as it happened very few others were either to know or care to know, at least for some years, either the name of the poet or the qualities of his poem. To Browning's father, however, the discovery of the authorship was of momentous import. It justified his proud bold notation in the family Bible of his son's birth, May 7, 1812, and made up for his own disappointments as an artist and a creative writer.

The elder Browning's life had not been easy. In 1778 his father,

[1] These too Browning destroyed when they were returned to him a few years after Eliza Flower's death.

also Robert Browning, descended from Dorsetshire's respectable yeomanry under Henry VII, married Margaret Tittle the daughter of West Indian property owners and herself born there, of English parentage. He entered the Bank of England through the influence of Lord Shaftesbury and from a clerk rose to the headship of a major department on a salary which enabled him to live in comfort and support his wife. In 1780 he distinguished himself in the defense of the bank during the Gordon riots and so allied himself with its interests that he had no difficulty later in placing his son, born in 1781, in the position at which he had started.

But there had been a number of vicissitudes in the young man's life before that. When he was seven years old his mother died leaving him with only the memory of her calm white face in the coffin. Five years later his father married again, a Miss Jane Smith who began to provide her husband with the large family customary at the time. The second Mrs. Browning was a woman of jealous temper who soon showed her resentment by banishing to the garret the portrait of her predecessor.

"You do not need two wives," she said to her husband.

She also distinguished herself by answering to the letter the description of the traditional stepmother, discriminating between her children and the earlier offspring and in every way working out her feelings against him. She always had some virtuous explanation for her deeds. When the boy begged his father to send him to the university, offering to pay the costs from a small income inherited from an uncle, the second Mrs. Browning prevailed upon her husband to refuse on the grounds that such an education would prove unfair to their sons, "For we could not afford to send them to college too." The youth's ambition to become a painter had been discouraged in the same way though not in so many words. When, one day, he proudly showed his father what he considered his first good finished picture, Mr. Browning turned away without comment. He knew that his acquiescence would have had to be revoked. Perhaps too, as a member of the good, stolid, conservative family of John Bull he had no regard for artists and wanted none in his family.

He sent his son instead to St. Kitts where the Tittles had their sugar plantation. A taste of the realities of West Indian slavery and a lucrative position on his mother's property would help to drive that artistic nonsense out of his head. The youth, however, soon developed such a hatred of the slave system that he gave up all thought of ever profiting by it. For a while he supported himself as best he could by teaching and then returned to England and his astonished and angry father. One can hear in the background the acid comments of the second Mrs. Browning on this bad coin forever turning up.

Not long afterward the young man was placed by his father as clerk in the Bank of England, doubtless as a last resort. The moment he began drawing a salary he was presented with a bill for everything he had cost his parent, including the midwifery expenses at his birth. The old man's mistrust of this wayward sheep in his family of lambs had not subsided when his thirty-year-old son declared his intention of marrying Miss Sarah Anna Wiedemann, then staying at Camberwell with an uncle.

At the news the honorable Mr. Browning whose library consisted of the Bible and *Tom Jones*, both of which he read over once a year and adopted as his guides in religion and life, betook himself to Miss Wiedemann's uncle and benevolently waited on him, "to assure him that his niece would be thrown away on a man so evidently born to be hanged!" When both uncle and niece were willing to take the risk despite his warning, Mr. Browning refused his sanction.

On February 19, 1811, his son made the first entry on the flyleaf of the large illustrated family Bible that was to hold the records of the new family: "Robert Browning married to Sarah Anna Wiedemann at Camberwell. . . ." A year later came the notation of the future poet's birth, followed on the 7th of February, 1814 by that of his sister, named after the mother but known as Sarianna.

Mrs. Browning, born in Scotland, was of German and Scottish parentage. Her father, a native of Hamburg, had come to Dundee where he married a Scotchwoman and founded a profitable business as a shipowner. The daughters born of the union, Sarah Anna and Christiana, were reared in the Scottish kirk and in all ways reflected the life about them so that Carlyle could speak of Mrs. Browning as "the true type of the Scottish gentlewoman . . . a divine woman." She inherited from her father a love of music far beyond the limitations of her training and it was one of the joys of her life to sit at the piano and let her exquisite sensitiveness guide her fingers over the keys. After her marriage she and her husband who had been brought up in the Church of England joined an Independent group in York Street where they would attend the evening services under the guidance of the Rev. Henry Melvill.

It was commonly believed during Browning's lifetime that there was Jewish blood in his ancestry. The theory was chiefly founded on his knowledge of Hebrew and Hebraic literature, as well as on his keen sympathy with Jews and Jewish lore. The elder Browning was also known to be a profound student of the Talmud and his mind teemed with Hebrew legend. Then, too, Browning's subjects, his "Saul," "Rabbi Ben Ezra," "A Death in the Desert," as well as allusions to Jews in other poems, lent substance to the surmises of those who would interpret as autobiography such lines from "In a Gondola" as:

> I am a Jew,
> And carry thee, farther than friends can pursue,
> To a feast of our tribe. . . .

Who but a Jew, they would ask, could have made such a comparison as Browning's when he said of the figures of St. Saviour's in Salzburg:

> You might conceive them
> A troop of yellow-vested white-haired Jews
> Bound for their own land where redemption dawns. . . .

Then too the Brownings were connected with the Rothschild Bank. His uncle Reuben Browning held an important post in its London office and was, besides, a friend of that other Jew, Lord Beaconsfield. Another Browning occupied a prominent position in the Paris Branch of the Messrs. Rothschild. Finally, to cap the argument, the Brownings, with their dark hair and prominent nose, looked foreign. The blue eyes could be explained somehow as exceptions from the norm.

The vexed question, of concern to everyone but the Brownings, had scarcely been laid temporarily aside when Dr. Furnivall, who founded the Browning Society in 1881, advanced another theory: The Brownings were part Negro. Indeed, Margaret Tittle, Browning's grandmother, had been much more than a Creole. There could be no mistaking the dash of Negro blood that darkened her son's complexion to such a degree that when he lived in St. Kitts he had been made to sit in church among the colored members of the congregation. Besides, wasn't he, Browning's father, always drawing Negro heads?

The portrait of Browning's grandmother painted by Wright of Derby showed a stately, fair-skinned woman whose features revealed nothing to support Dr. Furnivall's contention. Nonetheless his theory had its adherents and started a few literary tempests in which ink-wells and invectives were hurled. The Brownings held calmly aloof. What Mrs. Sutherland Orr had to say of the Furnivall speculation holds equally for the Jewish: "The poet and his father were what we know them, and if Negro blood had any part in their composition, it was no worse for them and so much better for the Negro."

Certainly in their all-embracing humanity they would have been the last to utter any disclaimer. As for Browning the poet, he was as much the inheritor of the Greek as of the Hebrew spirit in that largeness of acceptance that made all culture his own, all life his province. Besides, in the England of his day as of many generations the Bible was the rock and Greek thought the vivifying air of the spiritual climate. A Byron could write his Hebrew melodies and his Cain and also sing of Hellas. A Shelley for all his atheism could speak for love and for the soul in his Epipsychidion. A Tennyson was to find inspiration in the Old Testament singers as well as in a Ulysses and an Oenone. At the very time that the boy Browning was listening to the inexhaustible lore of that living encyclopedia, his father, who sped from Faust to the Talmud and from the Talmud to Homer with the ease of a fairy tale character on his magic carpet, the adolescent Miss Barrett was pausing long enough in her evocation of Greece to learn Hebrew sufficiently well to read her Bible in the original.

Meanwhile the Browning library at Southampton Street, Camber-well, was growing from hundreds to thousands of volumes as the acquisitive passion of the book-loving elder Browning gave him no peace unless he possessed as many as possible of those treasures for which, as someone said, he had the scent of a hound and the snap of a bulldog. Perhaps his love of books had been aggravated by the privation in his stepmother's home. However that was, he had an intellectual hunger which nothing could appease. Despite his desultory education he was an accomplished linguist who besides French and Italian knew Hebrew and Greek. Indeed, his Hebrew learning was so profound that he went to the sources for his research. At one time he engaged upon a Biblical genealogy, the Nomenclator, which began with Adam and ended with Zerubbabel. The two large volumes exhibit the tidy scholarship of a meticulous mind, precise in every detail of the scheme of red circles and yellow diamonds indicating the male and female characters, the whole astounding for the infinite patience it must have cost.[2] The question arises—for what? It gives one the same dismaying feeling of awe as at the cherry pit carved by the prisoner. The labor is excessive for its worth. In a sense the unwilling bank clerk, the artist and ambitious literary man who had not been given a chance, was the prisoner of his own frustration.

But frustration neither soured nor embittered the florid, compact, blue-eyed man by whose regular comings and goings the Camberwell neighbors might have set their clocks. He knew that for himself it was too late for anything but the pleasures of the dilettante, a dilettante, however, with unusual talents. But he could foster in the blood of his blood whatever was latent in it. If real achievement was not for him, he would make it possible for his child, thus canceling through him the wrong his own father had done him. Therefore, long before the light yellow hair with which his son was born had begun to darken, Mr. Browning began his tutelage of the genius. Mrs. Browning let him have his way though his methods must have struck even her wifely devotion as unconventional. But then Mr. Browning did not quite fit in with convention. He was an amiable eccentric of phenomenally wide interests, with a pleasant disposition and an almost fanatical attachment to his family. That close unit was his whole world—outside of the macrocosm of books.

And so the devoted pelican watched over his fledgling, alert for every propitious sign and ready to pluck at his breast for the lifeblood to nurture it. That expedient he did not have to resort to, however. Young Robert was healthy and strong and gave proof of intelligence. Whenever he was fretful Mr. Browning rather than his wife would soothe him to sleep. The lullaby was unusual—an ode of Anacreon sung to the tune of "The Cottage in the Wood." When the child was old enough to learn words Mr. Browning would string into jingles whatever knowledge he thought the young mind could assimilate. He must have been pleased when the boy who could not yet walk except by clinging to the edge of the dining room table would toddle round and round it, gleefully shouting extemporaneous rhymes. He also discovered very early his son's talent for drawing, a fact duly recorded under the picture of a cottage and rocks, drawn in pencil and colored with black currant-juice: *R.B. aetat two years and three months.* The currant-juice had been a concession to the infant who sucked his brushes.

---

[2] A sample of his industry in this direction is preserved in the Baylor University Browning Collection.

It was Mrs. Browning however who first became aware of her son's response to the music that was to be with him a lifelong passion. She had put the child to bed one evening and then had sat down at the piano in the twilight. She had been playing for some time when she became aware of two large wistful eyes fixed upon her and a little white figure almost lost against the oaken bookcase in the dimness. Suddenly the little boy ran to her and as she clasped him in her arms he sobbed from some unguessed depth of emotion, interrupting himself only to beg her to "Play! Play!" After this the parents lost no time in finding him a music master.

Conditions could not have been more favorable for a child's development. Young Robert had the security of a happy, united family, a sister near enough to him in years to make a congenial playmate, a father who could stimulate his intellect and nurture his imagination, and an adoring mother who was yet strong enough to shape his character. His surroundings, too, the Camberwell of the early nineteenth century, with its three-mile nearness to London and its "green half-hour's walk" to the Dulwich Gallery; with its hedgerows and oak groves and willow-shaded pastures; with its orchards and meadows and sky-dappled slopes had that happy mingling of the urban and the pastoral which offered constant excitement.

Southampton Street itself was like any village street, green and neat in its front lawns and secluded in the back gardens that made even the middleclass Englishman's cottage his castle. It boasted no great wealth but neither did it show poverty.

The houses of the richer families rose elsewhere in Camberwell. Not too far off, at Herne Hill, John James Ruskin of Ruskin, Telford and Domecq, wine merchants, had his comfortable home, in surroundings that made his son John fall in love with blue hills while yet in pinafores. The child, unlike Robert Browning, had no playmates of his own age. But then he had the trees and hedges of the ample grounds, the birds, the flowers and clouds, all of which were always to be dearer to him than the taskmasters of his real living, his adoring but stern parents who looked upon their son as the elect of the Lord.

Browning and Ruskin never met in their boyhood—Ruskin was seven years younger—but the shaping circumstances were similar. Their lives and works, however, could not have been more divergent. Ruskin, whose relations with people ended in tragedy, threw himself into the things he loved, the shapes of the visible world, man's creations, and the ideal of the good the true and the beautiful. Browning, equally responsive to the life about him but endowed with a passion which the author of *Modern Painters* felt only for abstractions, kindled to poetry through the spark of contact with men and women. People in good and evil were always to be infinitely more important to him than things.

In the years of discovery when every sense reaches out to experience, Robert Browning gave himself up to it, alive to everything, scorning nothing.

> I am made up of an intensest life,
> Of a most clear idea of consciousness
> Of self . . .
> Existing as a centre to all things,
> Most potent to create, and rule, and call
> Upon all things to minister to it.

It was as true of him, the boy, as at twenty when he wrote *Pauline*. Seeing, feeling, hearing, all contributed to that memory of experience, the reservoir of the creative imagination. He had moreover an appreciation of beauty that had startled even his too partial parents when, as a mere baby, after he had thrown into the fire a Brussels lace veil belonging to his mother, he gave as an excuse for his mischief: "A pitty baze, Mama!" The *pretty blaze*, of course, spared him any punishment.

Southampton Street held much to satisfy the interests of an intelligent child. The swallows and white-throats found the eaves and trees of the Browning property suitable for their nest building, to the delight of Robert and his sister. Besides, the garden yielded pets of all sorts including for a time two large snakes and a magpie. As he grew older he would go off on long walks across the meadows, but best of all to the Camberwell hill above the church from where he could see like a far off mirage the city of London, still for him unexplored. Often he would simply lie on the grass, becoming so much part of the nature about him that the birds would alight upon his body, as still as a rock. Yet all the while he missed nothing of the life about him.

His father, for whom the world of books held the greatest fascination, did not believe in wasting the shining hours on a mere walk. Thus, whenever they sauntered about the country together he would read aloud to Robert from some instructive work. Once when they were enjoying such an excursion up Nunhead Hill in Surrey, Mr. Browning regaled the boy with the whole of the lengthy dedicatory preface of Dryden's translation of Juvenal's satires. Surely they must have rested at intervals or retraced their steps. The reading would have outlasted the scaling of a Himalayan peak.

The boy took it all as most natural, as he did everything else, in an acceptance that spoke well for his physical and mental energy. He studied languages, music, singing, dancing. Later he rode and also had boxing and fencing lessons. Most of his learning he acquired at home although several attempts had been made to give him a conventional education. At a dame's school which he briefly attended his precocity made him unpopular with the parents of his fellow pupils who suspected favoritism in his obvious superiority over their sons. They would have been alarmed as well as suspicious had they known that the small fairhaired boy in his pinafore of brown Holland had already become so corrupted with learning—not, however, at that impeccable place—as to write verses in imitation of Ossian.

At the age of eight or nine Robert was sent to board at the school of the Misses Ready who served as the initiatory vestals to the shrine of learning presided over by their brother, the Rev. Thomas Ready at Peckham. From the young ladies' tutelage Robert emerged with very glossy hair, a rich repertory of Isaac Watts' hymns, and a parlor accomplishment which in later life never failed to amuse his friends. Once a week, possibly out of regard for the connection between cleanliness and godliness, the Misses Ready would see to it that their young charges brushed and oiled their hair. This was accomplished to the rhythm of edifying song. Browning never forgot one verse particularly, whose beat he would mark with the downward swoop of an imaginary hairbrush:

> Lord, 'tis a pleasant thing to stand
> In gardens planted by Thy hand . . .
> Fools never raise their thoughts so high,
> Like *brutes* they live, like BRUTES they die.

His attendance at the Rev. Thomas Ready's school was even less profitable than his stay at the young ladies' establishment. All he could remember of those years was the copy of verses he made to ingratiate himself with the Rev. Ready who must have been pleased to learn that

> We boys are privates in the Regiment's ranks;
> 'Tis to our Captain that we all owe thanks.

By the time Robert reached fourteen he had had enough both of the Captain and of the ranks and pleaded with his parents to let him continue his education at home. The limitations of the Rev. Ready's school were all too apparent to the cultured Brownings. They decided to do as their son wished.

Now Browning took up his studies seriously and gave direction to his reading. Besides a French tutor he had an Italian teacher and also a music master, John Relfe, musician in ordinary to His Majesty and a composer in his own right. Mr. Relfe enjoyed moreover a reputation as a pedagogue for his learned works on harmony and theory, a reputation further enhanced by his living up to his promise "to divest thorough-bass and composition of their intricacies." Besides, his *Muschedula* purported to reveal to his students "the whole arcana of the science." Robert who, as he said, had been studying the grammar of music when other children were learning their multiplication table, was more than ready for the revelation and received enough illumination for him to set to music a poem of Hood's as well as Donne's fanciful "Go and catch a falling star." Under Relfe he also became an accomplished pianist.

There is at this time no indication that he pursued the art which he had begun so auspiciously with black currant-juice at the age of two. But painting next to music now became an absorbing interest. Ever since he could walk the two miles from Southampton Street to the Dulwich Gallery, Mr. Browning had taken him there with a frequency that would have been exemplary in church attendance. The boy early selected his favorites in the collection of more than three hundred paintings which, through the generosity of Sir Francis Bourgeois at a time when the nation had been more concerned with defeating Napoleon than establishing an art gallery, gave the public a privilege which it was not to enjoy more fully until a quarter of a century later with the founding of the National Gallery.

Browning did not see eye to eye with his father, who was inclined to favor the "boors" of the Dutch school, those robust representations of bucolic scenes and hearty family groups, crowded canvases that almost broke through their frames with the vitality they tried to confine. Instead, he would stand reverently before the Rembrandt of Jacob's vision, the three Murillos, the classical Poussins—the "Armida" and "Jupiter's Nursing"—and the delicate Watteaus, pastoral too like the Dutch, but in what a different world!

The paintings of the Italian Renaissance, however, spoke to him most directly, especially that exquisite music lesson group (then attributed to Giorgione) in whose subtlety of expression and pose, in the lifted hand and the rapt look, music itself is portrayed as life holds itself in suspension. It was a prophetic choice. After discovering his affinity with the Renaissance he rescued from the family collection a picture of Caravaggio's "Andromeda" uncomfortable in the proximity of the "boors" in which his father had placed it, and hung it in his own room. From that moment "Andromeda" became a symbol in his life of the imagination.

It was his reading, however, that unlocked the gates of wonder for his ardent mind. Even before Robert could distinguish his letters Mr. Browning had turned him loose among his books, letting the pictures tell their story. But it was not long before the boy learned to read and then there was no stopping him. His father used to entertain his children with stories from that compendium of anecdotes and prodigies, Nathaniel Wanley's *The Wonders of the Little World*. Soon Robert had read it from cover to cover and repeated the performance at intervals, never tiring of the fascination of the seventeenth century divine, as entertaining for variety and curious lore as any Scheherazade. Moreover, most of the Wanley wonders had the merit of being true, and even as a child Robert liked a springboard of fact for his imaginative flights.

More frequently than Wanley even, the boy had in his hands the two-volume edition of *The Art of Painting* by Gérard de Lairesse. The copious prints filled him with delight. The text had the double virtue of giving him solid instruction while keeping him absorbed in lives and times other than his own. Later, when his knowledge of French opened up still other paths for his intellectual ranging, he tore through the *Biographie Universelle*, or at least through most of its fifty volumes, learning about Paracelsus and Narses and King Victor and King Charles, about places and men that from then on peopled his imagination.

Dante too he read, in Italian, seeing through the eyes of that great, embittered man who described hell as if he had indeed been there, the forms of dead lovers borne eternally by the winds of passion; the weird trees that had once been men and bled when their twigs were broken. He read too of the troubadour Sordello whose name rang a haunting note through his memory till he had to convert it into song of his own. And he met the pure woman image of Beatrice which unconsciously he was always to seek, not in the heaven to which Dante's love had translated her, but on earth.

Until his early adolescence, however, he had little association with any girl except his sister although at the age of seven he had shocked his parents by writing in his diary one Sunday, "Married two wives this morning." Whatever the event that had inspired the note, it was less momentous to him than to his parents, for he never referred to that Mohammedan marriage again.

He was a good-looking, rather too self-confident boy of fourteen when in 1827 he met Sarah and Eliza Flower to whom his mother had already introduced him through his manuscript *Incondita*. The young women, twenty-two and twenty-four at the time, were the daughters of Benjamin Flower, a martyr to religious and intellectual freedom, a man who had dared to criticize the political conduct of Bishop Watson many years earlier. As a result he had spent six months in prison, the House of Lords finding him guilty of libel. The liberals of the day had stood staunchly by him, at least in sympathy. One, who also had known the bitter taste of persecution, came to minister to him in his confinement. He fell in love with his visitor, Eliza Gould, and after serving his sentence he married her.

The three daughters born of their union inherited their parents' qualities of heart and mind. They were also beautiful and accomplished. Eliza, the musician of the family, played the piano and composed. Sarah wrote poetry. The third was skilled in drawing. They were no dilettantes but girls of genuine talent who were given a solid training and had the intelligence to take advantage of their association with the artists, writers, and political advance-guard drawn to the standard of the *Cambridge Intelligencer* which Mr. Flower published.

Among their closest friends was the Rev. W. Johnson Fox, a liberal and reformer, who had recently opened a new Unitarian chapel in South Place, Finsbury. He tightened the bond between himself and the Flowers by marrying their artist daughter. Besides preaching from the pulpit Mr. Fox was also a writer of trenchant articles on literary and social trends. The better to obtain a hearing he associated himself with the *Westminster Review* about to be launched by the father of the future social philosopher John Stuart Mill.

Browning could not have entered a more sympathetic circle. Everything he loved, everything toward which his idealistic youth reached out, that circle contained. Most important, he was warmly welcomed as an aspirant to Apollo's laurel bough. Eliza Flower saw such talent in the immature *Incondita* that she made a copy of the verses to show to Mr. Fox.

From the beginning Eliza more than Sarah found herself drawn to

the "poet-boy" as they were soon calling him. In spite of the ten years'
difference in their age they met as equals, Browning's maturity of
mind and feeling easily bridging the gap of time. But then, neither
the mind nor the heart has ever been known to defer to time. Sarah,
the younger sister, admired his "great power of conversation and
thorough originality." She also admitted that he was exceptionally
good-looking but for one flaw. "If nature had not served him an
unkind trick in giving him an ugly nose!" Also, she found him disturbing in his assaults upon her religious beliefs, the very center of
her devout life.

In Eliza Flower the poet-boy found perfect understanding at a
time when he most needed it, the time of conflict and self-discovery.
He was drawn to her by many affinities—her music most of all and
her love of poetry. That she included his poetry in that love made
him one of her elect circle, gave him a sense of belonging, a factor
of the utmost importance in the transition from boyhood to youth.
Then, too, Eliza had beauty of that rare quality that makes the body
the lamp of the soul. In the regularity of her fine, strong features she
might have posed for that lover of radiant faces, Benjamin Haydon.
The level brows accentuated the ample intelligence of her forehead.
The eyes large, luminous, and far apart expressed such spirituality
that the whole countenance absorbed light from them. The nose and
chin gave firmness to her feminine delicacy. The mouth was wholly
womanly, chaste yet sensual and lifted into a smile that made the
goddess not wholly unapproachable.

Her loveliness alone would have sufficed to enchant the boy already
in love with the Andromeda image. But Eliza was also kind. She
believed in him and in his future to the extent of finding friends for
his poetry. But more than everything else, she held the power to
touch the very quick of his being through music—"music, my life,"
as he wrote under the influence of her playing.

> For music, (which is earnest of a heaven,
> Seeing we know emotions strange by it,
> Not else to be revealed,) is as a voice,
> A low note calling Fancy, as a friend. . . .
>   This was not at first,
> For I scarce knew what I would do. I had
> No wish to paint, no yearning—but I sang.

His first true song was for her—and for Shelley the Sun-Treader
who, very shortly, came to dazzle his vision.

Chapter III: Pauline, the Sun-Treader, and the Critic

IT TOOK the enterprise of a piratical publisher, William Benbow and the fateful generosity of James Silverthorne, Robert Browning's favorite cousin, to introduce the poet-boy to Percy Bysshe Shelley through a volume of his lyrics brought out in 1826. Perhaps if James Silverthorne had known the effect that the *Miscellaneous Poems* would have had upon Robert, he would have refrained from giving him the book. Still, the way had already been paved for the reception of the Sun-Treader by the saturnine Voltaire who had long been lurking in Mr. Browning's library waiting for Robert to bring him to light.

The philosophical rationalist and the shining rebel, discovered almost at the same time, threw the boy off balance in a dervish whirl of enthusiasm. The first sign came when he questioned the Non-Conformist principles to which his family was attached and refused to go to hear the Rev. Henry Melvill's evening service. Worse was to follow when, with a devotion that was almost saintly, his mother bought him the birthday present he requested—everything of Shelley's that she could find. It was for *Queen Mab*, that omniscient fairy guide who under her innocent exterior carries a load of intellectual dynamite, to complete in Browning what the *Miscellaneous Poems* had begun.

Shelley had written *Queen Mab* in the ferment of his youthful idealism when the reformist ideas of Godwin's *Political Justice*, mingling with Volney's *The Ruins of Empires*, and the concept of man's perfectibility, sent up their bubbles from the depths of his creative mind to burst into lyrical expression. All he believed and all that he hoped for humanity found their place in the poem. The glory of empire is vain, he repeated with Volney. Power abused, religion, commerce, kept man in servitude for the advantage of the tyrannous few, he echoed with Godwin. Could any God see such injustice and tolerate it, he questioned for himself. "There is no

God!" he cried with the atheists, and with a bow to the Necessitarians he hailed "Necessity! Thou mother of the world!" Yes, Necessity was the true divinity, for unlike the God of human error, it required neither prayer nor praise. Necessity and Reason would save the world. "O Happy Earth! Reality of Heaven!"—when marriage would be sanctified without the intervention of law and perfected man enjoy a beautiful and useful life, unstained by the blood of the beast, until he sank happily into "the slow necessity of death." An eloquent and learned note inspired by John Newton's *Return to Nature*, added the persuasions of prose to the exaltation of poetry. Prometheus, Shelley argued, had been the cause of man's descent to the fleshpot by his gift of fire. Man must rise above his appetite, transcend as he had done all taste for "murdered fowl," and subsist on the fruits of the earth.

Browning's admiration for *Queen Mab* overflowed into action. Shelley was a vegetarian. He too became one. Surpassing his model whose customary meal consisted of bread and raisins, he ate his crust without the raisins. For two years he lived almost exclusively on bread and potatoes until his eyesight was impaired and he had, alas, to partake of murdered beasts.

His emulative zeal with regard to diet affected none but himself, but his conversion to atheism, an active, voluble, proselytizing atheism, was another matter. He talked about his unbelief to anyone who would listen and gave arguments for the necessity of atheism. (Surely he must also have read Shelley's undergraduate essay.) His wise and tolerant parents let him work out his ebullience, reassured by a confident knowledge of the quality of the wine. It was different when Browning carried his atheism to the Flowers in Hackney. The two young women had been brought up as believing though Non-Conformist Christians by their pious mother. After her death they had as their mentor their father's valued friend, Mr. Fox. Now the boy Browning, speaking with the tongues of men and of fallen Shelleyan angels, attacked the Scriptures and gave such powerful reasons for his skepticism that the fortress of belief, while it did not crumble, tottered for lack of support.

Eliza Flower, perhaps because she understood him better, contented herself with objective criticism of his impiety and kept up her gentle protests as late as *Pippa Passes* when she disapproved of Pippa's "God's puppets first and last are we." But Sarah, the more religious of the two, suffered the agony of doubt under the wily siege laid by

Browning. Finally she found herself so nearly lost that in November 1827 she wrote to Mr. Fox a letter that was a confession and a cry for help.

"My mind has been wandering a long time, and now it seems to have lost sight of that only invulnerable hold against the assaults of this warring world, a firm belief in the genuineness of the Scriptures . . . I did not discover the darkness in which my soul was shrouded until, in seeking to give light to others, my own gloomy state became too settled to admit of doubt. It was in answering Robert Browning that my mind refused to bring forward argument, turned recreant and sided with the enemy . . . And now as I sit and look up to the room in which I first had existence and think of the mother who gave it . . . the thought links itself with another—how much rather would she I had never been, than to be what I now am."

What is remarkable in Sarah Flower's struggle is not that she should have had it, but that a fourteen-year-old boy proved strong enough to shake the fortress of a belief buttressed by such strength as Mr. Fox's, her parents' teachings, and her own admirable integrity. What arguments did the atheist-libertarian employ to prove so compelling? By that time besides *Queen Mab* Browning had also read *Prometheus Unbound*, *Hellas*, and *Alastor*. The thunder of the rebel Prometheus that had rocked the very throne of the gods gained fire from the flaming hope of liberty in *Hellas*. The poet-boy vibrated to the thunder and flung up his face to the lightning. In *Alastor*, the spiritual autobiography of Shelley's questing youth, Browning saw himself. He set out to follow in the luminous tracks of the Sun-Treader, bent on beating down error and superstition. If in his progress to the goal of universal goodness, truth, liberty, and beauty he left a Sarah Flower on the wayside, grappling with the forces of doubt that he had pitted against her, he went on with a clear conscience, knowing she would be the better for the struggle—a conqueror, an illuminated being.

> . . . . I was vowed to liberty,
> Men were to be as gods and earth a heaven,
> And I—ah, what a life was mine to be!

The words were Browning's but the voice was *Alastor's*.

Sarah Flower returned to her piety, stronger for her soul's conflict yet never quite the same for the experience. Years later she reaffirmed her faith in her famous hymn, "Nearer, my God, to Thee," but in her poem, "Vivia Perpetua," published in her thirty-eighth year, the heroine martyr of Carthage relives the struggles of the Sarah Flower of 1827.

Eliza, on the other hand, Browning left untouched in her beliefs. The Shelley he shared with her was not the revolutionary but the gentler poet of *Rosalind and Helen*, of the lyrics and, of course, of *Alastor*, especially when the gratitude of the singer of *Incondita* toward the woman who had seen merit in it turned, in the future author of *Pauline*, into more personal feeling. From the first days of their acquaintance Browning wrote her boyish poems and sent her letters which she put away. In return she found him a hearing among her friends and, in Mr. Fox, a sort of literary father. Browning himself used still another word that implied respect as well as affection.

"The 'Master' is somebody you don't know," he was to write to Euphrasia Fanny Haworth. "W. J. Fox, a magnificent and poetical nature who used to write in reviews when I was a boy and to whom my verses, a book full, written at the ripe age of twelve or thirteen, were shown; which verses he praised not a little; which praises comforted me not a little; then I lost sight of him for years and years; then I published *anonymously* a little poem—which he, to my inexpressible delight, praised and expounded in a gallant article in a magazine of which he was editor."[1]

The anonymous poem was *Pauline*. Pauline was Eliza. The lover who pours out his "fragment of a confession" was Alastor-Browning, returned from his quest of self-knowledge victorious over his doubt and confident of salvation through faith and love.

The very framework of Browning's poem is in Alastor, the pure idealist who in his search for beauty dreams that

> . . . . a veiled maid
> Sate near him, talking in low solemn tones,
> Her voice was like the voice of his own soul
> Heard in the calm of thought . . .
> Knowledge and truth and virtue were her theme,
> And lofty hopes of divine liberty,
> Thoughts the most dear to him, and poesy. . . .

The description of the veiled maid fitted both Eliza and the Shelleyan yearnings of Browning's quickened soul. Knowledge and truth and beauty were indeed Eliza's theme. She herself had sprung from the lofty hopes of divine liberty. In the fusion of reality and imagination *Pauline* embodied in Browning's poetry what elsewhere

[1] From a holograph letter, undated, in the Baylor Browning Collection.

Shelley called Intellectual Beauty, at once love and spiritual aspiration. Only in such terms can one comprehend the full meaning of Pauline-Eliza in Browning's development as man and poet.

But first it is important to trace other influences that led to the writing of *Pauline*, this acorn that held in embryo the oak of Browning's poetry. Soon after his discovery of Shelley, it was a foregone conclusion that he should look for Keats. Shelley's *Adonais* would have incited him even without the pathos of Keats' death in want and despair in the gloomy Roman winter of 1821. Like everyone else Browning believed that the critics had killed him and his sympathy went out to the poet who, with Byron, the Pilgrim of Eternity, rounded out the trinity of his admiration. What would he have said had he seen the quatrain that Byron, the inveterate mocker, wrote to John Murray after Keats' death?

> Who killed John Keats?
> "I," says the Quarterly,
> So savage and tartarly;
> " 'Twas one of my feats."

It was not until 1827 that Browning read Keats, for it was then that he sent to the poet's publisher "and got a copy of each first edition—no second having been called for even then."[2]

Now with the Sun-Treader and the Pilgrim of Eeternity he had the beauty-loving Adonais who himself had created loveliness from shape and hue and odor and sweet sound. Fervor for liberty, romanticism and the awareness of the beauties of the visible world now worked together in the bubbling activity of Browning's ambition. It must have been at this time, when he knew that he was destined for poetry, that he prepared himself further by reading Johnson's *Dictionary* from A to Z.

Mr. Browning felt, however, that his son should be exposed once more to the higher learning which he himself had never ceased to respect. Since Oxford and Cambridge did not admit Dissenters[3] not to mention atheists, he listened favorably to the announcement that London itself would be having a university if public support warranted. According to the prospectus the University of London

[2] The uncertainty as to the time of Browning's discovery of Keats is terminated by Browning's letter to Julia Wedgwood dated Sat. Eve 1865 in which he writes: "Six years after his death I sent to his publisher etc." See *Robert Browning and Julia Wedgwood, A Broken Friendship as Revealed in their Letters.* Ed. Richard Curle. New York, Stokes and Co., 1937.

[3] As late as 1834 a Parliamentary bill admitting Dissenters to university honors in England was thrown out by the House of Lords.

proposed to be non-sectarian and moderate in its fees. Mr. Browning therefore promptly became a subscriber to the extent of investing one hundred pounds. In due time the cornerstone was laid by the Duke of Sussex and in 1828 the new edifice of learning on Gower Street opened its doors to the students, Robert Browning among them.

The sheep looked up and they were fed—all but the sixteen-year-old Browning. He had wandered too far afield in literary pastures and savored too many of the varied fruits of knowledge to be content with the common grass. He attended desultorily through the first term. He quit in the middle of the second.

For a time he sat in on Dr. Blundell's lectures in medicine at Guy's Hospital, only to learn that he had no vocation in that field. His indulgent parents let him have his way. Their son had vowed himself to poetry and they were willing to further his ambition.

His room in Hanover Cottage, the second Browning residence on Southampton Street, showed the loving care of his mother in all the little comforts it provided. He had his writing table, his books, and his predilected picture on which he would gaze as he lifted his eyes from his writing—

> .... Andromeda!
> And she is with me—years roll, I shall change,
> But change can touch her not—so beautiful
> With her dark eyes, earnest and still, and hair
> Lifted and spread by the salt-sweeping breeze ...
> As she awaits the snake on the wet beach,
> By the dark rock, and the white wave just breaking
> At her feet; quite naked and alone,—a thing
> You doubt not, nor fear for, secure that God
> Will come in thunder from the stars to save her.

The echo from Keats was no mere coincidence. The eternality of beauty was symbolized for Browning by that picture as it had been for Keats by the Grecian urn.

For all his dedication young Browning had enough of the leaven of Adam to rebel against the literary man. He had lived almost exclusively the life of the imagination. Now he set out "to look on real life, which was all new to me." Nearby lived his cousins, James and John Silverthorne, in Portland Place, Peckham Road, where their father had his thriving brewery. Their family like Browning's loved music and literature. The young men were also devotees of the theater as well as of lighter amusements that gave them the reputation of being gay, if not wild. It was with James who had introduced him to Shelley's poetry that Browning had most in common. He now went out with him to look on the real life he had missed. His parents never questioned him, confident that Robert would not betray their complete trust in him. After all he was a man and must enter into a man's life.

Except for Eliza Flower there is no evidence of any other woman to whom Browning was much attached but for a vague mention of his having fallen in love with a handsome girl who had visited at Hanover Cottage. That infatuation died almost as soon as it was born. His love of Eliza by the time he wrote *Pauline* had survived eight years of more or less continued rapport. It was to last until her death. It was a love compact of yearning and imagination, of admiration of considerable talents on both sides, and of common hope for the betterment of man. On Browning's part it was largely love for love's sake. From all indications it involved his imagination much more than his passions.

As for Eliza Flower, she had come upon the poet when he was too young for her ever to overcome an almost maternal protective affection. Perhaps the ardent youth may have fancied himself her lover. For the purposes of poetry that was desirable. But Eliza's disciplined virtue would have made such love impossible. Practically, however, the relationship satisfied the real need of the youth for a woman other than his mother upon whom to spend an as yet uncentered sexuality.

It is not surprising therefore that in *Pauline* he declared, to the horror of future Browning scholars:

> I am knit round
> As with a charm, by sin and lust and pride.

What? An admission of sin and lust on the part of one of the most moral men who ever lived? They forget the experience of the ascetic saint in the desert assailed by every temptation to which man is subject. Persons of chaste life will always be prey to the phantoms conjured up by a compensating imagination. Let it comfort Browning apologists that in the very next line to follow the woeful admission he confesses:

> Yet tho' my wandering dreams have seen all shapes
> Of strange delight, oft have I stood by thee.

The shapes of strange delight in the wandering dreams disprove beyond a doubt any connection with sin and lust except in the desert reaches of the imagination.

Despite the impassioned language of *Pauline* and the intimate form in which it is couched, the prototype of the dramatic monologue which Browning was to make his own, the poem, he later maintained, sprang not from a heart bursting for expression but rather from emulative ambition. The night of October 22, 1832, he had gone to Richmond with James Silverthorne to see Edmund Kean in Shakespeare's *Richard III*. The play and the actor so overwhelmed him that then and there he conceived the grandiose scheme of proving himself in every literary form. It was as if the tree of knowledge were his to deck like a Christmas fir with here a poem, there a novel, a speech, even an opera. (Why should not he, the musician, write an opera?) That he might not be accused of egotism he would conceal his identity under such spelling-book names as Brown, Smith, Jones, and Robinson.[4]

However, though a plan may spring from ambition the subject, even if wrapped and disguised like any Egyptian mummy, will contain a core of life. Therefore it is as a confession that *Pauline* has been rightly read. During the autumn when he had gone to see Kean, Browning was in the throes of an emotional upheaval wherein Shelley and Eliza Flower, atheism and faith, whirled about in a mind further agitated by the fever of creation. Eliza was then reading his copy of Shelley's *Rosalind and Helen*. Thus his love of the woman and of the poet became necessarily associated, together with what they represented in a sincere and ennobling rebellion in Shelley and an equally sincere and ennobling spiritual faith in Eliza. At any rate it was between the night of the Richmond performance and January of 1833 that *Pauline* was conceived and written.

Before he sent it out into the world Browning prefixed it with a lengthy quotation from Henricus Cornelius Agrippa. Since the quotation was in Latin he perforce limited the public whom he benevolently warned against the dangerous, heretical matters contained in his book. However, if such readers, granted that they could understand his warning, persisted in their quest of knowledge, he bade them ignore what did not please them and go on to the rest. For, he stressed in large letters, NAM ET EGO VOBIS ILLA NON

---

[4] The copy of *Pauline* in which he later jotted down this universal plan is in the Victoria and Albert Museum, the Forster and Dyce Collection.

PROBO, SED NARRO. *I do not advocate these things for you, but merely tell you about them.*

The words might have served as a motto throughout his life and appeased the critics who accused him of being abnormally fascinated by unpleasant subjects and characters. "I believe I unduly like the study of morbid cases of the soul," he admitted to Miss Wedgwood years later. "But remember," he added, "first that this is God's world, as he made it for reasons of his own, and that to change its conditions is not to account for them." It was the Browning of *The Ring and the Book* paraphrasing his quotation from Agrippa.

Browning scholarship has been inclined to pass over *Pauline* with apologies and sometimes contempt, perhaps because Browning himself was later ashamed of "this crab . . . of the shapely Tree of Life in this Fool's paradise" of his grand scheme. But besides containing poetic beauty enough to furnish forth a dozen poets of any age the work is of inestimable importance for adumbrating so much of the later Browning, not only in the daring of the images, the emotional power of the narrative, and the form of the dramatic monologue, but for the poet's stand on good and evil, finally developed to magnificent scope in his masterpiece on a Roman murder case.

Before *Pauline* went out to face the critics on March 7, 1833, Browning thought it wise to pave the way by sending twelve copies to Mr. Fox for distribution. He also begged him to review the poem himself in the *Monthly Repository* which Mr. Fox had recently acquired. Browning may have been influenced in his request by the ten-page article on Tennyson's poetry which had appeared in the January issue of the magazine. Mr. Fox responded nobly. At last the youth whose boyish *Incondita* had shown such promise proved himself a poet in *Pauline*. Mr. Fox's review came out in the April *Repository* and compared favorably in length with the Tennyson article.

"The poem," wrote Mr. Fox, "though evidently a hasty and imperfect sketch, has truth and life in it which gave us the thrill . . . which has never yet failed us as a test of genius . . . The whole composition is of the spirit, spiritual," he continued with keen perception. "The scene is in the chambers of thought; the agencies are powers and passions; the events are transitions from one state of spiritual existence to another. . . . In recognizing a poet," he concluded, "we cannot stand upon trifles, nor fret ourselves about such matters. Time enough for that afterwards, when larger works come before us.

Archimedes in the bath had many particulars to settle about specific gravities and Hiero's crown; but he first gave a glorious leap and shouted *Eureka!*"

Mr. Fox's own leap was glorious enough for the delighted Browning to tell him: "I shall never write a line without thinking of the source of my first praise." Two months later the *Monthly Repository* made another allusion to *Pauline* in a descriptive passage on Barnet Wood. "Last autumn L—— dropped a poem of Shelley's down there in the wood . . . and this spring someone found a delicate exotic-looking plant, growing on the very spot, with *Pauline* hanging from its slender stalk. . . ."[5]

It was a graceful linking of Browning with the poet-god he had renounced yet not ceased to love, and it comforted him in the general indifference to *Pauline* among the rest of the critics. *The Athenaeum* did indeed say in its brief notice in April that fine things abounded in the poem. But what was such mild praise against the damning of the *Literary Gazette* whose total review read: "Somewhat mystical, somewhat poetical, somewhat sensual and not a little unintelligible— this is a dreamy volume, without an object and unfit for publication." *Tait's Edinburgh Magazine* dismissed it as "a piece of pure bewilderment." Even so early the tag of unintelligibility attached itself to the poet.

Time passed but not a reader came forward to buy a copy. For unprofitableness Mrs. Silverthorne's thirty pounds might as well have been scattered over the Sahara where Keats not long before had wished his own poems thrown. There could have been little balm for the projector of the Brown, Smith, Jones, and Robinson scheme in his critical reception. In the consensus of disapproval even Mr. Fox's praise must have seemed partial and therefore to be discounted.

The sharpest blow came after Mr. Fox returned to him one of the review copies of *Pauline*, toward the end of October. In his efforts to obtain sympathetic opinion for his protégé, Mr. Fox had given the book to his assistant on the *Monthly Repository*, John Stuart Mill, who also contributed to the *Examiner* and to *Tait's*. The brilliant man of twenty-six whose sharp mind had already begun to cut through the shams of public opinion, took his task seriously. Therefore, before beginning his critique of *Pauline* he was not satisfied that he could do it justice until he had read the poem four times, making

[5] L—— is Eliza Flower. The book was Shelley's *Rosalind and Helen*— Browning's copy.

notes as he read. He was impressed but he was also annoyed. The love passages did not ring true. A morbid self-consciousness in the poet irritated his own forthrightness. As a member of the Fox circle he knew Eliza and Sarah Flower and, in fact, was far from indifferent to the older of the two, to whom he eventually proposed. Whether or not he knew that the poem's anonymity concealed Robert Browning and the name of Pauline that of Eliza Flower is mere conjecture. What he distinctly perceived was that for all his verbal passion the young man of the poem, the poet himself, loved not a real flesh and blood woman but a figment of his own creation.

With his customary thoroughness at the challenge of an idea Mill attacked it from all angles, and even though he was forestalled in his review by the magazine for which he intended it, he decided nevertheless to set down his opinions on the blank end pages of *Pauline*. It was this mirror, held up to him, into which Browning gazed in the depths of his disappointment:

"With considerable poetic powers, the writer seems to me possessed with a more intense and morbid self-consciousness than I ever knew in any human being."

Ariel faced himself and discovered Caliban. The shock of this first sentence was so great that twelve years later in one of his earliest letters to Elizabeth Barrett, Browning quoted it apologetically and incorrectly: "But I know myself—surely—and have always done so, for is there not somewhere the little book I first printed when a boy, with John Mill, the metaphysical head, *his* marginal note that 'the writer possesses a deeper self-consciousness than I ever knew in a sane human being. . . .' " Time, and the still rankling hurt, attenuated the "intense and morbid" to the less damning "deeper."

If Browning expected gentler treatment as he read on, he was quickly disabused. "I should think it a sincere confession," Mill's note continued, "though of a most unlovable state, if the 'Pauline' were not evidently a mere phantom. All about her is full of inconsistency— he neither loves her nor fancies he loves her, yet insists upon *talking* love to her. If she *existed* and loved him, he treats her most ungenerously and unfeelingly. All his aspirings and yearnings and regrets point to other things, never to her: then he *pays her off* toward the end by a piece of flummery, amounting to the modest request that she will love him and live with him and give herself up to him, *without* his loving her—*moyennant quoi* he will think her and call her everything that is handsome. . . . Then he leaves off by saying he knows he shall

have changed his mind tomorrow and despite 'these intents which
seem so fair,' but that having been thus visited once by doubt he
will be again—and is therefore 'in perfect joy' bad luck to him! as
the Irish say."

On the face of it, this indictment of Pauline's poet mingled more
animus than the circumstances warranted—unless Mill had penetrated the secret of the lovers' identity. However it was, its effect upon
Browning was shattering. It was bad enough to have one's mask torn
off. But to feel one's heart dissected and analyzed, and so bluntly,
filled Browning with shame for his work and for himself. After that
there was but small cheer to be found in what followed:

"A cento of most beautiful passages might be made from this poem,
and the psychological history of himself is powerful and truthful—
truth-like certainly ... If he once could muster a hearty hatred of his
selfishness it (the badness of his state) would go; as it is, he feels only
the lack of good, not the positive evil ... A mind in that state can
only be regenerated by some new passion and I know not what to
wish for him but that he may meet with a real Pauline. ..."

Then and there Browning disavowed his firstborn and never mentioned it except with repugnance. Yet in some of its lines he had
already foreshadowed his function as a poet, and that function he
would fulfill:

> I cannot chain my soul, it will not rest
> In its clay prison; this most narrow sphere—
> It has strange powers, and feelings, and desires,
> Which I cannot account for nor explain,
> But which I stifle not, being bound to trust
> All feelings equally—to hear all sides.

But in hearing all sides he himself, as when a child, would "go with
the tale" and become both the teller and the story. Never again would
he put into his poetry that creature of intensest life, Robert Browning.

Shelley he still loved with all the fire of his imagination, so far the
only real ardency he had experienced. The noble invocation to him in
Pauline would hold true for him for a long time.

> Thou must be ever with me, most in gloom
> If such must come, but chiefly when I die,
> For I seem, dying, as one going in the dark
> To fight a giant: but live thou for ever
> And be to all what thou hast been to me!

With Shelley the reformed atheist also embraced Christ, and there is no more touching disclosure in his poem than the poet's reference to Him:

> A mortal, sin's familiar friend, doth here
> Avow that he will give all earth's reward
> But to believe and humbly teach the faith
> In suffering and poverty and shame,
> Only believing he is not unloved.

Before that year ended Browning suffered the humiliation of having a bale of the unbound sheets of *Pauline* delivered to his house by the encumbered publisher.

He decided on a change of scene and thought of Russia.

Chapter IV: From Hope End to London

THE year 1832, notable in England for the Reform Bill and financial panic, brought revolutionary change to the Barrett family. Mr. Barrett had suffered monetary reverses and decided to sell Hope End. The decision, however, he kept to himself with his usual autocratic reserve until he had found a suitable furnished house in Sidmouth, Devonshire. When he made the announcement he expected obedience and he got it. He also demanded no show of emotion, no regret or tears. In that too his outwardly Spartan family obeyed him. Mrs. Barrett alone was spared that wrenching from the home where she had raised her children and known whatever satisfactions marriage to that Old Testament husband had brought her. She had died in 1828, in her forty-ninth year.

Her death had been like the departure of an unobtrusive guest. Henrietta took on the management of the house and everything went on as before. Whatever the children felt at her loss they left unexpressed but for Elizabeth who in writing of her years later penned a sentence that summed up that self-abnegating existence: "We lost more in her than she lost in life, my dear, dearest mother." It might have been the epitaph of Mrs. Barrett as of all long-suffering victims of a domestic tyrant. "One of those women who never can resist; but in submitting and bowing on themselves, make a mark, a plait, within—a sign of suffering."

Of that plait within, the one who had inflicted it was never conscious. After his wife's death, however, Mr. Barrett built his life more than ever about his children. Like the famous Roman matron, he could have said of them in his abnormal attachment, "These are my jewels." Not that he ever underestimated the importance of actual wealth. He prized it as the golden ladder that elevated him by so many degrees above his fellows. The present descent of several rungs humbled him in pride and power. But he would have been the last man in the world to betray his feelings, especially before his children who, like the despot's subjects, must not be shown the least sign of weakness. So on the family's last evening at Hope End, Mr. Barrett, grimly self-possessed, joined his sons in a game of cricket.

The removal, whatever the pangs it cost them, still had the excitement of adventure. It was a considerable caravan, excluding the two sons at Glasgow University but including the servants, that looked back for the last time on the receding minarets of Hope End. Elizabeth Barrett had spent most of the twenty-six years of her life in its woods and gardens and in the little green room always to be associated with her poetry. Her whole youth, her first dreams, her only affections, had been sheltered by that house. But her regrets at leaving it even she kept from her father.

Sidmouth, said Papa, would be a temporary alighting place. Two months, perhaps, or till he could find a more permanent home for them. It seemed hardly worthwhile to make the fatiguing journey of more than forty-eight hours for so short a stay, but the scenery was always interesting and the glimpse of Bath in the twinkle of its lights summoned up romantic associations.

When they reached the house they were going to occupy they found a building that could hardly have been called grand for all that the Grand Duchess Helena had lived in it the previous year. "Not a human being—and not even a rushlight burning," Elizabeth complained. The situation made up for what the house lacked in architecture. The sea, which the Barrett children saw for the first time, created ever-changing pictures in the frames of the drawing-room windows—four of them that let in air and sunlight. There was a garden behind the house with tall trees and a view of hills which made homesick thoughts turn toward Hope End, and Malvern, and the mornings with Mr. Boyd. But he too, the Greek scholar, had been moved to peregrinate and found a place near enough to the Barretts for Elizabeth to resume her reading with him.

Two months went by and then half a year, yet Mr. Barrett issued no order to pack. Miss Barrett dated her letters 1833 yet she was still in the Sidmouth of green lanes and thatched cottages and the expanse of that restless sea. She could write of the place as a nest among elms but she missed the majestic Herefordshire landscape. The grandeur was concentrated upon the ocean, she criticized nature. She enjoyed that ocean, however, on boating parties though she seldom ventured on anything more daring than sitting in the bottom of the boat.

Then one day Elizabeth wrote to one of her correspondents, "Of course you know that the Bill has ruined the West Indians . . . The consternation here is very great. Nevertheless I am glad, and always shall be, that the negroes are—virtually free."

Mr. Barrett had no such tolerance for the Abolition Bill. He declared that no one in his right senses would even think of attempting the culture of sugar any more and suggested that they had better hang weights to the sides of the island of Jamaica and send it to the bottom of the ocean at once. No longer very rich, he entered into some mysterious business that took him from home for days at a time. He also sent Edward to Jamaica to look after his West Indian interests during the confusion before actual emancipation. Edward's absence somewhat attenuated Elizabeth's rejoicing over the abolition of slavery, but not for long. She vibrated to freedom like a leaf in the wind, like the prisoner she was to her uncertain health and her father's tenacious affection. Besides, Edward would not be too long away. Meanwhile she went on outings in the Devonshire countryside, walking a little with her brothers and sisters but more often ambling along after them on a donkey.

The Sidmouth stay prolonged itself to three years, uneventful on the surface but to Elizabeth significant for inner growth, as the spirit sank deep roots and sent up promises in branch and blossom of the fruit that was to come. Mr. Barrett hovered over her in nervous solicitude. Death had visited the family twice. It threatened in one's own dwelling, as the Grand Duchess Helena's house proved with that malicious purposefulness which inert matter often seems to have. So Mr. Barrett was kept busy pulling down chimneys that threatened to tumble and reinforcing brickwork after the masons cautioned the girls not to lean too much out of the windows. There was no protection against the tiles, however, that would suddenly leave their moorings as if ripped out by some mischievous *poltergeist* and come hurtling over their heads.

But then, every mote of dust, every wind that blew, was a menace to Mr. Barrett's oldest daughter. Still, her health had improved in the milder Sidmouth climate, and perhaps for that reason Mr. Barrett did not hasten their removal. Elizabeth had become more necessary to him after his wife's death, and she would have succeeded Mrs. Barrett as the natural female head of the house but for her semi-invalid state. As it was, she retained the highest place in the order of his attachment and it pleased him that she showed herself worthy. Oddly enough, her physical dependence constituted a major virtue in his eyes. Yet with that she combined, thanks to her Spartan training, an almost masculine strength of mind, together with a sense of honor that made her rightly allude to herself as "an honest man on the whole." Mr. Barrett did not leave her womanly qualities out of account, however, for he was once overheard saying that she was "the purest woman he ever knew."

When his comment was reported to Elizabeth she smiled, knowing perfectly well what he meant—simply "that I had not troubled him with the iniquity of love affairs, or any impropriety of seeming to think about being married." Marriage was his great dread in connection with his daughters and, for that matter, his sons, as they grew up. He had established his family pattern and would not tolerate any change in the design.

Elizabeth Barrett had not reached the age when most women had already given a few hostages to posterity without feeling more than an impersonal curiosity about love and marriage. As an avid reader of novels from Bulwer's to those of Mrs. Trollope whom she found lacking in nobility of mind, she learned enough about life to make her aware of how little she was living it.

It was George Sand, however, whose career as writer and emancipated woman was evolving more fantastically than the plots of her *Lélia* or *Indiana*, who brought home most forcibly to Miss Barrett all that she was missing. It was no mere coincidence that made her call the heroine of a poetic tale written at about this time by the thinly disguised name of "Leila."

George Sand, only slightly older than herself, was already a Lilith in experience. The Frenchwoman's impulsive nature, her generosity, her love of humanity and her defiance of convention in appeasing her tempestuous senses, made her one with Byron in the English girl's admiration. Long before her compatriots had lowered the hands they had lifted in horror over the French "female" and her immoral books, Elizabeth Barrett had seen the true greatness of the woman who wrote them.

Her estimate if anything grew greater with the years. Although she was enough her father's daughter to have a poor idea of women's power and depth of mind as compared to men's, she made an exception of George Sand, and in the eloquent defense she wrote of her in 1845 there is, as in all expression of opinion, an element of autobiography. "One woman indeed now alive . . . and only *that* one down all the ages of the world—seems to me to justify for a moment an opposite opinion—that wonderful woman George Sand; who has something monstrous in combination with her genius, there is no denying at moments . . . but whom, in her good and evil together, I regard with infinitely more admiration than all other women of genius who have ever been. Such a colossal nature in every way,—with all the breadth and scope of faculty which women want—magnanimous, and loving the truth and loving the people—and with that 'hate of hate' too . . .—so eloquent, and earnest as if she were dumb—so full of a living sense of beauty, and of noble blind instincts toward an ideal purity—and so proving right even in her wrong."

One of the two sonnets which Elizabeth Barrett wrote to George Sand is even more revealing.

> True genius, but true woman, dost deny
> The woman's nature with a manly scorn,
> And break away the gauds and armlets worn
> By weaker women in captivity?
> Ah, vain denial! that revolted cry
> Is sobbed in by a woman's voice forlorn.
> Thy woman's hair, my sister, all unshorn,
> Floats back dishevelled strength in agony,
> Disproving thy man's name. . . .

George Sand was doing what she, Elizabeth Barrett, could never hope to do. Yet she felt the spiritual kinship between them. She too had breadth and scope of faculty. She too was magnanimous, loving the truth, loving the people, sympathizing with the Negroes suffering under colonial slavery rather than with Mr. Barrett the slaveowner, for the loss of a source of his income. She knew that she could be eloquent in her "hate of hate," hate of injustice and oppression, of man's inhumanity to man. As for the living sense of beauty, the instincts toward ideal purity, her whole life so far had been dedicated to their realization if not in fact, at least in the only existence that circumstances had made possible.

In one thing she differed from George Sand. There was nothing monstrous in combination with her genius. She was wholly a woman and in every sense womanly. It was as a woman that she would fulfill herself—despite "the gauds and armlets worn by weaker women in captivity." Her own armlets were of another metal and, as from some enchantment, invisible to the eye. But they were all the more binding for being intangible. Still she would prove to George Sand—"my sister"—that without denying her woman's nature she too would burn in a poet-fire, letting her woman-heart "beat evermore through the large flame."

For the present, because she felt the intensity of life only through books, she could not speak in her own voice. Therefore the year that saw the scarcely noticed publication of *Pauline* saw also her translation of *Prometheus Bound*. It had taken her only thirteen days to turn Aeschylus's tragedy from Greek into English and it had been wholly a labor of love. As such, perhaps, it should have remained unpublished, even without her honest recognition of its faults. But published it was, though unadvertised and, like *Pauline*, almost unknown. Her father's pride had suggested publication and she had acceded. For she, more than any of the other children, loved him, with a large admixture of gratitude in her affection because of his interest in her writing. It was further understood between them that whatever Elizabeth accomplished she owed to him, from the drawing of her first breath to the newest poem.

> For 'neath thy gentleness of praise,
> My Father! rose my early lays!
> And when the lyre was scarce awake,
> I lov'd its strings for *thy* lov'd sake.

Such incense, lavished upon Mr. Barrett on one of his birthdays, made him want more. Perhaps to keep Elizabeth in his debt actually as well as spiritually, he again paid for the publication of the book, even though she could easily have taken care of the expense. Only last year her Grandmother Moulton had remembered her with a bequest of four thousand pounds in her will.

Prometheus Bound found its way to the *London Quarterly's* critic who dismissed it in gentlemanly fashion as "a remarkable performance for a young lady but not a good translation in and by itself." The *Athenaeum's* pundit in commenting on his copy, disapproved on the grounds that "those who adventure in the hazardous lists of poetic translation should touch any one rather than Aeschylus, and they may take warning from the writer before us." Indeed, any lover of Aeschylus, letting alone a reviewer, would have been appalled by the temerity of a poet's throwing the Greek iambics into blank verse and the lyrics into rhymed octosyllabics. But that was the least of the translator's sins. The undertaking in itself was a piece of daring that only a cloistered young scholar would have attempted. Later she judged her work more severely than any critic. "It is the most miserable of all miserable versions of the class . . . This sin of mine has been my nightmare and my daymare, too."

And very tangibly. Like *Pauline*, *Prometheus Bound* was shipped home to the translator, unwanted and unmourned. At her insistent prayers Mr. Barrett finally agreed to hide away the reproach of the unsold copies in the wardrobe of his bedroom.

The group of poems bound together with the translation received no notice and deserved none. They were literary exercises kindled by no deep emotion, impelled by no passion that must break out in a lyric cry. Yet even as a very young girl Elizabeth Barrett was intensely passionate. Whatever she felt, she felt deeply and with lasting effect. Feeling, indeed, sometimes made her the victim of sentimentality. She would weep on hearing music and tremble at the sound of a loud voice. But she could be strong and contained in the grip of powerful emotion. She was compelled to learn such discipline under her father's anxious scrutiny.

Her face portrayed in youth tells its story of self-mastery. The eyes look straight out, earnest and intelligent, the lids slightly drooping as from the weight of the great brow, serene as a cloudless horizon. The nose, thin and shapely, shows extreme sensibility in the winged nostrils that one can imagine quivering easily. The mouth, in contrast, has a masculine firmness in the compressed lips that do not succeed in obliterating a curve of humor, dimpling the cheeks to a smile. The whole countenance expresses controlled strength which only the glossy curling hair softens to femininity. It is the face of one who could keep a secret.

In spite of her sheltered life there had been things which she had had to keep to herself—the occasion, for instance, when she heard the word *love* from the lips of a man for the first time. It had filled her with horror because that same man had only recently declared his passion to the very girl who was her friend and confidante. "I was very young then," she said when she could speak of it, "and the world did, at the moment, look ghastly."

It was an unfortunate experience for a romantic girl to have. She could not mention it to anyone, least of all to her friend. So she had to contain the scorn that was in her, letting it grow from contempt of one man to mistrust of the whole sex. Words that she overheard from her brothers' friends did not inspire her with any greater confidence. "I've ruined my prospects by marrying!" one whom everybody believed to be happy cried out in a sort of smoking-room frankness. Another, reputed to be a paragon of husbands, expressed himself cynically on the subject. "I should have done as well if I had not married *her!*"

As for the lot of women, what she had observed in her own family had not given her any illusions about marriage. Could she endure to live such a life as her mother's? Not that it differed from the lives of other women of their acquaintance. All of them had to bow to the lord of the house. Elizabeth had been a mere child when she overheard two women talking.

"The most painful part of marriage," said one, "is the first year, when the lover changes into the husband by slow degrees." The other agreed as a matter of fact is agreed to.

It had seemed to the child a terrible thing, even though she scarcely understood what was involved in the process that made a lover change into something that made marriage painful. Did love die, then? Was marriage a way to kill love? She could not bear to think it and for comfort she would quote to herself two lines from her reading:

Si l'âme est immortelle
L'amour ne l'est-il pas?

Perhaps love might be immortal like the soul. Still, unmarried in her advanced twenties, Miss Barrett chastened romance with doubt.

Sometimes the three sisters would discuss the possibility of marriage. What if the perfect suitor came, would Mr. Barrett still object? Would he do so on the grounds of religion? Of family?

"If a prince of Eldorado should come," Elizabeth conjectured, "with a pedigree of lineal descent from some signory in one hand, and a ticket of good-behavior from the nearest Independent chapel, in the other—?"

"Why, even *then*," said Arabel, "it would not *do*."

And they knew it was so. They indulged in speculation nevertheless and often when they had friends of their own age visiting, they would talk "the foolishness which women talk when they are by themselves," as the serious Miss Barrett apologized. One day the female seminary decided to discuss love. What should be the woman's attitude toward the object of it?

"Perhaps it's safest to begin with a little aversion," said one.

"Oh, no, it would be wiser to start with a great deal of esteem," said another.

"The best attachments come from mutual respect," offered a third.

Miss Barrett listened quietly for a while. "It seems to me," she offered, "that real love is love that has no cause at all for it, and

the more wholly unreasonable, the better. It is love itself that counts
and not the object of it."

The girls demanded an explanation and Miss Barrett gave it,
warming up to the subject as she talked. "The love which could
throw itself out on an idiot with a goitre would be more admirable
than Abelard's!" she burst out in conclusion.

Everybody laughed at the notion.

"That's pure affectation on your part," accused one.

"Why, it's immoral!"

"I hope," said a third sarcastically, "that you'll act out your theory
for the advantage of the world."

"I haven't virtue enough for that," Miss Barrett answered gravely.

The subject was dismissed as pure nonsense and all went back to
their tea.

People who saw a little more deeply than others would chide
Elizabeth: "You expect too much—you are too romantic."

She bridled at their penetration and flashed the shield of her
skepticism. "I cannot expect too much when I expect nothing at all!"

Men like her Uncle Samuel who used to assure her that he loved
her more than Mr. Barrett did, certainly understood her better.
From the first he had singled her out from the rest of the family
and spoiled her with gifts, among them a perfume locket of crystal
set in coils of gold which she always wore. He gave her what was
even more important, a simple affection that was not afraid to speak
out. He said to her once, unexpectedly: "Beware of ever loving! If
you do, you will not do it half. It will be for life and death."

The words impressed her enough for her to remember them the
rest of her life.

But what chance was there of her ever falling in love? In Sidmouth
she went little into society and the friends she made, the Herrings
and Sir John Kean, presented no threat of romantic involvement.
Sometimes she almost believed she wanted none. But in London, of
which Mr. Barrett was beginning to talk? In London surely life
would be different. They would see more people, entertain more,
learn more of the world than was bounded by the walls of their house.

By the end of the summer of 1833 the Barretts left Sidmouth and
moved to 74 Gloucester Place, Baker Street. With his customary
abruptness Mr. Barrett issued his mandate and his well-trained brood
migrated as unquestioningly as the flock of wild geese at the imperative honk of the leader. The big dingy structure was to be an interim

residence, until Mr. Barrett had found a suitable unfurnished house for the Hope End moveables. It took another three years—did Mr. Barrett believe in the mystical potency of the number?—before he was satisfied that the building at 50 Wimpole Street answered the requirements for a permanent home. It was on a street well known to him for at Number 87 the firm of Lindsell had printed his daughter's *Battle of Marathon.*

Their stay at Gloucester Place was notable for a number of things. The family, to Mr. Barrett's intense satisfaction, was now gathered again under one roof, what with Edward returned from Jamaica and the two student sons from Glasgow. George had come back with a degree but Stormie with a shamed face for not having had the courage to meet the examiners on account of his incurable stammer.

Mr. Barrett kept himself busy and for a good part of the day left the domestic citadel in charge of its denizens who enjoyed a sort of democratic freedom until his return. They knew vaguely that he had business in the city where, now that Jamaica had ceased to be Eldorado, he launched various speculative ventures. On one occasion they learned of his buying a quarry. Then it was commerce that occupied him, and they would hear of cargoes shipped to Russia and to Egypt. It had all the unreality of something happening in another sphere and they did not trouble themselves about it. They were comfortably off. They had servants, all the necessities and many luxuries, and they were beginning to feel the excitement of London through the visitors who now began to come to Gloucester Place.

Elizabeth Barrett as a matter of course had her private sanctum to which the noises of the active household ascended like the murmur of a swarm of bees, a soothing sound that made her seclusion the more delightful. Sidmouth had greatly improved her health. When she was not writing she would receive callers or go out to penetrate the mystery of London with some member of her family. At first she had not liked the change from the elm-shaded garden and sea to the city, "wrapped up like a mummy in yellow mist,"— picturesque but unhealthy, for it brought back the cough that the Devonshire sunlight had almost cured. But little by little she let herself be seduced by metropolitan life. As it happened, Mr. Boyd had also come to London, to the pleasant oasis of St. John's Wood, not too far away. She could thus still keep in touch with the Greeks and respond to the stimulation of London literary society.

Otherwise little came to interrupt the domestic routine. The

Barretts had always been plagued by falling chimneys. The Gloucester Place house had the distinction of treating them to a spectacular cataclysm in the genre. Elizabeth and Edward were sitting in the dining room, talking, of all things, about shipwreck, when they heard a terrific crash as the chimney came down through the skylight into the entrance passage. The force of the falling bricks broke the stone steps as they bounded. In addition twenty-four large panes of glass left the windows, frames and all. The maid, Sarah, had chanced to look up and had seen the nodding brickwork. By the time she had run shrieking into the drawing room for Mr. Barrett, it was already too late. Not that he could have prevented the accident. But he could thank God that none of his children was hurt.

With the air of London occasional currents from the outside world penetrated into Elizabeth's room and found their way into her poetry. A more personal note, less dependent upon the bookish life which she knew best made itself heard, as if in the midst of her derivative music her heart had begun to sing. One of its first songs was a threnody inspired when, after the death of Felicia Hemans, the poet who signed herself L.E.L. commemorated her in a poem. Laetitia Elizabeth Landon had won herself a certain fame by her perfervid poetry which, of course, Miss Barrett had read. Her own poem, in honor of Mrs. Hemans she wrote in the form of an address to L.E.L.—"Thou bay-crowned living one that o'er the bay-crowned dead art bowing. . . ."

The slow, solemn music of the lines came in a cadenced flow as if to accompany the pace of a processional. The tone was lofty, as the circumstances required, but it rose from human grieving, and the tears "dropping o'er the tranquil eyes, the tears not of their shedding," were warm, living tears. The personified abstraction intruded nowhere in the eight stanzas. The speech was the speech of life and the emotion sprang from the heart touched not only by the "moveless brow" of the dead but by the tribute of the "crowned and living one."

A bold experimentation in the music showed that Miss Barrett had for the present laid aside her classical lyre. She needed more than its limited strings for the solemnity of her dirge, more than its restrained resonance to sustain the elevation of her thought.

> Nor mourn, O living one, because her part in life was mourning;
> Would she have lost the poet's fire for anguish of the burning?
> The minstrel harp, for the strained string? the tripod for the afflated
> Woe? or the vision, for the tears in which it shone dilated?

The alarmed Mr. Boyd in his cautious pedestrianism called her back from such dangerous vaulting. He disapproved not only of the manner but of the matter. Her writing a poem in the same form on "Cowper's Grave" did nothing to cheer him. Deep emotion was something undesired and incomprehensible to him in the bareness of his house of life to which he would admit only the golden mean. "Whenever I feel sorry for anything," he confided to Miss Barrett, "I am inclined to fall asleep." She knew that he cared for her more even than for his own daughter. But he was so devoid of any sensibility that she could say, only partly in jest, "If he heard of my death he would merely sleep a little sounder the next night."

As she well knew, she herself was far from asleep emotionally. Like L.E.L., soul-awakened to romanticism, Elizabeth Barrett responded to every thought and emotion, eager to become in her own being the thought and the emotion. "Be thou, Spirit fierce, my spirit!" every romanticist has cried since Shelley. "Be thou me, impetuous one!" Miss Barrett was no exception. Therefore when L.E.L died a few years later, before her youth had tasted fully of the love she had sung, Miss Barrett wrote "L.E.L.'s last Question" on the words L.E.L addressed to her friends at home from the desolate Cape where she was found, whether self-slain or murdered no one ever knew. "Do you think of me as I think of you?" The poignancy of that cry had to be answered.

> It seemed not much to ask—"as I of you?"
> We all do ask the same: no eyelids cover
> Within the meekest eyes that question over:
> And little in the world the loving do
> But sit (among the rocks?) and listen for
> The echo of their own love evermore—
> "Do you think of me as I think of you?"

The question was her own as well as L.E.L.'s. Like the dead poet she too could have described herself as "thirsty for a little love." Would she find the grail and drink from it before youth faded? Or would she, like so many women, stop at the halfway station of renunciation?

Chapter V: Expanding Circles

THERE is nothing like travel to clear the head and restore mind and heart to health. It was undeniable that the misadventures of *Pauline* had affected its author, for even though he knew that the soul gains strength through struggle and failure, he could have wished his recent effort had been less beneficial to the inner man and more rewarding to the poet. His parents had understood what he had not spoken and therefore encouraged the voyage to Russia which he proposed. The project was not too farfetched. At that time England was carrying on a brisk commerce with that colorful and mysterious country. Even Mr. Barrett, as we have seen, was exploiting the market with the cargoes of wool or coal which he sent to Odessa. Like him many another who lost a source of income by the emancipation of the slaves in the British West Indies, South Africa, and other colonies in 1834, sought to make good his losses by commercial investment.

Robert Browning's interest in Russia was diplomatic, however. Through his uncle Reuben Browning of the Rothschild banking firm, the family had become acquainted with the Chevalier George de Benkhausen, Russian Consul-General to St. Petersburg. At the very time that the youth was suffering most from his literary dejection and in revulsion was considering adopting a different career, the Russian Consul was recalled to St. Petersburg on an urgent mission. Would Robert Browning, he suggested, accompany him as an unofficial secretary? There might be a future. One could see the world, gain experience of life and people, even find oneself.

The best inducement was Browning's desire for change, any change. On March 1, 1834 he left his family and set out on his adventure, carrying with him in his luggage a Bible, the gift of his mother. At twenty-one he was an attractive youth with something of the continental in his ivory-tinted skin and dark hair worn long and in sculpturesque waves. He carried his head high and moved his slim body with grace. Although he was not tall he gave the impression of height.

The packet steamer on which he sailed landed its passengers at Rotterdam and from there on the rest of the journey of more than fifteen hundred miles was covered by relays of horses, pulling behind them the lumbering diligence with the travelers and their baggage. The Consul-General was not in so great a hurry as to ignore the treasures of art and architecture of the cities they traversed. Browning looked, studied and remembered with that same receptivity which as a boy, while he lay in apparent idleness in the meadows, had imprinted on his memory every note of the thrush singing "each song twice over" every petal of that

> . . . slight flower growing alone, and offering
> Its frail cup of three leaves to the cold sun.

Now it was pictures, buildings, and landscapes that he memorized— the portrait of Charlemagne, the oldest known of the emperor, which he saw in the Council Hall of the Rathhaus in Aix and later described in *Sordello*; the Castle of Ravenstein "that sleeps out trustfully its extreme age on the Meuse," which lent its romantic atmosphere to *Colombe's Birthday*; the versts of pine forest in Russia, that took forty-five years to be recalled, yet in spite of the lapse gave vivid color to *Iwàn Iwànovich*. Nothing escaped his watchful senses or failed to find its place in the storehouse of his memory.

A play too, now lost but for its title and a facetious description of it by Browning, came out of the two-month expedition. *Only a Player-Girl* never reached the boards but found oblivion in Browning's "russet horror of a portfolio," a receptacle which, like Dante's inferno, received sins and sinners in its various pockets and kept them confined till their author redeemed them or gave them quick extinction in the fire. "*Only a Player-Girl*," he wrote, "was Russian, and about a fair on the Neva, and booths and droshkies and fish-pies and so forth, with the palaces in the back ground . . . and the sayings and doings of her (the player-girl) and the others—such others!"

The society frequented by the Chevalier de Benkhausen included nobles and diplomats, if also player-girls and others. Among them Browning met Sir James Wylie who insisted on referring to him as "M. l'Italien." The mistaken nationality flattered the young man. He remained in St. Petersburg long enough to witness the annual spring ceremony celebrating the thawing of the Neva. It was not as splendid as the symbolic wedding of the Doge to the Adriatic on Ascension Day, but there was something of barbaric pageantry in the singing boatmen, the vividly dressed women and the ceremonial cutting of the ice which released the river from its winter imprisonment and furnished the city with water, a bowl of which the Czar raised to his lips in a half-Christian, half-pagan sacrament.

By the first day of May Browning was safely back in England. The trip had accomplished its purpose—so well, indeed, that he applied for a diplomatic post in Persia. For a while the plan rested on the knees of the gods, and then it fell to where all unfulfillment goes, for better or for worse. But surely there was rejoicing in the halls of the muses.

In the stimulating surroundings of his father's library the would-be diplomat soon forgot his disappointment. He went out a great deal and counted a new friend in the twenty-seven-year old Frenchman, Comte Amédée de Ripert-Monclar, a brilliant talker, a talented artist, and an amateur historian. The count too had reached Southampton Street through the Rothschild bank channels via Robert's uncle, William Shergold Browning.

A strong intellectual affinity must have existed between the two youths to make the Shelleyan rebel consort with a man of active Royalist sympathies. At that time England was full of French refugees from the 1830 three-days' revolution that succeeded in deposing the Bourbon Charles X and electing Louis Philippe, the Duke of Orleans, as a constitutional monarch. With Charles X hundreds of his followers fled to England. But the overthrow of the Bourbon scarcely constituted a revolution as in 1793. It simply meant the transfer of governmental power from one political faction to another. Louis Philippe soon proved that he was a Republican in name only.

Comte Amédée, a Bourbon sympathizer, served as an intermediary during the summer months between the Royalists in France and their brothers in exile. He was often at the Brownings' and soon knew enough about Robert and his ambitions to suggest a subject for his next poem—Theophrastus Bombast von Hohenstein, better known by his nom-de-guerre of Paracelsus.

The suggestion caught Browning's fancy and he was soon rummaging through the home library in search of material. His father had not failed him. On the shelves, together with the ever reliable Biographie Universelle he found Melchior Adam's Vitae Germanorum Medicorum, published in 1620, and Frederick Britiskius' three-volume edition of the writings of Paracelsus. The polyglot had no difficulty in making the sources his own.

It would be a mistake, however, to look upon Browning as a bookworm in spite of his heavy drafts upon learning. Culture for him was an extension of the mind to the endless vistas of man's achievement. Every language acquired, every book read, opened out another casement through the walls of ignorance, giving the mind a view of the beginning when the world was without form, of remote ages when man was without speech to tell his dreams, without fire to light the blackness till a daring one stole a spark from the gods. Knowledge made every age as real as one's own and oneself a participant in its story. Browning could be a Saul with the Hebrews, a Greek with the Greeks, singing and believing that

> . . . never morn broke clear as those
> On the dim clustered isles in the blue sea,
> The deep graves and white temples and wet caves.

Yet these were single views, and only that man could count himself enlightened who lived in a house of many windows. The complete man must do more than look out. He must also have direct, red-blooded contact with the great world of reality.

For six months Browning studied, wrote, and lived, doing all with inexhaustible energy. He also found time to sit for his portrait to Monclar, who has left the picture of a dandified young man with a clean-cut profile prominently featuring the nose which had so displeased Sarah Flower, a fine mouth, a manly chin, and the eyes and brow of a poet. One can understand why people stopped to admire his hair, lustrous and becomingly arranged on the well-shaped head. The light beard along the cheek and chinline is the amiable affectation of a young man who did not need it to be remarked in the world.

It was Browning's literary father, Mr. Fox, who found a publisher for the new poem, but it was his real father who paid the printing costs to Effingham Wilson of Royal Exchange. There was no cloaking the poet in anonymity this time. When *Paracelsus* appeared in the midsummer of 1835, the title page carried the name of Robert Browning. He had no fear that any Mill would penetrate the heart of his mystery even though the poem contained as much of himself as *Pauline*, and Shelley still hovered over it in spirit if not in word. The characters, Paracelsus the seeker after knowledge, and Aprile the knight errant of love, are given a local habitation as well as a name. They speak for themselves, at least on the printed page, in a spiritual drama that remains, in spite of Browning's denial, essentially his own.

He had reached a parting of the ways. Was he, the poet, to aspire to the ultimate in knowledge for its own sake, surrendering all to it, the warmth of human companionship and affection, or like Aprile should he seek only love? But there were many kinds of love as he showed through that sweet singer. The noblest he himself had found in Shelley's Intellectual Beauty. It is Browning's translation of that love which Paracelsus finally recognizes as perfect in communion and understanding. However, Browning asserted optimistically what Shelley had begun to doubt shortly before he died, when he wrote in his unhappiness:

> I loved—oh, no, I mean not one of ye,
>   Or any earthly love, though ye are dear
> As human heart to human heart may be;—
>   I loved, I know not what—but this low sphere
> And all that it contains, contains not thee,
>   Thou, whom, seen nowhere, I feel everywhere.

For Browning then and to the close, love remained as pervasive as the circumambient air.

It took him four thousand lines of blank verse and three songs to reveal in this drama of the soul that knowledge without humanity is selfish and sterile.

> I go to prove my soul!

cries Paracelsus as he sets forth.

> I see my way as birds their trackless way.
> I shall arrive! what time, what circuit first
> I ask not: but unless God send his hail
> Or blinding fire-balls, sleet or stifling snow,
> In some time, his good time, I shall arrive.

It was verse which rushed with the force of a torrent, carrying thought to an impact that frothed up into related thought, making it shine in the light of an amazing intellect. The music of the songs on the other hand, had the sweet, sinuous grace of some nostalgic air played on a harpsichord. The content was startlingly modern. Aprile's "I hear a voice" was important too for its formulation of Browning's reiterated conviction that to do was a prime necessity in life. A haunting echo of genius wasted or unused comes as from some limbo of unfulfillment in the voices that Aprile hears, bidding him do what they had not done.

Couldst not sing one song for grace?
Not make one blossom man's and ours?
Must one more recreant to his race
Die with unexerted powers,
And join us, leaving as he found
The world, he was to loosen, bound?
Anguish! ever and forever;
Still beginning, ending never!

Had Browning never written anything but *Paracelsus*, he would have changed the world to the extent of contributing this robust credo to the song of life. But he went further. For he now boldly announced his theme of the soul's travailing through vision, struggle, and defeat to final triumph, which he was to treat in variations in his most important work.

In gratitude to Comte Amédée for suggesting the subject Browning dedicated *Paracelsus* to him.

It is a foregone conclusion that Browning's literary godfather should have responded generously to this new demonstration of the genius he had so early discovered. But not even the anxious author expected anything like the praise that filled nearly a dozen pages in the *Monthly Repository*. The busy editor had let four months go by before he spoke; his review more than justified the delay.

Still, no matter how gratifying the commendation of friends may be it is doubly agreeable coming from strangers. The chief merit of criticism as of diagnosis lies in objectivity, and so Browning had every reason to be pleased with the three columns devoted to his poem in the September issue of the *Examiner* which the twenty-three-year-old literary barrister, John Forster, had been moved to write. Two of its sentences alone should have sufficed to heal the hurt inflicted by Mill. "We may safely predict for him (Browning) a brilliant career, if he continues true to the present promise of his genius. He possesses all the elements of a fine poet."

Yet such is the unreasonableness of the artist that, as Byron remarked, one unfavorable review will rankle long after a dozen good ones are forgotten. The bad one, as it happened, was the first to be rushed into print, exactly a week after *Paracelsus* appeared, with that precipitancy to warn away readers which the adverse reviewer seems to have. The whole review consisted of one paragraph. "There is talent in this dramatic poem . . . but it is dreamy and obscure. Writers would do well to remember by way of example that though it is not difficult to imitate the mysticism and vagueness of Shelley we love him . . . not *because* of these characteristics, but in *spite* of them."

The chastening parental tone was identical with that in which the critic of the same magazine, the *Athenaeum*, had warned Miss Barrett on the foolhardiness of translating Aeschylus. Both Miss Barrett and Browning, however, were rapidly pulling away from such leading strings and turning deaf to such warnings, trusting rather to their inner guidance and growing independence.

The following year, Coburn's *New Monthly Magazine* did much toward making both Browning and Miss Barrett known to the world. In the March issue John Forster, who felt he had not yet done justice to the author of *Paracelsus*, published an article of twice the length of his original review in which he declared: "Without the slightest hesitation we name Mr. Browning at once with Shelley, Coleridge and Wordsworth." With Shelley! For Browning that was indeed touching hands with immortality! As if that were not enough, Forster went on: "He has entitled himself to a place among the acknowledged poets of the age. . . . He has written a book that will live."

But Browning's contemporaries were hard to convince, and very few invested the six shillings necessary to make the book their own. For that reason Browning always spoke of the work as a failure although he confessed his true estimate by describing himself on the title pages of successive volumes as "the author of *Paracelsus*." It was only right, for *Paracelsus* not only admitted him into the company of the foremost literary men of his day, but also opened his way to a new field.

In July of 1836, the *New Monthly Magazine* published a ballad of twenty-seven stanzas called "The Romaunt of Margret." When Elizabeth Barrett had finished writing it she knew with that unfailing sense of the artist that she had produced something for more than her limited audience. Still, she had misgivings about trying the literary market. At that time Richard Hengist Horne was being very much talked about for his poetry which caused as much stir because of its author's eccentricities as for its merits. Miss Barrett had read and admired it. Through Mrs. Orme, an acquaintance of hers, she sent the manuscript of her poem to Mr. Horne, requesting him to tell her frankly whether he considered it good. His answer was eloquent. He forwarded it at once to Bulwer, then editor of the *New*

Monthly Magazine, and Miss Barrett thus made her first professional appearance in a periodical. In October Bulwer published another balladic poem, "The Poet's Vow," for which Miss Barrett had chosen as the motto: "Oh, be wiser thou, instructed that true knowledge leads to love."

It was not to Wordsworth, from whom she had borrowed the motto, but to Tennyson, of whom she had not read a line, that her work was subsequently compared by the critics. The unjust accusation of her adopting too many Tennysonianisms enraged her, but the association worked toward her advantage. Of the two poems "The Romaunt of Margret" was by far the better. A mood of desolation and eeriness is established by the opening verses and sustained as the narrative unfolds. The theme of "failing human love" is as old as the oldest ballad, and the style with its refrain, equally familiar. The touches of nature are entirely her own, as well as the pathos and the power of the telling. One stanza illustrates both her vividness and her occasional lapse in taste.

> "He *loved* but only thee!
>   *That* love is transient too.
> The wild hawk's bill doth dabble still
>   I' the mouth that vowed thee true:
> Will he open his dull eyes,
>   When tears fall on his brow?
> Behold the death-worm to his heart
>   Is a nearer thing than *thou,*
>   Margret, Margret.

What is remarkable about the poem is that it antedates by many years the work in the genre by Dante Gabriel Rossetti and William Morris. Also, it began to win her a popular audience which Browning long hoped for in vain.

For both poets it was a time of creative fervor and expansion. Browning went out into the world. The world came to Elizabeth Barrett. In the merging circles of new friendships they had acquaintances in common. They shared admirations. But for them the meeting was still far off, though their names reached them as echoes in the hubbub of society. Both were working on large projects: Browning on a long poem, *Sordello,* which he had begun shortly after the publication of *Pauline* and interrupted for *Paracelsus,* and Elizabeth Barrett on what she described to Mr. Boyd as "my drama of the Angels."

Browning was to find *Sordello's* progress checked again by an entirely different undertaking. Late in 1835 he had dropped in at Mr. Fox's after dinner and there met the actor-manager, William Macready whose eloquent pauses had already become legendary in the theater. He responded immediately to the youth whose work he had not yet read but of whom he had heard through his other friend, Forster. So very much impressed was he that he recorded the meeting in his diary the same evening, November 27, finding Browning "more like a youthful poet" than any man he had ever seen, and admiring the intelligence of his face. "I took Mr. Browning on," he noted, "and requested to be allowed to improve my acquaintance with him." Browning reciprocated with equal cordiality. By the end of the evening they had exchanged cards and Browning promised his new friend a copy of *Paracelsus.*

Within the next week Macready had not only received but read the poem and delivered himself of his opinion. It was a work of great daring, he found, starred with poetry of thought, feeling, and diction, if occasionally obscure. He was not slow either in discovering its dramatic power. "The writer can scarcely fail to be a leading spirit of the time," he prophesied, setting to work at once to turn that spirit to his advantage as well as of the art for which he lived.

He was in despair over the state of the theater. A great tragic actor, he was always looking for new roles to redeem contemporary drama from the morass into which it had sunk, only to fall back upon plays grown stale with use, to which not even he could give the vitality of a run of more than a few performances. He was also contemplating leaving Drury Lane for Covent Garden. Perhaps with the change of locale might come a change in fortune.

For him the theater, glorified by Shakespeare, represented the highest art. In its service he was willing to put up with the miseries, disappointments, and humiliations which all too often he had to confide to his diary. He could not help dreaming of a golden age of drama, however, even in his dejection, and for that reason gathered about him young and promising literary men like Forster and now Browning. "It would indeed be some recompense for the . . . heartsickening disgusts which I have endured in my profession, if by its exercise I had awakened a spirit of poetry whose influence would elevate, ennoble and adorn our degraded drama."

He was thinking specifically of Browning in that awakening. The poet had met his admiring critic Forster at a New Year's gathering at Macready's house in Elstree. The two had at once struck up a friendship. Already vast plans engaged them in endless discussion, the most tangible of them the promise that Browning would write for Macready a tragedy on Justinian's general, Narses.

"May it be!" Macready hopefully suspired in his diary.

But *Sordello*? What of *Sordello*, the poem of the development of a soul with which Browning intended to answer Mill and other critics for the failure of *Pauline*? He had been writing and rewriting, casting and recasting this poetic saga of the medieval troubadour, keeping his father working overtime on historical research and making himself thought-sick over its many involvements. For more than two years he had been struggling to bring it to an end and still it grew in complexity and dimensions like another labor of Hercules. It was therefore halfheartedly that he abandoned it temporarily for Narses. When would he ever finish it?

Justinian's general failed to come to life and for a time no one else suggested himself as a subject for tragedy. As it chanced, Forster who had been working on a biography of Thomas Wentworth, Lord Strafford, fell ill in the middle of it and Browning like a good friend brought it to completion in time for it to be published early in May, 1836. Impatiently Macready waited for his play, although in the meantime he had accepted Sergeant Talfourd's classical drama, *Ion*, which was to inaugurate the actor's accession to Covent Garden.

The opening on May 26 occurred auspiciously on Talfourd's birthday and he had reason to be elated. The audience was like a gathering of a literary Olympus. In one of the boxes sat Wordsworth with Walter Savage Landor beside him. Other poets and writers, actors and actresses, artists and beautiful women occupied conspicuous seats, their presence testifying to the importance of the occasion. John Forster, both as Macready's friend and as critic for the *Examiner*, had to be there. With him was Robert Browning, aspiring dramatist.

Ion received such acclaim that its success was assured. Thus the evening party which Talfourd had arranged at his house on Russell Square to celebrate his birthday also served to mark his triumph and Macready's. As a token of regard the actor was placed between Wordsworth and Landor. But he would have preferred to dispense with the honor, complaining in his journal of "Wordsworth who pinned me." Ellen Tree, the actress, was also one of the guests and so was Miss Mitford, the "tragic" writer, with her careless chit-chat but with a shrewd eye for possible sponsors for her tragedies, and contributors to her elegant annuals. At the other side of the table sat Forster and Browning, listening with the respect of youth to the pronouncements of their elders but now and then making themselves heard.

As the night wore on toasts were proposed and drunk. Then to Browning's amazed delight, Sergeant Talfourd raised his glass to the author of *Paracelsus*. Landor, like a god of the Greeks, bowed his magnificent head and drank to the younger poet. But Wordsworth, with great generosity for one who had cut only a few pages of Keats' early poems and thrown the book aside, rose and, leaning over the table, said: "I am proud to drink your health, Mr. Browning."

Saul was indeed among the prophets.

Late that night as the guests were taking their leave, Macready touched Browning affectionately on the shoulder and pleaded, unaware of the implied slight to *Ion*: "Will you not write me a tragedy and save me from going to America?"

To avert such a calamity to the English stage Browning soon afterward informed Macready that he had decided to write a play on the subject of Strafford. "He could not have hit upon one that I could have more readily concurred in," the actor rejoiced.

When Macready was making this notation in his diary, the much harassed poet was writing to a recently found friend, a literary lady and neighbor of the actor's at Elstree, Euphrasia Fanny Haworth, thirty-five, unwed and susceptible: "I am going to begin the finishing Sordello—And to begin thinking about a tragedy (an Historical one, so I shall want heaps of criticism on 'Strafford')—and I want to have another tragedy in prospect . . . I want a subject of the most wild and passionate love, to contrast with the one I want to have ready in a short time. I have many half-conceptions, floating fancies: give me your notion of a thorough self-devotement, self-forgetting; should it be a woman who loves thus, or a man? What circumstances will best draw out, set forth this feeling? . . ."[1]

Browning's very objectivity in wanting "a subject of the most wild and passionate love" proved him as yet untouched by either love or passion.

Miss Haworth meanwhile was expressing herself in sonnets two of which, "To the Author of *Paracelsus*," found their way to the *New Monthly Magazine* for September, 1836. The first described the poet and foretold his future:

[1] From holograph letter, Baylor Browning Collection.

He hath the quiet calm and look of one
Who is assur'd in genius too intense
For doubt of its own power; yet with the sense
Of youth, not weakness,—like green fruits in spring,
Telling rich autumn's promise—tempering
All thought of pride. . . .

The second voiced a yearning:

. . . . Then, poet give to me
No splendour, but one feeling true and kind
That, if unskill'd wholly to comprehend
Thy scope of genius—I may call thee friend.

The feeling true and kind of an uncomplicated friendship was exactly what Browning gave her, no more, no less.

Chapter VI: *De Profundis*

M R. JOHN KENYON was too fat, too old, and too dignified to
be cast in the role of Cupid even by a prankish chance. Yet
that was exactly the part reserved for him in one of the most inspiring
of life's romances. He came, one day, like a benevolent fate, knocking
at the door of the house on Gloucester Place, with the privileges of
blood kinship as a pretext and his importance in the world as his
calling card. He did not come to see his distant cousin Mr. Barrett,
but his still more remote kin, Mr. Barrett's poet-daughter whose
name Mr. Kenyon had been hearing with more and more frequency
in the literary circles that were his chosen milieu, both as a patron
of the arts and as a practicing bard of sorts. Indeed, his friend
Wordsworth had made a rather ambiguous pronouncement on his
writings. "I cannot say it is precisely poetry, but it is something as
good,"—which satisfied Mr. Kenyon's modest muse.

By the conventions of that unusual family Mr. Kenyon was admitted as Miss Barrett's special guest, both Mr. Barrett and the rest
accepting the fact by a tacit understanding which made everything
right provided Mr. Barrett's tenor of life was not disturbed. The
rules and regulations were few but explicit. The children might have
whatever callers they chose if only they did not trouble him with
introductions or inflict their visitors upon him at dinner. On the
latter subject he was inflexible—none of their guests at dinner, a
function which had almost the sacrosanctity of a ritual supper.

But the *bon viveur* Kenyon had no need of the fare of Gloucester
Place, and soon afterward, of Wimpole Street. His table was as
renowned as his cellar and to that all the gourmets of England could
testify, if the literary great who drank of his wine and ate of his
food were not too much concerned with higher things to mark the
delight of their palates. Though in body something of a Silenus in
his mid-fifties and weighing over two hundred pounds, he had an
exquisiteness of soul that made his bulk vibrate like a reed to beauty.
Even while engaged in dining, one of his keenest pleasures, he would
not overlook the aesthetics of the table. Everything must be well

cooked, gracefully served, and thoroughly enjoyed. Once when he introduced his dinner guests to the as yet unknown luxury of some canvasback ducks, prepared as only his cook could prepare them, he exhorted while serving: "Do not talk, pray, but eat and think." He said the words in all seriousness and with equal gravity his guests complied. After all, at what other table could they dine so well?

Like Mr. Barrett, Mr. Kenyon had derived most of his money from the West Indian sugar plantations. Like him, too, he had been taken to England from his native Jamaica and educated at English schools, though he never took a degree. He married a wife with a considerable dowry and bought a house in Somerset, near Nether Stowey, among the Quantock hills associated with Coleridge. That was long after the visionary Pantisocrat had tried to make prosperity and poetry meet in the little cottage to which he had taken his wife, his children and Nanny the servant, "scientific in vaccimulgence"— a useless talent on a farm that could not afford a cow. It could not afford many other necessities as well, so that by the time John Kenyon settled among the meadow and dingle, fir and heather of Nether Stowey, the extended palm of need was reached out to him by Coleridge's household. He could well exercise his generosity. After the death of his wife he married a still richer one, Caroline Curteis, whose only brother, even wealthier than herself, seemed vowed to bachelorhood—a golden prospect in case he died before his sister. Not that John Kenyon harbored such thoughts. He was one of those men, however, endowed with Midas' touch without the disadvantages.

Coleridge was dead by now—he had died in 1834—but the need remained. Unobtrusively Mr. Kenyon helped, there as elsewhere, in heart-warming friendship rather than charity. Indeed, he the devotee of greatness, the feeder of lions, as he was called, the zealous but pedestrian versifier of abstract virtues and historic cities, the worshiper of Apollo and the muses, possessed genius only in friendship. But in that he had few equals. He knew everyone in London and de-lighted in a private mathematical play of personalities, bringing people together, enlarging circles, and rejoicing in the combinations and permutations that ensued. In 1835 when he appeared on the Barrett doorstep he had begun to resume his genial hospitality after a decent period of mourning for his second wife who had recently died.

In his gifted relative, Miss Barrett, with her poetry and her ro-mantic ill-health, he found a challenging figure for his mathematics.

He found also a witty talker, erudite without being a blue-stocking, and of a winning naturalness. He was amazed at how young she looked, no older than a girl about to be brought out. As for her poetry, he had no doubt of the qualities in it which, if developed, would make her known to the large audience he knew she deserved. Unambitious for himself, he was ambitious for her.

After Elizabeth had begun showing him her work and confiding her plans to him, he saw to it that her name reached not only his poet friends but those editors who could help to spread it. He introduced it casually at large dinners, or he would drop it into the unsuspecting ear of a compiler of gift books, those elegant songsters which, with the pet canary, no ladies' chamber could be without. Thus, Miss Barrett would be presented with a fanciful picture—for art shared honors equally with literature in the annual—and requested to write a poem appropriate to the subject. The compensation, of course, was nominal since the compiler had to receive some reward for the labor. And so for five pounds and a fine copy of the book, priced at two guineas, the poet gave wings to imagination and the midnight oil did the rest.

Miss Barrett, always the dedicated poet even when writing to order, gave to her commission from the indefatigable Mary Russell Mitford the wealth of her fancy and scholarship, impressed possibly by Miss Mitford's assurance that the splendid annual contained only the choicest poets and would surely "be seen on the table of almost every rich person of taste in England." Hence when Miss Barrett's narrative poem, "A Romance of the Ganges," appeared, it had besides a romantically colored description of the Hindu festival of the flame-boats, a touching story of love betrayed and the pediment of three learned notes, so that no rich person of taste in England could possibly fail to derive the fullest profit from the exotic tale. None could say that Miss Mitford had not received her money's worth.

John Kenyon was pleased with the results of his propaganda. A few more friends like Miss Mitford for Cousin Ba and her career would be prosperously launched. He was not blind to her possibilities as a social lioness either. She charmed him by the grace of her person and brought a twinkle to his eyes behind their formidable spectacles by her witty sallies, when she did not widen them by some profoundly learned allusion.

By slow degrees he got her to leave her room for the parlor. Then

cunningly he led her out of the parlor to the park and then the zoo
to look at the giraffes and the Diorama. Finally he enjoyed the
triumph of seeing her at his dinner table with her brother Edward
for moral support.

It was a resplendent gathering, such a gathering as Browning had
enjoyed at almost the same time at Macready's. Wordsworth, however, did not drink to the poetry of Mr. Kenyon's relative as he had
to take it on trust, not having read any of it. But he flattered Miss
Barrett by having her "hear his conversation"—not particularly
"prominent" conversation, as she commented, especially when followed by the brilliant Landor's. But then, how could the Lake Poet
compare with the Greek god, "in whose hands the ashes of antiquity
burn again?" To her Landor represented the spirit of Greece returned
to earth in the flesh to make known its ancient glories to the world
once more. He stood large in genius to Wordsworth's "eminent
talent."

Edward distinguished himself by bearding the leonine Landor
during a coruscating piece of oratory, when he accused him of ambitious singularity and affectation. Yet even her too biased affection
did not make her agree with her brother.

Oddly, her estimate of Wordsworth and Landor coincided with
Browning's. But then both she and Browning were closer to Greece
than to the realities of their day in the strangely isolated education
they had received as children.

Elizabeth Barrett's health did not thrive in the fogs of London and
the cold damp winter brought back her lung symptoms. The removal
to Wimpole Street the walls of whose houses looked "so much like
Newgates turned inside out" did little to cheer her. Too soon the
exciting ventures into the brilliant night world had to cease. Besides,
Papa, though proud of her success with the great as reported with
amusing asides by Edward was not pleased to have his singing bird
turn to a moth.

He did his best, however, to render her back bedroom as little like
an invalid's as books and attractive furnishings could make it. The
bed was disguised as a sofa. A large table placed out in the room
toward the wardrobe end of it had a convivial look. There were
several armchairs conveniently arranged. The washing table, masked
as a cabinet, further abetted the deception by a row of shelves above
it. The chest of drawers too was crowned with shelves, fashioned by
"Sette and Company," from papered deal and crimson merino. The

busts of Chaucer and Homer guarded the departments of English and Greek poetry. Three other busts, unidentified, consecrated the wardrobe. The window, like that of the Hope End cage, had green curtains and a flower box planted with scarlet runners, nasturtiums, and ivy, the last Mr. Kenyon's gift. Once he also brought back for her from Rydal Mount some geranium cuttings from Wordsworth's garden. These she treasured for poetry's sake. She had also put away two Greek epigrams of Landor's which the Hellenist had recently given her. Thus the symbols grew in her poetic life wherein the busts of the famous dead gradually outnumbered the living whom she admitted into her privacy.

If her life in the world was necessarily restricted, she lived intensely within, setting down in black and white in her minuscule hand-writing—as a saving to her energy—the visions that seethed in her imagination, more than ever active in her enforced physical inactivity. The results of her industry she published in 1838 in her volume *The Seraphim and other Poems.* It was the first book to which she affixed her name.

The theme of the title poem, "from which Milton would have shrank!" as one reviewer exclaimed, was indeed a bold one, compara-ble in daring to Byron's *Cain* with which it had other kinships, both good and bad. Like *Cain* too it might be called a drama in that it is a dialogue between two Seraphim, Ador and Zerah, who look down on Calvary during the Crucifixion and comment on what they see. The rhymed verse of varied meter alters with the emotion of the speakers whose dialogue is interrupted at the final agony of Christ by Earth, crying:

> I have groaned, I have travailed: I am weary.
> I am blind with my own grief, and cannot see
> As clear-eyed angels can, his agony;
> And what I see I also can sustain,
> Because his power protects me from his pain.
> I have groaned; I have travailed: I am dreary,
> Hearkening the thick sobs of my children's heart . . .

The very weariness of matter groans in that refrain, the utter helplessness of earth caught between man her creature and God her Maker. The immortal tragedy is retold with profound emotion by the seraphic beholders, but the author has not yet learned to make immortal poetry of it. It has passion without force and a facility which discipline has only begun to curb. Yet here and there some startlingly effective passage, a phrase, an image, gives earnest of latent power still to be expressed.

Had *The Seraphim* been published alone, it would have overawed the reader rather than won him. As it was, the volume contained among shorter poems like "The Poet's Vow" and "Isobel's Child," the "Romaunt of Margret" which with other works in the same vein had begun to win Miss Barrett the influential magazine reader. The public is always intimidated by intellect, especially in a female poet, and *The Seraphim* had more than its share of it—a sinewy intellect which, if it had to be classified, was more masculine than feminine, despite the *Athenaeum's* welcoming of the volume in the words of Henry Chorley as "an evidence of female genius and accomplishment." It was only when Elizabeth Barrett allowed her woman's heart to speak out without interference from the mind with which she too was impressed, that she fulfilled herself and reached poetic greatness. But that time was still to come. For the present it was enough that she began to be mentioned with Tennyson whom like everyone else she was now admiringly reading.

Suddenly, whether because the London climate was at last taking its toll or because, as Elizabeth believed, she had ruptured a blood vessel in the lungs, her health grew so much worse that the whole family was thrown into confusion. It was one thing to have a romantic invalid ensconced and privileged in her shrine. It was quite another to be faced with serious illness. The doctors were summoned and duly wrote out their prescriptions, which made Mr. Barrett snort with contempt when he saw how little they helped his daughter. Nevertheless he worried about her condition and when a change of air was suggested he went so far as to begin giving it consideration in the family councils that he democratically held without, however, yielding one autocratic inch.

Again the months passed before he could resolve to break up the family. By the autumn of the following year Elizabeth was so much worse that he agreed to have her moved to Torquay in the hope that the milder climate and the nearness to the sea which had benefited her in Sidmouth would help her again. He fixed upon No. 1 Beacon Terrace, the house occupied by an aunt of Elizabeth's. Edward accompanied his sister. It was also arranged that Arabel and Henrietta take turns staying with her. For them it was a welcome holiday from their father. Elizabeth, however, parted from him tearfully, but he promised to come to see her often.

The regimen of fresh air, sunshine, and nourishing food was supplemented by medical authority with opium, "To keep the pulse from fluttering and fainting and to give the right composure and point of balance to the nervous system," Miss Barrett was told. Obediently she took the prescribed doses although no one had anything illuminating to say about her illness or its causes. One of the doctors, William F. Chambers, physician in ordinary to Queen Adelaide, suggested it might be poetry, as if it were a disease. "A sort of fungus of the brain," the invalid commented roguishly when he made an elaborate ceremony of carrying her inkstand out of the room. "You will have such a pulse tomorrow," he said.

The pulse showed no variation; neither did the doctor's opinion. "Nobody can be properly well who exercises poetry as an art," he maintained. "I've studied the physiology of poets. It's true even of men. But for women, it is a mortal malady. As for you, Miss Barrett, I've never known a system approaching yours in excitability—except Miss Garrow's. Yes, Miss Garrow is a young lady who wrote verses for Lady Blessington's annuals. I don't give her two years, for all she's dancing quadrilles . . . You must mend your ways, Miss Barrett, take to reading a course of history, for example."

She was amused by the opinion of Dr. Chambers who after all had scant knowledge of literature. But she was scandalized when she overheard Mr. Kenyon, who had also come to winter at Torquay, remark in all seriousness within her hearing: "What if genius should be nothing but scrofula?"

But then, for all his verses, Mr. Kenyon was not really a man of letters, she told herself. He was rather a sybarite of letters, which did not diminish him in her affection. She learned to know how to take his well-meant advice and drew such a lifelike thumbnail sketch of him as would have done honor to the most expert writer of characters. "Do you think he ever knew what mental labor is? . . . No more than he knows what mental inspiration is. And not more than he knows what strife of the heart is. . . . He seems to me to evade pain . . . the secret of all being that he has a certain latitudinarianism (not indifferentism) in his life and affections, and has no capacity for concentration and intensity. Partly by temperament and partly by philosophy he contrives to keep the sunny side of the street— though never inclined to forget the blind man at the corner." As it happened, both in Torquay and later, the urbane latitudinarian would frequently leave his predilected sunny side of the street to spend a few hours with that being of vibrant intensity who was slowly but inevitably shrinking into a shadowy corner of life.

Spiritually, however, the lamp was kept burning. When Miss Barrett was not writing she was reading, to the annoyance of Dr. Chambers who fulminated against her intellectual fare, especially the Greeks. In an impish mood she had her solemn Plato bound to resemble a novel, so for a while she could study in peace and satisfy the good doctor at the same time.

The presence of Edward was a source of joy, making her illness seem almost worthwhile. In fair weather she would join him outdoors and even on boating parties as at Sidmouth, with the friends Edward so readily made. He was a gay, life-loving youth, inclined to strain at the leash and to run wild in the intoxication of freedom. At his age his father had been married more than a decade, yet in his life of thirty-two years Edward had been permitted no bond closer than that of his family. To Elizabeth he represented perfection in the male sex, this wholly unselfish youth who willingly gave up the excitement of London to amuse her with his bright talk. He was the one being on whom she could lavish her wealth of heart and mind and know it was generously returned. For his part he was very proud of his sister. He had seen how such men as Wordsworth and Landor had paid court to her. He was also impressed by the volume of mail that had begun to come to her after the appearance of *The Seraphim*. She was on her way to fame. As for Elizabeth, she derived more satisfaction from his pleasure than from her success. "My sympathies drooped toward the ground like an untrained honeysuckle," she confessed, ". . . but for one, in my own house."

She had to battle with her father for his consent to part with that one. To begin with Edward was suffering under paternal displeasure at that time for having dared to fall in love and, worse, to mention marriage. A Jovian No had been thundered. But Mr. Barrett desired to make it more emphatic by his forbidding presence and therefore sent urgent requests for his son to join him in London. When at last Edward was about to leave, Elizabeth, weakened as she was by fatigue and illness, burst into tears, whereupon her sympathetic aunt sat down at once and wrote a letter to Mr. Barrett, saying that he would break his daughter's heart if he insisted on wanting Edward back.

Mr. Barrett acted strictly according to his nature. He yielded to women's tears but he did not conceal his disapproval. "Under such circumstances," he pronounced, "I do not refuse to suspend my purpose, but I consider it to be very wrong in my daughter to exact such a thing." He knew that Elizabeth loved her brother better than himself—she was too honest to conceal it either from her father or from the rest of the family—and an edge of jealousy cut into his magnanimity. But for Elizabeth the only important fact was that she would not be parted from Edward—not for the present.

Suddenly in April of 1840 news came from the West Indies that Samuel, the second of the Barrett sons, who had been looking after the family property, had died in February. He had always had a streak of wildness in him and passions not easily controlled. The easy licentious life of Jamaica, away from family influence, made him indulge his protest to Mr. Barrett's rigorous puritanism to the full. Several times he was recalled to England for a moral lesson, but a year or so earlier he had been sent back to the colony and its unlimited temptations. Elizabeth, who had always feared the dangers to him from his dissipation, had sometimes ventured on advice. But it was yellow fever that killed him at the age of twenty-eight.

The family was paralyzed under the blow, the first that seriously broke up their united circle. Elizabeth, because she was the weakest, felt it most. Mr. Barrett bore his grief dumbly. But Jamaican affairs had to be looked after, especially now that Samuel was gone. The next in line, Stormie, was sent to replace him.

Week after week went by. Sometimes Elizabeth was better, sometimes worse. The only constant thing was the medical men's refrain that they would not answer for her life. One day when she needed the reassurance of a deep affection Edward took her hand and said words that she remembered as long as she lived—that he loved her better than them all and that "he would not leave me . . . till I was well."

It was several months after Samuel's death that, with the warmer weather, she was beginning to show improvement. Soon she might leave her bed for the sofa and then perhaps go out with Edward to the boating parties he loved.

On Saturday, the 11th of July, a beautiful calm sunny day, Elizabeth saw Edward leave on such a party with two young men, Captain Carlyle Clarke and Charles Vannek whom he had met in Torquay. They intended to go to Teignmouth on the *Belle Sauvage*, a fleet little yacht that had distinguished herself on a number of regattas. With the help of the experienced pilot, William White, whom they had aboard, the three youths had no doubt that what with the favorable weather and the *Belle*'s mettle they would have their run and be back in Torquay before dusk. They were full of laughter and exhilaration and Captain Clarke pinned a *boutonnière* on his coat as they went off.

Elizabeth had been very uneasy when Edward left. They had had a trifling argument that morning during which pettish words had been uttered on both sides, and when he said good-by the cloud had not been dissipated. She knew, however, that the moment she saw him again all would be well.

Impatiently she waited for the hours to pass, but as the afternoon turned into dusk her impatience became anxiety. The *Belle* should have been back by that time unless, possibly, the young men, tempted by the weather, had decided to make a longer run of it.

As the night wore on Henrietta and Arabel came more frequently into Elizabeth's room to conceal their uneasiness by talking about the calm sea and fair winds. But they only succeeded in showing that their alarm was as great as hers. The night somehow passed. The following morning brought even fairer weather. The sun shone on a sea as smooth as glass, a sea so innocent that it seemed to have no purpose but to reflect the heavens. As Elizabeth was confined to her bed her sisters drew back the window curtains so that she might see for herself that such a sea could harm nobody.

One by one the other boats that had sailed with the *Belle* came back, but she was nowhere on the horizon. Somehow that day too went by, an anguished Sunday, spent in alternate hope and despair. Then a rumor spread that a boat answering the description of the *Belle* had been seen to capsize in a storm in Babbacombe Bay. There appeared to be four men on board, according to the two Exmouth seamen who had seen the shipwreck. Even then, for lack of definite proof, the girls still hoped. But as Edward had not yet returned they notified their father.

The truth of the rumor became too evident when several days later the *Belle* was sighted floating on her side. Soon afterward the body of Captain Clarke was recovered with the flowers still fast in his buttonhole. Mr. Barrett sent out searching parties all along the coast for miles, offering a reward to anyone who would bring him news of his son. At last, three weeks after the *Belle's* ill-fated run, another body was found floating near Torbay and was pulled to shore. Mr. Barrett identified it as Edward's.

The stricken father was magnificent in his wordless grief and for that reason the more awesome to his children. To Elizabeth, near death at the terrible discovery, his silence accused her more than any speech. Edward, best beloved of all human beings, was dead and she had killed him. Her tears, her aunt's letter written for her sake—they had been as much the cause of his death as the boat's capsizing. Because of her selfish love her father's house was bereft of its cornerstone and she herself deprived forever of an affection that until then had filled her life. "I killed him! I killed him!" The words assailed her consciousness with every dash of the waves against the shore. And always, hard and silent as a rock, there was her father, accusing. If only he had spoken! If he had said again that it had been very wrong of her to exact Edward's staying. If he could have let himself be human enough in his anguish to cry out: "If it had not been for you the crown of my house would not have fallen!" He never did, and she never ceased blaming herself.

Edward had hardly been buried when the sea yielded up the corpse of the pilot, William White. Charles Vannek was never found.

For months Elizabeth hung between life and death—"the only time in which I have known what absolute despair is." She now took opium not only to regulate her pulse but to bring her sleep. But even then it came cruelly with memories that gave her no peace even in her unconsciousness. Edward was gone. Edward who had taken her hand in his and told her he would not leave her, not till she was well—Edward had left her forever only ten days after giving her that promise. She saw herself and her father standing side by side by that closed grave and that unclosing sea. From then on water was never to be without the memory of that death.

Yet as a result of their common grief father and daughter were drawn more closely to each other. Where the other children had shrunk back from the hardness of that rock, she had heard the fountain within it, and now it ran with tears. She saw her heart struggling toward him. She saw herself thrust off, dropping away, turning again and clinging. He was her parent, she told herself, and she loved him for that, but more dearly for his fine qualities despite the miserable "system" that made him appear worse than he really was. Perhaps God had meant to strike their hearts together by that shock. She resolved, even in her nearness to death, to make up to him for his loss by her own love—and she did love him better, she knew, than all those left to her to love.

With Edward and Samuel dead, Mr. Barrett recalled Stormie, his oldest son now, from Jamaica where the youth had barely arrived.

Fifteen months, harrowed by the accusations of the relentless sea, went by before Elizabeth returned to Wimpole Street. She made the hard journey home against the doctors' orders, by slow stages in an invalid's carriage, to prove her love for her father. He understood. He spoke gently to her again. He took an interest in her work. At night, before retiring, he would come to her room and, kneeling at her bedside, pray aloud. She found herself listening for the sound of his footstep on the stairs. She took comfort from his prayers. The doctors told her, and she believed them, that from now on she could hope for no life but that of an invalid. Thoughts of her own death went through her mind. In her emotionally overwrought state she would cling to her father and tell him: "My best hope is to die beneath your eyes."

Of Edward's death she could not trust herself to speak, to him or to anyone else. Like the mourning dove she sang, but only to herself, in a lament out of the depths of her despair. "De Profundis," too private to be published until many years later, was laid away even from the most loving eyes. Its weary stanzas with their monotonous refrain in the last line had the leaden beat of a pendulum marking time too slow in passing. What was there to live for now that the beloved face was dimmed, the tongue hushed, the heart caught away from life? Nature that thinks kindly of the bird in June and in midwinter keeps the red fruit ripening for it among the snowy branches—what did it hold for her?

> No bird am I to sing in June,
> And dare not ask an equal boon.
> Good nests and berries red are Nature's
> To give away to better creatures,—
> And yet my days go on, go on.
>
> I ask less kindness to be done,—
> Only to loose these pilgrim-shoon,
> (Too early worn and grimed) with sweet
> Cool deathly touch to these tired feet,
> Till days go out which now go on. . . .

Only resignation remained in the half-life that now was hers.

Chapter VII: Magnificent Failure

MAY 1, 1837 dawned as a red-letter day for Robert Browning. Two events were taking place simultaneously: the publication, *not* at his aunt's or his father's expense, of the text of *Strafford*, and its opening at Covent Garden, with Macready in the lead and a beautiful actress of twenty, Helen Faucit, in the part of Lady Carlisle. Mr. Vandenhof and Mr. Dale acted respectively the roles of Pym and King Charles.

The handsomeness of the book itself would have gratified any playwright even though it was modestly bound in drab paper. But the title page with its attribution of authorship to "Robert Browning, author of 'Paracelsus'" gratified the poet. True, he had just fathered the tragedy. Yet he knew, even if for ten years he was to carry on an unequal love-affair with Melpomene, that he belonged to poetry. It was only fair that the play should have been dedicated to the man who had asked Browning to write it, and so it was, "with affectionate admiration . . . by his most grateful and devoted friend," under the date of April 23, 1837. Had Browning, in augury, chosen Shakespeare's birthday?

However, Macready too had selected that date in his diary for some confessions on *Strafford* which he undoubtedly needed to make for the good of his soul. He had looked at the changes Browning had made in the last scene and "found them quite bad—mere feeble rant—neither power nor nature, nor healthful fancy . . . I felt certainly convinced that the play must be utterly condemned."

After his initial enthusiasm the moody tragedian had blown hot and cold on the subject of *Strafford*. At first he had welcomed the idea of a drama on the impeachment, condemnation, and execution of the faithful earl who loved his monarch enough to sacrifice his life for him, even knowing him to be unworthy. He saw the dramatic possibilities of Strafford's surrendering friendship, patriotism, and the love of Lady Carlisle for his king's sake, and visualized the magnificence of his role when, as the earl about to be executed, he pleads for the life of the king who had betrayed him. But between the shadow of an idea and the substance of a finished play lay a mountain of temperamental obstacles.

First Macready was worried by the baseless gossip that Browning had written the play in only ten days. (As a matter of fact, the harassed poet was to struggle over it for nearly eight months while the neglected *Sordello* languished in the red portfolio.) When, considerably more than five months after the Talfourd dinner, the poet brought him the nearly finished tragedy, Macready was sufficiently pleased to offer only minor suggestions for the fourth act, whereupon he drove off to the Garrick Club, leaving Browning to sweat out the scenes.

A month later, in December, Macready flirted with Bulwer's *Duchess de la Vallière*, letting three more months elapse before he returned to *Strafford*, only to find it admirable and disappointing at the same time. But when he read it to Osbaldiston on the 20th of March, 1837, and the manager of Covent Garden "caught at it with avidity," agreeing to produce it on very favorable terms, Macready's optimism rose, only to fall again in a feverish instability that frayed Browning's nerves as well as his own. Then, shortly before the play went into rehearsal, Macready worked over it with Forster, staying up with him until four o'clock, only to receive Browning's coolness for his pains, while the friendship between the poet and his admiring critic suffered a severe strain.

The rehearsals made matters worse. Miss Faucit complained that her part was too meager and Osbaldiston that the production was too costly. The actors revealed a remarkable obtuseness, not to mention ignorance, and the bedevilled author poured out his troubles to the loyal Eliza Flower who wrote to another confidante: "Browning seems a good deal annoyed at the go of things behind the scenes and declared that he will never write a play again as long as he lives. You have no idea of the ignorance and obstinacy of the whole set . . . Think of his having to write out the meaning of the word impeachment, as some of them thought it meant poaching."

On the eve of the *première* Macready poured out his litany of complaints which, fortunately, Browning never learned of. After comparing the young playwright unfavorably with Shakespeare he concluded: "There is a sad want of judgment and tact in the whole composition. Would it were over! It must fail—and it grieves me that I am so placed."

It was certainly not a pleasant prospect to have a fiasco on his

benefit night. "Browning will efface its memory by the production of
Sordello," he mused gloomily. "But it will strike me hard, I fear."

The author had no such foreboding when with his father and a
retinue of well-wishing friends he waited for the curtain to rise, as
the custom was, shortly before seven o'clock. He was flattered by the
full house, although of course the splendid attendance was largely
attributable to Macready and the lovely new actress, Miss Faucit.
Like any dramatist in the same situation he hoped that the play
counted for something too. He had done his best with it, despite
Macready's moods and the usual backstage contrarieties. Now it was
up to the public to give its verdict.

Judging by the applause the public of that first night approved.
Behind the scenes, in the euphoria of compliments and congratula-
tions, of friends wishing one well and rivals putting a fair face on
envy, *Strafford* seemed to have carried the day. "The play was a grand
escape," Macready told Browning, "and you ought to regard it as
such." After that there was silence except that in his diary three
days later Macready noted, laconically for him, that the *Morning
Herald* for that day had pronounced the play "the best that had been
produced for many years."

The *Herald's* compliment to the dramatist was perfervid praise
against the tepid reception from the other critics, most of whom
expressed more dispraise than plaudits. If the *Literary Gazette* spoke
favorably of the play's vigor, it found the dialogue plodding. Even
the *Examiner*, from which Browning had expected friendliness since
it was Forster who wrote the review, told him roundly that as a
drama *Strafford* failed, albeit the author revealed possibilities in the
field. A tone of politeness on the whole predominated about the
play itself. It was quite otherwise with the treatment of the actors
but for Macready and Miss Faucit who, despite her youth, had given
an understanding interpretation of Lady Carlisle. The performance
of Vandenhof as Pym one critic found "positively nauseous with his
whining and drawling." As for Mr. Dale as King Charles a rude
journalist not only suggested that he should have been thrown off
the stage but added, "Anything should have been done rather than
such exhibitions should be allowed to disgrace the stage of a national
theatre."

Evidently Osbaldiston had expected a long run for *Strafford* since
his terms provided an honorarium of twelve pounds per night to the
author for twenty-five nights and ten pounds per night thereafter.

For the first and second performances Covent Garden was filled to capacity. On the third the audience fell off. On the fourth it was so alarmingly small that the management wondered whether or not to go on with the play. Another performance was scheduled nevertheless for May 11, but the actor who played the part of Pym deserted and so the run came to an abrupt end. It was played once more, however, on the 30th of the month for the benefit of Edward Fitzball and not again until the Browning Society revived it in 1886.

In spite of the poor financial returns *Strafford* had been more profitable to Browning than any of his previous work. As a book it also received one of the longest notices Browning had had so far, in the *Edinburgh Review* for July, but only to be condemned for its dramatic shortcomings. *Paracelsus*, meanwhile, no doubt helped by Browning's reminder on the title page of his drama, steadily gained him admirers. Perhaps after all he should not let himself be waylaid from his true function. Somewhat chastened, he returned to *Sordello*. Macready, for his part, listened to the call from across the ocean and accepted an offer to appear in America. Browning had failed to save him from that fate, alas!

According to an announcement in the printed *Strafford* Browning's poem on the thirteenth century Italian troubadour was described as nearly ready. But the year closed and not one of the six books which, as the notice informed one, comprised *Sordello*, appeared either through Longman, Rees, Orme, Brown, and Green, who had published the play, or through any other firm. In July, however, after Browning had picked up the threads of that most tangled narrative, he read the disconcerting information that Mrs. W. Busk had forestalled him. Her *Plays and Poems*, just out, was receiving the consideration of the *Athenaeum's* reviewer, a gentleman who kept up with the literary output. After dealing with Mrs. Busk's long poem in six cantos entitled *Sordello*, the critic inquired: "Is this founded upon the same subject as that chosen by the author of *Paracelsus* for his announced poem?"

There was nothing Browning could do but stop short in consternation. How much of the Sordello story had Mrs. Busk told? Had she treated it historically? Poetically? With understanding of the medieval poet's mind? He had been working on his poem at intervals for four years. It was an obscure subject culled out of Dante, amplified by the ever reliable *Biographie Universelle* and marvelously aided by Daniele Bartoli's *De' Simboli Trasportati al Morale*, issued

by Browning's Italian tutor, Angelo Cerutti, in 1830. How much
would Mrs. Busk's poem affect his work in progress? How much
would it affect his father's? For the elder Browning had also been
captivated by Sordello to the extent of projecting a novel in a lengthy
and complicated synopsis, full of intrigue, pirates, fair womanhood
in distress and brave knights, as ready with their swords as with their
lutes.

The genial antiquarian never wrote his novel but the outline
remains, a mute testimony to his unfulfilled ambition. Browning,
however, had worked too long on *Sordello* to give it up merely
because someone else had handled the subject. Besides, it was so
personal a poem in spite of its source in history that *Sordello* has
justly been recognized as blood-brother to the nameless speaker in
Pauline—a kinship which Browning unconsciously admitted in the
very opening when, accounting for the narrative form, he apologizes:

> . . . . Never,—I should warn you first,—
> Of my own choice had this, if not the worst
> Yet not the best expedient, served to tell
> A story I could body forth so well
> By making speak, myself kept out of view,
> The very man as he was wont to do.

He had not been too lucky at keeping himself out of view in his
first attempt. Hence now he would tell anyone who wished to hear
the story of

> Sordello compassed murkily about
> With ravage of six long, sad, hundred years.

So, in those magnificently evocative lines, he introduced his hero.

But work as he might, Browning, whether because of Mrs. Busk's
innocent mischief or through his own disappointment over *Strafford*,
failed to draw *Sordello* out of the murk into reality. He therefore
decided to go to Italy so that by visiting the scenes known to his hero
he might restore inspiration and give his creation new life.

His parents sped him on with their blessing and a garnished purse.
He sailed on Good Friday, the 13th of April, 1838, on the *Northern
Castle*, Captain Matthew Davidson. Among his belongings he carried
his well-thumbed copy of Bartoli's *De' Simboli*. Constantly with him,
though unseen, he had Sordello.

He covered much land and water during his three months' voyage.
On the 30th of May he landed at Trieste. The following day he was

in Venice from where he visited, and fell in love with, "delicious Asolo" to be forever associated with his name. Then Vicenza, Padua, and again Venice and its environs, the stamping ground of the Eccelini family, linked with Sordello's fate. At one place he almost held history by the hand when a canon told him how a few years earlier he had seen the huge skeleton of Alberic, son of Eccelino Monaco, unearthed from a barrow. Browning lingered at Verona in Sordello's almost palpable presence and then started back for home pausing on the way at Trent, Innsbruck, Munich, Salzburg, Frankfort, and Mayence. On the voyage down the Rhine he visited Cologne, then Aix-la-Chapelle, Liege and Antwerp.

He saw few Italians long enough to know them but those he did see he liked. He also carried away with him scenes of suffering and want that roused the Shelleyan humanitarian. Henceforth he would speak out the griefs of the inarticulate. *Sordello* would be his mouthpiece for what he had seen in twisted bodies and warped souls.

Being Browning he missed nothing of the works of God and man. He recorded his disappointment in Canova's sculptures but to make up for it he carried away enough local color to vivify many a poem besides the one that had sent him traveling.

Captain Davidson took such a fancy to his passenger, the only one on his ship, that he offered him a free voyage to Constantinople. It was not often that he had the good fortune to carry such an engaging conversationalist to fill the tedium of the long watches. Browning was anxious to get back to work, however. In spite of his intention to "finish my poem among the scenes it describes" he confessed that except for a passage of a play jotted down as they sailed through the straits of Gilbraltar, he "did not write six lines while absent." They were lines which, as it happened, had nothing to do with Italy and were addressed to "My English Eyebright," Miss Haworth, with whom he continued to carry on a very proper literary correspondence.

"I called you Eyebright," he explained in a letter soon after his return, "meaning a simple sad sort of translation of Euphrasia into my own language. Folks would know who Euphrasia or Fanny was."

How cautious for one who had nothing to fear from such revelation!

For a long time he kept the home circle entranced by the variety of his adventures. One especially he told to Sarianna who told it to a Mr. Dow, who delivered it to Forster who in turn related it to Macready, the whole becoming so distorted in the repetition that

Browning felt obliged to write the true account to Miss Haworth.
Browning has always been charged with being a poor writer of prose.
There is such vividness in his description of a wreck at sea, such telling selection of detail, such observation, such dramatic balance of
pity and horror, and, as in all Browning's writing, such power, that
by this one passage he proves what he might have done in prose
narrative.

"The captain woke me one bright Sunday morning to say there
was a ship floating keel uppermost half a mile off. They lowered the
boat, made ropes fast to some floating canvas and towed her
toward the vessel. Both met half-way, and the little air that had risen
an hour or two before, sank at once. Our men made the wreck fast,
and went to breakfast in high glee at the notion of having 'new
trousers out of the sails,' and quite sure she was a French boat,
broken from her moorings at Algiers, close by. Ropes were next hove
(hang this sea-talk) round her stanchions, and after a quarter of an
hour's pushing at the capstan, the vessel righted suddenly, one dead
body floating out. Five more were in the forecastle, and had probably
been there a month—under a blazing African sun . . . don't imagine
the wretched state of things. They were, these six, the 'watch below'
(I give you the results of the day's observation)—the rest, some eight
or ten, had been washed overboard at first. One or two were Algerines,
the rest Spaniards. The vessel was a smuggler bound for Gibraltar.
There were two stupidly-disproportionate guns, taking up the whole
deck, which was convex and—nay, look you, these are the gun rings,
and the black square the place where the bodies lay.[1] Well, the sailors
covered up the hatchway, broke up the aft-deck, hauled up tobacco
and cigars, good lord such heaps of them, and then bale after bale
of prints and chintz, don't you call it, till the captain was half
frightened—he would get the ship's papers, he said. So these poor
fellows were pulled up, piecemeal, and pitched into the sea, the very
sailors calling to each other to 'cover the faces.' No papers of importance were found, however, but fifteen swords, powder and ball
enough for a dozen such boats, and bundles of cotton, etc., that would
have taken a day to get out. But the captain vowed that after five
o'clock she would be cut adrift. Accordingly she was cast loose, not
a third of her cargo having been touched. And you can hardly conceive the strange sight when the battered hulk turned round, actually,
and looked at us, and then reeled off, like a mutilated creature from

---

[1] Browning makes a drawing here.

some scoundrel French surgeon's lecture-table, into the most gorgeous and lavish sunset in the world."

Sordello kept him in a torment through the rest of the year and part of the following spring. In May of 1839 he delivered himself of his seven-year labor. Ideas for new poems conceived in Italy had had to wait until his release from that formidable pregnancy. Perhaps because *Sordello* had cost him so much anguish in the radical changes he had had to make, he expected more from it than from anything he had so far produced. It was a spectacular work, longer by more than sixteen-hundred lines than *Paracelsus* and infinitely more complicated in the story, the setting, the history, and the character of the pro-tagonist who, indeed, underwent as many transmutations as a chameleon in the altering landscape of his author's brain. Browning was satisfied with his work. He had accomplished in *Sordello* what he had failed to do in *Pauline*—traced the progress of a soul toward self-realization through apparent failure to the ultimate resolution of the conflict between head and heart.

The public he had made for himself with *Paracelsus* looked forward to the announced *Sordello*, which came out early in March, 1840. The enterprising Edward Moxon was the publisher but Browning's father paid the costs. That neither father nor son suffered from an unrealistic view of the reader of poetry is evidenced by the modest issue of five hundred copies at six shillings sixpence—sixpence more than the price of *Paracelsus*. But how much more it had cost Brown-ing in agony of creation, not to mention the trip to Italy!

It is a sad fact, tragic indeed to one who must learn it from his own pain, that the worth of a masterpiece is not established by the time and anguish that go into its making. The spontaneous lyric cry of a Sappho can challenge with its insubstantial syllables the epic that consumed another's lifetime. Yet in the final estimate her few roses will outweigh the rock.

Browning, lord of creation in his own right as a poet, had fashioned a crag, alluring with the flowers of poetry at its feet—gracious de-scriptions such as only he who identified himself with the least as with the grandest in nature could write, from within outward, as it were. But he made the ascent so steep, he interposed so many pitfalls for anyone who would follow, distracted him so often with a caution to mark this, pause here awhile, that the other, in peril of losing his wits as well as his footing, gave up the climb almost as soon as it was begun. Had he portrayed Sordello as the minstrel-warrior, even if

harnessed in the accoutrements of Browning's philosophy of life, the
poem might have been acceptable to the reader, as no doubt Mrs.
Busk's had been. But Browning became so much engrossed in the
interminable wrangles of the Guelfs and the Ghibellines, in the
conflicts of Emperor Frederick with other historical figures, not to
mention his own philosophy, that he lost the sweet singer in the
clash of arms, the lover in the soldier, and himself in the profundities
of his own speculation.

Yet he had known how to make the reader almost fall in love at
first sight with the young Sordello, even as he had, and waken hopes
of enchantment to come.

> His face,
> —Look—now he turns away! Yourselves shall trace
> (The delicate nostril swerving wide and fine,
> A sharp and restless lip, so well combine
> With that calm brow) a soul fit to receive
> Delight at every sense: you can believe
> Sordello foremost in the regal class
> Nature has broadly severed from her mass
> Of men, and framed for pleasure, as she frames
> Some happy lands, that have luxurious names,
> For loose fertility . . .
> You recognize at once the finer dress
> Of flesh that amply lets in loveliness
> At eye and ear . . .

Too soon, however, that soul fit to receive delight at every sense was
sundered by conflict in the effort to reconcile vision with reality, the
head with the heart. Sordello lost his peace of mind. He became
introspective.

> He slept but was aware he slept,
> So, frustrated: as one rainsick made pact
> Erst with the overhanging cataract
> To deafen him, yet still distinguished plain
> His own blood's measured clicking at his brain

The problems of good and evil tormented him. The struggle toward
future perfection challenged yet made him turn a longing eye toward
the lures of the present, which also was a stepping stone toward the
ideal to come. And so the soul broke into exclamatory invocations.

> O life, life-breath,
> Life blood,—ere sleep, come travail, life ere death!

This life stream on my soul, direct, oblique,
But always streaming! Hindrances? They pique.
Helps? Such . . . but why repeat, my soul o'ertops
Each height, than every depth profoundlier drops?
Enough that I can live, and would live! Wait
For some transcendent life reserved by Fate
To follow this? Oh, never! Fate, I trust
The same, my soul to; for, as who flings dust,
Perchance (so facile was the deed) she chequed
The void with these materials to affect
My soul diversely: these consigned anew
To nought by death, what marvel if she threw
A second and superior spectacle
Before it? What may serve for sun, what still
Wander a moon above me? What else wind
About me like the pleasures left behind,
And how shall some new flesh that is not flesh
Cling to me?
        . . . . Oh, 'twere too absurd to slight
For the hereafter the to-day's delight!
Quench thirst at this, then seek next well-spring; wear
Home-lilies ere strange lotus in my hair!

Before such passages—and it is one of the least involved—the contemporary reader, while awed by the strange lotus of Browning's offering, looked even upon the home-lilies with suspicion. No, such daring of diction, such cragginess, such loftiness of thought, such startling new poetic tensions were not for him. He wanted something to amuse him and he was, instead, not only made to think but actually to meditate. No, no, there was no time for the demands Mr. Browning made upon him. It was far pleasanter to read the musical Alfred Tennyson, far pleasanter indeed to look for some new offering from Miss Barrett, now that she had done with being classical and wrote verse romances which she affectedly called romaunts. But she would soon abandon even that affectation. No, no, no, Mr. Browning expected too much if he meant one to exercise mental labor over his verse—and to have to pay for it, too!

Very soon Browning discovered that the poem which was to have proved his genius only availed to obscure it. His name from now on became a synonym for the unintelligible and if *Sordello* was mentioned, it was only to furnish a witticism for the diner-out. Have you heard about Douglas Jerrold and *Sordello*? Well, our incomparable wit was ailing and had been told by his doctor not to read too much.

One morning Mrs. Jerrold left him to do some shopping and during her absence a parcel of books arrived from London. The sick man took *Sordello* which was among them and began to read. Line after line, page after page, Jerrold read, and the more he read the more bewildered he became. Suddenly the terrible thought struck him that his illness had deprived him of his faculties. The cold sweat burst from his brow, so he stopped reading and waited, brooding, for his wife to return. At last she came and without ceremony he thrust the book into her hands crying, "Read this, my dear!"

She read the first page and turned to the second, her face clearly showing her dismay. "Bother the gibberish!" she exclaimed throwing the book from her. "I don't understand a word of it."

"Thank heaven!" cried Jerrold. "Then I am not an idiot!"

The story of Jerrold's reaction was double-edged in its effect. Everyone knew how impatient he could be with the followers of the Lake Poets and with the Lake Poets themselves for their straining toward simplicity which sometimes came very close to inanity. Some sentences of his on Wordsworth had very nearly shattered the Rydal Mount sage's serenity. "He reminds me of the beadle of Parnassus," Jerrold had written, "strutting about in a cocked hat. . . . He is only fit for those old tabbies, the Muses. His Pegasus is a broken-winded hack, with a grammatical bridle, and a monosyllabic bit between his teeth."

Perhaps for a young poet there was balm to be drawn from being damned with the great. Still, one could have wished that the age had been more discerning, or at least that the rising poets had seen a portent for the future in *Sordello*. But even Tennyson found in it matter for jest. The only lines he understood, he said, were the first and the last—"Who will, may hear Sordello's story told. . . . Who would has heard Sordello's story told"—and they were both lies.

A still younger generation of poets, however, the future Pre-Raphaelites, were to uncover the embers their elders had slighted and kindle their torch from a fire of which those others had seen only the smoke.

Meanwhile the book at Moxon's sold very slowly. Fifteen years later a little more than half of the original edition still remained in stock. Yet how much harm to Browning's literary reputation the few copies of his magnificent failure that went out into the world had managed to do!

Those who read *Sordello* to the end may have been struck by the airy child who appears toward the close:

> Lo, on a heathy brown and nameless hill
> By sparkling Asolo, in mist and chill,
> Morning just up, higher and higher runs
> A child barefoot and rosy—See! the sun's
> On the square castle's inner-court's green wall
> —Like the chine of some fossil animal
> Half turned to earth and flowers; and thro' the haze
> (Save where some slender patches of grey maize
> Are to be overleaped) that boy has crost
> The whole hill-side of dew and powder-frost
> Matting the balm and mountain camomile:
> Up and up goes he, singing all the while
> Some unintelligible words to beat
> The lark, God's poet. . . .

Unseen, yet not far behind, is that other child of Asolo, Pippa, whose eidolon he is.

Chapter VIII: "Or From Browning Some Pomegranate"

IN PROPORTION as Miss Barrett withdrew from the world the world came to her. She wrote more than ever as if to drown in conscious creative thought her grief and guilt over her brother's death. "The associations of Torquay lie upon me . . . like a nightmare," she confided to Mr. Boyd after her return to Wimpole Street. "Part of me is worn out; but the poetical part—that is, the love of poetry—is growing in me freshly every day." The magazines eagerly took the results of this fresh growth. Her public, like Tennyson's, now included America where an enterprising publisher printed fifteen hundred copies of her poems. "If I am a means of ultimate loss to him, I shall sit in sackcloth," she cried in gratitude. "I love Americans, a noble and cordial people," she added at more good news from across the ocean.

Details of her private life reached her readers. She appealed to the public imagination, and little by little the legend grew of the caged nightingale that sang the more sweetly for her pain. Little did anyone guess the truth behind such verses as:

> If I dared leave this smile, she said,
>   And take a moan upon my mouth,
> And tie a cypress round my head,
>   And let the tears run smooth,
> It were a happier way, she said.

Admirers wrote to her and not content with prose addressed her in verse. Many offered to lighten her solitude with their company but Miss Barrett was adamant. She refused to see anyone, even Mr. Horne with whom she had been corresponding since the publication of her "Romaunt of Margret." Mr. Horne was soon to achieve both fame and notoriety for his poem *Orion*, a name also applied to him. "The farthing epic," people dubbed that original work after Horne with wry humor set its price at a farthing—possibly as a commentary on the public evaluation of the poetic art—yet forbade its sale to anyone who mispronounced its title.

To make up for her refusal to see him Miss Barrett not only redoubled her correspondence with him but also engaged, always from a distance, in an active literary collaboration.

One little being soon became her constant companion, a glossy Titian-haired—the vulgar called it liver-colored—cocker spaniel. Flush was the gift of Miss Mitford who had brought it one day, a no less exciting bundle than the packet of gossip of the great and near-great with which she always came provided. The diminutive, homely woman with her immense forehead and heavy brows over a meager face, with her fading curls bobbing under her bonnet, was always as welcome as the town crier. Without the loudness of voice she had the advantage of remarkable breath control and would deliver her anecdotes with intolerance of even an exclamation from her auditors.

"Have you heard the latest about Mr. Horne?" she would inquire without pausing for an answer. "Well, the other night he poured libations on his bare head out of the water glasses at a great dinner! And then, being in the midst of sportsmen, all talking of pointers' noses and spaniels' tails, he exclaimed aloud—'If I were to hold up a horse by the tail?' Imagine the consternation of the gentlemen! Then, later, going to a fashionable evening party, what does our Mr. Horne do but throw himself full length on the satin sofa, for all the world as if doing a somerset? As for his affairs of the heart, dear Miss Barrett! He has a positive mania for heiresses. He will go out at half-past five and propose to Miss M, with fifty thousand pounds, and being rejected, will come back to tea the same evening and fall in love with Miss O, with forty thousand. He went away for a few months and on his next visit if he didn't do as much for Miss W, on the promise of four blood horses! Likely as not he will see a prospect in Miss R, who, after all, has hounds!"

Miss Barrett enjoyed the chatter of the little old maid who went everywhere and saw everything like the hardiest diner out, making nothing of the peril to her life in taking the terrible new invention, the train, to come to London. Yet what frustration in that outwardly busy life! Married women envied her freedom and the career which threw her among the most prominent figures of the day. They read her novels, the threads of whose plots were drawn together like so much netting. They wept over her tragedies. They bought her annuals, as unfailing and as rewarding as the winter holly. They were even to accord the accolade of a minor masterpiece to her sketches, *Our Village*. But those who knew her story pitied her.

She was the daughter of Dr. Mitford who in his strikingly handsome youth had made his beginnings with the quack, Dr. Graham, the advocate of mud baths and high priest of the Temple of Health in the Adelphi, where he also experimented with the forces of magnetism and electricity. It was the mud bath that won him notoriety. In order to gain clients Dr. Graham would give public demonstrations during which he would be immersed in mud to the chin. With him in the mud-bath appeared a beautiful young lady whom he called Vestina, Goddess of Health, although but a few months earlier she had been an ordinary mortal nursemaid. During her immersion Vestina saw to it that the only visible part of her, the head, would be dressed in the height of fashion with powder, flowers, feathers, and ropes of pearl, adornments which she was never to lack after she became Lady Hamilton. As Vestina she presided over Dr. Graham's evening lectures, "assisting at the display of the celestial meteors, and of that sacred and vital fire over which she watches," the doctor advertised. "The descriptive exhibition of the apparatus in the daytime is conducted by the officiating junior priest"—the future Dr. Mitford.

Something of the charlatan and the charlatan's laxity with money clung to Dr. Mitford throughout his life. In his hands it seemed to have a motive power of its own, like quicksilver. Marriage and its responsibilities did not curb his extravagance. Something always happened to keep him temporarily in funds. The most extraordinary shower of gold descended upon him when his daughter Mary, at the age of ten, found herself the winner of a twenty-thousand pound lottery prize. Before she had got over the wonder of it Dr. Mitford had already squandered the better part of the money. Yet with his genius for profligacy he lacked the talent to keep himself safe from debtor's prison from which his daughter was often to rescue him.

It was an odd shifting of roles between the daughter and the father. She was still a young girl when she assumed the duties of a parent toward this incorrigible child. He was, however, a wily child who made her believe she was the privileged of the earth for having such a charge. So she coddled and spoiled and supported him, and because the lightning of fortune does not strike in the same place twice, she took up the pen and put it down only when it had earned its quota for the day. She worshiped poetry and considered herself a poet, but that devotion Dr. Mitford as her financial beneficiary did not encourage. So she arranged other people's verses into saleable garlands and herself stuck to more profitable fields. As the years sped and youth lay irretrievably behind her, she fell into a sensible spinsterhood, consoled by her greenhouse at Three Mile Cross, her garden, her pony stable, and her dogs. The cocker spaniel which she had presented to Miss Barrett was her prized pet, the son of a champion for whom Dr. Mitford had refused twenty guineas at a time when he scarcely owned as many pence.

Flush was no ordinary dog. As the fosterling of a literary lady, he soon adjusted himself to Miss Barrett's habits. If his canine heart beat faster whenever flowers were brought into the house and he was seized with yearning for the open fields, he never showed it. If, on his leashed walks, he met a spotted spaniel like Mr. Pritchard's gentle bitch and he was reminded of the brief romance that had made him a father when he was scarcely more than a puppy, he gave Wilson the maid no intimation.

It was distinctly understood that Flush was Miss Barrett's dog, distinguished from Folly, Henrietta's King Charles, and from Cataline, the Cuba bloodhound who lived below stairs, a sort of Cerberus of the kitchen regions. Flush enjoyed the privileges that Miss Barrett enjoyed, as well as her seclusion. As for Miss Barrett, she doted upon the droll little creature who, with his rather prominent golden eyes, high rounded forehead, and long, hanging silken ears, reminded people very much of herself. Sometimes as she watched him lying at the foot of her couch, a privileged place that some of her epistolary admirers would willingly have exchanged with him, she hoped that he would learn to love her enough to forget the carefree life of Three Mile Cross.

But then, if he could not run about as he had done in the country, he was recompensed with favors that no dog had ever had. He was fed on the daintiest of food which he learned to eat with the delicacy of a lovelorn young lady, scorning this, and condescending to have that—cream cheese, for example, which he tolerated only if Miss Barrett salted it herself. He drank his water out of a purple bowl, signifying no doubt his regal status; his milk was sugared to his taste. On feast days he had his special macaroons and on the whole was so pampered that little by little his tastes had to be studied if one wanted him to eat at all. Mr. Barrett, both amused and annoyed, grumbled that the creature had been utterly spoiled. "No dog in the world could be of his own accord and instinct so like a woman!"

There was nothing his mistress would not do for Flush, especially

when he would gaze at her with reproachful eyes fit to break anybody's heart, "because I refuse to give him my fur cuffs to tear to
pieces." But she would pacify him by twining strings of coral round
his neck. He was a source of endless amusement. The first time he
saw himself in a mirror he began to gnash his teeth at the interloper.
"But he learnt by experience what that image means," Miss Barrett
explained with pride at his intelligence, "and now he contemplates
it, serene in natural philosophy."

Everyone who came to see her soon realized how much Flush
meant to her and respecting the tacit *love me love my dog*, sought
to ingratiate the not always friendly favorite. Mr. Kenyon would
carry a lump of sugar for him which "Flush leapt to accept, *ore
rotundo*," Miss Barrett noted, as if the knowledge of Latin were
also one of Flush's accomplishments. But then his understanding
transcended language. He learned to read her very thoughts in a
mute devotion that would have been remarkable in a human being.

Flush had his faults, of course. He was always overturning cologne
bottles which brought its own punishment by lacerating his nostrils
with unbearable scents. He also went rummaging where he had no
business to be, causing endless havoc among Miss Barrett's assortment of vanities. But Mr. Kenyon put an end to the mischief by
giving Cousin Ba a table with a rail round it to protect her odds and
ends from Flush's paws. As time went on Flush became, besides a
distinct personality, an affectionate companion who knew when to
amuse his mistress and when to lie quietly while, silent and absorbed,
she traced her hieroglyphics on sheet after sheet of paper. "My time
goes to the best of music when I read or write," she said of herself at
this period. "And whatever money I can spend on my own pleasures
flows away in books."

As it was, her Uncle Samuel who died in 1837 had left her a
legacy of some four hundred pounds a year. She was the only one
of the Barrett children to be so remembered, but then, she had always
had his affection. It may be that by his bequest he intimated that
since in her circumstances she could not marry, he wished to make
certain that in any event she would be provided for.

She was far from unattractive, however, despite her recent suffering. Indeed, one of her female admirers painted an engaging picture
of her at about this time, in a fluttery yet vivid prose, as a slight
and girlish figure, "very delicate, with exquisite hands and feet . . .
lips like parted coral . . . large, dark eyes with such eyelashes, resting

on the cheek when cast down, when turned upwards touching the flexible and expressive eyebrow."

Whatever prompted Mr. Samuel Barrett's generosity, his legacy gave Elizabeth an independence whose importance she did not yet fully appreciate. For the present it was enough that she had money to spend on books, Indian shawls—a prime requisite for young ladies confined to their rooms—and whatever else the family budget was not expected to provide. Together with the four thousand pounds left her by her grandmother, her little capital could care for her adequately under any circumstances and even enable her to help those less fortunate than herself.

Indeed, one of the friends she made at this time, by correspondence only, through Miss Mitford, would have had no difficulty in swallowing up her whole fortune in the service of his art. Benjamin Robert Haydon was in difficulties when they began their letter writing. A painter of canvases which although they usually measured thirteen feet by eleven were nevertheless too small to hold his subjects, he had impoverished himself and his family in the pursuit of impossible ideals. A friend of Keats, he had jealously tried to dispute Leigh Hunt's influence over the young poet. Yet when Hunt had been in trouble and in prison, Haydon had had his huge "Judgment of Solomon" carried to Horsemonger Lane that the prisoner might be exalted by Glorious Art. He had waged bitter battles in the name of beauty, wasting his energies in endless polemics. But some of his triumphs, like England's final recognition of the Elgin marbles, a treasure that had been dumped like so much offal in a Park Lane barn, gave him the impetus to fight on. His pleas for their preservation had reverberated throughout Europe. Goethe had echoed it, Canova had taken up the cause. In the face of such advocacy the nation had no alternative but to purchase the marbles. "It has saved the marbles but it will ruin you," Lawrence prophesied on Haydon's success.

By 1842 the warning had almost been verified. Haydon's epic canvases, no longer popular, served only to increase his more epic debts. But he painted on, sinking to his knees before Glorious Art in a high-minded purpose that for the moment made him forget his starving family and the constant threat of debtor's prison.

At this stage Miss Barrett's letters brought him what he needed more than money—hope and the resolve to carry on the fight for the things in which, strangely, they believed with equal fervor. Soon he was calling her his "dear Aeschylus Barrett." She responded by paying him the tribute he most desired by writing poems to his canvases. Before the first year of their correspondence closed he had deposited with her for safe-keeping, in the uncertainties of his daily living, his lecture papers and his journals in three great trunks, together with "two jars of oil, twenty-seven years old."

Although the letters are reticent on the subject, some of Miss Barrett's money may have gone the way of other sops in the maw of Haydon's insatiable debts. Books were a major expense, especially now that she was writing for the magazines. But she baulked at having to pay fourteen guineas for a copy of *Poetae Christiani* which she needed for her *Athenaeum* essay, "The Greek Christian Poets." She wrote the essay nonetheless, to the delight of Mr. Boyd who saw his lamb returning from her romantic straying to the classical fold where he would have kept her.

All the poets whom they had read together made their appearance in that essay, garbed in rich yet restrained prose, as with a beautiful humility Miss Barrett introduced them to the English reader, evaluating their spiritual contribution, as valid then as for a future day in the immortality that only thought, in this instance, noble thought, can have. Most of the names must have been Greek indeed, even to the learned reader, for not everyone had had the advantage of being guided by a Mr. Boyd. But after perusing the essay no one had any doubt of the significance of the Greek Christian poets or of Miss Barrett's love and knowledge of her subject. The style had loftiness and distinction, as well as the quality of communicating the author's enthusiasm.

The essay found such favor that the editor, Mr. C. W. Dilke, suggested an article on English poetry surveying the art from Chaucer to Wordsworth and other contemporary practitioners. It was a large order but Miss Barrett, a literary David, would have taken on any Goliath. For that matter there was scarcely a poet whom she had not read. As for Chaucer, she had engaged on a project to modernize him—with Mr. Horne, Monckton Milnes, Leigh Hunt and other bold collaborators—at the suggestion of none other than Wordsworth. She now set to work at once on "The Book of the Poets," which the *Athenaeum* published in the summer of 1842.

Mr. Kenyon watched his cousin's activity with an approving eye while Miss Mitford, whenever she happened to be visiting at the same time watched him, gathering material for her entertaining word-hoard. "Our dear friend, you are aware," she would retail to Mr. Horne, "never sees anybody but the members of her own family, and one or two others. She has a high opinion of the skill in reading, as well as the fine taste of Mr. Kenyon and gets him to read her new poems aloud to her. . . . So Mr. Kenyon stands upon the hearth-rug and uplifts the manuscript and his voice, while our dear friend lies . . . upon the sofa, with her long black tresses streaming over her bent-down head, all attention. Now dear Mr. Kenyon," she bubbled on, "has lost a front tooth—not quite a front one, but a side front one— and this, you see, causes a defective utterance, an amiable indistinctness, a vague softening of syllables into each other, so that silence and ilence would really sound very like one another. . . ."

Besides lending Cousin Ba his voice, even if amiably indistinct in pronunciation, Mr. Kenyon brought her books and current news of writers. Had she read Browning's *Pippa Passes?* Ah, yes? He wondered, because the little pamphlet of *Bells and Pomegranates* that contained it had come out in April of 1841, before her return to London. But then, of course, it was published by Edward Moxon, who was her publisher also. He had met Browning in 1839, he thought it was, at a dinner at Sergeant Talfourd's, and had suddenly remembered that the poet's father had been an old schoolfellow of his. Oh, yes, they had met quite often here and there at dinners since then. Wouldn't Cousin Ba like to meet young Mr. Browning? He's very learned in Greek, you know. You'd have much to talk about together. Ah, your health? Yes, your health. The reason you refused to see Mr. Horne. But Mr. Browning is not a whit like Mr. Horne, you know, not a whit. Not at all eccentric. Ah, you admire *Pippa Passes?* An excellent, a most excellent work. *He* thought very well of your "Greek Christian Poets," you know. Yes, indeed, he expressed approval. . . .

Not long afterward Mr. Boyd learned from Miss Barrett that "Mr. Browning the poet" had commended her article. But let not Mr. Boyd think it was praise from the undiscriminate. "Mr. Browning is said to be learned in Greek," she informed him, "especially in the dramatists." Unconsciously she had already made the association between herself and Browning in their common interests, poetry and Greek.

There is no definite clue as to when Miss Barrett had begun to read Browning. It is on record that she admired *Pippa Passes* enough for her to confess to him several years later in a rather embarrassed prose for one usually so fluent: "*Pippa Passes*, which I could find in my heart to covet the authorship of, more than any of your works. . . ." It is safe to assume that by 1842 she was reading whatever she could find of his, except of course, the embarrassing *Pauline*, which Browning ruthlessly suppressed. Since she was writing about contemporary poets she had to acquaint herself with his poetry to make any intelligent allusion to him. What she read impressed her enough to write this coda to a review of Wordsworth's latest volume shortly after her article on the English poets: "In the meantime the hopeful and believing will hope—trust on; and, better still, the Tennysons and the Brownings, and other high-gifted spirits, will work, wait on."

It may be Browning never saw this mention of himself in Mr. Dilke's magazine. If he did, the link with Tennyson and other high-gifted spirits would have solaced him in the continued apathy with which not only his first issue of *Bells and Pomegranates*, but also the second and third, containing the *Dramatic Lyrics* of November 1842 had been received. Yet the *Dramatic Lyrics* comprised poems whose very names will continue to conjure up Browning for the form and stamp that make them unalterably his own—miniature masterpieces like "My Last Duchess," "Soliloquy of the Spanish Cloister," "Cristina," "Porphyria's Lover"[1] as well as "In a Gondola," "Waring," and the "Pied Piper of Hamelin," and "Incident of the French Camp."

Now at last Browning was speaking with his own true voice. Still England remained as deaf as in January 1836 when, disguised under the signature of "Z," he had told the story of Porphyria's strangling in her own yellow hair in Mr. Fox's *Monthly Repository*. Somehow it seemed as if the six years that had passed had made no difference but for the almost forgotten triumph of *Paracelsus* of which he patiently reminded the public on the title page of every issue of *Bells and Pomegranates*. John Forster noticed the *Dramatic Lyrics* favorably in the *Examiner* for old friendship's sake, though he need not have commented, "Mr. Browning is a genuine poet, and only needs to have less misgiving on the subject himself." It is not pleasant to have one's secret hurts exposed.

The fourth and fifth numbers of *Bells* contained plays, *The Return of the Druses* on the subject "of the most wild and passionate love" and *A Blot on the 'Scutcheon*, which vanished almost as soon as it was shown at the Drury Lane, breaking the friendship with Macready. Since his return from America the actor's disaffection had

---

[1] They bore other titles in the original *Bells and Pomegranates*.

been on the ascendant toward the persevering playwright whom he would have wished hard at work on poems like "The Pied Piper" which Browning had written to amuse little Willie Macready when the child was sick. "The Piper" had served a double purpose. It had kept Browning from writing plays and it had entertained little Willie for weeks making illustrations for it.[2]

Evidently poetry did not occupy Browning sufficiently to please Macready who had never quite overcome his mortification over what he considered the *Strafford* fiasco—no fiasco to the playwright, however, who soon brought him another verse drama, *King Victor and King Charles*, on a political situation like the first. Macready read it, not too sympathetically, and ended by finding it a great mistake. "I called Browning into my room and most explicitly told him so," he wrote in his diary for September 5, 1839.

He nearly convinced Browning that the play was worthless. But only for the boards, and so Browning published it in the second issue of *Bells*. No sooner had Macready disposed of the unvictorious *King Victor* than the prolific youth came round with another dramatic work, passionate this time, and nonpolitical. Macready read it, still with a jaundiced eye, and complained in his journal, "Browning came here before I had finished my bath, and really wearied me with his obstinate faith in his poem of *Sordello*, and his eventual celebrity, and also with his self-opinionated persuasions upon his *Return of the Druses*. I fear he is for ever gone."

But he wasn't, either in time or in Macready's sense, for with astounding celerity Browning submitted another play, *A Blot in the 'Scutcheon* which, he assured his friend, had plenty of action, "drabbing, stabbing, *et autres gentillesses.*" (If only Bulwer, whose *Lady of Lyons* had been shown thirty-three times and whose *Richelieu* furnished the greatest triumph of Macready's Covent Garden career, had been as productive!) Macready took his time about reading the manuscript. Indeed, a year passed before he made himself acquainted with that monomaniac of family honor, Thorold, Earl of Tresham, and his motherless sister Mildred who in her innocence had allowed herself to be seduced by the neighboring nobleman, Henry, Earl Mertoun. Young Henry had honorable intentions, however, and wished to marry Mildred. But Thorold who had been informed of his sister's trysts, not suspecting that her lover was also her suitor, kills him and himself dies of poison.

Neither the subject nor the treatment was to Macready's liking.

[2] These delightfully naive pictures are at the Baylor Browning Collection.

Still he needed fresh material for the stage. After consulting with Forster, he agreed to let him submit it to his friend Charles Dickens, well qualified to judge of the passions of the human heart. Dickens let another year go by before giving his verdict, but when he did, it turned the scales in Browning's favor.

"Browning's play," wrote Dickens on the 25th of November 1842, "has thrown me into a perfect passion of sorrow. To say that there is anything in its subject save what is lovely, true, deeply affecting, full of the best emotion, the most earnest feeling and the most true and tender source of interest, is to say that there is no light in the sun, and no heat in the blood. It is full of genius, natural and great thoughts, profound and yet simple and beautiful in its vigor . . . I know no love like it, no passion like it, no moulding of a splendid thing after its conception like it. And I swear it is a tragedy that MUST be played; and must be played, moreover, by Macready. There are some things I would have changed if I could (they are very slight. . . .) But the tragedy I shall never forget, or less vividly remember, than I do now. And if you tell Browning that I have seen it, tell him that I believe from my soul there is no man living (and not many dead) who could produce such a work."

For reasons best known to Forster and Macready, Browning never received the message that would have heartened him through that discouraging period, nor did he know of the letter until he read it in Forster's *Life of Charles Dickens* in 1873. Suddenly, however, Browning heard from Macready that he accepted the tragedy for production. Accordingly, the play went into rehearsal, to the relief of its author who had chafed under his well-meaning friends' queries as to when Macready would present it to the world. As if to make up for lost time, the play that had languished unread and almost forgotten for twenty-four months was rushed through production in half as many days. Macready's interest during the preparation was scarcely more than tepid, however. Harassed as he was by threat of bankruptcy, he feared he might have another failure on his hands and so he kept Browning busy on a thousand and one alterations. Also he was loath to risk his reputation by appearing in another possible fiasco. Thus a few days after the play was in rehearsal, he blandly announced that the part of Thorold which Browning expected him to play, had been entrusted to a comparatively unknown actor, Mr. Phelps. No wonder that during this trying period nerves were strained, tempers ran high and Macready's diary contained outspoken censure of the unmanageable playwright. "Went to Drury Lane theatre. Found Browning waiting for me in a state of great excitement. He abused the doorkeeper and was in a very great passion. I calmly apologized for having detained him . . . But his dignity was mortally wounded. I fear he is a very conceited man."

Then Mr. Phelps fell ill during rehearsals. Macready, who now saw the possibilities of the part of Thorold, decided to understudy it after all, with the intention of performing it if Phelps continued ill. Phelps recovered and showed no inclination to give up the stellar role. He would do the part if he died for it, he told the manager.

By this time Macready wanted nothing more ardently than to play Thorold. But when the decision was put before Browning he declared himself quite satisfied with Mr. Phelps. In a passion Macready crumpled the manuscript and dashed it to the ground. That night, the eve of the *première*, he poured out his irritation. "Browning . . . in the worst taste, manner and spirit, declined any further alterations, expressing himself perfectly satisfied with the manner in which Mr. Phelps executed Lord Tresham. I had no more to say. I could only think Mr. Browning a very disagreeable and offensively mannered person. *Voilà tout.*"

That was indeed that, so far as their friendship was concerned.

Perhaps Macready found vengeful satisfaction in the small audience for Phelps' three performances, and self-righteous justification in the criticism of the play, especially the harsh review of the *Athenaeum* for February 18, 1843. "If to pain and perplex were the end and aim of tragedy, Mr. Browning's poetic melodrama . . . would be worthy of admiration, for it is a very puzzling and unpleasant piece of business. The plot is plain enough but the acts and feelings of the characters are inscrutable and abhorrent . . . A few of the audience laughed, others were shocked. . . . It is impossible that such a drama should live even if it were artfully constructed, which this is not. . . ."

There was one reader, however, who was not stirred except to anger by such verbal lashings. Miss Barrett had read enough of Browning to see the injustice done him and bravely came to his defense. "There is truth on both sides," she wrote to the American Cornelius Matthews who since 1842 had been publishing her poems in *Graham's Magazine*, "but it seems to me hard truth on Browning. I do assure you I never saw him in my life—do not know him even by correspondence—and yet, whether through fellow-feeling for Eleusinian mysteries, or whether through the more generous motive of appreciation of his powers, I am very sensitive to the thousand and one stripes with which the assembly of critics doth expound its vocation over him, and the *Athenaeum*, for instance, made me quite cross and misanthropical last week. The truth is—and the world should know the truth—it is easier to find a more faultless writer than a poet of equal genius."

The affinity, as perhaps Mr. Kenyon could not help noticing, went beyond mere literary fellow-feeling. He was certain of it when Ba asked him for one of Browning's notes to keep for an autograph. Later, when the *New Spirit of the Age* on which she had collaborated with Mr. Horne appeared, she had been sent copies of the eight portraits it contained. Although her room was already crowded with busts, she had five of the portraits framed. Browning's was among them.

"Is it a good likeness?" she asked Mr. Kenyon.

"Rather like," he said noncommittally.

The mathematician of human relationships, however, grew ambitious. Several times he had attempted a meeting between Miss Barrett and Browning, and once the poet had accompanied him to the very door. But when John Kenyon went in to announce Browning he was told that Miss Barrett was too unwell to see anyone, and so the disappointed visitor had to leave, feeling, however, as if he had been "close, so close to some world's wonder in chapel or crypt, only a screen to push it and I might have entered, but there was some slight and just sufficient bar to admission, and the half-opened door shut."

Still the name of Browning, together with his poetry, invested him with a tangible reality in the ivy-shaded back bedroom of Wimpole Street. There the vitality of *Bells and Pomegranates* brought color to the invalid's cheeks and strengthened her belief in the nobility of her vocation, his vocation also.

It was in a signal moment that she wrote in her poem, "Lady Geraldine's Courtship," the lines:

> Or from Browning some pomegranate which, if cut deep
> down the middle,
> Shows a heart within blood-tinctured, of a veined
> humanity.

Part Two

O LYRIC LOVE

Chapter IX: "I love your verses . . . dear Miss Barrett"

TO THE microcosm of the individual the year 1844 was no more remarkable than any other year. It had its births and deaths, its revolts as in Calabria and the Bandiera uprising in Naples, and its revolutions as in Greece. Sensational events marked it, such as the lynching of the Mormon leader Joseph Smith at Carthage, Illinois, on the charge of treason, and the trial of Daniel O'Connell for sedition, in Ireland. Gold was discovered in South Australia, drawing thousands of immigrants. In England the Queen opened the Royal Exchange. A group of dry-goods clerks in London, under the influence of current humanitarian ideas, founded the Young Men's Christian Association. Public sentiment, abetted by the novels of Charles Dickens, put an end to the shameful Fleet Prison.

Science and industry made giant strides. The encroaching railroad which threw Wordsworth into a fever when it threatened to desecrate the Lake Country received serious attention from Gladstone, who passed a bill requiring the companies to provide proper accommodations. Since the necessary evil promised to yield profits, the government was also advised to acquire all existing railways in the course of the next twenty years. The conquest of distance by the iron horse, however, diminished to insignificance when the American Samuel F. B. Morse harnessed electricity with his space-conquering telegraph. His first message, "What hath God wrought!" complete with exclamation point, traversed beyond his primitive forty-mile line to astonish the world. In England that still mysterious power had its serious students, among them Faraday who published his *Experimental Researches in Electricity*. In another field Charles Darwin was pursuing investigations of his own, the results of which he issued anonymously under the title *Vestiges of the Natural History of Creation*. Anonymity did not protect him against the storm of protest that arose from this, his first enunciation of the theory of the origin of species. Elsewhere the Quaker chemical genius, John Dalton, died after a life dedicated to research that culminated in the eventual development of the atomic theory.

On a lower scale science, new and misunderstood, made holiday for the charlatan and his deluded followers. Mesmerism was the current fad. In the desire to appear open-minded during such novel experimentation, believers easily turned into converts, and when a convert was of the importance of a Harriet Martineau, the "science" flourished. Miss Martineau had an unimpeachable reputation. She possessed the intellect of a man and the courage of ten. Believing herself to be dying of cancer, she submitted herself to the terrifying experimentation of the mesmerist and her article in the *Athenaeum* in November 1844 told the rest. From an invalid, more confirmed than her friend Miss Barrett, to the extent of renouncing bonnets and parasols in her despair of ever going out again, she became once more the intrepid walker, covering her five miles a day with the zest of a Dickens—all through the good offices of the mesmerist and the "magnetic trance" into which he put her in the course of the cure.

Yet though her recovery was remarkable it was nothing to what the mesmerist accomplished with her maid, a girl who would ordinarily have hesitated to say Boo to a goose. The gentleman had only to put his hand on the bump of imitation on the girl's head for her to translate anything one said to her into Greek, Latin, Italian, and German. The wonder of the "apocalyptic girl" ably publicized by the missionary enthusiasm of her mistress went so far that other maids, like Miss Mitford's Jane, fell into prophetic trances even without the help of the mesmerist originally called to cure Jane of deafness. The girl's ears remained as shut as before, but what was mere deafness against the advantage of her "seeing behind her" during her trances? That convenient faculty might even have served domestic economy by giving warning of Dr. Mitford's hand reaching out toward the cracked teapot in depredation of his daughter's small economies.

In gratitude for her own "cure" Miss Martineau spread the gospel right and left in spite of the polemics her article called forth from unbelievers. But then these doubters could well be ignored in the triumph of the near conversion of such a personage as Archbishop Whately who came to call on her. There was nothing Miss Martineau desired so much, however, as the performance of some such miracle as her own on Miss Barrett. What prestige for mesmerism if the foremost female poet of the day should suddenly be made to leave her invalid shawls and appear at evening parties in the decolletage of a lady of fashion!

Again and again she wrote to Miss Barrett, describing her recovered self as the strongest of women capable of "walking fifteen miles one day and writing fifteen pages another day without fatigue." But Miss Barrett shrank from any suggestion of consulting a mesmerist, even when Miss Martineau implied the heroism of such an act—heroism comparable to her own when for the sake of truth she exposed herself to public misunderstanding and alienated her family who could not forgive her for getting well by such means. The recollection of Godiva, she told Miss Barrett, had given her strength. But while believing in mesmerism, Miss Barrett feared her father's immediate displeasure more than she desired health obtained by the recollection of Godiva's heroism. So she folded her shawls more becomingly about her and placated Miss Martineau by tactful refusals. She would never—alas! —qualify for the brave parliament of women that the feminist Miss Martineau was even then advocating.

What Miss Barrett refused to do one of her sisters managed to accomplish, despite Papa's unsleeping watchfulness. Through the offices of a mesmerist she fell into a trance and told Elizabeth of her sensations. Elizabeth was so horrified at the idea of having one's will at the mercy of another's that she had her sister promise never to try the experiment again.

The mesmerists, hydrotherapists, and other healers so victimized the public that the *Lancet* published a long article on quackery in which the lambs found themselves damned equally with the goats. The *Times* felt that the article was entirely justified and at the height of the Martineau sensation lent the *Lancet* support by quoting a long section from it. "There is scarcely a peer of the realm who is not the patron of some quack pill or potion: and the literati too are deeply tainted. We have heard of barbarians who threw quacks and their medicines into the sea: but here in England we have a Browning, a prince of poets, touching the pitch which defiles and making Paracelsus the hero of a poem. Sir E. L. Bulwer writes puffs for the water doctors . . . Miss Martineau makes a finessing servant-girl her physician-general: and Richard Howitt and the lady aforesaid stand god-father and mother to the contemptible mesmeric vagaries of Spencer Hall."

The sweet incense of "prince of poets" failed in its effect for Browning when he saw his *Paracelsus* mentioned with Miss Martineau's tranced maid. The year 1844 which had wrought wonders big and little in the world had brought no miracle into his life. He was thirty-two, unloved, unmarried, unloving and unrecognized. True, the discriminating had seen, since his earliest work, the advent of a high-gifted spirit as well as of a new and daring poet. He had followers among the literate few. But to the general public he was the writer of the obscure *Sordello*, of unsuccessful plays, of incomprehensible philosophical poetry.

Even *Pippa Passes*, that varied and moving drama of the simple girl, the silkwinder of Asolo whose innocent songs on her one day's holiday affect the lives of the guilty lovers; of the sculptor Jules who believed himself duped by the girl he was going to marry; of the young Carbonaro Luigi plotting an assassination, and of the holy Monsignor planning Pippa's own ruin—even that gem in Browning's poetic crown was generally ignored. Yet though the world might feel that it could dispense with his gift of poetry, it made itself the poorer for ignoring his gift of love, his love of the many-faced, unknown, perhaps unknowable humanity—the love which like Pippa, the innocent and unconscious force, influences the destinies of those it reaches. But the world spun on unheeding. Meanwhile no American publisher came to Browning with flattering offers. No English house showed willingness to chance the initial expense of printing his books. Every issue of *Bells and Pomegranates* since 1841 had been paid for by his father who would continue to do so until the last pamphlet of 1846. Few, comparatively speaking, came forward to buy his poetry, even in the cheap shilling book. Had he depended upon it for his livelihood even the garret would have been beyond his means. And yet Browning had already produced a bulk of poetry which for daring, scope, and originality of thought would have made his place secure among the greatest.

Of that fact he was confident or he would have abandoned the pen altogether. Not long since, however, he had made a little money from his dramatic writing—his imagination in later years augmented the sum to five hundred pounds—when the actor-manager Charles Kean, Macready's strongest competitor, commissioned the poet to provide him with an acting vehicle. With reminiscences of his travels stirring in his mind, Browning produced the blank verse drama, *Colombe's Birthday*. The action, such as it is, has for setting the duchies of Juliers and Cleves. The heroine, the reigning duchess, is confronted with a choice between marrying an overlord and keeping her estates, or of taking a man of inferior rank and losing all for love. Colombe chooses love.

As a play it is one of Browning's most readable but unfortunately one of his least dramatic. When he read it over to Kean and his wife who was to play the part of Colombe, they both expressed their pleasure in it. But there was no talk of immediate production. Kean spoke vaguely of Easter of next year—a postponement of thirteen months!—and even then he was not certain that he could do it. It meant that meanwhile the play would lie stifling in the russet portfolio. "I *must* print," Browning declared. "I must print or risk the hold, such as it is, I have at present on my public."

Colombe's Birthday accordingly saw the light as the sixth number of *Bells* in April 1844. Its publication cost him the friendship of Forster who took it upon himself to review it in such terms, possibly out of loyalty to Macready, that Browning was mortally wounded. "There can be no question as to the nerve and vigor of the writing or of its grasp of thought," Forster admitted in the *Examiner* for June 22. "Whether the present generation of readers will take note of it or leave it to the uncertain mercies of the future, still rests with Mr. Browning himself. As far as he has gone, we abominate his tastes as much as we respect his genius."

No wonder Browning reeled under the blow, gloved though it was with the velvet of compliment! What had he, the poet who spoke for the "warped bodies and souls" of his fellow men, what had he, the singer of good and evil, in common with Forster the self-confessed prude?

It was painful nevertheless to lose another friend. For all his going out into society Browning was beginning to find himself a rather lonely man. As early as *Pauline* he had boasted of his self-sufficiency. Still, he had expanded both as man and poet in the warmth of Eliza Flower's understanding. But the relation had been attenuated through the years to an infrequent correspondence. The friendship of his English Eyebright, Miss Haworth, had also become largely epistolary since his break with Macready when he discontinued his visits to Elstree. But then Browning had never really needed the friendship or love of women. The devotion of his mother and of Sarianna, companion and amanuensis, gave him as much of feminine influence as he required. He adored them both. As for love itself, he had lived it through its sublimation in his poetry rather than in actual experience. Sex was another matter. As a youth of strong, virile emotions, it

may well be that when he went the rounds with his Silverthorne
cousins he saw more of life than his fond parents suspected. In any
case it is scarcely conceivable that a man of his ardent nature should
have remained virginal through his third decade. He wrote too
vividly of passion. Indeed, many a virtuous subject of Queen Victoria,
whose nuptials in 1840 Miss Barrett had celebrated with commend-
able propriety in "Crowned and Wedded," must have been jolted
out of complacence by the stanza in "Confessional" where Browning has a young girl, tortured at the rack, cry out before her tor-
mentors:

> I had a lover—shame avaunt!
> This poor wrenched body, grim and gaunt,
> Was kissed all over till it burned,
> By lips the truest, love e'er turned
> His heart's own tint: one night they kissed
> My soul out in a burning mist.

More incandescent still is the wonderful, consuming dialogue of
the guilty lovers in *Pippa Passes*. What a shock to a public brought
up on bloodless abstractions, on the decent allusion and the inevitable
drawing of the curtain, on the polite euphemism of unpleasant fact,
as pantaletted as Victorian piano legs were soon to be! What a
revelation to see eternal urges presented in their eternally constant
aspects of commonplace suddenly turned to miracle—to see everyday things like wet boots, dust on a sill, a glass of wine, a thunderstorm, become the stuff of rapture. Yet that is the magic that Browning performs as the lovers relive in words the beginning of their
passion.

> Ottima: . . . . The Past, would you give up the Past? . . .
>   The garden's silence! Even the single bee
>   Persisting in his toil, suddenly stopt;
>   And where he hid you only could surmise
>   By some campanula's chalice set a-swing:
>   Who stammered—"yes, I love you?"
> Sebald: And I drew
>   Back; put far back your face with both my hands
>   Lest you should grow too full of me—your face
>   So seemed athirst for my whole soul and body . . .
> Ottima: So lay we till the storm came.
> Sebald: How it came!
> Ottima: Buried in woods we lay, you recollect:

> Swift ran the searching tempest overhead;
> And ever and anon, some bright white shaft
> Burst through the pine-tree roof, here burnt and there,
> As if God's messenger thro' the close wood screen
> Plunged and replunged his weapon at a venture,
> Feeling for guilty thee and me: then broke
> The thunder like a whole sea overhead—
> While I stretched myself upon you, hands
> To hands, my mouth to your hot mouth, and shook
> All my locks loose, and covered you with them . . .
> Sebald, as we lay,
> Rising and falling only with our pants,
> Who said, "Let death come now! 'tis right to die!"

That is not the language of the saint in the desert. It is incarnate passion speaking.

Love itself, however, the great gift of heart, soul, emotion, imagination, of self complete yet yearning for completion, Browning had given to no woman. So far he had found none to whom to give it. His was a nature as fastidious as it was generous. When it gave it surrendered wholly, but the recipient must be equal to the gift since with Browning love and worship were one. It was not without self-knowledge that he described in *Sordello* such persons as himself, who have

> A need to blend with each external charm,
> Bury themselves, the whole heart wide and warm—
> In something not themselves; they would belong
> To what they worship.

Ideal or person, once they dedicated themselves to the beloved object, it was forever.

Browning was too honest not to question himself on his failure to love. As he admitted later in a bit of self-analysis, he often wondered at "having for many years now made up my mind at the impossibility of loving any woman." He had fought not a little against it, but in the end he had acquiesced, accounted for it to himself "and become, if anything, rather proud of it than sorry." For lack of love he devoted himself to friendship which transcended sexuality and satisfied his soul.

In 1840 the Brownings had left Camberwell which had become overpopulated and commercialized and moved to an old-fashioned three-storied cottage at Hatcham—past the Kent Road, past the turnpike at New Cross and down a lane with a hedge to the right. "There you will descry a house resembling a goose-pie," Browning directed his friends. "Only a crooked, hasty and rash goose-pie." But the house had a garden and trees and a view of hills which could be easily reached by a few minutes' walk.

At Camberwell in the late 'thirties he had made friends with a number of youths of the same age and inclinations, Alfred Domett, Christopher Dowson, Joseph Arnould who had won the Newdigate prize at Oxford in 1834, a mysterious Captain Pritchard whose habitat none ever discovered, Arthur Young and several others, all banded together in a club which they called "The Colloquials." Of them all Alfred Domett, a year older than Browning, became his friend, the closest he had ever had. Domett was vital, adventurous, handsome and a poet. His face with its expressive chin and veiled eyes bespoke the conflict of the active man and the dreamer. He was impatient for life yet loitered on the way to study the blossoms on the hedgerows. At eighteen he went up to St. John's College, Cambridge, but left at the end of four years without a degree but with a volume of poems for publication. The book scarcely created a ripple and quickly sank to oblivion. Perhaps because like all literary innocents he had hoped too much for it he was disappointed and, eager for a change of scene, started off for Canada. Later he wandered across Italy and the Tyrol, and produced another poetic volume, Venice, in 1839. It was probably their common interest in literature and Italy which drew Browning to Domett, although he must have known that with Domett poetry would be nothing more than an amiable avocation. Domett himself realized it too. Between the voyages facilitated by his shipowning father and the climbs up Parnassus, he prepared himself for a career by reading for the Bar.

The friends saw each other often, first at Hanover Cottage and then at Hatcham, in a manly comradeship that was not ashamed to admit affection. They would talk for hours in the large low upper room that was Browning's library or, in expansive moments, go together into the sanctum adjoining it, Browning's study where he would read some new poem for his friend's approval or criticism. Sometimes they would join the family in the drawing room. Then Browning would sit at the piano and play. There was nothing Browning did not share with his friend, even his love of Shelley whose bust, modeled from life by Mrs. Leigh Hunt, stood on the landing where he could see it whenever he left his room or went back to it. "Ah, *that* was a poet!" he would exclaim to Domett as they passed the wild, sad, prophetic face framed in its maenad locks.

The year Browning published the first *Bells* Domett was called to the Bar. He was not too busy to watch over Browning's literary fortunes. The blindness of the critics to the beauties of *Pippa Passes* goaded him on to write a violent diatribe against them, but this defense was seen by "The Colloquials" only as no printer came forward to make it available to the public. Such loyalty was not without its reward in the esteem of the grateful poet.

Those were difficult years in England, marked by disaffection in the working classes and oppressive measures by the Government, especially after a crazed potboy, like an incarnation of social unrest, attempted to assassinate the Queen. The Chartist movement tried to organize the discontent into practical action by a monster petition signed by more than a million people who demanded universal suffrage, secret ballots and women's rights. The bulky scroll was rolled into Parliament where it was looked at, marveled on—and denied. Again in 1842 the Chartists presented their claims, this time in a petition that contained three and a half million signatures and made a cylinder of such proportions that it had to be cut into segments to pass through the doors. Once more Parliament rejected it. Then followed a strike with two more attempts on the life of the Queen. When calm reigned again, it reigned over the same conditions of power and privilege, poverty and unemployment.

Under the circumstances it was scarcely surprising that the youth of the nation responded wholeheartedly to the falsetto of Tennyson's hero in "Locksley Hall" and dreamed with him of virgin lands where

> . . . the passions cramped no longer shall have scope
> and breathing space;
> I will take some savage woman; she will rear my dusky race.
> Iron-jointed, supple-sinewed, they shall dive and they
> shall run,
> Catch the wild-goat by the hair and hurl their lances in
> the sun;
> Whistle back the parrot's call and leap the rainbows of
> the brooks,
> Not with blinded eyesight poring over miserable books.

Alfred Domett was one of the first to join the great exodus, leaving England for New Zealand. Browning missed him, so much indeed that he who hated writing letters not only corresponded with him frequently but set to work on "a fancy portrait" of him in "Waring" recalling their walks up and down London town, their lighthearted chatter, their adventures. The rollicking rhythm, the absurd rhymes, are the mock hilarity of one striving too hard to restrain the sigh. They also show Browning in that maddening jocular vein that could devise such rhymes as "rhinoceros" and "toss Eros," or "Mizpa" and "it is, Pa," tricks that set the teeth on edge and shorten patience. Though these are not in "Waring" one can find other examples to break the molars on:

> Meantime how much I loved him,
> I find out now I've lost him . . .
> His eyes that just a little wink
> As deep I go into the merit
> Of this or that distinguished spirit—
> His cheeks' raised colour, soon to sink,
> As long I dwell on some stupendous
> And tremendous (Heaven defend us!)
> Monstr'-inform'-ingens-horrend-ous
> Demoniaco-seraphic
> Penman's latest piece of graphic. . . .

Heaven defend us indeed!

Yet though the mood was light the longing was real enough. Something of its depth is discernible in the letter Browning sent Domett in November of 1843, a year and a half after Alfred's departure: "There you walk past our pond-rail (picking up one of the fallen horse-chestnuts) and now our gate-latch clicks, and now— . . . 'Tis worth while running away to be so wished for again."

So friendship substituted for love. But it was not enough. Not for that energetic, quick-pacing youth whom women turned to look at. Not for the treasure he had to spend in tenderness and devotion, nor for the fervor of his heart and brain.

As once before in dejection he thought of Italy as if a change from London murk to the southern sunlight would alter his state of mind. Bartoli's De' Simboli, that useful handbook, accompanied him again when he sailed for Naples, late in the summer of 1844. His absence, at least in one quarter, was not unmarked. "Mr. Browning is not in England," Miss Barrett wrote to one of her friends, ". . . so that whatever you send for him must await his return from the east or west or south, wherever he is."

It was a slow voyage lasting from early in August to September, the

rocking of the boat making him long for a good gallop across the
Hatcham fields on his horse York in the stables at home. With the
unpredictability of the creative mind the thought of his horse, combined with the echo of Virgilian meters, blended with memories of
previous travels. And so that favorite of all schoolboys, the rollicking
ride of the three young heroes bearing good news from Ghent to
Aix, was conceived. The inspiration must have come urgently to
Browning, perhaps while musing over the familiar pages of *De'
Simboli*, there under the bulwark of a vessel off the African Coast,
for he wrote the poem in pencil on the flyleaf of the book. There
was no historical foundation for the story but the ride with its adventures might well have taken place in the chronic turmoil of
European history.

When Browning arrived in Naples the whole region was still
agitated over one of those heroic rebellions that had been breaking
out like signal flares to liberty in Italy's struggle against the Austrian
tyrant. Two young men, Attilio and Emilio Bandiera, sons of Admiral
Bandiera in the service of Austria, suddenly threw over their posts
under their father and joined the ranks of Mazzini and Young Italy
which already counted its martyrs by the hundreds. Many had been
executed without pretense of trial, many more were confined in
makeshift prisons. The two youths, therefore, planned to sail from
the island of Corfu where they had taken refuge after their flight, and
with a band of followers make an assault on the prisons of the
Calabrian coast. They carried out their plan with some success,
raiding the jails by force of arms and hiding away with their liberated
comrades among patriotic sympathizers. Their band, however, concealed its Judas who sold out to the enemy. The two leaders and a
number of their followers were seized, imprisoned, and then put to
death. But the enemy could not silence their cry of *"Viva l'Italia!"*
as they died, nor keep the people from making of their name a battle
shout for the fight that was only beginning.

Browning, still companioned by the libertarian Shelley even though
in *Sordello* he had begged him not to come too near, sided with the
people in their struggles. For that matter he had been on their side
in all his works and could not conceive of a poet who would not
espouse their cause against tyranny. He looked upon it as a defection
when a man who like Wordsworth had once been a fighter for liberty
became the belled cat of the ruling powers. What business had a once-
revolutionary poet with bag-wigs and ribbands and court appearances?

How could such a man consent to mewing occasional verse when he had once been the clarion of liberty?

With such thoughts in mind he planned "The Italian in England," the gripping narrative of the perils of an Italian patriot, and "The Lost Leader" for which he admitted he had used Wordsworth as "a sort of painter's model." It was a damning portrait when it was finished. Removing the lost leader from the company of Shakespeare, Milton, Burns, and Shelley, Browning charged:

> He alone breaks from the van and the freemen,
> He alone sinks to the rear and the slaves!

But Wordsworth was more distressed by the menace of modern invention to the landscape than by the Corn Laws grinding the people down.

Browning therefore communed with his beloved shade, visiting the places where Shelley had once been. From Naples he went to Rome to stand over those few square feet of ground on the violet-studded slope of the English Cemetery where, near the pyramid of Cestius, the body of Keats and the ashes of Shelley are brought together in death. Nearby a burial plot was reserved for that adventurer and worshiper of genius, Edward Trelawny, who had set the torch to Shelley's pyre. Browning had a letter to Trelawny whom he intended to visit in Leghorn.

Meanwhile in Naples he had met a young Italian, Signor Scotti, personable and talented, with whom he struck up an agreeable friendship. Not the least of Signor Scotti's talents was the ability to bargain down his fellow countrymen who deemed it a point of honor to fleece the visiting foreigner. "I hear him disputing our bill," Browning wrote home. "He does not see why we should pay for six wax candles when we used only two."

Together they had visited Sorrento and Amalfi and eventually Rome where Signor Scotti charmed the Contessa Carducci, an old friend of Browning's, by his beautiful manners and still more beautiful person. Soon afterward Browning and Signor Scotti had to follow their respective itineraries. They parted with mutual regret. Then suddenly came the shocking news that for some unknown but certainly powerful reason Signor Scotti had taken his own life. What tragedy, what secret anguish had tortured that outwardly gay youth?

Before leaving Rome Browning visited the jewel-like church of the virgin Santa Prassede, near Santa Maria Maggiore. The builders had lavished all the art of ornamentation upon it, sparing no expense to make every niche and chapel a thing of such beauty that the people called the church the Garden of Paradise. As often in holy edifices, the interior held a number of monuments of the notable dead. One of the richest was the tomb of Cardinal Cetive. The excessive ornamentation of that tomb which housed only the bones of a mortal, and the surrounding extravagance, striking upon Browning's knowledge of Renaissance Italy, its worldliness, hypocrisy, and intense love of adornment, roused his quiescent imagination. Either then or on his return to England he wrote that concise masterpiece on the corrupt yet beauty-worshiping Renaissance spirit, "The Bishop Orders his Tomb at St. Praxed's Church."

On his way home through northern Italy Browning delivered his letter to Trelawny. Here was one who had lived in the intimacy of Shelley at Pisa, this Corsair who had been drawn there by Byron's fame but who had succumbed to the spell of Shelley. Browning was eager with questions. What had Shelley said, those last days? What had he been writing? What did he look like? He had heard much about Shelley from Leigh Hunt who with Byron and Trelawny had stood by watching the funeral pyre on the desert Italian shore, while the restless brain seethed in the burst skull and the great heart, laid bare, refused to burn. There were so many things he wanted Trelawny to tell him. But Trelawny told him nothing. A mutual antipathy kept them awkward and dumb. They parted as they had met, utter strangers.

Except for ideas for new poems stirring in his mind, Browning's spirits had not been lifted by this second Italian voyage. It was December. The old year was dying, with little remembered happiness in it for him to regret its passing. He had written poems, epics, plays, yet he was frustrated, no matter what he did. His glowing promise seemed to have been spent. He loved his family, and they adored him. He had pleasant acquaintances. He went out a great deal at night. Yet life outside his study held nothing that put any eagerness into his step to meet it.

Then one day early in the new year, while reading Miss Barrett's *Poems* which had created a sensation on their appearance during his stay in Italy, his heart leapt. His name with Wordsworth's and Tennyson's was mentioned in her poem, "Lady Geraldine's Courtship." Not only that. With exquisite perception Miss Barrett had seen the quality of humanity in his work and himself, and in a bold figure suggested by his own *Bells and Pomegranates*, had paid him a priceless compliment. Existence took on meaning. Even the two skulls on their brackets by his window where life nonetheless triumphed in the spiders that spun their webs in the gaping jaws—even those fearful reminders of mortality now affirmed the intense joy of living.

Miss Barrett's two volumes, he found, had been sent to Sarianna by Mr. Kenyon. On meeting him several days after his discovery Browning naturally brought up the subject that had been uppermost in his mind, and asked Mr. Kenyon: "If I were to write now—?"

Mr. Kenyon's shrewd eyes glinted behind his spectacles. "Why, under those circumstances," he said, "Miss Barrett would even be *pleased* to hear from you." As if his encouragement had been insufficient, he wrote Browning a note to urge him further. The corpulent Cupid had shot his bow.

On the 10th of January, 1845 Robert Browning in his study, with the picture of Andromeda before his eyes and the silent skulls reaffirming life, took up his pen to write. It was a letter and it began, "I love your verses with all my heart, dear Miss Barrett,—and this is no off-hand complimentary letter that I shall write, no prompt matter-of-course recognition of your genius, and there a graceful and natural end of the thing. . . ."

Chapter X: "In the spring we shall see "

". . . and there a graceful and natural end of the thing," Eliza-beth Barrett read with growing wonder and agitated pulse on the night of January 10th. "Since the day last week when I first read your poems, I quite laugh how I have been turning and turning again in my mind what I should be able to tell you of their effect upon me, for in the first flush of delight I thought I would this once get out of my habit of purely passive enjoyment, when I do really enjoy, and thoroughly justify my admiration—perhaps even, as a loyal fellow-craftsman should, try and find fault and do you some little good to be proud of hereafter!—but nothing comes of it all—so into me it has gone, and part of me it has become, this great living poetry of yours, not a flower of which but took root and grew. . . ."

She read the words but she could scarcely believe them. When Wilson the maid had brought in the tray with its usual accumulation of mail, she had felt no more excitement over the unfamiliar hand-writing than over any communication from a stranger. Many had been writing to her, especially since the publication of those two green-bound volumes, *Poems*, which Moxon had issued with that deprecating shrug which speeds an uncertain venture. She had pub-lished no book since *The Seraphim* six years earlier.

Poems, like her earlier work, had been a tribute to her father. Guilt and love mingled in her lengthy dedication whose words the reader might translate to filial piety. To Mr. Barrett they spoke clearly of her dependence, contrition, and affection. He forgave much of the past as he read: "When your eyes fall upon this page . . . and you start to see to whom it is inscribed, your first thought will be of the time, far off, when I was a child, and wrote verses, and when I dedi-cated them to you. . . . Of all that such a recollection implies of saddest and sweetest to both of us, it would become neither of us to speak before the world. . . . Enough, that what is in my heart when I write thus will be fully known to yours. . . . Somewhat more faint-hearted than I used to be, it is my fancy thus to seem to return to a visible personal dependence on you, as if indeed I were a child again; to conjure up your beloved image between myself and the public, so as to be sure of one smile; and to satisfy my heart, while I sanctify my ambition, by associating with the great pursuit of my life its tenderest and earliest affection." She had signed it "Your E.B.B."

These public declarations were manna to the patriarch's hungry ego. His favorite child was his without fear of rivalry. The one she had preferred above him was under the ground, and with him lay buried many a hope. Unashamedly and before anyone who chose to read, the child on whom he had fixed his most tenacious affection, declared him to be her tenderest love, for whom she wrote her poetry, for whose sake she strove and was ambitious. She admitted a closeness between them that spoke from heart to heart without need of words. She made him, her fifty-eight-year-old father, the sum and crown of her life.

What was extraordinary in Mr. Barrett's reading of the inscription was its total accuracy. At thirty-eight Elizabeth Barrett had given up all thought of change in her mode of living. Love—it was something to write about, always with rue for the burden of unhappiness it carried, whether fulfilled or without hope. Like her own heroine in "Catarina to Camoens," she could have cried:

> On the door you will not enter
> I have gazed too long: adieu!
> Hope withdraws her peradventure;
> Death is near me, and not you.

Her Camoens, however, had never come and gone. The only bridegroom who would ever enter her chamber she fully believed would be death. For her the sole love possible dwelt in that house on Wimpole Street. Her strangely haunting verses, the half mystical "Confessions" which with a few others in the same manner oddly anticipated Christina Rossetti, contained a stanza sprung from a heart already convinced of its narrow scope in earthly affections.

> "The least touch of their hands in the morning, I keep
> it by day and by night;
> Their least step on the stair, at the door, still throbs
> through me, if ever so light;
> Their least gift which they left to my childhood, far
> off in the long-ago years,

> Is now turned from a toy to a relic, and seen through
> the crystal of tears.
> Dig the snow," she said,
> "For my churchyard bed:
> Yet I, as I sleep, shall not fear to freeze,
> If one only of these my beloved shall love me with
> heart-warm tears,
> As I have loved these."

Being large-hearted and noble of spirit, she could not limit her sympathies. For lack of the one who would have filled her heart, she made room in it for all humanity. Nothing happened in the outside world but that its echoes penetrated her chamber. She took sides— for the oppressed—in the agitation over the Corn Laws. She knew about the Chartist movement and approved. When she read the report of Horne's commission which had been investigating child labor in the mines and factories, her whole nature rebelled against such crime as the research exposed. Lord Shaftesbury's ringing speech against the inhuman conditions in the exploitation of childhood had scarcely made its effect upon Parliament when Elizabeth Barrett's plea, in *Blackwood's Magazine* for August 1843 stirred up the whole nation. Men and women read her "Cry of the Children" and were not ashamed to weep. Mothers blessed her who had never known motherhood and yet could speak for their anguish. It was a noble poem, strong, direct, brave and human.

Since she was Elizabeth Barrett, she prefixed it with a quotation from *Medea*. But there was no need to know Greek to understand the horror of the crime which, in the gentlest language, with the simplest of everyday images, she condemned. Clergymen read the poem from the pulpit. Little children learned it by heart to plead for their unhappy fellows.

> Do you hear the children weeping, O my brothers,
> Ere the sorrow comes with years?
> They are leaning their young heads against their mothers,
> And that cannot stop their tears.
> The young lambs are bleating in the meadows;
> The young birds are chirping in the nest;
> The young fawns are playing with the shadows;
> The young flowers are blowing toward the west;
> But the young, young children, O my brothers!
> They are weeping bitterly.

They are weeping in the playtime of the others,
    In the country of the free. . . .

Sentimental, said those who think it bad taste to be made to feel. The generous-hearted rubbed their eyes and thanked the poet for being made to see. Whatever the individual reaction, "The Cry of the Children" roused public feeling to such a degree that Parliament passed the first of the acts regulating child labor. It was something accomplished in the much that still remained to do.

In America, Poe found in the poem "a horror sublime in its simplicity—of which Dante himself might have been proud." He was even less temperate in his praise of the American edition of Miss Barrett's poems. Indeed, he went so far as to dedicate a volume of his tales to her. To Miss Barrett's consternation, however, she found that while dedicating the book to her, he did not fail to abuse her in its preface. In the same spirit Poe wrote a review of her—"the two extremes of laudation and reprehension," she complained. "You would have thought it had been written by a friend and foe, each stark mad with love and hate, and writing the alternate paragraphs." Hence when she saw herself described as "the noblest of her sex" by Mr. Poe, she wondered whether she should not thank him by saying, "Sir, you are the most discerning of yours." In the particular copy of the book that she received from the American poet she found that "the deteriorating preface which was to have saved me from vanity-fever . . . is cut down and away—perhaps in this copy only."

For all his critical instability Poe had a genuine admiration for Miss Barrett. "You ought to come to New York," Mrs. Osgood wrote to her, "to see Mr. Poe's wild eyes flash through tears when he reads your verses."

Miss Barrett's feelings were hardly reciprocal. Though she did not go so far in scorn as in describing Mrs. Osgood's book of poetry—"of the most gorgeous, all purple and gold"—she had little to say in praise of Poe except, "There is poetry in the man though, now and then, seen between great gaps of bathos." As for the "Raven," she said, "(It) made me laugh, though with something in it which accounts for the hold it took upon people such as N. P. Willis and his peers."

So poets may misunderstand one another.

Although there was no woman at the time who had so captured the public in England and America to that extent Miss Barrett rightly said of herself: "A bird in a cage would have as good a story."

It was gratifying to have the powerful reviewers praise her poems, to be called "extraordinary" by one and to inhale the rare incense of *Blackwood's* which declared, "Her genius is profound, unsullied, and without a flaw." She knew her many flaws, some blameless because she had not yet attained the perfection for which she strove, some conscious, both in the license of rhythm and particularly rhyme, because she attempted to break down formal limitations. "I have written these poems as well as I could," she said of her new volumes, "and I hope to write others better. I have not reached my own ideal." And she was truthful when she added that she loved poetry itself more than she loved her own successes in it—such as waking one morning, like Byron, to find herself famous.

In consequence there was a longer line than ever of those who wished to be admitted into her privacy. But she was firm in her prohibitions. Her family, with Wilson as well as the butler who had his instructions, barred the door to intruders as effectively as the guardians of the crown treasure.

There was one strong-willed woman, however, whom neither they nor Miss Barrett availed to keep out. Mrs. Anna Jameson, a literary celebrity in her own right though not in the poetic field, and an ardent feminist like Miss Martineau, felt that she owed it to herself and the author of *Poems* to meet. She called, was refused admittance, and left a note. Undeterred, she came again, leaving another note. Miss Barrett was vanquished. Mrs. Jameson was, after all, a toiler in the vineyard too. Her books, *The Diary of an Ennuyée*, and *Characteristics of Shakespeare's Women*, had won her a deserved recognition, and her writings on art, in which she was very learned, helped to make people aware of beauty, a good thing in the increasing "uglification" of London with the growth of industrialism.

So one November afternoon, while Elizabeth listened with a heart that "beat itself almost to pieces," as it always did at the sound of an unfamiliar step on the stairs, Mrs. Jameson made her appearance. The two became friends immediately although at first Miss Barrett was taken aback by that brusque, oddly commanding Irishwoman with a colorless complexion, pale eyes, lips barely defined, no perceptible eyebrows, and red hair. She was about Miss Mitford's age, but there any similarity ended. One could tell at once that there was no gentle sentiment about her. That, for instance, one could never exchange letters with her about one's pets, or enclose the feathers of one's canaries as friendship tokens in the correspondence, as Miss Barrett had done with Miss Mitford. Mrs. Jameson's talk was as sharp and precise as herself, and vigorous to a degree. But with that formidable manner her thoughts, Miss Barrett found, were clear as glass, even if she could not always agree with them. Mrs. Jameson's belief in the superiority of mind in women, for instance, and her denunciation of "carpet work" in which her sex indulged.

"It is positively injurious to the mind because it leads us into fatal habits of revery," she maintained.

Miss Barrett begged to differ on the injuriousness of carpet work, saying not a word, however, "for the poor reveries which have frayed away so much silken time for me." But Mrs. Jameson was inclined to make a magnanimous exception for her who, as it happened, was innocent of all knowledge of the art.

"Oh, but you may do carpet work with impunity," she flung at parting. "Yes! *Because* you can be writing poems all the while!"

Thus the days passed in writing and receiving visits from "dear Mr. Kenyon" when he was in town, from Miss Mitford and now Mrs. Jameson, from Mr. Barrett, of course, for the intimate moments of conversation and prayer, and from a mysterious character, a strange, embittered, selfish, jealous man, possibly a relative for the privilege he enjoyed of coming and going freely in that otherwise inhospitable house. He idolized Elizabeth and was critical of her. "I am lifted halfway to the skies, and made a mark there for pellets," she complained. For whatever reason, perhaps because she pitied his twisted nature and was touched by his jealous devotion, she had borne with him for years and still allowed herself to be worshiped and insulted in one and the same breath. She gave him no name in her allusions to him, then called him Chiappino after she had encountered his double in Browning's *A Soul's Tragedy*.

That, however, was still in the future. Meanwhile one hour went by like another and day closed into night with such set monotony that she thought of dates only for the convention that required them at the head of a letter. Very often she omitted them even there. As for time, it scarcely mattered any more. Two years ago her watch had snapped its spring; she left it, broken and silent, in a drawer. The clocks in the neighborhood struck for the most part out of hearing and if the wind did carry the sound, it was in a jangle of confusion. She had the pulse of her own life to mark the passing time and the testimony of her published work to show that she had not wholly wasted it.

Now unexpectedly in the dead of that monotony came a letter

from New Cross, Hatcham, which, as she held it to read, infused her with life through the fingertips and made all the bells round about peal in unison. Time suddenly mattered. She must read, read on quickly, to return to the beginning and rescue the words drowned in her too ready tears.

"Now, talking with whoever is worthy," the letter continued, "I can give a reason for my faith in one and another excellence, the fresh strange music, the affluent language, the exquisite pathos and true new brave thought." All this about the weaving of her own poor reveries! "But in this addressing myself to you—your own self, and for the first time, my feeling rises altogether. I do, as I say, love these books with all my heart—and I love you too."

Bold words for the unmet Robert Browning to write. But somehow she did not take them amiss. After all Mr. Kenyon had spoken of him with more frequency than she had thought necessary. And to think that, as Mr. Browning said in his letter, they might have met years ago! He had been at her very door—and had not been admitted. "I went home my thousands of miles, and the sight was never to be?" The question mark had a peculiar eloquence. "Well, these Poems were to be, and this true thankful joy and pride with which I feel myself, yours ever faithfully, Robert Browning."

He admired her poetry. He spoke of her fresh strange music and true new brave thought. The innovator, the new voice of the age made her his kin by his generous words.

It was not the first time she had enjoyed his praise. Soon after composing "The Dead Pan" she had sent the manuscript to Mr. Kenyon who showed it to Browning. The bold conception, the magically suggestive images of the dead gods of Hellas when the One in Sion "hung for love's sake on a cross" spoke the directest language to Browning. How could he have failed to thrill to such a subject as he might have chosen, unfolding in visions that could have sprung from his brain musing over the godly dead?

> Do ye sit there still in slumber,
> In gigantic Alpine rows?
> The black poppies out of number,
> Nodding, dripping from your brows
> To the red lees of your wine,
> And so kept alive and fine?
> Pan, Pan is dead.

> Ha, Apollo! floats his golden
> Hair all mist-like where he stands.
> While the Muses hang infolding
> Knee and foot with faint, wild hands?
> 'Neath the clanging of thy bow
> Niobe looked lost as thou!
> Pan, Pan is dead.

How trivial was the flaw of the weak word "fine" against the genius of those "faint, wild hands"—for that matter, against the effectiveness of the poem as a whole! Browning had written Kenyon a note of admiring praise which the mathematician of personalities sent on at once to Cousin Ba. Such delight as she felt had to be shared, so she had forwarded the note to Mr. Horne.

If then her pleasure had been great, it was overshadowed by what she now experienced. With the need of the lonely to communicate she had to tell someone of the advent of a marvel in the room where so little ever happened. But she could not trust herself to speak of it that night. The following morning she wrote a number of letters. In one she announced, in the midst of feminine inconsequentialities: "I had a letter from Browning, the poet, last night which threw me into ecstasies—Browning, the author of *Paracelsus* and king of the mystics." It revealed little enough of what the letter had meant but it helped to relieve the burden of sudden, unbearable joy. Was "the king of the mystics" thrown in to preclude any suggestion of earthly relationship, after the admission of her ecstasies?

Her answer to Browning was also written that day, the 11th of January. It was twice as long as his, but then she had had years of practice in the art in which she exercised her natural gaiety and wit and her "usual insolence," as Mr. Kenyon fondly teased. There was scarcely any levity and but little of her whimsical charm in that first epistle. Almost, one would have thought she was writing to the king of the mystics and needed to be adequately astral.

"I thank you, dear Mr. Browning, from the bottom of my heart," she began cordially enough till sudden embarrassment cooled her. "You meant to give me pleasure by your letter—and even if the object had not been answered, I ought still to thank you. But it is thoroughly answered." That might be, but her stiff declarativeness gave no such indication. "Such a letter from such a hand!" she exclaimed in the next sentence. The exclamation point released her. In the flow of her uninhibited prolixity she went on to tell him how she felt. "Sympathy is dear—very dear to me: but the sympathy of a poet, and of such a poet . . . Will you take back my gratitude for it?—agreeing, too, that of all the commerce done in the world, from Tyre to Carthage, the exchange of sympathy for gratitude is the most princely thing."

Even so early—she had not had his letter twenty-four hours—she was associating with him the words *king* and *princely* that set him above his peers, and the gift of his sympathy beyond the ordinary commerce of the world.

As her pen flew across the page she gained naturalness and even the boldness to ask for the criticism he had offered on her "master-faults." Not that she would slavishly accept it. "I do not pretend to any extraordinary meekness under criticism and it is possible enough that I might not be altogether obedient to yours." There it was—her usual insolence again! After a brief flight on Buffon's dictum that style is the man she descended to what, in Browning's letter, had sunk into her heart. "Is it indeed true," she asked, "that I was so near the pleasure and honor of making your acquaintance? and can it be true that you look back upon the lost opportunity with any regret?" Was it overbold of her to respond thus clearly to that question mark, so meaningfully placed in his letter? ". . . I would rather hope (as I do) that what I lost by one chance I may recover by some future one. Winters shut me up as they do a dormouse's eyes; in the spring, *we shall see* . . ." Her delicacy would not let her go further in proffering an invitation.

She closed with a return to formality but with genuine feeling. "I will say that while I live to follow this divine art of poetry, in proportion to my love for it and my devotion to it, I must be a devout admirer and student of your works. This is in my heart to say to you—and I say it. And, for the rest, I am proud to remain your obliged and faithful Elizabeth B. Barrett."

The most indifferent reader would have been struck at once by the friendliness in the letter and the desire to continue the correspondence were it only on the subject of master-faults. The far from indifferent Browning read much more in it—and indeed it was there for him to interpret. The door to Miss Barrett's house while not flung wide was not irrevocably shut. With the opening of the dormouse's eyes in the spring, there might be a space made between the formidable portals of Number 50 Wimpole Street large enough for him to slip through. So far he knew the street as a dead uniformity of respectable middle-class houses, their doorknobs and knockers catching the sun in their high polish, their elaborate curtains hanging in studied folds. He knew it as a neighborhood of moneyed propriety, snobbish in its butlers, decorous in its parlor maids, impeccable in outward decency. A neighborhood of starched shirts and striped morning trousers, of pedigreed dogs and opulent tables. A neighborhood that, since it could not actually obliterate the commercialism of Oxford Street and the shame of Shoreditch, did the practical thing by ignoring them. It was worlds away from the chapel of his imagination and yet, and yet—After all, it was the deity that made the chapel.

He noted that with subtle reticence Miss Barrett had made no allusion to his impulsive "—and I love you too." Also, that she took seriously his "try and find fault" with her poetry which to her as to him was the *divine art* that justified existence. Altogether the letter encouraged him to write to her as freely as he felt. The keynote, as he saw, must be for the present their respective work.

But when he answered her two days later, he plunged headlong into intimacy which he was too honest to mask. "My poor praise was nearly as felicitously brought out as a certain tribute to no less a personage than Tasso, which I was amused with at Rome some weeks ago, in a neat penciling on the plaster-wall by his tomb at Sant'Onofrio—'Alla cara memoria—di—Torquato Tasso—il Dottore Bernardini—offriva—il seguente Carme—O tu!'—and no more, the good man, it should seem, breaking down with the overload of love here! But my 'O tu' was breathed out most sincerely, and now you have taken it in gracious part, the rest will come after."

It was a bold stroke which he knew she would understand, especially in the exhortation of that familiar *tu*, even if again she would pass over it in silence.

The remainder of the letter concerned itself with their poetry. "But of this soon—for night is drawing on and I go out, yet cannot, quiet at conscience, till I repeat (to *myself*, for I never said it to you, I think) that your poetry must be, cannot but be infinitely more to me than mine to you—for you *do* what I always wanted, hoped to do, and only seem now likely to do for the first time. You speak out, you—I only make men and women speak—give you truth broken down into prismatic hues, and fear the pure white light, even if it is in me, but I am going to try. . . ."

All of it Miss Barrett read with quickened heart. Robert Browning was truly the poet she had always known him to be. The glimpses of the man that now emerged between the lines disturbed, excited, and a little frightened her. Could she, when the time came, resist, as she had resisted "Orion" Horne, this man who closed his letter with: "I will joyfully wait for the delight of your friendship, and the spring, and my Chapel-sight after all!"

Outside it was still January for all the pretense of sunlight and verdant groves on the transparent blind that blocked the view from her windows.

Chapter XI: "I who am scarcely to be called young now . . ."

SINCE Mr. Barrett's prayers were matters between himself and God none could know what he gave thanks for or besought. Certainly he had many reasons to be grateful. He was still a wealthy man in spite of his Jamaican losses and but for the terrible strokes which after the death of his wife had deprived him of Edward and Samuel, his family was intact. Most wonderfully in those days of high infant mortality his children but for little Mary had been spared to reach maturity. In the case of the girls a Jane Austen mother would have invoked the Almighty for providential husbands before that maturity degenerated into a negative virtue. As it was, in 1845 Elizabeth was only one year away from forty, Henrietta was thirty-six and Arabel thirty-two. Most of the sons were of an age when they should normally have had families of their own. Yet all remained unmarried and dependent upon their father. He was not ungenerous. He dressed his daughters well, allowing them many luxuries with the necessities, and he paid for the education of his sons. But for reasons of his own he kept them on rather short tether financially—"constrained *bodily* into submission—apparent submission at least—by the worst and most dishonourable necessity, the necessity of *living*."

The sons had their professions and would eventually establish themselves independently. Thanks to her legacies Elizabeth had money of her own. Henrietta and Arabel could look to no one but their father for their keep unless they married, which was the last thing Mr. Barrett encouraged or desired.

They were both attractive young women.

> The shadow of her face upon the wall
> May take your memory to the perfect Greek . . .

Elizabeth wrote of Henrietta who otherwise had little of the classical in her temperament. Gay, fun-loving, fond of music, she played the piano and was a fanatic for the polka. Arabel, gentle, serious-minded, active in charities and other good works, would have made an ideal wife for a curate, though perhaps too pretty with her long-lashed eyes and abundant curls. Her talent for painting Mr. Barrett had not encouraged. She went from water colors to oils without instruction and stopped there. If, whenever Arabel looked at the huge "Holy Family" attributed to Andrea del Sarto that Mr. Barrett had bought and hung over the drawing-room mantel, or if when she dusted her box of paints she regretted her unused talent, she made no audible complaint. Mr. Barrett would have paid little heed, even if she had.

Everything was cut and dried, as in an herbalist's sampler in that arid mind. He had his moments, however, when he would unbend to human act and speech. When that same "Holy Family" was acquired, he had Stormie and Alfred almost break their backs carrying it upstairs for Elizabeth to see. He could also be wryly witty. At Elizabeth's accounts of Mr. Horne's peculiarities he remarked: "Perhaps he is going to shoot the Queen and is preparing evidence of monomania,"—a comment that Ba found amusing enough to repeat. He also said of her transparent blind with its castle and walks and peasants and groves that it looked like the back window of a confectioner's shop, a criticism which was softened for her when she saw how much moved he was when the sunshine lighted up the picture.

There were other moments however that were not so pleasant, when his voice shook the chandeliers and sent the dogs skulking under the tables, moments when Elizabeth would rather have been struck than listen to that maniacal frenzy. One scene haunted her though it had happened years ago. Henrietta at that time had fancied herself in love and had confided in her sisters, swearing them to secrecy until she had obtained Mr. Barrett's consent. When she summoned up enough courage to speak to him all the vials of wrath were unloosed. "Oh, the dreadful scenes! And only because she had seemed to feel a little," Elizabeth recalled with a shudder. "I hear how her knees were made to ring upon the floor, now!" The poor girl was carried out of the room in hysterics while Elizabeth who had got up to help her fell flat upon her face in a fainting-fit. Arabel, seeing one sister distraught and the other apparently dead, added to the havoc by her own shrieks. But nothing softened the man who suffered on love and marriage "an obliquity—an eccentricity, or something beyond," as his most understanding daughter charitably put it.

In the violence of that storm Henrietta who had too much softness to be able to assert herself gave up her suitor, though not the thought of love. She attracted masculine admiration and saw no harm in accepting it. Mr. Barrett's monomania, however, had taught her to adopt a fickleness which she did not feel. Elizabeth whose poetic romaunts of the adoring wife who disguised herself as a page to follow her husband, of Catarina whose love was stronger than death, of many another heroine faithful to the last, was scandalized by Henrietta's levity. She who had not yet been touched by love could think of it only as sacred and eternal.

But she had too much sense of humor not to be amused by the tragicomedies which were sometimes enacted under the eyes of the "Holy family." In the previous autumn Henrietta who now played the guitar as well as the piano, had been so bold as to give a little polka while Mr. Barrett loitered unsuspecting in Cornwall. The house did not fall on its knees as Elizabeth had half expected, and the family had some lively diversion. They were still young, those seven boys and three girls, and youth can make everything bearable. Besides, their common lot only bound them closer in that long-standing secret alliance against the tyranny of the unreasonable father. No small part of that unreasonableness was his granting of certain unusual privileges. The boys might come and go as they wished provided they made no permanent attachments while the girls could receive visitors, male or female at the proper calling hours.

There was in consequence a great deal of activity at the front door on the part of the butler throughout the day, what with Miss Henrietta's morning visits and Miss Elizabeth's afternoon callers. Duties had been especially taxing two years ago when three of Miss Henrietta's suitors decided to make the drawing room their jousting field. For several months they charged and feinted and tested one another's mettle, while Miss Henrietta with remarkable composure—one might have said boredom—watched from a distance and sometimes watched not at all, going about her household affairs as if the frays in the drawing room were none of her concern. Arabel and Wilson brought up bulletins to Miss Barrett. The brothers who happened to be about kept the scores although it was difficult to determine who held the advantage in the eyes of a maiden who would have thrown her ribbon to each impartially—when Mr. Barrett was not looking.

At last, worn out, one of the suitors ungallantly quit the field, taking his revenge by dubbing his former rivals Perseverance and Despair. For a while the remaining two tried each other's endurance,

Henrietta showing a little more interest now that the field was limited. Speculation went on in all quarters. The brothers weighed the qualities of the opponents. Miss Barrett wondered how far Henrietta would commit herself with her half a yes, her quarter of a yes, and her inability to utter a good round *no* in the right place. To her amazement, when Despair in a crisis presented his suit, Henrietta rejected him.

It was too much for Despair. Seeing himself cast out of the by now homelike drawing room, he appealed against the judgment. Henrietta who for once had said *no*, weakly returned to the *status quo* of her ambiguous yes. Neither she nor Despair could have behaved more mildly or beautifully.

"Despair is at least a gentleman," approved the brothers.

At this stage Perseverance, an army man and a cousin two or three times removed, decided to speak up. Facing Henrietta he declared with violent reiterations: "You love me! You love me without knowing it! You love me, and if you don't you should!" Thereupon, since Henrietta did not contradict him, he elbowed Despair into the street, swearing, "If she marries another I'll wait till she becomes a widow, trusting to providence."

Too well bred to elbow back, Despair accepted his defeat. Later Henrietta was touched to hear that he had bought a new horse to solace himself for losing her and that he was taking music lessons to heal his melancholy.

Now that his suit was neither rejected nor accepted, Perseverance changed his strategy. Every morning he would wait at a safe distance till he saw the stately Mr. Barrett leave the house, then run to ring the bell. The butler let him in without question—he had done so often enough before—and was possibly grateful that he had to go to the door once instead of three times. Perseverance would then sit out all of four hours in full view of the family and whatever visitors chanced to call, indulging in unrestrained sobs whenever Henrietta veered toward a negative and unmindful of the rudeness of the brothers who grew tired of having their privacy so constantly invaded.

Two years had passed since he had adopted the military tactic of the siege, and Miss Barrett conceded, "He sits now sole regnant." On being taxed with instability Henrietta would weep a little in remorse and answer gently: "I'm taken by storm and cannot help it." It had been a very lengthy storming. If it did not accomplish its purpose it proved at least that Captain Surtees Cook had earned his nickname.

Miss Barrett pondered the domestic comedy. Was it love, that taking on and off of an emotion on the part of Henrietta? Could it be love, that easy consolation in horses and music on the part of a rejected suitor? As for Captain Cook, no doubt he was sincerely attached to Henrietta. But was that love, she asked again. Everybody seemed satisfied with the state of affairs—everybody, that is, except Mr. Barrett who was carefully kept in ignorance of everything.

Perhaps Captain Cook was the right man for Henrietta. He was highly thought of by his fellow officers and he did not have a low opinion of himself. Yet though aware that Henrietta had been "in love" with someone else at one time it did not prevent him from pressing his own suit. Did that not show want of refinement and sensibility? Could there be love without them? Miss Barrett was appalled by what he had recently said to Henrietta. "I always persevere about everything. Once I began to write a farce which they told me was as bad as could be. Well! I persevered! I finished it." Neither he nor Henrietta had found anything wrong in the statement. Well, indeed! No doubt the young man was handsome and in other ways charming. No doubt he overawed the susceptible feminine heart in his regimentals. Miss Barrett had never seen him and was perhaps not likely to do so—such was the regime of that unusual household. So the little dramas went on.

Meanwhile in Miss Barrett's room where Mr. Kenyon's ivy had managed to survive the winter, another drama was unfolding, on paper as yet and with Flush and Lily Wilson as the best apprised of them all. Every day, on Wilson's coming in with the mail, there was only one letter that Miss Barrett looked for, her face lighting up when she found it. Wilson noticed too that Miss Barrett wrote most often to Mr. Browning of New Cross. A taciturn girl, she knew when to put two and two together and be quiet about it. She had been Miss Barrett's personal maid long enough to know that she would find out in due time all there was to learn. Miss Barrett never kept anything from her. They were as familiar as it was proper for an impeccably correct maid to be with a kind and indulgent mistress, who, moreover, paid her very good wages: sixteen pounds a year. In the family's estimation she entered the category of an expensive servant. But they all agreed that Wilson was worth her keep.

There is no record as to when Wilson went into service with the

Barretts nor of how she had made her way from Sheffield, where her family lived, to Wimpole Street, her adopted world. She was young, untouched in person and morals, and as little given to verbal communication as a blank book. For her the Barretts represented the whole of society and Miss Barrett its finest flower. Beyond the immediate neighborhood lay utter darkness and the perils of poverty and crime. Respectability was Wilson's religion and the Wimpole Street domicile its shrine. She questioned nothing and accepted everything. The Barretts, Miss Elizabeth in particular, could do no wrong. Even Flush enjoyed special grace. Was he not a Barrett dog?

Flush no doubt felt much the same as Wilson, and for good reason. Twice he had had the bad luck to be spirited away by the dog-stealers to dreadful regions of vile smells, harsh voices, and boots with kicks in them. There had been no cheese on toast, with or without salt, for him, no chicken nicely roasted, no coffee with muffins in it, for that matter not even water during those dreadful days when he had waited trembling, wondering how the world of his mistress' room and the clean quiet street had changed into this horror. But both times he had been restored to Miss Barrett after transactions too complicated for him to understand. Mr. Barrett fumed at the six and a half guineas of his ransom and the threat of ten which the dog-stealers impudently said they would demand if they caught Flush again. But the money was paid and Flush was fed, bathed, and led up the stairs to his sobbing mistress. After these experiences he developed a suspicion of strange men especially if they carried anything like a sack or a stick. He also learned to appreciate the security of that room whose only sunshine came in a narrow strip that fell upon the floor, a strip to lay his nose along, with both ears out in the shadow. Still, it was safe and his mistress was with him.

Before the day that had brought Browning's first letter Miss Barrett, watching Flush pityingly as he enjoyed his sunshine, would muse on the lack of it in her own life. All the heaps of letters that she had received from strangers—"because I am a woman and have written verses"—what did they mean except that those men were merely amusing themselves to see what would come of it? Some wrote from kind motives, she knew. "Well . . . how could it make for me even such a narrow strip of sunshine . . . ?" One after the other she had thrown the letters into the fire. "Not for me . . . in any way. Not within my reach." Flush came nearer and she was grateful to him.

"Yes, grateful . . . for not being tired." Grateful when he chose to stay with her all day rather than go downstairs. Grateful for that matter to her own family, "For not letting me see that I was a burthen. . . ."

Yet everything had changed in the course of the weeks though the outward circumstances remained the same. The same visits, the same talk. Miss Martineau with her ear trumpet, Miss Mitford with her innocently scandalous chatter. Mr. Kenyon seemed to gaze at her more searchingly these days, she thought. Or was it guilt that made her think so? And why feel guilty in an impersonal correspondence? (But was it impersonal?) She was in an agony of apprehension lest one or the other of her visitors should ask her about Browning. They had done so, often before, and she had answered with no embarrassment just as she related the latest news about Orion who had been *headlong* twice in Germany recently, once in tumbling from Drachenfels and again while skating on the ice of the Elbe. She had even written to Browning about it. But somehow she was tongue-tied where Browning was concerned.

His letters came too often for her to say nothing about them to her family. Besides, her very silence on the matter would have been *interpreted*. (She had made no secret of her other correspondents.) Henrietta and Arabel were told, therefore. So were the boys and Mr. Barrett. To her father Robert Browning became "the Pomegranate man" possibly in reference to her lines in "Lady Geraldine's Courtship." At any rate whenever Mr. Barrett alluded to the poet he always employed the name which, if humorous, was also slyly derogatory.

The colloquy between Miss Barrett and Robert Browning meanwhile went on, as the letters flew between Wimpole Street and New Cross. In his study where he sat most of the day trying to finish some incomplete *Bells*, Browning would find himself instead picking up one or the other green-covered volume of Miss Barrett's poems, "as if it were so much trefoil to feel in one's hands this winter-time." Never before had he waited so eagerly for spring. He watched the days go by, noting that the white-throat had begun to sing now, and sighed, "Spring is to come!" On the 26th of February he began his letter, "Real warm Spring, dear Miss Barrett, and the birds know it; and in Spring I shall see you, surely see you—for when did I once fail to get whatever I had set my heart upon?"

His eagerness to see her, his constant reminder of the hope she had held out in her first letter aggravated her almost morbid qualms of their meeting face to face. He was Paracelsus, she told herself, contrasting their lives. She was a recluse "with nerves that had been all broken on the rack, and now hang loosely-quivering at every step and breath." He had drunk from the cup of life with the sun shining on it. She had lived only within herself, or with sorrow for a strong emotion. She had grown up in the country, with few social opportunities, whereas he had lived in London and traveled abroad. Her heart had been set in books and her whole experience in reveries. Yes, books and dreams were what she lived in. It almost seemed to her now that she was confronted with his intense vitality, that she had seen no human nature, and that her brothers and sisters of the earth were only names to her. She thought of herself as someone dying who had not read Shakespeare, and it was too late.

And so she answered him: "Yes, but, dear Mr. Browning, I want the spring according to the new 'style' (mine) and not the old one of you and the rest of the poets. . . . A little later comes my spring; and indeed after such severe weather, from which I have just escaped with my life, I may thank it for coming at all. How happy you are, to be able to listen to the 'birds' without the commentary of the east wind, which, like other commentaries, spoils the music."

She left the subject long enough to speak of "Luria" and of Carlyle for whom Browning had a warm and simple friendship. "He fills the office of a poet—does he not?—by analysing humanity back into its elements, to the destruction of the conventions of the hour." So she wrote of the Cheyne Row prophet tormented by man's imperfection as much as by the lion of dyspepsia gnawing at his vitals. "That is—strictly speaking—the office of the poet—is it not?—and he discharges it fully."

No one would have been more astonished than Carlyle at being called a poet, a tribe which, Plato-like, he would have banished from his ideal republic. Indeed, the burden of his song to Browning was that he should write prose. But to Miss Barrett it was a term of the highest praise. Anyone Browning loved must belong to the company of the elect. "But how I do wander!" she interrupted herself. "I meant to say, and I will call myself back to say, that spring will really come some day I hope and believe . . . and that then I shall be probably fitter for certain pleasures. . . ." One moment she resolutely shut the door. The next she let in a ray of light.

"Is it true that your wishes fulfill themselves?" she asked. "And when they do are they not bitter to your taste—do you not wish them unfulfilled?" Even if they met he must be warned not to expect too much from the meeting. "Oh, this life, this life! There is comfort in it, they say . . . but the brightest place in the house, is the leaning out of the window—at least, for me."

What struck Browning most was her phrase about the weather, from which she had barely escaped. Was she as ill as her words implied? From talk he had heard here and there he had been led to believe that she suffered from a spinal injury. She said nothing of such a condition but blamed east winds instead. Her phrase raised his hopes on the one hand yet gave him grave concern on the other. "I seem to find of a sudden—" he began his answer to her, ". . . anyhow, I do find now, that with the octaves on octaves of quite new golden strings you enlarged the compass of my life's harp with, there is added, too, such a tragic chord, that which you touched, so gently . . . 'just escaping' etc. But if my truest heart's wishes avail, as they have hitherto done, you shall laugh at East Winds yet. . . ."

Since besides themselves the letters discussed literature, Browning went into a long passage on *Prometheus* generously strewn with Greek quotations, and closed: "Are you not my dear friend already? . . . And pray you do not 'lean out of the window' when my own foot is only on the stair; do wait a little for Yours ever, R.B." The underscoring implied even more of his growing feeling for Miss Barrett than his poetically eloquent figure of the golden strings.

Startled by his forthrightness, Miss Barrett withdrew into the impersonality of poetic discussion. "And tell me too, if Aeschylus is not the divinest of all the divine Greek souls?" She reassured him at once about her health, however. "I am *essentially* better, and have been for several winters; and I feel as if it were intended for me to live and not die . . ." She was not despondent by nature, she assured him. "Anguish has instructed me in joy, and solitude in society . . . and altogether, I may say that earth looks the brighter to me in proportion to my own deprivations. . . . And I do like to hear testimonies like yours to happiness. . . . Still it is obvious that you have been spared, up to this time, the great natural afflictions . . . or your step would not be 'on the stair' quite so lightly. . . . Remember that as you owe your unscathed joy to God," she added a little sententiously, "you should pay it back to His world. And I thank you for some of it already. . . . How kind you are!—how kindly and gently you speak to me! . . . Although I am aware that you unconsciously exaggerate what I can be to you, yet it is delightful to be broad awake and think of you as my friend."

The letter that had begun with caution closed with such unaffected warmth that Browning expressed his happiness and asked roguishly: "Is it too great a shame if I begin to want more good news of you? . . . Always when you write, though about your own works, not Greek plays merely, put me in, *always*, a little official bulletin-line that shall say 'I am better' or 'still better' will you?"

By that simple request the literary correspondent flung wide the door to the intimacies of friendship. Browning knew, however, that whatever relations resulted between him and Miss Barrett, Poetry or Art as they both wrote of it with a generous use of the capital, would figure as one of the most important elements. To both their work so far had been the pedestal of their lives, the sure footing that held them above the ordinary level of living yet broadened their view to encompass all of life. It was their poetry that had initiated their correspondence although an instinctively felt affinity had played its part. Poetry, therefore, was the warp and woof of the sturdy fabric of friendship turning into love whereon their emotion now began to weave the designs. That they confided so freely to each other their work and plans proved their spiritual kinship.

In a previous letter Miss Barrett had told Browning of a grand project which was ultimately to be realized in *Aurora Leigh*: ". . . The writing of a sort of novel-poem—a poem as completely modern as 'Geraldine's Courtship', running into the midst of our conventions, and rushing into drawing-rooms and the like . . . and so meeting face to face and without mask the Humanity of the age, and speaking of the truth as I conceive it . . ." Browning now answered her. "The poem you propose to make . . . is the only effective piece of service to be rendered God and man; it is what I have been all my life intending to do, and now shall be much, much nearer doing, since you will be along with me."

No declaration of the permanence of his feeling for her could have been stronger than his association of his lifework with hers. To prove it he began to give her his unpublished poems to read and criticize.

"And now enough of Greek," he interrupted himself after a long digression. ". . . You think—for I must get to you—that I 'unconsciously exaggerate what you are to me.' Now, you don't know what *that* is, nor can I very well tell you, because the language with which

I talk to myself of these matters is spiritual Attic. . . . I never yet mistook my own feelings. . . . Of what use is talking? Only do you stay here with me in the 'House' these few short years." Then once more the desire that had been uppermost manifested itself. "Do you think I shall see you in two months? . . . I may travel, perhaps," he added, not wholly without guile.

Her morbid fears reawakened. Once more she made apologies and pleaded with him to try to understand. "If you think that I shall not *like* to see you, you are wrong, for all your learning." She reminded him of her secluded life and then made an admission, boldly, because painful. "There are few of the youngest women in the world who have not seen more, heard more, known more, of society than I, *who am scarcely to be called young now.*"

Well, it was said. She knew from Mr. Kenyon that Browning was a young man. She could see that he was handsome as well as young from the picture hanging on her wall. She dropped the subject of age as soon as she had mentioned it and went on to the compensations of her seclusion. "I have had much of the inner life . . . but how willingly," she added (one can almost hear her sigh), "how willingly I would as a poet exchange some of this lumbering, ponderous, help-less knowledge of books, for some experience of life and man, for some. . ." The rest she left in suspension.

Anyone with half the perception of Browning would have under-stood the hunger for life crying out from the very silence of the page. She felt perhaps that she had admitted too much for im-mediately she went on to say, answering a question he had pre-viously asked: "Like to write? Of course, of course I do. I seem to live while I write—it is life for me." And yet, and yet . . . "If you mean 'to travel' "—she suddenly referred back to his letter—"why, I shall have to miss you. Do you really mean it?" she asked on the heels of her bravado. This time she signed herself "Ever and truly yours."

Henceforth formality was banished from their letters. Very early she had asked him to treat her *en bon camarade*, "taking no thought for your sentences (nor for mine) . . . nor for your blunt speaking (nor for mine), nor for your badd speling (nor for mine) . . ." Now the restrictions are also lifted from the expression of their emotions. They begin to make little admissions, slightly veiled at first, half-uttered avowals of how much they occupied each other's thoughts. They are concerned about each other's health, especially after Brown-ing admitted to suffering from a recurrent headache—"one little wheel in my head that keeps on its—" and he drew the musical staff and the exact pitch of the sustained note of pain. "This sunny morning," he writes, "is as if I wished it for you. . . . Tell me if at ten this morning you feel any good from my heart's wishes for you." Then again, "I heard of you, dear Miss Barrett, between a Polka and a Cellarius the other evening, of Mr. Kenyon—how this wind must hurt you! And yesterday I had occasion to go your way—past, that is, Wimpole Street, the end of it,—and, do you know, I did not seem to have leave from you to go down it yet. . . ."

A little later he wrote lightly so as not to alarm her, "I have been surprised, rather, with something not unlike illness of late—I have had a constant pain in the head for these two months, which only very rough exercise can get rid of . . . Just now all of it is gone, thanks to polking all night and walking home by broad daylight to the surprise of the thrushes in the bush here." The thrushes of course brought thoughts of spring, real spring, evident on every bush and tree. "Surely the wind that sets my chestnut-tree dancing, all its baby-cone-blossoms, green now, rocking like fairy castles on a hill in an earthquake,—that is South West, surely!"

She little heeded what wind was blowing in her real worry over his health. "So when wise people happen to be ill," she reproved him, "they sit up till six in the morning and get up again at nine? Do tell me how Lurias can ever be made out of such ungodly imprudences. If the wind blows east or west, where can any remedy be, while such evil deeds are being committed? . . . And where is the reasonableness of it in the meantime, when we all know that thinking, dreaming, creating people like yourself, have two lives to bear instead of one, and therefore ought to sleep more than others. . . . You have to live your own personal life, and also Luria's life—and therefore you should sleep for both . . . Polka, for the rest, may be good, but sleep is better. I think better of sleep than I ever did, now that she will not easily come near me except in a red hood of poppies. . . . You will not persist, (will you?) in this experimental homicide."

When she did not hear from him for six days she wrote again, after hearing from Mr. Kenyon that Browning had been quite ill. "I had been thinking so of seeing you on Tuesday . . . with my sister's eyes—for the first sight," she wrote on his canceling an engagement at Mr. Kenyon's where Henrietta was to have met him. She could not sleep, she told him, unless she found out how he was.

He reassured her at once about his health. But he had been ill enough to announce to his friends that his London season was over for the year. "I shall be worried no more, and let walk in the garden, and go to bed at ten o'clock . . . and one day, oh the day, I shall see you with my own, own eyes."

How could she delay the meeting? Aeolus had called back the east wind, the thrush was singing, the baby-cone-blossoms of the chestnut were full blown. As if everything in nature were not reminding her of her promise, Browning spoke it out. "When I am to see you—I will never ask you! You do not know what I shall estimate that permission at . . ."

No, she could not longer delay. On the 16th of May she wrote, after apologizing for making such a piece of work of the meeting: "If you care to come to see me, you can come . . . It is my gain . . . and not yours, whenever you do come." But he must not be left to believe, if he believed it, that he would be happy in what he found. "There is nothing to see in me; nor to hear in me—I never learnt to talk as you do in London. . . . If my poetry is worth anything to any eye, it is the flower of me. . . . The rest of me is nothing but a root, fit for the ground and the dark. . . . Come, then. There will be truth and simplicity for you in any case; and a friend. . . ."

As she wrote the tears streamed down her face.

Chapter XII: Andromeda's Eyes

THE date of the meeting was fixed for Tuesday afternoon, the 20th of May. "If on Tuesday you should be not well, pray do not come," Miss Barrett wrote to Browning in her last note before the interview.

Mr. Barrett and the family knew that the poet of *Bells and Pomegranates* would be calling upon Miss Barrett at three o'clock. Mr. Barrett went about his business as usual, thinking nothing of it. Just another literary person come to do homage to his famous daughter. The boys teased her because in anticipation of Browning's arrival she had taken down his portrait from its nail under Wordsworth's and hidden it away. They were not fooled by the fact that she had also pulled down Tennyson's, and they made a great to-do opening drawers and boxes to find the missing pictures.

As the time approached she was left alone in her room, alone, that is, but for Flush. No doubt she wore her most becoming dress and perhaps Wilson had taken particular pains arranging the dark, glossy hair in a cascade of curls on either side of that fragile face with its fine brow and eyes. The time as at all fateful meetings must have dragged endlessly and then sped with the fleetness of Dr. Faustus' last minute.

The doorbell rang. There was the sound of steps on the stairs—Henrietta's, light and familiar, and then an energetic running pace. Henrietta introduced the visitor and quickly left. Flush, the only other present at the interview, could not speak. The busts of the famous dead looked down upon the two and maintained their eternal silence. What Miss Barrett and Browning said between three and four-thirty o'clock, the duration of his first visit, no one ever learned. The date and the time are known because Browning made a note of them on the envelope of Miss Barrett's latest letter.

Had he stayed too long? Had he talked too loud? (They all told him at home that he spoke too loud, a habit he had formed from having often to converse with a deaf relative.) The thought troubled him, and in the note he wrote Miss Barrett the following day he apologized.

"Indeed there was nothing wrong—how could there be?" she replied. "And there was everything right—as how could there not be?" To his prayer that he might be permitted to call on her from time to time she gave her consent. "Why it must obviously and naturally be delightful to me to receive you here when you like to come. . . ."

To read the constraint that crept into their letters one might imagine they had been disappointed. Nothing was farther from the truth. Their spirit had received a shock that stunned; they needed time to recover. The first thing he noticed about her was the beauty of her eyes, as in his own Andromeda—"dark eyes, earnest and still." They were extraordinary eyes which even in a facetious description of herself to Haydon convey a remarkable quality. "I am 'little and black' like Sappho, en attendant the immortality—five feet one high . . . eyes of various colours as the sun shines,—called blue and black . . . afidavited for grey—sworn to for hazel—and set down by myself . . . as dark-green-brown—grounded with brown and green otherwise. . . ."

But it was their expression that counted most. Browning saw and was never to forget them nor that grave face which suddenly lighted up with the play of her thoughts, nor that soft blurred voice, nor "her thousand sweet and attaching qualities."

As for her, she compared the real Browning with his portrait and cried denial. No! The picture had not his character in any line of it. Perhaps a little hint of his fine face in the forehead and eyes. But no, it was not like him at all, though Mr. Kenyon had vouched for the resemblance. Eventually, after she had grown tired of her brothers' teasing, she pasted the picture in her copy of Paracelsus. But by then she had no need of images to visualize him. From the moment she had looked at him she had him as if etched upon her mind. It was more than a mere evocation of him. "When you came, you never went away," she told him when she could make the admission.

To her father she had spoken of the phenomenon much earlier—the morning after the meeting. "It is most extraordinary how the idea of Mr. Browning does beset me! I suppose it is not being used to see strangers, in some degree—but it haunts me. It is a persecution."

Mr. Barrett, understanding only what it pleased him to understand, smiled and said, "It is not grateful to your friend to use such a word."

She did not know what was happening to her and she was fright-

ened. She felt Browning had a power over her and meant to use it,
as if she could not breathe or speak differently from what he chose
to make her. He seemed to read her thoughts as he read the news-
paper and she dreaded her own transparency. Why had he insisted
on meeting her? She would have been happy to have gone on writing
to him and receiving his letters, each keeping a secret identity safe
and inviolable. But had she not in a rash moment admitted: "How
willingly I would as a poet exchange some of this . . . helpless knowledge of books, for some experience of life and man . . . ?" What other
impulsive things had she written which she could not remember?
She had warned that he might exaggerate what she could be to him,
however. On that reed she leaned her strength and found it further
bolstered by his restrained note of May 21st. She waited impatiently
for his reply to her tactfully worded letter so that she might be
assured of the continuance of the relationship which had brought
the only sunshine into her room for the past four months.

His answer came on the 23rd. She read it and trembled. She
blotted the words from her mind but her pulses still beat in feverish
agitation. Tristan, drinking the love potion, had at first been aware
only of the paralyzing shock to his being. During the pause suspend-
ing life itself he was reborn—the lover—and the heart found voice.
It was that voice which until then Browning had lifted in singing
imaginary loves that now spoke for him. The thing which he had
foreseen once he saw the woman with whose spirit he had already
fallen in love, came to pass. He loved her and he told her so. In what
words, only he who wrote them and she who read them ever knew.

At first she thought of answering the letter at once, but she could
not. She was too much shaken either to think clearly or to write.
She knew only that she was nearing forty—had she not written of
her age to him in a strange prevision of what was now happening—
that the bars of her prison were as much home to her as the confines
of a canary's cage; that he was a genius with much to accomplish;
that he was generous, impulsive, vital and young—very young despite
his thirty-three years. She could not accept the love, the life, he gave
her in the headlong liberality of his youth. The fact that she too had
been deeply moved by the meeting—more deeply than she would
as yet avow—made it imperative for her to open his eyes if love
had blinded them.

All night long she could not sleep. The memory of his words
pounded in her brain. She was feverish. The fear that she might

become delirious and betray herself to Arabel who slept in her room added its own torment. The following morning she tried in vain to answer him. Not till that night did she manage to find enough composure to write what would discourage any wild dreams on his part, yet retain the friendship she could not easily live without.

"You do not know what pain you give me in speaking so wildly," she bravely attacked the subject. "And if I disobey you, my dear friend, in speaking, (I for my part) of your wild speaking, I do it, not to displease you, but to be in my own eyes, and before God, a little more worthy, or less unworthy, of a generosity from which I recoil by instinct and at the first glance, yet conclusively. . . . Listen to me then in this. You have said some intemperate things . . . fancies,—which you will not say over again, nor unsay, but *forget at once*, and *for ever*, *having said at all*; and which (so) will die out between *you and me alone*, like a misprint between you and the printer. . . . For me to listen to 'unconscious exaggerations' is as unbecoming to the humilities of my position, as unpropitious . . . to the prosperities of yours. Now if there should be one word of answer attempted to this; or of reference; *I must not—I will not see you again*—and you will justify me later in your heart. . . . Your friendship and sympathy will be dear and precious to me all my life, if you indeed leave them with me so long or so little. Your mistakes in me . . . I put away gently and with grateful tears in my eyes; because *all that hail* will beat down and spoil crowns, as well as 'blossoms' . . . You are not displeased with me? *No, that* would be hail and lightning together."

All her honesty and unselfishness are in that letter, written with a candor, a strength, and dignity that, if Mr. Barrett had ever seen it, would have justified him in his Spartan discipline. The struggle it had cost her is implicit in the dots and dashes, the underscoring, the finality of "If there should be one word of answer attempted . . . I will not see you again." It must have taken great moral courage to risk losing the source of her greatest happiness by giving up Browning rather than endanger his "prosperities" by encouraging his love.

The threat of her never seeing him again so frightened Browning that he was not only willing to counteract the effect of his declaration but to do it as thoroughly as his inexperience with women thought possible. He had offended by speaking wildly. He would make amends by judicious agreement, making Miss Barrett understand at the same time that his sin had not been as great as she made it. On no account must she go on believing he had meant more than ordinary compliment, however immoderately he had written. He answered her in panic haste.

Panic too lent him a certain bravado as he began, "Don't you remember I told you, once on a time, that 'you knew nothing of me?' whereat you demurred—but I meant what I said, and knew it was so. To be grand in a simile, for every poor wreck of a Vesuvius or a Stromboli in my microcosm there are huge layers of ice and pits of black cold water—and I make the most of these two or three fire-eyes, because I know by experience, alas, how these tend to extinction—and the ice grows and grows . . . Still I am utterly unused . . . to dream of communicating anything about *that* to another person . . . when I make never so little an attempt, no wonder if I *bungle* notably."

There, that should set Miss Barrett's fears at ease, though the apocalyptic picture of fire-eyes and pits of black cold water was calculated rather to turn them to awe of his elemental personality. Perhaps he should make himself clearer, attempt a more direct explanation.

"Will you think me very brutal if I tell you I could almost smile at your misapprehension of what I meant to write?—Yet I *will* tell you, because it will . . . exemplify the point I have all along been honestly earnest to set you right upon . . . my real inferiority to you; just that and no more . . ." The words Miss Barrett had interpreted as a declaration of love he would now have her believe were only expressions of praise. Perhaps he had overstated. "I forgot," he went on, "that one may make too much noise in a silent place by playing the few notes on the 'ear-piercing fife' . . . Will you forgive me . . . ?"

For the purposes of apology as well as explanation the letter should have ended there. But Browning's uneasiness made him overload the argument. He wrote on and on, trying to elucidate his character, declaring that his ambition was "to be a Poet, if not the Poet" yet speaking of himself a little farther on as a "mild man-about-town." "Indeed," he expatiated, "my own way of worldly life is marked out long ago, as precisely as yours can be, and I am set going with a hand, winker-wise, on each side of my head, and a directing finger before my eyes . . . I shall be too much punished if, for this piece of mere inconsiderateness, you deprive me . . . of the pleasure of seeing you . . . Remember me for good," he closed, "and let me not for one fault, (and that the only one that shall be) lose any pleasure . . . for your friendship I am sure I have not lost. . . ."

An afterthought occurred to him, however, and he appended it in a

long footnote. "And by the way, will it not be better, as co-operating
with you more effectually in your kind promise to forget the 'printer's
error' in my blotted proof, to send me back that same 'proof' if you
have not inflicted proper and summary justice on it? When Mephistopheles last came to see us in this world outside here, he counseled
sundry of us 'never to write a letter,—and never to burn one'. . . ."

Whether or not Miss Barrett's feminine pride was hurt at having
to accept Browning's explanation, she clutched eagerly at the opportunity of resuming the status quo. So the following day, Sunday, she
wrote him: "I owe you the most humble apologies dear Mr. Browning, for having spent so much solemnity on so simple a matter,
and I hasten to pay it; confessing at the same time . . . that I am
quite as much ashamed of myself as I ought to be, which is not a
little."

That she was not quite recovered emotionally she betrayed by
her grammatical slip.

She was too much the woman, however, to give the impression
of being greedy for flattery. "You will find it difficult to believe me
perhaps when I assure you that I never made such a mistake (I
mean of over-seriousness to indefinite compliments) no, never
in my life before—indeed my sisters have often jested with me
. . . on my supernatural indifference to the superlative degree in
general . . ." But there had been something in his letter, a relation
of two things in it, as she recalled—for she would not reread it—
something that justified her interpretation. She had to put in that
small extenuation both for honesty and as a dab of balm to her own
hurt feelings. He must admit he had been obscure, at least in this
case which he explained in one way and which she could reasonably
have interpreted in another.

"A good deal of what is called obscurity in you," she went on,
"arises from a very subtle association; so subtle that you are probably
unconscious of it . . . and the effect of which is to throw together on
the same level and in the same light things of likeness and unlike-
ness—till the reader grows confused as I did, and takes one for
another."

Browning might interpret that as he chose. She did want him to
understand one thing in justice to herself. "I wrote what I wrote so
unfortunately, through reverence of you, not at all from vanity on
my own account." Perhaps he was right in saying she did not know
him. "I was certainly innocent of the knowledge of the 'ice and

cold water, . . . and am only just shaking my head, as Flush would, after a first wholesome plunge."

She returned the offending letter. "I would venture to advise you to burn it at once . . ." she said, "and never mind Mephistopheles." She also arranged for their next interview.

Browning's relief at the happy ending expressed itself in a delightfully maladroit note throbbing with contrition. "There! And now, 'exit prompt-side, nearest door, Luria'—and enter R. B. . . . as boldly as he suspects most people do just after they have been soundly frightened!"

The appointment had to be postponed because of an incursion of Barrett relatives but Miss Barrett and Browning saw each other soon afterward. What constraint there had been vanished at the first look they exchanged. But so did every resolve on Browning's part to hold his hands winker-wise against Miss Barrett's potent fascination. He was in love for the first time and he was helpless. What he could and did control was any show of feeling in her presence, his fear of offending again by his impetuousness acting as a curb. Thus on his visits he would sit facing her, with Flush's golden eyes fastened upon him, with Flush's ears twitching at the unaccustomed ringing of his voice in that quiet place where, in lonely hours, his mistress fancied herself another Mariana in the moated grange, listening to the mouse in the wainscot. Browning's whole being was keyed up to Miss Barrett's least response as each varying theme found expression in her muted utterance. She seemed so ethereal. Yet she had the intellect of a man behind that great brow leaning against the hand as small as a child's as, with her elbow propped on the cushions, she gave him thought for thought in a dialogue ranging over spirit and fancy, not omitting a pleasant meander among the foibles of common humanity.

At first Browning called once a week, later twice. The intervals between the visits they bridged over with letters in which they continued their colloquy. If, when Browning entered Miss Barrett's room, he never went away, she in turn wholly possessed him. For that reason he had to be more than ever careful not to startle her renewed trust. He acted *en bon camarade*, therefore, concealing from her the depth and breadth of her dominion over him.

It is not to be wondered at that his headaches grew worse, so much so that Miss Barrett was alarmed. "You *will* have advice, will you not? It cannot be prudent or even safe to let a pain in the head go on so long. . . . So you will see someone with an opinion to give, and take it? *Do*, I beseech you." Her letters showed as much solicitude for his health as his for the least improvement in hers. And she was improving, amazingly, in her effort to please him.

"And you—you have tried a new journey from your room, have you not?" he countered.

"Instead of writing this note to you yesterday . . . I went downstairs—or rather was carried—and am not the worse," she answered like a pleased child.

Another thing about her illness which troubled him greatly he did not dare mention until she herself gave him the occasion. Before their meeting she had alluded to sleep coming to her only "in a red hood of poppies." Later she made other references to her use of opium. In those experimental days when the harmful effects of the drug were not generally known and it could be bought without a prescription, it was considered almost as a household remedy in one form or another. The doctors recommended it freely and the suffering were grateful for the oblivion it brought. With an uncanny understanding of its effects after continued use, Browning mistrusted its immediate benefits and disapproved of Miss Barrett's dependence upon it. Perhaps his months at Guy's Hospital had helped to open his eyes. Whatever the origin of his knowledge, he spoke out when the opportunity came.

"I never dared, nor shall dare inquire into your use of that for, knowing you utterly as I do, I know you only bend to the most absolute necessity in taking more or less of it—so that increase of the quantity must mean simply increased weakness, illness—and diminution, diminished illness. . . . You speak of my silly head and its ailments . . . well, and what brings on the irritation? A wet day or two spent at home; and what ends it directly? Just an hour's walk! So with *me*. Now,—fancy me shut in a room for seven years. . . ."

"That you should care so much about the opium!" she replied in astonishment. "Then *I* must care, and get to do with less—at least. On the other side of your goodness and indulgence . . . it might strike you as strange that I who have had no pain—no acute suffering to keep down from its angles—should need opium in any shape. But I have had restlessness till it made me almost mad. At one time I lost the power of sleeping quite—and even in the day, the continual aching sense of weakness has been intolerable—besides palpitation—as if one's life, instead of giving movement to the body, were imprisoned undiminished within it, and beating and fluttering impotently to get out. . . . So the medical people gave me opium— a preparation of it called morphine, and ether—and since then I have been calling it my amreeta draught, my elixir—because the tranquillizing power has been wonderful . . . The need has continued in a degree until now, and it would be dangerous to leave off the calming remedy, Mr. Jago says, except very slowly and gradually. But slowly and gradually something may be done . . . After all, the lotus eaters are blessed beyond the opium-eaters. . . ."

"All the kind explaining about the opium makes me happier. 'Slowly and gradually' what may *not* be done?" Browning encouraged her. "Then see the bright weather while I write!"

How naturally he scattered the petals of the red hood of poppies and opened wide the sickroom to the sun!

But the dependence of years was not to be so easily shaken off, however valiant the effort. At the time Miss Barrett was taking forty drops of laudanum a day—"And *cannot do with less,*" she wrote to a family friend, Mrs. Martin, emphasizing the words. "That is, the medical man *told me* . . . saying so with his hand on the pulse. Dearest Mrs. Martin, more than I thought at first of telling you I have told you," she added with an intimation of guilt.

Yet why the guilt? From the first, when the doctors had diagnosed her illness as a weakness of the chest, they had prescribed the remedy and she had taken it without question, certainly with no moral compunction. Why should she have had any? Coleridge had made use of it. Miss Martineau too, before mesmerism. For that matter, as the offspring of generations of West Indian planters she must have heard of the comfits the Jamaican ladies would never be without, those agreeable pills made of sugar and opium which they took for all their little ills. She, goodness knows, had reason enough for taking the drug. Mr. Barrett, the most moral of men, saw no wrong in it. Such approval from supreme authority would have allayed any qualms his daughter might have had.

An odd fact in connection with her medicine is that she had to provide it at her own cost. "My greatest personal expense lately has been *the morphine,*" she wrote to Browning.

Why did not her father buy it for her? In the same letter she mentioned that her expenses in dress had never exceeded twenty pounds a year, even when she was well. Yet Miss Mitford and other witnesses mentioned her fine, stylish clothes which must have amounted to much more than twenty pounds a year especially in the days when she had gone to Mr. Kenyon's dinner parties. Mr. Barrett, therefore, must have contributed toward their purchase. Why did he let her bear the expense of the morphine? Did he look upon it as something too negligible to bother with—or did he think that such an outlay should be borne by his financially independent daughter who in all likelihood would never have other use for her money than this care for her health? The significant fact was that he knew of his daughter's use of opium in various forms by her doctors' orders, that he approved of her doing so, and that he let her buy the drug for herself. Such sanction would have made everything right in his daughter's eyes.

Something strange, however, had been happening in the course of Miss Barrett's contact with Browning, scarcely perceptible at first but for little phrases tucked away in the lengthy letters, meaningful echoes of words carried over from their conversations. Man of honor that he was, Browning respected the limitations she set upon their friendship. But soon both he and she began to ignore them. After jesting about Wordsworth's appearance at court in finery borrowed from the banker poet Samuel Rogers—"to the manifest advantage of the Laureate's pocket, but more problematic improvement of his person,"—Browning took the opportunity to sign off, "And now I am yours." A week later his boldness progressed to his kissing her hand—in writing and, most respectfully, in Italian. But kiss her hand he did. What gave the words significance one passage revealed: "I take the opportunity of mentioning the course I shall pursue with (Horne) and any other friends of yours I may meet . . . the course I understand you to desire, with respect to our own intimacy. While I may acknowledge, I believe, that I correspond with you, I shall not, in any case, suffer it to be known that I see, or have seen you. . . ." Why did Miss Barrett feel it necessary to conceal from her friends that she was seeing Browning?

Try as they might, they could not keep their secret from their benevolent Cupid, Mr. Kenyon, who swore a solemn oath, nor from Miss Mitford, whom Miss Barrett on pain of appearing a hypocrite had to take into her confidence, but only on the bare fact of having seen Browning. Their meetings now had a thrilling conspiratorial air—provided Mr. Barrett did not peer too deeply into it. Toward him too Miss Barrett began to observe a certain caution. No more comments now on how she was obsessed by the thought of Browning.

They wrote more freely to each other. One day in June he sent her a yellow rose because, he explained with a touch of jealousy, "You let flowers be sent to you in a letter." She quickly reassured him. "The 'flower in the letter' was from one of my sisters . . . But I thank you—for this, and all, my dear friend."

The intimate little words, the delicate innuendoes did their work, drawing them toward each other though on the surface their letters, when not discussing their work, went into interminable analyses of character, always with self-depreciation on Miss Barrett's part. Browning would have none of it and chided her, but she always returned to speak of her inferiority to him, her lack of advantages, her illness, her age. He replied on that last with simple directness. On reading her *Essay on Mind* he had noted the date of publication. "I did indeed see, and wonder at, your advance over me in years—what then? I have got nearer you considerably—since then—and prove it by remarks I make at favorable times." The soul is ageless, he demonstrated in a paragraph full of dashes and parentheses. It was still through the little words that they spoke most clearly to each other.

"*Vivi felice*, my dear friend. R. B."

"May God bless you my dear friend, my ever dear friend! E. B. B."

"God bless you, my best, dearest friend—think what I would speak—ever yours, R. B."

Like a chaperone the word *friend* stood by to keep check on a love that could no longer be denied.

In August Miss Barrett confided to Browning the tragedy of her life, Edward's drowning. The letter itself showed the anguish it had cost her. He understood her agony. He understood also her trust in him. "Remember how you wrote in your 'Gismond'," she said,

> What says the body when they spring
> Some monstrous torture-engine's whole
> Strength on it? No more says the soul.

. . . You never wrote anything which *lived* with me more than *that*. It is such a dreadful truth. But you knew it for a truth, I hope, by your genius, and not by such proof as mine . . . Do not notice what I have written to you, my dearest friend. I have never said so much to a living being,—I never *could* speak or write it."

Yet she had spoken and written it to him. She had taken consolation from words of his. He was so overwhelmed by his feelings that he could pen only a brief note of gratitude for allowing him to participate in her grief. His headache came upon him violently. When she did not hear from him again the following day she wrote him, worried: "I do not hear; and come to ask you for the alms of just one line, having taken it into my head that something is the matter. . . . You could not be vexed with me for talking of what was 'your fault' . . . in having to read sentences which, but for your commands, would have been blotted out. . . . No, you could not misinterpret so. . . ."

Her reference to his impulsive love letter, which they had discussed on their previous meeting, released him of any further obligation to be silent. He spoke out. "Can you understand me so, dearest friend, after all? . . . I believe in you absolutely, utterly.—I believe that when you bade me, that time, be silent—that such was your bidding, and I was silent—dare I say I think you did not know at that time the power I have over myself, that I could sit and speak and listen as I have done since? Let me say now—*this only once*—that I loved you from my soul, and gave you my life, as much of it as you would take,—and all that is done, not to be altered now: it was in the nature of the proceeding, wholly independent of any return on your part. . . . As it is, the assurance of your friendship, the intimacy to which you admit me, *now*, make the truest, deepest joy of my life—a joy I can never think fugitive while we are in life . . . If I thought you were like other women I have known, I should say so much!—but—(my first and last word—I *believe* in you!)—what you could and would give me, of your affection, you would give nobly and simply and as a giver—you would not need that I tell you—(*tell* you!)—what would be supreme happiness to me in the event—however distant. . . ."

Chapter XIII: Trial Flights

ELIZABETH BARRETT read Browning's tender reiteration of his love and once more panic mingled with her joy. What had she said to make him again throw his life at her feet? She had been honest with him yet he refused to see the reason for her rejecting anything but friendship. She was *unworthy* of him. How often she used the word trying to prove the unworthiness by citing endlessly the catalogue of her faults and disadvantages—her "peculiar situation," her invalidism, her age, her father's "system," his abnormal attachment to his family, her inexperience. There was nothing she omitted to keep that impetuous, that recklessly generous youth from forcing the door of her prison and sharing it with her. That he might pull her out of it filled her with dread, not so much for herself as for him who, because he was the deliverer, would have to drag behind him one not only unaccustomed to fly but even to walk. "And so may God bless you! and me in this, just this," she had written him, "that I may never have the sense, intolerable in the remotest apprehension of it, of being in any way, directly or indirectly, the means of ruffling your smooth path by so much as one of my flint-stones!"

This time she did not threaten him with never seeing him again. She called him repeatedly "my dearest friend" and in matchless phrases that burst to sudden flower in her writing, told him again why she could not listen to his love. ". . . My dearest friend—you have followed the most *generous* of impulses in your whole bearing to me—and I have recognized and called by its name, in my heart, each one of them. . . . You once wrote to me, oh, long before May and the day we met: that you 'had been so happy, you should now be justified to yourself in taking any step most hazardous to the happiness of your life'—but if you were justified, could *I* be therefore justified in abetting such a step,—the step of wasting, in a sense, your best feelings, of emptying your water gourds into the sand? . . . Your life! If you gave it to me and I put my whole heart into it; what should I put but anxiety, and more sadness than you were

155

born to? What could I give you, which it would not be ungenerous
to give?"

His love, rooted in generosity, was met by her selfless abnegation
—not rejection—for feelings too deep to come readily to the surface
told her that she could never deny that love. Selflessness is the soul
of an abiding attachment. Without it love is as brief as the pleasure
of the senses. From the first these two thought only of the other
and of the other's good. Not that passion did not play its part. Both
Elizabeth Barrett and Robert Browning were intensely sensual. The
hot blood of a Jamaican ancestry mingled in their veins and passion
was their very life's breath. But a self-imposed discipline governed by
a high valuation of truth and beauty kept Browning morally intact.
As for Miss Barrett, a high romanticism unimpaired by a keenly
perceived reality made her turn her eyes above what she had come
to believe would never be hers in this world. Her poem, "A Denial,"
seems almost to echo her letters at this time.

> We have met late—it is too late to meet,
>   O friend, not more than friend!
> Death's forecome shroud is tangled round my feet,
> And if I step or stir, I touch the end.
>   In this last jeopardy
> Can I approach thee, I, who cannot move?
> How shall I answer thy request for Love?
>   Look in my face, and see.
>
> I love thee not, I dare not love thee! go
>   In silence; drop my hand.
> If thou seek roses, seek them where they blow
> In garden alleys, not in desert sand.
>   Can life and death agree,
> That thou shouldst stoop thy song to my complaint?
> I cannot love thee. If the word is faint,
>   Look in my face, and see.
>
> Meantime, I bless thee. By these thoughts of mine
>   I bless thee from all such!
> I bless thy lamp to oil, thy cup to wine,
> Thy hearth to joy, thy hand to an equal touch
>   Of loyal troth. For me
> I love thee not, I love thee not!—away!
> Here's no more courage in my soul to say,
>   "Look in my face, and see."

The desperate repetition of "I love thee not" confessed how deeply even then she loved him. She did not show Browning this poem, but she did bid him look in her face, and see.

Browning waited. He believed to the depths of his being, "I was made and meant to look for you and wait for you and become yours for ever." He knew she was created for him, predestined for him "In my time, and then not in Timbuctoo but Wimpole Street, and then . . . the strange hedge round the sleeping Palace keeping the world off—and then. . . . All was to begin, all the difficulty only begin. . . ."

He had made a beginning, gone past the hedge to the very chamber of the enchanted princess. He had spoken but had not yet awakened her to the desire of his heart. He needed a more powerful charm than his voice alone. He needed an expression, a proof of his love, and then she would respond and become his forever, as he was hers. He knew it as surely as he had known when he saw her name and his in the same magazine, that as long as people lived, "our names will go together, be read together." In his complete faith in that eternity he could be patient and wait.

So he listened as Elizabeth told him that Dr. Chambers had ordered her to Pisa for the winter to reap the benefit of her improved health but that her father, after agreeing at first, had changed his mind. Little by little she gave Browning the full catalogue of her father's "peculiarities" stressing, however, his goodness and devotion. As the weeks passed, up and down went the barometer of Mr. Barrett's decision between his desire to see his daughter recovered and his reluctance to have his family broken up. He may also have been influenced by the memory of another vacation that Dr. Chambers had prescribed and by its consequences in tragedy and death.

When for a time it seemed as if Mr. Barrett would send his daughter to Pisa and she communicated the information to Browning, he wrote to her more cheerfully than he felt: "So, wish by wish, one gets one's wishes . . . for one instance, you will go to Italy." A line of music followed, punctuated by a question mark. Thus wordlessly and with Browningesque allusion, the lover expressed what he could not speak. If Miss Barrett knew the words of the opening bars of Glück's aria from *Orfeo* she would have read her lover's question: "Che farò senza Euridice? Che farò senza il mio ben?[1] Indeed,

---

[1] It. What shall I do without Euridice? What shall I do without my darling? *Mio ben* is literally *my good*.

what would Orpheus do in the absence of the source of all the present good in his life? What a delightful glimpse into Browning's rich and subtle character!

Miss Barrett may have answered him in person. She made no comment in her letters.

Again the plans underwent the usual fluctuations. Pisa became Malta and Malta, Madeira, the only constancy residing in Mr. Barrett's inconstancy. Torquay was much too present in his mind. He could not bear to think of parting with one or another of his sons, not to mention his daughters who would have to accompany Ba.

"Don't think too hardly of poor Papa," she begged Browning. "You have his wrong side, his side of peculiar wrongness . . . just now. When you have walked round him you will have other thoughts of him."

The thoughts Browning had of Mr. Barrett he set down in vigorous words. Ba—she allowed him now to use her pet name—had written of scenes, of bitter feelings on Mr. Barrett's part. "I really almost smile in the midst of it all," she wrote, "to think how I was treated as an undutiful daughter because I tried to put on my gloves —for there was no worse provocation. . . . He complained of the undutifulness and rebellion (! ! !) of everyone in the house—and when I asked him if he meant that reproach for me, the answer was that he meant it for all of us . . . I told him that my prospects of health seemed to me to depend on taking this step, but that through my affection for him, I was ready to sacrifice those to his pleasure if he exacted it . . . And he would not answer that. I might do my own way, he said . . . For his part, he washed his hands of me altogether."

"I truly wish you may never feel what I have to bear in looking on quite powerless and silent," Browning answered, "while you are subjected to this treatment . . . I think I understand what a father may exact, and a child should comply with. . . . And you ask whether you ought to obey this no-reason? I will tell you: all passive obedience and implicit submission of will and intellect is by far too easy, if well considered, to be the course prescribed by God to Man in this life of probation—for they evade probation altogether, though foolish people think otherwise . . ." After proving his thesis with unanswerable argument he ended by convincing himself. Enough for him of passive obedience and implicit submission. Once for all he would make himself clear. "You are in what I should wonder at as the veriest slavery—and I who could free you from it, I am here scarcely daring to write . . . Now while I dream, let me once dream! I would marry you now and thus—I would come when you let me, and go when you bade me—I would be no more than one of your brothers—'no more' . . . I deliberately choose the realization of that dream—of sitting simply by you for an hour every day—rather than any other, excluding you. . . . And it will continue but a dream. . . ."

Even if her situation had been other than it was, she could not have remained deaf to the manly despair in the last sentence despite its apparent resignation. If in her filial duty she had not been aware of it before, she saw now how dissimilar was Browning's love in its utter unselfishness from Mr. Barrett's willfully blind devotion that wanted her with him at the expense of her life. In what little things too Browning's love showed itself! For instance, in his offer of a cloak for shipboard when it seemed almost certain that she was sailing. But she had to refuse the cloak for fear of the tempest that would have broken over their heads if Mr. Barrett had ever found out its source. It showed itself in his plundering his mother's garden for the flowers that brought light and beauty into her room. It showed itself in the cakes—Sarianna's cakes—with which he propitiated the jealous Flush who enjoyed privileges that Browning envied. In how many ways did that princely lover prove his devotion! And now—now he made the sacrifice of his future in her service.

She saw him before she received his letter, as everybody had been out when it arrived and it had not been delivered to her room. She esteemed him the more for not betraying by his behavior that he expected her to be different, to have an answer for him in word or look. What abundant amends she found in his generosity for all the difficulties of her personal life! Her tears fell on the page as she thought of the small bitterness that had made her unhappy for several days. "The tear-marks went away in the moisture of new, happy tears." Should she, in her circumstances, accept the gift of his future? Could she?

When she answered she made a valiant attempt not to take "a base advantage of certain noble extravagances." Somehow the words seemed false against her true feelings. "And now listen to me in turn," she then wrote from the truth of her being. "You have touched me more profoundly than I thought even you could have touched me. . . . Henceforward I am yours for everything but to do you

harm—and I am yours too much, in my heart, ever to consent to
do you harm in that way. If I could consent to do it, not only should
I be less loyal, but in a sense, less yours. . . . A promise goes to you
in it that none, except God and your will, shall interpose between
you and me,—I mean, that if he should free me within a moderate
time from the trailing chain of this weakness, I will then be to you
whatever at that hour you shall choose—whether friend or more than
friend—a friend to the last, in any case . . . Only in the meanwhile
you are most absolutely free—'unentangled' (as they call it) by the
breadth of a thread . . . And now if I ask a boon of you?"

Browning's reply was a cry of exultation allowing scant breath to
her alternative. "Think for me, speak for me, my dearest, my own!
You that are all-greatheartedness and generosity, do that one more
generous thing. . . . My own now! For there it is!—oh, do not fear
I am 'entangled'—my crown is loose on my head, not nailed there—
my pearl lies in my hand—I may return it to the sea if I will!—What
is it you ask of me this first asking?"

The boon turned out to be the restitution of the letter she had
sent back for him to burn. He was unable to grant it. "Could you
think that that untoward letter lived one *moment* after it returned
to me?"

From now on there was a tacit engagement between them. He
felt free to use her intimate name, but it was long before she
could get herself to call him Robert. Even then she had to write
it first. "It is a white name to take into my life. Isn't this an Hebraic
expression of a preferring affection, 'I have called thee by thy name?'
And therefore, because you are the best, only dearest!—Robert."

They could speak to each other without reserve now and so they,
who had never loved, released the pent-up wealth of their emotions,
untarnished in a spiritual virginity, and poured it out in a golden
shower. At last each had found a peer in height and depth of passion.
The capacity for loving, Elizabeth Barrett admitted, was the largest
of her powers. With equal truth it could be said of Browning. Ever
since Elizabeth had come upon Mme. de Stael's words, she had repeated them to herself in her few experiences with the human heart:
"*Jamais je n'ai pas eté aimée comme j'aime.*" She could never say
them truthfully again.

What they said to each other sank into their hearts with the echo
of their words. What they wrote remains as a lasting record of love
at its purest, noblest, most human and civilized. They had no thought

of posterity as they penned their letters. They were only continuing
with the same spontaneity their interrupted talks for which, somehow, Browning's visits never seemed long enough. Now their discourse
had the rapture of poetry chanted antiphonally.

She wrote: "Your beautiful flowers!—none the less beautiful for
waiting for water yesterday . . . And while I was putting them into
water, I thought that your visit went on all the time. Other thoughts
too I had, which made me look down blindly . . . on the little blue
flowers, while I thought what I could not have said an hour before
without breaking into tears . . . To say now that I never can forget;
that I feel myself bound to you as one human being cannot be more
bound to another; and that you are more to me at this moment than
all the rest of the world is only to say in new words that it would be a
wrong against *myself*, to seek to risk your happiness . . . You are not
like other men, as I could see from the beginning—no." Later she
wrote: "Whatever I can feel is for you—and perhaps it is not less for
not being simmered away in too much sunshine as with women
accounted happier. *I* am happy besides now—happy enough to die
now."

He answered: "When I come back from seeing you . . . there
never is a least word of yours I could not occupy myself with. . . .
There is nothing in you that does not draw out all of me. You
possess me, dearest, and there is no help for the expressing it all, no
voice nor hand, but these of mine which shrink and turn away from
the attempt. . . . Dearest, I believed in your glorious genius and
knew it for a true star from the moment I saw it; long before I had
the blessing of knowing it was MY star, with my fortune and futurity
in it. . . . Yet, if you can lift me with one hand, while the other suffices
to crown you—there is queenliness in *that*, too!" Later he wrote: "I
want ALL of you, not just so much as I could not live without . . .
And now I will dare—yes, dearest, kiss you back to my heart again,
my own. There—and there!"

Again she said: "You cannot guess what you are to me—you cannot
—it is not possible . . . It is something to me between dream and
miracle, all of it—as if some dream of my earliest brightest dreaming-
time had been lying through these dark years to steep in the sunshine,
returning to me in a double light. Can it be I say to myself, that you
feel for me *so* . . . Could it be that heart and life were devastated to
make room for you?—If so it was well done,—dearest! They leave
the ground fallow before the wheat."

And he: "I *do*, God knows, lay up in my heart these priceless treasures—shall I tell you? I never in my life kept a journal . . . In my last travel I put down on a slip of paper a few dates . . . on such a day I was on Vesuvius, in Pompeii, at Shelley's grave . . . But I have, from the first, recorded the date and the duration of every visit to you; the number of minutes you have given me, and I put them together till they make—nearly two days now; four-and-twenty-hour-long-days, that I have been *by* you . . . For, love, what is it all, this love for you, but an earnest desiring to include you in myself, if that might be; to feel you in my very heart and hold you there for ever, through all chance and earthly changes!"

When he wrote to her again only two days later, he was suddenly seized with an embarrassment that stammers through his sentences: "Give me, dearest beyond expression, what I have always dared to think I would ask you for—one day! Give me, wait—for your own sake, not mine who never never dream of being worth such a gift—but for your own sense of justice, and to say, so as my heart shall hear, that you were wrong and are no longer so, give me so much of you—all precious that you are—as may be given in—"

What? the scandalized reader asks.

"—as may be given in a lock of your hair. I will live and die with it, and with the memory of you—this *at* the *worst!* If you give me what I beg—shall I say next Tuesday—when I leave you, I will not speak a word. If you do not, I will not think you unjust . . . but I will pray you to wait and remember me one day—when the power to deserve more may be greater. . . . Good night, now. Am I not yours—are you not mine? And can that make you happy too?"

The same embarrassment came over her when she replied to his request, in a Victorian near-prudery that for once and once only, made them the children of their period. "I never gave away what you ask me to give you to a human being except my nearest relatives and once or twice or thrice to female friends—never, though reproached for it; and it is just three weeks since I said last to an asker that I was 'too great a prude for such a thing' . . . And, prude or not, I could not—I never could—*something* would not let me. And now, what am I to do? . . . Should you have it, or not? Why, I suppose . . . yes . . . Oh, You—who have your way in everything! . . . Which does not mean that I shall give you what you ask for, *tomorrow* . . . Some day I will send it perhaps. . . ."

It was a week before she gave him a lock of her hair, and when he received it, it was in a ring that was the symbol of her troth. Before that she had demanded a fair exchange in kind because, "You have come to me as a dream comes, as the best dreams come, dearest—and so there is need to me of 'a sign' to know the difference between dream and vision. . . ." His hair she put into the locket her uncle Samuel had given her as a child. How well she remembered his telling her to beware of loving. "If you do . . . it will be for life and death." She knew it was true.

For life and death, therefore, they made plans and marriage was the chief of them. "Did my own Ba, in the prosecution of her studies," he wrote, "get to a book . . . wherein Voltaire pleases to say that '*si Dieu n'existait pas, il faudrait l'inventer*'? I feel, after reading these letters,—as ordinarily after seeing you, sweetest, or hearing from you—that if marriage did not exist, I should infallibly invent it. I should say, no words, no feelings even, do justice to the whole conviction and *religion* of my soul."

But there were also worldly matters to consider, and Browning who so far had had few, if any, financial worries, began to give serious thought to the future. "If I *wished* to be very poor, in the world's sense of poverty," she reassured him quickly, "I could *not*, with three or four hundred a year of which no living will can dispossess me." The "no living will" was as ominous as it sounded. "I might certainly tell you," she had earlier clarified Mr. Barrett's position, "that my own father, if he knew that you had written to me *so*, and that I had answered you *so*, even, would not forgive me at the end of ten years."

Strong words. But they still underestimated Mr. Barrett's incapacity to forgive.

Browning, however, returned to the "worldly matters." He would sacrifice everything, "this careless 'sweet habitude of living'—this absolute independence of mine.—I feel sure that whenever I make up my mind to that, I can be rich enough and to spare—because along with what you have thought *genius* in me, is certainly talent . . . I have tried it in various ways, just to be sure that I was a little magnanimous in never intending to use it." Why, he cited as an example of his talent for the kind of literature that pays, some of the very papers which had laughed *Paracelsus* to scorn, had praised to the skies an elementary French book on a new plan that he had written for his French master! "So that when the only obstacle is that there is so much *per annum* to be producible, you will tell me," he said.

Miss Barrett would have none of such practical nonsense, and told him so. It would amount to "a sacrifice of duty and dignity as well as of ease and satisfaction—to an exchange of higher work for lower work—and of the special work you are called to, for that which is work for anybody . . . Do me the little right of believing that I would not bear or dare to do you such a wrong."

They concentrated instead on what was more to the purpose, the recovery of her strength. That did not prevent Browning, however, from casting about for a paying occupation to fatten the bachelor's purse which had enabled him to support his Muse without worry. He thought seriously of reading for the Bar, like Arnould. He again pulled strings, hoping to land a diplomatic post. Then he applied to the influential Monckton Milnes, suing, pleading, coaxing, cajoling for any post, no matter how small, in the British Museum. "I will work like a horse," he said. Nothing came of his efforts and his worried Muse was jubilant as Miss Barrett, had she known, would have been.

Meanwhile she planned with him a strategy of freedom. Neither spoke of why it was so important for her to leave her couch and be carried downstairs to the drawing room. But they knew that every moment's absence from her cage meant a trial flight to the outside world. Little by little she trusted herself to stand, then to walk from her sofa to the chair without assistance. At every step she reported progress and he cheered her as one does a child learning to walk. Indeed, in her withdrawal after Edward's death she had unconsciously returned to the helplessness of infancy and the consequent security of dependence. Now she had to train herself forward to adult womanhood. As she leaned more on Browning she learned to detach herself from her father.

Browning was "in ecstasies" at her progress. He who had never seen her except reclining on her couch dreamed of meeting her, standing on stairs and galleries and passages generally, "and spiral heights and depths, and sudden turns—and above all, landing places —they are my heart's delight—I would come upon you unaware in a landing-place in my next dream!"

On such encouragement she overcame the hardest of all barriers, the self-induced psychological fear. "Now *walk*, move, *guizza, anima mia dolce*.[2] Shall I not know one day how far your mouth will be from mine as we walk?" he asked her poignantly.

_____
[2] *Guizzare*, almost untranslatable, means to move fleetly, in a flash. Earlier he had played amusingly on the Italian word. "Dart, my sweet soul," would be the closest approximation.

"Now, I shall tell you what I did yesterday," she announced soon afterward in great elation. "It was so warm, so warm . . . that I took it into my head to call it April instead of January, and put on a cloak and walked downstairs into the drawing room—walked, mind!"

Her brother Stormie had been so startled at this apparition that he cried, "So glad to see you!"—as if she were some person he was meeting for the first time.

Chapter XIV: Fugitive Angel

IN THE autumn of 1845 Browning had shown Miss Barrett a
number of new poems for the seventh issue of *Bells and Pomegranates* which came out in November as the "Dramatic Romances
and Lyrics." One of the poems, of two brief stanzas, spoke as it was
meant to do to her deepest self. Browning said nothing of the source
of his inspiration, nor did she let him know by the merest word that
she understood to whom he alluded in his

> Nay, but you, who do not love her,
>   Is she not pure gold my mistress?
> Holds earth aught—speak truth—above her?
>   Aught like this tress, see, and this tress,
> And this last fairest tress of all,
>   So fair, see, ere I let it fall?

For some time she too had been writing of their love, secretly,
letting no flash escape of the treasure she was slowly amassing in a
series of sonnets destined to become part of the spiritual heritage of
the world. But she had no such thought as she wrote. Her whole
being had been convulsed by a terrific emotion. In the upheaval her
soul's aridity had been shattered and from the wounds, as from the
clefts made by an earthquake, great bursts of living flowers blessed
what had been so frightening. Emotionally she had become a woman.
As a poet she was realizing unconsciously, as with all true greatness,
the dream of speaking from her own heart to the heart of the world
in the language of a sublime, ennobling universal experience.

From the first when she realized that the mystic shape who drew
her backward by the hair was not Death but Love, she had been
tracing the miracle of her rebirth in its every stage. As in all wonder-
working she had had her anguish and her trials. The butterfly is not
born in the splendor of its rainbow wings. As groping worm and as
blind chrysalis it is wrapped in silence and the dark till it is summoned to the light and freedom. Her chrysalis had been a sheath as
manifold as the wrappings of a mummy, as layer upon layer of guilt

and grief and fear bound her, still living, in the trappings of an unnatural death.

Then *he* had come, and having come had spoken, and in the breath of the animating voice she had awakened and burst her bonds. But she had not at once found wings. Her burdened heart had held her down.

> I lift my heavy heart up solemnly,
> As once Electra her sepulchral urn,
> And, looking in thine eyes, I overturn
> The ashes at thy feet. Behold and see
> What a great heap of grief lay hid in me . . .

One can almost see the origin of this sonnet in the letter in which she told Browning of Edward's death. How could she burden him with her burden? Her generous impulse had been to send him from her, from the danger of her still living grief.

> . . . those laurels on thine head,
> O my beloved, will not shield thee so,
> That none of all the fires shall scorch and shred
> The hair beneath. Stand farther off, then! Go.

In equal generosity he stood fast. The liberal and princely giver not only would not go but gave her the "gold and purple" of his heart. The face of all the world was changed for her by his love, but it was long, very long, before she would take his gift in her unworthiness before such giving.

> If thou must love me, let it be for nought
> Except for love's sake only,

she pleaded, fearful that if he loved her for her smile or her way of speaking or for any transient thing, the love itself might prove transitory. Every flicker of emotion she fanned into a flame of poetry. At the very time that Browning was showing her his verses and they were exchanging locks of hair she was writing two sonnets on the event—the only two which, for coming too close to Victorian sentimentality, remove them from the high place that the others will forever hold.

Phrases from their conversation or from their letters she picked up and dressed for immortality. The letters themselves she chose as the subject for one of the sonnets which gives better than any chronicling the progress of their love.

> . . . This said, he wished to have me in his sight
> Once, as a friend; this fixed a day in spring
> To come and touch my hand . . . a simple thing
> Yet I wept for it; this . . . the paper's light . . .
> Said, *Dear, I love thee;* and I sank and quailed
> As if God's future thundered on my past.
> This said, *I am thine,* and so its ink has paled
> With lying at my heart that beat too fast;
> And this . . . O love, thy words have ill availed
> If what this said I dared repeat at last!

This was the twenty-eighth sonnet. She had sixteen more to write. Was it to them she alluded in her letter to Browning of the 22nd of July, 1846 when she said: "You will see some day at Pisa what I will not show you now. Does not Solomon say that 'there is a time to read what is written'?"

In the prose of living doubts still assailed her on her deserving Browning's devotion, although now they expressed themselves no longer in fits of hysterical anxiety during which she stamped her feet with impatience to receive the "candid" letter which she felt must come—the letter with its "confessional of an illusion." She would think, to soften the shock, "People say that women *always* know . . . certainly I do not know, and therefore . . . therefore. . . ." The candid letter never came. Instead, there was Browning, more tender, more devoted, more generous than ever. Now she tormented herself with thoughts of another woman, younger, beautiful, and she reiterated her plea to him to give her up. It would not be much worse, she tried to comfort herself, than it was before she knew him. She would at least have the memory of him to keep forever. She finally confessed her fears to him. "The chief *pang* was the idea of another woman—! From *that* I have turned back again and again, recoiling like a horse set against too high a wall." The wonder of it never ceased to amaze her. "Why did you love *me,* my beloved, when you might have chosen from the most perfect of all women and each would have loved you with the perfectest of her nature? That is my riddle in this world." But she need have had no doubt. He did indeed belong to what he worshiped, and he both loved and worshiped her.

Like all lovers, however, he too had moments of wanting to question the future, not because he lacked faith but rather to share with supernal forces the thought that filled his life. He was among his books one day, thinking of her, when he had a fancy to try divination on the first volume he chanced to pick up. "What will be the event of my love for Her?" he questioned the book that fell under his hand, opening it on a random passage. The volume, of all inauspicious ones, turned out to be Cerutti's Italian grammar. He hoped he might come upon a word like *conjunction* or at least a possessive pronoun. To his amazement his eyes lighted upon the sentence in an exercise for translation: "If we love in the other world as we do in this, I shall love thee to eternity." At the cost of being called superstitious he related the event to her.

Through the intervening months, in spite of the London winter, she had been getting stronger. Mr. Barrett had won out in keeping his family at home intact. The diurnal ritual of breakfast, work in the city, dinner and prayer at night and Treppy's Sunday visits filled the days agreeably for him. He was pleased too that the family was increased by little Lizzie Barrett, a niece, who kept Ba company in her room and entertained them all with her naive observations. She was a pretty child of ten or eleven who, everyone maintained, was the portrait of Ba at her age.

Nobody was startled any more at Ba's appearances downstairs where she would arrive wrapped in a cloak as if for an outing. With the pleasanter weather, she began to go out in the carriage. One of her first visits was to Treppy who spread a table with such Creole lavishness that she might have fed the whole Barrett family and not just Ba who in her excitement scarcely touched anything.

Then one night in June, 1846, when Henrietta was driving out to dinner, Ba and Lizzie and Flush took their places in the carriage and went through Hyde Park, along the Serpentine whose shining surface in the dusk was scarcely ruffled by the breeze. Flush kept his head out of the window in ecstatic enjoyment till he had the frightful vision of someone washing a little dog in the river when he turned back into the carriage with dilated eyes and ears quivering. All the while in the twilight when the water seemed to hold the only light left, Ba thought of one who was the whole world to her, "And the stars besides." As they returned home, the gas light was in the shops—another strange sight for the erstwhile recluse.

On the surface life went on as before. She had her usual visitors, the breakers-in upon genius and those whom she received as friends. But she was now very nervous in their presence. Inadvertently, in one of her letters to Miss Mitford, she had mentioned that Browning loved her. "But you are not to repeat it—for, of course, it is simply the purest of philanthropies." Had Miss Mitford kept the secret? If not, to whom had she revealed it? Elizabeth trembled every time she saw her or received a letter from her, but finally convinced herself that since Miss Mitford understood nothing of love, she probably believed Miss Barrett's early fervor had sunk into the socket. They had never agreed about Browning anyway, Miss Mitford always dwelling upon his obscurity while Ba talked of the light. "I never should think of asking her for sympathy," she said to Browning. "She is one of the Black Stones, which, when I climb up toward my Singing Tree . . . will howl behind me and call me names."

In that climbing she needed someone to take into her confidence for she and Browning had been making plans for going together to Italy. How they would manage it they were not yet clear. But if they did, then someone not of her family—she could not expose any of her brothers or sisters to her father's fury—had to be on hand to help carry out the scheme. Mr. Kenyon too she excluded out of a sense of honor. She could not take advantage of his trusting generosity to the extent of turning her father forever against him. So far the execution of the plan though not the plan itself was nebulous enough.

"Let me say humbly," Browning wrote, "I should prefer to go with you to Italy or any place where we can live alone for some little time, till you can know me, and be as sure of me as of yourself . . . And if now you do not understand,—well, I kneel to you, my Ba, and pray you to give yourself to me in deed as in word, the body as the heart and mind . . . I cannot, I think,—if I know myself—love you more than I do . . . but I shall always love you thus. . . ."

Marriage of course was implicit, though Ba in periodic attacks of self-depreciation offered to release him—offers which periodically he patiently rejected or ignored. Certain of his love for her and of hers for him she remained unsure of her power to hold him. Only a few weeks earlier one of her brothers, coming home from the Flower Show, retailed the latest gossip from informants who claimed to be intimate friends of the poet's: "Mr. Browning is to be married immediately to Miss Campbell."

As it happened Browning had neither seen nor heard of Miss Campbell before. "It must be a simple falsehood and not gossip or distortion of fact," he explained. His honesty made him go further. "I told you of the one instance," he reminded her, "where such distortion might take place,—Miss Haworth, to avoid mistake."

Would Ba never believe that she was the only woman he had ever loved? "It is a fact," he went on to exculpate himself where no guilt existed, "that I have made myself almost ridiculous by a kind of male prudery with respect to *young ladies* . . . In fact never seeing any attractiveness in the class, I was very little inclined to get involved in troubles and troubles for nothing at all. And as for marrying . . ." He, the keenest psychologist of the age in his writings, was frankly at a loss to handle the woman in the genius Miss Barrett. All he could hope to do was to give her greater confidence in herself and that, he knew, was best accomplished by having her lean upon the rock that was his love. "I am altogether your own, dearest . . . Now you call the rock a rock . . . It *is* a rock . . . not large enough to build a house on, not small enough to make a mantelpiece of, much less a pedestal for a statue, but it is real rock, that is all."

Because fundamentally she knew it she pursued the plan of marriage and Italy against the greatest odds, not the least of which was Mr. Barrett's renewed affection. There had been little talk this year of a Pisa journey. In the pleasant lull he resumed his nightly visits to Ba and lately had even called her "My love" and "My Puss"—his old endearments before his great anger.

"Anything but his kindness, I can bear now!" she cried to Browning, in an intuitive flash that kindness can be converted to the deadliest weapon.

Could she ever make him understand that her father was an upright man, faithful to his conscience, a man whom he would respect and perhaps love in the end? "The difficulty, almost despair, has been with me to make you understand the two ends of truth—both that he is *not* a stone and that he *is* immovable as stone."

Browning's masculine directness suggested the course of approaching Mr. Barrett and presenting his claim like a gentleman, since the good old days were past when as in the novels he might have rescued his lady's father from a dozen ruffians with blacked faces springing out from behind a hedge.

Ba turned away in terror from the idea. "We must be humble and beseeching *afterwards* . . . and try to get forgiven," she said. Not that she had not thought of telling Mr. Barrett. But there was one great danger. "We should be separated, you see, from *that moment,*" she warned, "hindered from writing, hindered from meeting—and I could evade nothing, as I am—not to say that I should have fainting fits at every lifting of his voice . . . I shut my eyes in terror sometimes . . . Only I wish this were Christmas Day, and we . . . even at Salerno . . . in the 'bad air.' "

Matters came to such a state of tension that even Flush felt it and disgraced himself by fastening his teeth on the leg of that kind Mr. Browning who brought such delicious little cakes to woo him. Ba made excuses for the favorite by saying that he mistrusted Browning's umbrella, but she slapped his ears and would not have anything to do with him all the while she arranged Browning's flowers. She could not bear the beseeching eyes of the poor little wretch, however, and she soon forgave him.

"Oh, poor Flush,—do you think I do not love and respect him for his jealous supervision—his slowness to know another having once known you?" said that perfection of lovers when Ba apologized for Flush's bad behavior. "I do not sorrow over his slapped ears, as if they ever pained him very much—you dear Ba!"

Two weeks later, with no umbrella to incite him, Flush tried to take another bite of Mr. Browning's leg. And after Mr. Browning had brought him a peace offering, too! This time it was Wilson who whipped him, in a fit of poetical justice. "Because it was right," she said to her mistress.

Flush's behavior, however, merely reflected the general uneasiness, as Ba's letter more than implied when she wrote to Browning: "Nobody heard yesterday of either your visit or of Flush's misdoings. . . ."

She had reason to be troubled about their secret which like King Midas's ears showed more than she realized. For some time Mr. Kenyon, instead of his taking his place against the mantelpiece to read aloud, would look at her piercingly and ask questions all the more pointed for their casualness.

"Did you see Browning yesterday?"

"Ye-es."

"I thought so. I intended to come myself, but I thought it probable that he would be here . . ." His naked look—he had broken his glasses and carried them in his hand—seemed to pierce through to her very thoughts. "Is there an attachment between your sister Henrietta and Captain Cook?" he suddenly asked.

"Why, Mr. Kenyon—what extraordinary questions, opening on unspeakable secrets," she faltered.

"But I did not know that it was a secret. How was I to know? I have seen him here very often, and it is a natural inquiry." The inference was obvious enough.

Then her Chiappino friend began to make drama of his own. On meeting Browning on the stairs he made a jealous scene when he next saw her, referring sarcastically to the poet as her "New Cross knight." Lately on her enclosing a copy of Browning's poems to him, Chiappino distressed her by sounding the tragic strain, asking for a last interview and promising to remove himself forever from her life. Though she pitied him, she was also at the end of her patience, as she exclaimed to Robert: "How was I especially to condole with him in lawn and weepers on the dreadful fact of your existence in the world?—Poor Chiappino!" But also dangerous Chiappino to one so jealously guarded as herself.

Treppy too gave her Creole intuition free play, especially when she called one day and Arabel told her that Mr. Browning was with Ba.

"Hm! It is much better that I should not go to Wimpole Street at this time," she complained to Arabel who had taken her out walking, "when there are so many secrets. Secrets indeed! You think that nobody can see and hear except yourselves, I suppose!"

"Oh, Treppy, you're always fancying secrets where there are none," Arabel interposed loyally.

"Well, I don't fancy anything now. I know, just as you do. Something was said too about Ba's going to Italy."

"And do you think that she *will* go to Italy?"

"Why, there is only one way for her to go—but she may go that way. If she marries, she may go."

Treppy had come so close to the truth that when Arabel reported the conversation Ba was truly frightened, not only for her sake but for Treppy's. Her impulse from the first had been to tell her all but, as she rationalized, Treppy must have it in her power to say after the event, "I did not know this"—and for very good reasons. "To occasion a schism between her and this house," she explained to Browning, "would be to embitter the remainder of her days."

The circle of anxiety widened till it included Mr. Barrett himself. On an August day, during Browning's visit, a violent thunderstorm had broken. Ba had always been afraid of thunder and with cause. Herefordshire at the foot of the Malvern Hills had been famous for its terrific storms, and the people round about Mr. Barrett's Turkish house looked upon its metal spires as provocation to all the lightnings of heaven. When Ba was a young girl a storm of extraordinary vehemence even for those parts had shaken the house so that they all thought it had been struck. Ba, who was looking out of the window, saw what had really happened. A tree close by had been hit by lightning, "the bark rent from the top to the bottom—torn into long ribbons by the dreadful fiery hands . . . torn into shreds in a moment, as a flower might be, by a child . . . The whole trunk of that tree was bare and peeled—and up that new whiteness of it, ran the finger-mark of the lightning in a beautiful rose-colour . . . the fever sign of certain death." Two young women on a holiday party were also killed in that storm—"each sealed to death in a moment with a sign which a common seal would cover—only the sign on them was not rose-coloured . . . but black as charred wood."

From that day Ba shuddered at the thunder and covered her eyes at the lightning, to the disgust of Mr. Barrett who called such con-duct disgraceful in anybody who had ever learned the alphabet.

While Browning was with her Ba found to her amazement that she had little fear of the storm. But as the downpour continued and the afternoon wore on, she would not hear of Robert's going out in the rain, even though she began to feel very uneasy. Papa would soon be returning. Perhaps that was he just now whose foot she heard on the stairs. The uneasiness turned to dread, the later it became, and she found herself looking at Papa's face as she imagined it through the floor. At last the rain abated and Browning left. She was stifling, what with the heat and her stays, so she put on a dressing-gown "to get rid of the strings" and lay down on the sofa, scarcely breathing in the oppressive air that the storm had not lightened.

At about seven Mr. Barrett came up to her room. Seeing her in her white robe, he looked as if the storm had passed into him. "Has this been your costume since the morning, pray?" he asked.

"Oh no—only just now, because of the heat."

"Well," he went on forbiddingly, "it appears, Ba, that *that man* has spent the whole day with you."

She explained as quietly as she could that Mr. Browning had meant to leave much earlier, but that the rain prevented him. What bothered Mr. Barrett was that Ba might have been ill with fear, "And only Mr. Browning in the room." An outrageous state of affairs. After this she wondered whether she could dare let Browning come on his next visit.

Obviously they must resolve their difficulties, and soon. Some weeks earlier Browning had suggested that Ba make Mrs. Jameson her confidante. Mrs. Jameson was not of the family and therefore en-joyed a certain immunity from Mr. Barrett's possible vengeance. Also she had a better understanding of the poetic tribe than Miss Mitford who, in her own disappointment, always referred to them as "those good-for-nothing poets and poetesses." Not that Mrs.

Jameson was free of prejudice for she stoutly maintained: "Artistical natures never learn wisdom from experience." Still, both as writer and artist she disproved her dictum, so Ba allowed herself to be taken out by her on excursions and also drawn out of herself in confidences.

Mrs. Jameson thereupon tactfully offered to take her along to Italy, together with her young niece to whom she was giving "an artistical education." Surely Mr. Barrett would permit her to go in the company of two ladies?

But Mr. Barrett would not. When later Mrs. Jameson again touched upon the subject and Ba intimated that in all likelihood she *would* be going to Italy at some time, the Irishwoman asked pointedly: "On what do you count?"

"Perhaps on my own courage," she answered.

"Oh, now I see clearly!" Mrs. Jameson exclaimed.

For all the clearsightedness nothing happened to make the dream of Italy a reality. Suddenly an unhappy event brought home to Miss Barrett the tragedy of human existence. On the 23rd of June Mrs. Jameson, in her capacity of art expert, had taken Miss Barrett to see the private collection of the banker poet Rogers. Through Mrs. Jameson's well-meant instruction on how Rubens painted landscapes, and various other mysteries, Miss Barrett was able to concentrate in a quiet enjoyment of the Titians, Mantegnas, Rembrandts, Tintorettos, Raphaels and a statuette of Michelangelo's, whose clay, she thought was still "alive with the life of his finger." Then they came to a halt before a modern painting which made Miss Barrett thrill—Haydon's Napoleon at St. Helena.

For some time her correspondence with Haydon had lapsed and during a year or more she had scarcely heard from him until a week earlier when he asked her to shelter his boxes and pictures. He had sent three notes, the first in a light vein, the second begging her not to attribute to him a want of feeling. In the third he wrote of the new background he was painting for a picture which made him feel as if "his soul had wings," and, he reiterated, as how often before, that he knew he could not, and would not die. She had not yet answered him.

Before she could write to him on the following day, she had a letter from Browning with the news of Haydon's death. He had learned of it from the *Times*, "which barely says that B.R.H. died suddenly at his residence—yesterday morning . . . and it is believed that his decease was hastened by *pecuniary embarrassment* . . . He is called the *unfortunate gentleman*—which with the rest implies the very worst, I fear."

Browning was right. Haydon, burdened by more than he could bear, and prevented by circumstances from serving the Glorious Art for which he lived, had taken his own life. Miss Barrett was shocked into self-accusation. Could she have averted what had happened? In his last letter Haydon had written that Peel had sent him fifty pounds, adding, "I do not want *charity* but employment." Should she not have understood his extreme need in that very defiance? Yet she had done nothing. Again and again she had been told—"Oh, never by you, beloved," she said to Browning—that to give money to Haydon was to drop it into a hole in the ground. "But if to have dropped it so, dust to dust, would have saved a living man—what then?" Her head and heart ached over the tragedy that might have been averted by her inactive hand.

When the artist's suicide note, methodically titled "Last Thoughts of B. R. Haydon" was read, together with his will, Miss Barrett learned to her consternation that he had left her his manuscripts with the request that she arrange for their publication with Longman. During their correspondence Haydon had sent her a good part of his memoirs to read and had suggested Longman, even though Miss Barrett assured him that she had no influence whatsoever with any publisher. The name must have come to him at the last, together with the thought of his trusted "Aeschylus Barrett."

She turned at once to Browning for help. "Whatever is clearly set for me to do, I should not shrink from under these circumstances . . . But if Mr. Sergeant Talfourd is the executor, is he not obviously the fit person?"

She was frightened by the task for which she felt wholly inadequate, both as a woman and as one historically ignorant of the persons and times of which he wrote. "In fact," she said of the manuscript, "it was—with much that was individual and interesting—as unfit as possible for the general reader—fervid and coarse at once, with personal references blood-dyed at every page . . . I should not know how one reference would fall innocently, and another like a thunderbolt on surviving persons."

After weeks of suspense Miss Barrett, through Browning's agency with Forster and Talfourd, was relieved of what might have proved an onerous burden. Eventually the memoirs were published, a posthumous monument self-erected by a man too big for his mold, whose very faults, in Miss Barrett's words, partook of nobleness.

Orion Horne too had something to say of Haydon, which Miss Mitford clipped for Miss Barrett from the *Daily News*:

> Mourn, fatal Voice, whom ancients called the Muse! . . .
> Mourn for a worthy son whose aims were high,
> Whose faith was strong amidst a scoffing age . . .
> Mourn now with all thine ancient tenderness,
> Mingled with tears which fall in heavy drops
> For One who lost himself, remembering thee.

Miss Barrett was much affected by it and found it worth more than twenty of Mr. Horne's ballad-books.

The turmoil over the Haydon papers added to the general unrest and warned the lovers that they must take the decisive step. Browning told his parents of his intention which they met with sublime understanding. Whatever he did was right in their eyes, which Mr. Browning further demonstrated by offering Robert financial aid.

"May God help us and smooth the way for us . . ." said Ba. "May your father indeed be able to love me a little, for my father will never love me again."

As if to gain strength for the great venture she went out more often to walk in the park, to hear music in a distant church, to visit Mr. Boyd in St. John's Wood, to see the Great Western Railway with Mr. Kenyon who perhaps wanted to introduce her to the iron horse that she might one day have to ride. She was thrilled by the great roaring grinding thing— "a great blind mole it looked for blackness"—while Flush, no hero ever in the face of the new, leaped upon the coach-box for safety.

They got out of the carriage to see the train closer. It began to rain. The raindrops falling on her face and clothes delighted her more even than the sight of the railroad. "It is something new for me to be rained upon, you know," she told her love, who heard in those words a promise that she would not fail him.

How grateful he had been, he remembered, when once she had crossed the room to look up Shelley's age in a book, and was not tired. Now she crossed London to see the trains arrive. . . . He recalled also how in the beginning he would sometimes shorten his visit to reach the time of taking her hand. Soon, God willing, she would be his and there would be no more parting.

They discussed ways and means and their itinerary. "If we go to Southampton, we go straight from the railroad to the packet," she spoke like a seasoned traveler, ". . . if I accede to your *idée fixe* about the marriage." She still teased him. "Only do not let us put a long time between that and the setting out, and do not you come here afterwards—let us go away as soon as possible afterwards at least."

He agreed. It did not seem right to either of them that after their marriage he should call at Wimpole Street asking for "Miss Barrett."

In her talks with her friends she was appalled to discover how very much they knew, even Mr. Boyd in his rayless dark. Perhaps for that reason. "He like a prisoner in a dungeon, sounds every stone on the wall round him, discerns a hollowness, detects a wooden beam."

"Are you going to be a nun?" he asked her one day without warning. On her next visit he put the question precisely right. She confessed. He approved but, as she knew, less out of love for Browning than for anger toward her unreasonable father.

"Was I not acute?" he asked her proudly at parting. She could not grudge him his triumph.

Mrs. Jameson for reasons of expedience was gently eased out of her proffered companionship. "But you will go to Italy?" she asked Miss Barrett.

"Perhaps—if something unforeseen does not happen." Miss Barrett had no wish to tempt the gods by too much assurance.

"And with efficient companionship?"

"Yes," she faltered.

Mrs. Jameson saw more clearly than ever. A fortnight later she called again. On Miss Barrett's saying that she had been making no special preparations for her projected Italian trip Mrs. Jameson remarked laughing, "Very sudden then, it is to be. In fact, there is only an *elopement* for you."

"But, dearest," Ba protested to Browning, "nobody will use such a word surely to the *event*! We shall be in such an obvious exercise of right—surely nobody will use such a word."

The only person whom Ba finally took wholly into her confidence was Lily Wilson, loyal, taciturn, and dependable. It was a brave decision for the young woman to make, to set out for a foreign land with her mistress, for goodness knows how long, and live among people of strange tongues and stranger ways. Miss Barrett in any case could not have left her behind. Wilson would have been cast out into the street before sunset as the first measure of Mr. Barrett's reprisal. Besides, Miss Barrett needed a woman with her in her new life, and who could care for her better than the faithful Wilson? True, she was an expensive servant, she told Browning, "But she is very amiable and easily satisfied." There was also a consideration that never left her consciousness. "I must manage a sheltering ignorance for my poor sisters at the last."

There was still another being she had to think about, her own Flush who in Pisa must guard the house, as Browning had said in jest. Ba wanted Browning to say it and mean it, in spite of Flush's naughty behavior toward him of late. "You will let him come with us to Italy . . . will you not, dear, dearest? In good earnest, will you not? Because, if I leave him behind, he will be teased for my sins in this house."

Of course Browning agreed. Did he not *love* Flush?

With Flush's future in Italy assured, Ba made preparations for herself. She bought boots for the glorious walking life in the sunshine, hiding them away, and got her belongings together, the jewelry that was her own, the books she could not be without. They were to leave for Italy toward the end of September.

Lo, on the 2nd of the month Flush was spirited away by the dog-stealers.

"Here is a distress for me, dearest!" she wailed to Browning. "You were a prophet when you said *take care!*"

How the rogues had been able to catch Flush from under her very eyes she could not understand. He had gone with her and Arabel in a cab to Vere Street, where he followed them as usual into a shop and out of it. She had seen him close at her heels when she stepped up into the carriage, but when she looked round and said, "Flush?"—there was no Flush.

Her brother Henry was sent out at once to the captain of the organized banditti who by this time had good reason to know the Barretts well. But by evening Flush had not yet been brought in. Henry made the tactical error of telling the captain that this time they were resolved not to give much, whereupon the captain mapped out his own strategy. Poor Flush meanwhile was the innocent pawn.

"All this night he will howl and lament, I know perfectly. . . . Poor darling Flush, with his fretful fears, and pretty whims, and his fancy for being near me. . . . Write to me—and pity me for Flush," she lamented to Robert.

"How sorry I am for you, my Ba!" he wrote sincerely. But he could not forbear a slight revenge at the expense of the rival who, he had no doubt, had by this time been recovered. "Poor fellow— was he no better than the rest of us, and did all the barking and fanciful valour spend itself on such enemies as Mr. Kenyon and myself, leaving only blandness and waggings of the tail for the man with the bag?"

For Ba's sake, however, he hoped for the best for "Our friend and follower, that was to be, at Pisa."

Flush's plight for the moment took precedence over every other concern. " 'Our friend and follower that was to be,'—is that then, your opinion of my poor darling Flush's destiny?" Ba inquired aghast.

She was very much worried about her pet. That the dog-stealers now had Flush Henry had ascertained. That this time they would exact their ten pounds Ba knew for a certainty. She knew also that she would pay it. "Get Flush back, whatever you do," she admonished Henry who had found it very hard to be civil to the gang captain in a room hung with pictures, and was now talking of setting the police against the thieves.

"I can't run any risk and bargain and haggle," she explained to Browning. "There is a dreadful tradition in this neighborhood, of a lady who did so having her dog's head sent to her in a parcel." As for Flush's allowing himself to be caught blandly with waggings of the tail—let not Browning believe that for a moment. Indeed, on a previous occasion the dog-thief had said of Flush (whose record belied it) that he was a most difficult animal to get, he was so mistrustful. "If he could have bitten, he would have bitten," she defended him. ". . . He was caught up and gagged—depend upon that."

Browning was appalled by a state of affairs that kept ruffians in paintings and expensive cigars by victimizing tenderhearted women through their pets, and pleaded with Ba, on principles of abstract justice, not to give in to the demands of the dog-thieves. He was for adopting quite another procedure, siding in that with Henry. Not one shilling would he give the knaves. "You are responsible for the proceedings of your gang, and you I mark," he would say to the captain, a wretch named Taylor. "Don't talk nonsense about cutting off heads or paws. Be as sure as that I stand here and tell you, I will spend my whole life in putting you down . . . and by every imaginable means I will be the death of you and as many of your accomplices as I can discover. . . . And for the ten pounds—see!" Whereupon he would give them to the first beggar in the street. "You think I should receive Flush's head?" he asked Ba.

Of course he understood that Ba could not approve the procedure he suggested. "But all religion, right and justice, with me," he maintained, "seem implied in such resistance to wickedness and refusal to multiply it a hundredfold—for from this prompt payment of ten pounds for a few minutes' act of the easiest villainy, there will be encouragement to—how many acts in the course of next month?"

It was all very well to defend abstract principles, Ba felt, but meanwhile poor darling Flush was going thirsty and hungry and breaking his heart with worry. Several days had passed and he remained unransomed. "A man may love justice intensely," she argued with Robert, "but the love of an abstract principle is not the strongest love now—is it? . . . Do you mean to say that if the banditti came down on us in Italy and carried me off to the mountains, and sending you one of my ears, to show you my probable fate if you did not let them have—how much may I venture to say I am worth?—five or six scudi . . . would you answer, 'Not so many crazie'; and would you wait, poised upon abstract principles, for the other ear, and the catastrophe—as was done in Spain not so long ago? Would you, dearest? Because it is well to know beforehand, perhaps." Justice or no justice, "If people won't do as I choose, I shall go down tomorrow morning myself and bring Flush back with me."

Browning made haste to say that he had spoken as he had under the impression that Flush was safe by her side. Still, he went on to defend his argument, bringing in God, Mahomet, and Hampden to reenforce his position. Manlike, he also managed to introduce Ba's Chiappino friend. If that gentleman were to assure Ba that "In the event of your marrying me he would destroy himself,—would you answer as I should, 'Do so and take the consequences?'—and think no more about the matter? I should absolutely leave it, as not my concern, but God's."

To Ba, kept awake by a dog shut up in a mews somewhere behind the house, yelling and moaning, and reviving Flush's misery to torment her, the most important thing was the release of her poor little beast. When her dinner was brought to her she scarcely touched it. The thought of the starving Flush's beseeching eyes was too much for her.

At last, what with abstract principles of justice on one side and lukewarmness about spending any more money on that wretched animal on the other, Ba set out for Shoreditch with Wilson to handle the situation herself. The cab drove them through vile streets,

unfamiliar even to the cabman who had to ask directions at a public
house. At the name of the street two or three habitués, coming out
to look at them, said: "Oh, you want to find Mr. Taylor," whereupon
one unsolicited benefactor ran before the cab to show them the way.

Ba saw neither Flush nor Mr. Taylor, but she did see that gentleman's wife—"an immense feminine bandit—fat enough to have
had an easy conscience all her life." The woman agreed to send her
spouse to Wimpole Street for the negotiations, and Ba returned
to the cab with Wilson who was not sure that they would get out
of it all with their lives.

Mr. Taylor actually kept his appointment and in the goodness of
his heart asked for only six guineas. But while the business was being
concluded in came Alfred who called Mr. Taylor a swindler, a liar,
and a thief, the truth of which the bandit could not bear. He flung
out of the house swearing, "As I hope to be saved you'll never see
your dog again."

Ba had to be restrained by main force from following Mr. Taylor
to Shoreditch in her dread of his inflicting the threatened martyrdom
on her poor Flush. She was called mad, obstinate, willful—as many
names as Mr. Taylor by her distracted family. Finally Sette managed
to get her back into her room again on the promise of going in
person to deliver the dog.

At eight o'clock that night, lean, dirty, and much the worse for
his sojourn of five days among the thieves, Flush was restored to
Wimpole Street. The first thing he did was to dash up the stairs to
Ba's door. Then he drank his purple cup full of water, filled three
times over. When anyone said to him, "Poor Flush, did the naughty
man take you away?" he put up his head and moaned and yelled,
Ba wrote to Browning. The letter ended cryptically with the post-
script: "I have been to the vestry again today."

It was the 7th of September. Browning had not been well for
several days, a sign that he was emotionally upset. They had been
seeing each other less frequently since the dressing-gown incident,
exercising a wise caution in the midst of so many alerted suspicions.
They had talked of marrying in a few weeks at the neighboring
church of St. Marylebone. Ba's visit to the vestry was no doubt a
practice call to nerve her against too severe a strain on the great day.
Suddenly, with fulminant authority, Mr. Barrett issued an order
for a general exodus to the country, to be effective almost at once so
that the Wimpole Street house could be painted and repaired.

On Wednesday night, the 9th of September, Ba sent Browning a hasty note to inform him of the new complication. "Now—what can be done? . . . Decide, after thinking. I am embarrassed to the utmost degree as to the path to take . . . Therefore decide! . . . I will do as you wish—understand."

"What a glorious dream!" he replied. ". . . We must be *married directly* and go to Italy. I will go for a license today and we can be married on Saturday." He outlined the plans, the very words throbbing with his happiness. Late in July he had written to her: "I wish I could take my life, my affections, my ambitions, all my very self, and fold over them your little hand, and leave them there . . ." In a matter of days he would have his wish.

But how could they make their final arrangements, obtain the ring, have their witnesses ready? This time luck favored them. That Friday all the Barretts except Ba were going to Richmond for a picnic. Thus, free on all sides but for Flush and Wilson, the lovers determined on the procedure for the following day, praying to God that all would go well.

A little past ten o'clock on Saturday morning, the 12th, Miss Barrett and Wilson left Wimpole Street on an unspecified errand, after instructing Arabel and Henrietta to call for Ba at Mr. Boyd's after lunch. All night long, with every nerve awake, Ba had not closed an eye. Before going to bed she had had a quiet talk with Wilson, telling her what she expected of her the following morning. Wilson, devoted and affectionate, never shrank for a moment. "I shall always be grateful to you," said Ba with tears in her eyes.

As the two women made their way toward the fly-stand on Marylebone Street, Miss Barrett staggered so that they had to stop at a chemist's for sal volatile before she could go on. They arrived at St. Marylebone's where they found Browning already waiting with his cousin James Silverthorne. It was a quarter of eleven. By half-past the hour, with Wilson and Silverthorne as witnesses, Elizabeth Barrett and Robert Browning were married. They remained scarcely a few minutes together. Wilson was sent home at once to allay suspicion. Then Ba drove on to Mr. Boyd's. On arriving at New Cross Browning wrote on the envelope of his last letter from Miss Barrett the date and hour of the marriage and the number ninety-one, indicating their ninety-first meeting.

To Ba it all seemed like a dream. Fortunately when she arrived at Mr. Boyd's she found him engaged with a medical man so that she had time to lie quietly on the sitting-room sofa to collect herself. Very considerately Mr. Boyd gave her some Cyprus wine to drink and when her sisters delayed in coming, he had her eat some bread and butter to keep her from looking too pale in their eyes. Arabel and Henrietta arrived in a high state of alarm. Though they knew nothing they suspected much, but so great was the family reticence that they could speak only by innuendo.

"What nonsense! What fancies you do have to be sure," Ba brazened it out.

Much as she disliked doing so, she had taken off her wedding ring and put it away. To dispel further suspicions she went with them as far as Hampstead Heath in the carriage, and talked as naturally as she could. On the way back, as they drove past the church where only a few hours earlier she had been married, she could scarcely see it for the mist before her eyes.

She wrote that day to Browning and he to her. They would continue communicating by letter only until Ba left Wimpole Street to join him—forever. Even without their earlier agreement that he could not ethically ask for Miss Barrett when she was Mrs. Robert Browning, it would have been too much to demand of Ba to make any pretense at a composure she could not feel in a household which, what with the coming removal, some visiting relatives and the constant callers, came close to being a bedlam. Sunday was especially trying, when Ba had to sit by while her brothers and sisters plus Treppy and two or three other women were all laughing and talking at once. Yet Ba, whose head felt as if it would split, did not dare protest for fear of rousing suspicion. She put up with the noise as long as she could. But when the bells began to ring and one of the provincial ladies asked, "what bells are those?" Ba made her escape as unobtrusively as she could after Henrietta answered: "Marylebone Church bells."

She had hardly sat down to write to her husband when in came Mr. Kenyon with his new spectacles, looking as if his eyes had expanded to their rim all the way around.

"When did you see Browning?" he asked the moment he stepped across the threshold.

"He was here on Friday—" she answered truthfully, quickly changing the subject. The rest of the visit passed in agreeable talk with no more pitfalls till he was about to leave. "When do you see Browning again?" he inquired.

"I do not know," she replied, once more with strict adherence to fact if not to truth.

The Barrett pattern of delay after decision held in the removal to the country as always before. The days passed and still nothing happened. Ba and Browning, however, employed the time usefully by getting their boxes ready and framing announcements of their marriage to be sent to the papers as soon as it was safe to do so. Another dozen letters passed between them before the 19th of September. On that day Ba, in a state near collapse, was preparing to leave her room for the last time, with Wilson and the future guardian of the Pisan home.

"Oh, Flush, if you make a sound I am lost!" she whispered to him as they started for the stairs.

Flush was a miracle of understanding. All the way down those two flights and out through the front door not a sound came from him who ordinarily shook the rafters with his rejoicing at even temporary liberty.

Unobserved the three walked around the corner to Hodgson's the bookseller on Great Marylebone Street. There Mrs. Browning found her husband waiting. The boxes had been sent ahead. Browning soon brought a cab from the neighboring stand and husband and wife, Wilson, and Flush who had so nearly missed the great adventure, drove off to Nine Elms to catch the five-o'clock train for Southampton—and a new world.

"Take care of *my life* which is in that dearest little hand," Browning had written to her a few hours after their marriage.

"By tomorrow this time, I shall have you only, to love me—my beloved," she answered in her last letter. "You only! As if one said God only. And we shall have Him beside, I pray of Him."

To the last her thoughts had been with her father and the blow she knew the news of her marriage would be. With the exception of this act she had submitted to the least of his wishes all her life long. "Set the life against the act, and forgive me, for the sake of the daughter you once loved," she worded her plea to him.

Would he forgive? Or would he wish that she had died years ago, like Sam, like Edward? She knew the storm would come and endure. But she hoped he would forgive in the final calm.

The shock to Mr. Barrett was greater even than his daughter had imagined. Although after his wife's death he had tried to keep her memory alive by having her room and everything that had belonged to her preserved as if she were still among them, he ruthlessly sought to obliterate every trace of his daughter.

He must have had bitter thoughts indeed when he came to his favorite portrait of her. The artist was a dire prophet who had painted her as a fugitive angel.

Part Three

FREEDOM, LIFE, AND TRIUMPH

Chapter XV: Flush and an Anniversary

IT TOOK nearly a day's traveling by land and sea to go from London to Paris. When the newly wedded pair arrived there with an ailing and very mistrustful Wilson, they found that Mrs. Jameson had already preceded them with her seventeen-year-old niece Gerardine Bate, whom she was at last launching on a long-promised artistical education. Mrs. Jameson had almost given up hope that her friends would ever take wing for what she insisted on calling their elopement, and it was with an incredulous stare that she read Browning's note announcing their marriage and their arrival. In a gust of enthusiasm she swept them off into the little Hotel de Ville on the Rue de l'Évêque where she was stopping.

Immediately a change came over the romantic Gerardine. The sight of the two poets, recently married and in an aura of happiness, made her want the same bliss for herself—not with Browning, for in the eyes of the adolescent he represented great age, but with some personable youth, in fact any youth. Mrs. Jameson, who adored her, noticed her sudden burgeoning and was alarmed.

To the Brownings Paris meant the gate to their Italian Eden. They loved it but their eyes turned yearningly southward, to the Pisa of their many months' planning. As it was, although Ba had borne the journey amazingly well and far better than Wilson, she had a day of illness that threw Browning into "a fit of terror" and made him decide to leave for Italy as soon as possible. Mrs. Jameson with Geddie set out with them. Like her niece, she too had a romantic streak. Besides, it was not often that one had the luck to be caught in the wake of an amatory venture that was sure to make history.

Already the "elopement" had set all England buzzing, as she knew by the letters that were beginning to arrive. She contributed her mite to the current excitement in breathless epistles to her friend Lady Byron who, like all victims of unhappy marriages, had an inordinate curiosity about the affairs of others. "My poet and my poetess—a pretty pair to go through this prosaic world together," Mrs. Jameson wrote on the way to Pisa. They were, indeed, "a charming fugitive pair" but would they find permanent happiness, she questioned, in her mistrust of the poetical temperament. "He is in all the common things of life the most unpractical of men, and the most uncalculating, rash—in short the worst manager I have ever met with; she in her present state, and from her long seclusion almost helpless. Now only conceive the ménage that is likely to ensue and without fault on either side."[1]

Mrs. Browning would have been ill-pleased had she seen Mrs. Jameson's prognostication to a woman whom she intensely disliked as she did Mary Shelley—both of them for having failed, in different ways, the poets they had married. She would have been annoyed too by the comments of others who knew both her and Robert. Wordsworth, for instance, exclaimed: "So Robert Browning and Miss Barrett have gone off together! I hope they can understand each other—nobody else can!"

When letters began to arrive from London they contained much that would have saddened both her and Browning had they not been so deeply in love. Mr. Barrett, they learned, had plunged into an extravagance of dinner parties at which he exhibited a jarring gaiety that was only the frothing up of his heart's bitterness. He would not suffer anyone to mention Elizabeth, and himself ventured no comment except to John Kenyon in a revealing phrase: "My daughter should have been thinking of another world."

Oddly his sons stood by him in his displeasure whether because they agreed with him or out of diplomacy only they could know. Henrietta and Arabel felt a sympathetic relief for their sister's sake. Arabel, vowed to a life of good works, knew she would never incur her father's hate through any man. Henrietta took hope from the act for herself and Captain Surtees Cook who not long since had ventured to oppose Mr. Barrett's demands for passive obedience in respect to marriage by asking, meekly it is true, and as if solely for information: "Are children then to be considered slaves?" Well, Ba had answered for them all.

Mr. Kenyon, as was to be expected, approved. Yet he did not lose sight of the risks Ba had incurred. "I considered," he wrote, "that you had imperilled your life upon this undertaking and I still thought you had done wisely." Then he told them what all lovers rejoice to hear: "I know no two persons so worthy of each other. . . . If the thing had been asked of me, I should have advised it, albeit glad

[1] From the Baylor Browning Collection of autograph letters, etc.

that I was not asked." Still, he had cause to be gratified. Had he not helped to bring about that marriage of poet hearts and poet minds?

It was Carlyle's letter, however, which gave the Brownings the greatest pleasure. It was not often that the harsh prophet turned from his cursing of the world's unrightness and attuned his voice to blessing. But bless he did, in words warm with affection for the young man he had known for many years and for the wife he had chosen. "Certainly, if ever there was a union indicated by the finger of Heaven itself, and sanctioned and prescribed by the Eternal Laws under which poor transitory sons of Adam live, it seemed to me, from all I could hear and know of it, to be this. Perpetually serene weather is not to be looked for by anybody," he warned with the voice of experience, "least of all by the likes of you two—in whom precisely because more is given, more also in proportion is required; but unless I altogether mistake, there is a life partnership which, in all kinds of weather, has in it a capacity for being blessed. . . ." Who could fear the world's malice after such benediction?

The little party, with Flush sitting prominently in the lumbering vehicles, went by easy stages from Paris to Orleans where letters from the Browning family awaited them. Miss Browning sent Ba a traveling writing-desk with the note, "E.B.B. from her sister Sarianna." Mrs. Browning sent love, while Mr. Browning closed his letter to Robert with, "Give your wife a kiss for me."

Meanwhile Wilson was making rapid progress in overcoming her insularity. The French no longer scared her and she had managed to learn how to ask for warm water and coffee and bread and butter for her mistress. From Orleans they went on to Avignon where they stopped for a few days to make a pilgrimage to Vaucluse, sacred to the memory of Petrarch who six centuries earlier had there sought solitude. Geddie accompanied them, more out of fascination for the two living poets than for the one long dead. There, at the source of those *dolci acque* which the Italian poet had sung, she saw Browning take up his wife in his arms and, wading through the shallow waters, seat her upon a rock in the middle of the stream. From the bank Flush watched apprehensively. Seeing his mistress in peril of death, he gallantly plunged, determined to perish with her, and was laughingly baptized in the name of Petrarch.

Life glowed with adventure for the happy pair. Their dream of Pisa would be realized in a few days. For them the small decrepit

Italian town was not only the land of dreams but the shrine of English poetry, the place which for a time had harbored Byron and Shelley and still held the imprint of their feet upon its soil. As they sailed from Marseilles to Leghorn, only a few miles from Pisa, the voyagers looked on sights that had been reflected in Shelley's large, nearsighted eyes and in the smoldering pupils of the Pilgrim of Eternity. Those waters had borne them on many a run till the treacherous Gulf of Spezzia swallowed up the bark *Ariel* and her master Shelley.

Browning remembered how Leigh Hunt had told him that when the destructive waters yielded up their prey the volume of Keats' poems which he had lent Shelley was found in his bosom, together with the right hand that pressed it there. He had been reading the "Eve of St. Agnes" before the end.

Past Viareggio they sailed, where Shelley had been washed ashore. Those yellow sands set with a backdrop of pines and mountains had been the scene of his body's burning, as the air quivered with the double heat of fire and sunlight, and a seabird circled over the whitening ashes. From that golden shore after the burning, Byron, sick with horror, had dived into the sea and swum off to his boat knowing that his days too were numbered.

At Pisa itself where the Brownings took rooms in the Piazza del Duomo, Shelley's presence was almost tangible. He had wandered through those narrow quiet white streets cut through by the winding Arno and its bridges and shut in by a bulwark of mountains. Like them he had had to shade his eyes against the shimmer of the sunlight on the marble walls of the houses. He had like them looked on the leaning tower, the Cathedral, and the wonderful Baptistery, a stone's throw from the Collegio Fernandino where they lived. In the autumn he too had walked between the garlands of vines, spanning the tree trunks and dropping their bunches of purple grapes. He may have reached up as they did to the golden globes of the orange trees overhanging the walls where the green lizards flitted— *guizzavano*—as Browning saw with delight that Ba was beginning to do. (He knew now how far her eyes and lips were from his as they walked together.)

Not far from their house, along the river, the Palazzo Lanfranchi, which Byron had occupied with his last mistress, the Countess Guiccioli, hid behind its pillared entrance memories of the disordered life he had lived. Tradition had it that Ubaldo Lanfranchi, Arch-

bishop of Pisa, whose palace it was, had in a former century transported the shiploads of soil from the Holy Land which covered the
Campo Santo. Most important to Browning, however, was the knowledge that in that atmosphere Shelley had breathed and written, and
that a Pisan girl, Emilia Viviani, had inspired him to his highest
expression of Intellectual Beauty in *Epipsychidion*.

How much more fortunate than Shelley was he in his wife! What
complete understanding he had with Ba whom he grew to love more
and more each day. Not long since they had talked of Mary Shelley
who had published a book on her Italian impressions. Ba, despite
her desire to be just, had broken out into a tirade. "The Mary dear
with the brown eyes, and Godwin's daughter and Shelley's wife,
and who surely was something better once upon a time—and to go
through Rome and Florence and the rest, after Lady Londonderry's
fashion! The intrepidity of the commonplace quite astounds me
. . . Once she travelled the country with Shelley on arm. Now she
plods it, Rogers in hand—to such things and uses may we come at
last."

Ah, no! Not Ba! As they were knit together by their common
living he saw more clearly than ever the worth of his stolen jewel.
Was there ever a woman comparable to Ba? One with her genius,
her gaiety, her will power that had worked a miracle in raising her
from a life-in-death to the fullness of living and made him the most
blessed of men? On her side Ba could not apprehend her good
fortune without wonder. "It is strange for *him* to love me with
increase and in this way," she wrote to Henrietta from Pisa. In her
humility she could not attribute to anything within herself the pure
fact of his adoration, and laid his worship to his powers of self-
deception as a poet. "It is not a bad thing . . . for a woman to be
loved by a man of imagination. He loves her through a lustrous
atmosphere which not only keeps back the faults, but produces continual novelty, through its own changes." But Browning would have
none of such casuistry. "Always he will have it that our attachment
was 'predestined from the beginning' and that no two persons could
have one soul between them so much as we."

Theirs was moreover a joyous, youthful relationship. Ba's seclusion
had kept her emotionally untouched except in her imagination so
that the heart she brought to Browning was a young girl's for him
to awaken and teach and cherish. Her candid letters then and later
gave in a few spontaneous phrases intimate glimpses of their absolute

happiness. "This morning," she wrote in the third month of their marriage, "when we were at breakfast, sitting half into the fire and close together, and having our coffee and eggs and toasted rolls, he said suddenly in the midst of our laughing and talking, 'Now! I do wish your sisters could see us through some peep-hole of the world!' 'Yes,' said I, 'As long as they do not hear us through the peep-hole!' For indeed the foolishness of this conversation would . . . Certainly we are apt to talk nonsense with ever so many inflections and varieties . . . He amuses me and makes me laugh . . . such spirits he has, and power of jesting and amusing—alternating with the serious feeling and thinking."

He was also tender and patient and strong. He had to be, to make up to her for the loss of her family—the father who answered none of her letters, the brothers who took his part. It was only now that Mr. Barrett was turned against them that the two realized how very close had been the attachment between father and daughter. Browning saw Ba's suffering but could do nothing to allay it except by silently demonstrating that everything which her father had given in considerateness and understanding and strength he also gave her —with selfless love. But the rigid habit of dependence was too strong for Ba to break without a struggle. It was all the more difficult because the bonds were of the spirit, forged when illness and unhappiness had found her at her weakest. In 1838, soon after she had been removed to Torquay, she had written to Miss Mitford about a recurrent dream that came to her whenever she was disturbed by her father's absence. "I never told him of it, of course, but when I was last so ill, I used to start out of fragments of dreams, broken from all parts of the universe, with the cry on my lips, 'Oh papa, papa!' I could not trace it back to the dream behind, yet there it always was very curiously, and touchingly too, to my own heart."

The implications of the dream still held even though she now had a basis of comparison between her father and the husband whom she agreed with Mr. Kenyon in describing as an incarnation of the good and the true. What would she have felt if in her bliss she had learned that her father had expressed himself as preferring her "to be dead rather than alive and happy?"

They saw few people in Pisa except for Mrs. Jameson and her Geddie. But they too soon took their departure in the manner of a reconnoitering vanguard. Robert was quite content to remain alone with his wife and, in fact, looked upon the inevitable intrusion of society as a threat. "Those people will spoil all our happiness, if once we let them in,—you will see!" he said. "If you speak of your health and save yourself on that plea, they will seize upon me. Oh, don't I know them!"

"But, dearest," Ba placated him. "I am not going to let anybody in! If one of us lets them in it will be Wilson, most probably. But we need not suffer it. I desire it quite as little as you."

"There's that coarse, vulgar Mrs. T. . . . I do hope, Ba, if you don't wish to give me the greatest pain, that you don't receive that vulgar, pushing woman—"

"Well, now we are at Mrs. T. You will have your headache in a minute. . . ."

Ba herself was in flourishing health. In spite of it her husband would not let her walk upstairs but insisted on carrying her. With Wilson he took charge of ordering the dinners—thrushes, Chianti, and roasted chestnuts—of laying the fires and looking after all house-keeping details. "When I am so good as to let myself be carried . . . and so angelical as to sit on the sofa, and so considerate, moreover, as *not* to put my foot in a puddle, why, my duty is considered done to perfection," Ba jested.

There was good reason, however, for Browning's redoubled care at this time. Though he knew too little about the matter to be certain, though Ba assured him that he was entirely wrong, and though Wilson only suspected the condition of her mistress, he was hopeful that the marriage might be bearing fruit. Meanwhile he hovered about Ba in happy solicitude aided by Wilson who was gradually shedding her mistrust of the foreigners in whose country she found herself. Flush alone was unconcerned. He highly approved of Pisa, especially of its roasted chestnuts. He went out every day now and spoke Italian to the little dogs—an acquirement Wilson found somewhat more difficult with the human Pisans. But she was learning.

As winter gave way to spring there could be no more doubt about Mrs. Browning's state. At her least indiscretion Browning would cry out: "You want to kill me! You're playing with my life!" And he did not speak altogether in jest. Mrs. Browning bore the discomfort well and whenever she felt too weak she would take the remedy that Dr. Jago had prescribed. Wilson had her misgivings about the wis-dom of such a course and asked whether it would not be wise to consult a medical man. Mrs. Browning was reluctant to take a

strange doctor into her confidence and did nothing. Toward the
end of March she began to feel ill. In her ignorance she concluded
that she must be suffering from a strange form of influenza brought
on, as she thought, from having walked barefoot on the chilly tiles
one night when Wilson had been unwell. As her symptoms became
more alarming Browning called in Dr. Cook. Mrs. Browning, in the
fifth month of pregnancy, was having a miscarriage.

All the while she was in bed, deathly pale and very feeble, her
husband ministered to her with such devotion that Wilson lost her
reserve enough to exclaim: "I never saw a man like Mr. Browning
in all my life!" He had such gentleness, such goodness. On the last
day of the month Ba was sufficiently recovered to walk from the bedroom into the parlor—"all dressed and ringleted, and looking in the
glass on the road, saw myself a little blanched, but otherwise rather
improved than not!" Small comfort after the great disappointment.

Dr. Jago whom Mrs. Browning consulted about the morphine
gave the opinion that "*in such a case* . . . the morphia did no harm
at all!" But the Brownings had been so badly frightened that they
preferred to heed Wilson's misgivings. At any rate, in his letter to
Mrs. Jameson, Browning, in describing Ba's progress confided, "This
good, moreover, has been nature's doing, without strengthening
medicine of any kind."

By the middle of April of 1847 they left Pisa for Florence, soon
to be the center of their life in Italy. It was the cheapness that lured
them. For two hundred and fifty pounds a year, they were told, they
could live in excellent apartments, keep their own carriage and two
horses, and a man servant as well. Just before their departure a
priest came to visit them in full canonicals to bless the house and
its inhabitants. Browning met him in the passage. The good man was
startled at seeing an Englishman, but Browning, taking off his hat,
requested him to go on as if they were not there. "Nobody's blessing
could do any body any harm," he said.

They had hardly settled in rooms near Santa Maria Novella when
they started out for Vallombrosa, the sprawling white, square-towered
monastery set like a snow flat among the high green mountains.
They left Florence at four o'clock in the morning, partly to escape
the heat, mostly for the fun of adventure. Mrs. Browning, Wilson,
and Flush, together with the luggage, were packed in basket sledges
drawn by white oxen, while Browning rode alongside on horseback,
keeping pace with the lumbering beasts. From the city to Pelago

the road stretched evenly before them, but from there on to Pontas-
sieve, five miles distant, they found themselves in a landscape that
might have served Salvator Rosa for his weirdest imaginings. It was
a primeval world of mountains cleft suddenly by deep ravines, black
but for the shimmer of water at the bottom. Rocks of fantastic shapes
twisted like monsters turned motionless by enchantment. Beech
forests hung as if in midair, their branches mingling with the thick
foliage of the chestnut, while over them the eagles glided, watchful.
All about they saw stretches of pines rising supernaturally silent, out
of soil black as ink. It was terrifying and beautiful.

When they reached the monastery—it had taken them four hours
to travel the five miles—they received a very lukewarm welcome. A
new abbot had been installed, a righteous man jealous of his sanctity
and of the peace of mind of his monks. The presence of women
therefore was as welcome as a host of devils. The Brownings had
contemplated lingering pleasantly for at least a few weeks in the
mountain retreat. But after three days Browning was told that the
monastery could shelter them no more. In vain he used all his eloquence. At most the Lord Abbot could give him two more days. He
then pleaded his case with the "meditating monk" he had befriended.
The holy man shrugged and turned up his palms in a gesture of
impotence. "While I am abbot, I will be abbot," his superior had
told him. So he was abbot, and the tourists had to think of turning
their face toward Florence.

They had enjoyed their stay in spite of the fetid bread, "which
stuck in the throat like Macbeth's amen," said Ba. She had learned
the trick of pretending to eat it then slyly dropping it under the
table. As for the eggs and the milk they had counted on, "The hens
had got them to a nunnery and objected to lay . . . and the milk
and the holy water stood confounded." But beef, oil, and wine
were plentiful and Ba, in her restored health, did not have to be
coaxed.

With them at Vallombrosa had been G. W. Curtis, an American
journalist and a former member of Brook Farm. One day while they
were all together, Browning sat at the monastery organ which Milton
had played two hundred years earlier, and roused it to stirring peals.

Browning had to have music. Knowing it, Ba persuaded him to
rent a piano for their lodging in the Via delle Belle Donne. It cost
them ten shillings a month, including the hire of the music. It was
worth a hundred times that for the pleasure it gave them. Here house-

keeping was on a slightly grander scale than at Pisa where the heavy mugs used to distress Wilson. They had real cups now, and the dinners delivered by arrangement with the neighboring *trattoria* had enough courses to satisfy not only Lucullus but Flush.

"It is something *like!*" Wilson approved as she saw her mistress eating turkey, sturgeon, stewed beef, mashed potatoes and a dessert of cheese cake—the dinners served at the rate of two shillings six-pence a day for everything. They profited by the discoveries they had made in Pisa on the art of housekeeping. They also had their eyes opened to the systematized cheating of the foreigner by the Italian tradespeople who had mistaken them for millionaires for their sublime indifference to being taken in on all sides. But they were learning, if not always without cost.

No sooner had they settled in their apartment, piano and all, than they realized to their dismay that Florence's sunshine was beyond their reach since none of it penetrated their windows. They had taken the place on a pre-signed contract for six months, but Ba was so unhappy there that Browning, doing his usual poet's work in the way of domestic economy, took another lease on a suite of sunny rooms at Casa Guidi, facing the church of San Felice, happily named. The Grand Duke's palace lay exactly opposite the Piazza Pitti. From their balcony the Brownings had an enviable view of the many color-ful activities of the square, a place of fairs, pageants, and parades. The palazzo Guidi itself was on the Via Maggio. A minute's walk from its arched portal, in the blazing sunshine, led to the beautiful Boboli Gardens back of the Pitti Palace.

Their first apartment at Casa Guidi was a furnished one which they made homelike with the household goods they had brought from England. But as they came to know Florence—"the most beautiful of cities, with the golden Arno shot through the breast of her like an arrow"—Florence, home of art and poetry, whose every stone marked a tradition of glory, they knew that it was their heart's dwelling place. One had only to stand at the windows to look out on beauty—the vivid life of the square from the front balcony, the flowering orange and camellias from the rooms that faced the garden. Churches and galleries held treasures of art. The Cellini Perseus holding aloft the head of Medusa stood only a short walk away, in the Loggia de' Lanzi, whose square had heard the last words of Savonarola from the pyre, and witnessed the final defiance of the martyred Giordano Bruno. Farther on Giotto's campanile soared into the air, singing in its wonderful harmony of breadth and line. In the piazza, Brunelleschi, forever contemplative in stone, gazed skyward on the dome for God's house that he had designed in a magical combination of vision and mathematics. Over all, the Italian sky created endless variations of color and light.

They were supremely happy. Even Wilson was becoming cosmopolitan enough to venture into the museums to look at the wonders that Mr. and Mrs. Browning found so enthralling. Her first experience had nearly cured her of art forever, so shocking had she found the two Venuses, a marble one and another, painted by Titian, right overhead—the first *nearly*, and the other *stark*, naked. She told Mrs. Browning all about them, and of how her modesty had kept her from going beyond the door of the Tribune. After Mrs. Browning's laughing explanation Wilson said she thought she would try again— but not until the troublesome modesty had subsided. She had more leisure in Italy than she had had at Wimpole Street. A little Italian maidservant, Annunziata, worked about the house and sometimes took Flush out for a walk. A man of all work was being considered for the larger apartment at Casa Guidi which the Brownings were planning to furnish from the proceeds of their poetry.

They were both writing again, a fact which Browning's friend, Joseph Arnould, communicated to Alfred Domett. "I would to God he would purge his style of obscurities," Arnould sighed, "that the wide world would, and the gay world and even the less illuminated part of the thinking world, know his greatness even as we do."

As it happened, Browning was preparing a revised edition of his poems. Moxon was politely, but not enthusiastically, interested. In the financial account he sent the Brownings, it was easy to see which of the two poets he preferred to print. "I say nothing of my wife's poems and their sale," Browning wrote to him. "She is there, as in all else, as high above me as I would have her." He believed it. But he also believed in himself, a belief that Mrs. Browning fostered with the faith of her impeccable judgment as well as her love.

Since the *Dramatic Romances and Lyrics* of 1845, Browning had published the eighth and last issue of *Bells and Pomegranates* containing *Luria* and *A Soul's Tragedy*. That had been in April 1846. He had had for these two plays the advantage of Ba's suggestions and criticism. He had also received her candid opinion that she did not find drama the happiest medium for poetic expression, even though she admired the plays. The critics barely noticed the works.

As for the public, he might as well have dropped his booklets into a well. He himself considered his plays failures. The general consensus, except on the part of those few who illumine an age's darkness, would have included the rest of the *Bells* in the description. Yet *Dramatic Romances and Lyrics* had contained enough to make the poetry-loving public shout for joy, as Ba did when she exclaimed on reading them for the first time: "Now if people do not cry out about these poems, what are we to think of the world?" Only that it was deaf to everything but its own tumult and blind to any light but the dazzle of the Golden Calf.

Criticism was scant and tepid. Buyers seemed to avoid them for fear of contamination. Yet the yellow-wrapped pamphlet of scarcely two-dozen pages contained besides a large part of *Saul*, "The Flight of the Duchess," the poem inspired by the tomb in St. Prassede's church, the delicate "Garden Fancies" as well as "The Confessional" and "The Laboratory" with another handful of poems that have since enriched the makers of anthologies.

On his leaving England Browning had known that one phase of his poetic career was over and another beginning, just as in his emotional life the best was yet to be. Not that he thought of his poetry in terms of comparison. He had written with integrity and to the best of his ability. He would continue to do so. But just as his life had found greater depth and intensity, so too would his work. Meanwhile as conscientious artist, he labored to improve what he had done while waiting for the poetry of his life to mature into lasting art.

Mrs. Browning's finest poetry so far, the sonnets, the last of which was dated two days before her marriage, no eyes had seen but her own. In one of her letters to him she had intimated their existence in veiled terms and doubtless she would have shown them to him but that one day he chanced to say something against putting one's love into verse. Acutely sensitive, she put away the manuscript for the auspicious moment.

Like Browning, she was preparing another edition of her work with which Mr. Chapman was to inaugurate his new publishing house in October of 1850. She was also gathering impressions and writing. From the moment she had set foot in Italy she espoused the cause of Italian freedom. Austria became her enemy and with all the fervor of her soul she threw herself on the side of the Piedmontese. For that matter, the spirit of liberty burned in every Italian breast, taking on ardor with the accession of the former Bishop of

Imola to the Papal throne. More than Mazzini, more than Garibaldi or Daniele Manin, Pio Nono—Pius IX—became the accepted leader of the Italian people when, scarcely a month after his accession, he freed the hundreds of political prisoners rotting in the dungeons of his predecessor.

"Viva Pio Nono!" echoed through the streets.

"Viva!" Mrs. Browning took up the cry, justifying such Papist support by telling her friends in England that he was, after all, a liberator, a great man who rode about the streets on a mule and dreamed night and day of doing good, humbly. "Think of such a Pope!" she exclaimed.

She even considered going to Rome to express by her pilgrimage what a man she held him to be.

Browning, less headlong, reserved his opinion not only of Pio Nono but of Leopold II, Grand Duke of Tuscany, their neighbor at the Palazzo Pitti, across the square—"Our good Duke," to Ba who put him on par with His Holiness in liberalism.

But in 1847, in spite of the Pope and the Grand Duke, Italy was still suffering under the tyrannical system established by the Congress of Vienna. "Death to the Austrians!" rang from the crowds at political demonstrations throughout the unhappy country. But the Austrians and their oppression did not die. The people grew more restive and demanded action which it was not in the power of the pontiff to give. "They want to make a Napoleon of me—a poor priest," he said, cognizant of his impotence.

Liberty, however, had become as essential to the Italian people as the air they breathed, till it seemed as if it were the alternative to death. Already hundreds had given their lives for it, like the Bandiera brothers, whose story, heard from her husband, perhaps, had made Mrs. Browning set them up high in her libertarian pantheon. Other heroes like them had taken up the individual fight in the absence of an efficient, organized large movement. The movement too, however, was beginning to rise and grow. Men, women, and children were keenly alive to the ferment in the air. One would almost have thought that liberty was the first word taught to the young. Mrs. Browning heard it and responded by echoing back her sympathy through her poetry.

One day she sat down and began a long poem, *Casa Guidi Windows*—the drama of the Italian struggle as she saw it enacted on the great square.

I heard last night a little child go singing
    'Neath Casa Guidi Windows, by the church,
"O bella libertà, O bella!" . . .

A little child, too, who not long had been
    By mother's finger steadied on his feet,
    And still "O bella libertà," he sang. . . .

She must have begun the poem soon after her letter describing
Florence "with the golden Arno shot through the breast of her."
Just as in her love sonnets she had transmuted to poetry many of the
emotions and even phrases of her letters to Browning, in *Casa Guidi
Windows*, on which she was to work for the next three years, she
turned her impressions to vivid imagery and her passions to lasting
art. In the poem the line of prose is expanded to

    . . . Golden Arno as it shoots away
Through Florence's heart beneath her bridges four,—
    Bent bridges seeming to strain off like bows,
    And tremble while the arrowy undertide
    Shoots on. . . .

The 12th of September marked their first wedding anniversary,
but long before the day Browning mentioned it so often that she
felt as if they were celebrating it many times over. Her happiness
was unbounded. But who could have been other than happy with a
husband who spoiled her as Robert did? Robert, Robert. Her letters
were starred with the name she had once been in awe of using and
with Robert's many acts of tenderness and devotion. After three
o'clock dinner he would wheel a comfortable chair into the dressing
room, the coolest in the house, and make her sit in it. Then he poured
eau de cologne into her palms and on her forehead and fanned her
till her eyes closed of themselves for the siesta. That had been during
the hot months of the summer, but he found other ways of minis-
tering to his love. As their *great day*, as Robert called it, approached
they twitted each other about claiming the flitch of bacon promised
by custom to people a year married who had never quarreled. "Only
I say to Robert, it will scarcely be a fairly divided recompense"—so
much did she owe him. The debt was on his side, he insisted, and
made her very happy "by saying again and again such things as can't
be repeated nor forgotten, besides, that never in his life, from his
joyous childhood upwards, had he enjoyed such happiness as he

had known with me . . . There has not been a cloud nor a breath," she wrote to Henrietta. "The only difference is from happy to happier, and from being loved to being loved more. . . ."

As if Florence had resolved to observe their anniversary on a magnificent scale, it held a demonstration on Piazza Pitti to celebrate an act of libertarian generosity on the part of Grand Duke Leopold. He had chosen that day to give his people a National Guard, despite the mandates of Austria. The rejoicing of the Italians, and for that matter, of the forty thousand strangers who had poured in, together with the deputations from the different Tuscan states, expressed itself in processions, music, and general good will of kisses and embraces.

Ensconced on a throne of cushions on her balcony, amid flowering plants and a tall datura branch arching overhead, with Robert beside her making skeptical remarks on the sincerity of rulers in general and the Grand Duke in particular, Ba watched the seething square. As far as the eye could see, the windows rippled with silks of blue and scarlet. Banners floated everywhere. Hands waving handkerchiefs or throwing flowers vied with exultant faces from every balcony and doorway as endless deputations filed past. The Magistracy came first with their insignia; then the lawyers and the priesthood—the friars with worldly-wise sidelong glances—and finally the people's representatives from every state of Tuscany. Siena's she-wolf bristled on the folds of her banners, and Pisa's heraldic hare, and Massa's golden, and Pienza's silver, lion, and the prancing steed of Arezzo. Last came the sympathizing lovers of Italy from other nations, the English, the Greek, the French, raising aloft their standards to the exultant clamor of the grateful Italians.

The Austrians alone were missing, by order of the police who had warned them to stay away and not stir up trouble, as they had done in Rome recently in order to justify the interference of the Austrian government. "It is hateful and loathsome," cried Ba. "Metternich puts out his fangs, trembling in his hole, poor reptile, for his power in Italy."

Directly opposite, at the windows of the Ducal Palace, Leopold stood with his family to receive the thanks of his people. His eyes brimmed with tears at the affecting sight.

For three hours the deputations kept arriving. Ba grew tired and so did Browning who had a cold and was looking very pale. At his usual hour Flush stood up before his master and barked to be taken out for his walk. The excitement below had subsided so Browning, not well enough to take Flush out himself, sent him forth with Annunziata, for the usual run.

The moment the two set foot out of doors a little dog passed by, one of those pert Florentines with turned-up tails. Not only did Flush run, but he ran away after the little dog. Upstairs without him returned Annunziata. *"Dov'è Flush?"* her mistress asked, as memories of London and Mr. Taylor came into her mind. "Where is Flush?" Browning inquired.

"Oh, è niente," said the girl lightly. *"Tornerà presto, presto."*

But flush did not come back *presto, presto*. Hours passed and no Flush, and on their wedding day, too! As it grew dark, Ba's eyes filled with tears as she remembered the new collar he was wearing in honor of the occasion. Not that she suspected the Florentines, but what about the forty thousand strangers? . . . Browning forgot his headache and scoured Piazza Pitti—in vain. Flush might just as well have been spirited away in the dog-stealer's sack for all one could find of him.

Late that night as Robert and Ba were watching the illumination that closed the day's festivities, she was deeply affected by "children two years old, several of whom I heard lisping 'Vivas!'" (Was it next day that she thought of them and wrote, "I heard last night a little child go singing . . . ," beginning her most important poem since her marriage?)

Sadly they went to bed, full of melancholy imaginings about Flush. Alas that they should have been so trusting!

In the morning, however, while Ba was dressing, there was a dash against the door of the room. "It's either Flush or the devil," she cried.

It was Flush looking very guilty and very tired.

"Quite disgraceful for a respectable dog like him," said Robert reproachfully.

Chapter XVI: The Claimant

IT WAS not Flush alone who breathed in romance and liberty with the Italian air. Wilson too found herself assailed in her exemplary modesty and little by little began to raise her eyes from the pavement to the noble height of Signor Righi, ducal guard at the Palazzo Pitti. He was a notable man, imposing and indeed handsome, with an open amiable countenance. He, on his side, was not averse to the attractions of the *forestiera*, a word which, to the Italian mind, implied the ring of the exotic as well as of gold. All foreigners were rich, for how could they travel and live in expensive apartments and keep dogs and carriages?

To Wilson the magnificence of the towering Signor Righi counted for more than wealth or position. He was well educated, moreover, and the son of a medical man. He could also, of course, be said to have position, for not everyone who came was chosen to grace the uniform of the ducal guard. How like one of those embarrassing statues he was that her mistress went to the galleries to see! Pretty soon Wilson was wearing a betrothal ring—and so was Signor Righi, observing Italian custom. Mr. and Mrs. Browning were happy for Wilson's sake. They were pleased as well with her sudden enthusiasm for Florence and the strides she was making in the language. What had been so potent in Signor Righi to stir Wilson's natural passions? Surely not the fact that he was "six feet long" as the Italians would have it.

"I have too high an opinion of Wilson to believe that she has chosen him on the mere strength of his externals," Mrs. Browning defended her. Whatever the fascination it was all for the best and everyone was happy.

Mrs. Jameson alone was none too pleased with the combined effect of Italy and the Brownings upon Geddie who was constantly falling in love. To the adoring aunt, however, Geddie was virtue itself unmoved and inviolable, a rock against which all males were tempted to hurl themselves.

"Geddie has such charming qualities," she would say, "that three out of five men would be in love with her at once."

Browning, while seeming to agree, would make sly comments about "this Gerardine as pure as the angels who couldn't be trusted to walk down the street by herself lest she should run away with the first man at the corner."

"Oh, not you, Browning, of course!" Mrs. Jameson would follow her single track. "I am aware that under no possible circumstances could she have been calculated to please you—I only speak of ordinary men."

Aunt and niece left Florence for Rome where the worst happened. Geddie herself—Mrs. Jameson was convinced of the girl's culpability this time—Geddie had fallen in love. She actually admitted her offense, remained unrepentant and set her, Mrs. Jameson, at defiance! Back in Florence she poured out her troubles into her friends' ears. Geddie, think of it! Madly in love with a bad artist! An unrefined gentleman!! A Roman Catholic converted from Protestantism!!! A poor man!!!! With a red beard!!!!!

"The truth is," she ended her list of tribulations, "the dear child who never thought in her whole life before of love and marriage, has had it all put into her head at once by the sight of your and Browning's happiness. Oh, I see it! I understand how it was!"

"But he is so good and generous!" Geddie spoke up for her swain, Robert MacPherson. "And handsome too, and likely to be a good artist when he tries . . . And likely to turn back again from being a Roman Catholic. Why, he left off smoking just to please Aunt Nina and was very firm!"

In spite of anything "Aunt Nina" Jameson could do or say, Geddie clung to her red-bearded artist and later triumphed by marrying him.

It is easy to see that the life of the Brownings had no lack of excitement. They began making friends. Hiram Powers, the American sculptor, went often to see them, and so did Miss Boyle, a niece of the Earl of Cork who lived with her mother at Villa Careggi and shared the Brownings' chestnuts and mulled wine of an evening. "And a good deal of laughing she and Robert make between them!" They became acquainted with the Hoppners who had known Byron and Shelley. Later George Stillman Hillard, another of Mrs. Browning's American admirers who like Poe but without his Chiappino reservations had praised her work, called upon them at Casa Guidi. Finally they met William Wetmore Story and his wife and a lifelong friendship began with advantages to both sides in intellectual pleasures and social intimacy.

The literary Jesuit, Father Prout—Francis Mahony of *Fraser's Magazine*—now chiefly remembered for his *Bells of Shandon*, always could be counted upon to drop in whenever he was in Florence. It was one of the Brownings' jokes that wherever they went they would be sure to meet the wandering ecclesiastic. On their wedding journey they had scarcely reached Leghorn when, behold, the first object that met their gaze in the harbor was Father Prout standing upon a rock, contemplative.

One evening on their arrival in Florence, Browning came in from a walk, with an "Ah, ha! I have been kissed by somebody since I saw you last!"

Ba gasped with joy thinking that by some miracle one of her sisters had made her way to Italy. But no. It was Father Prout spending an hour or two in the city on his way to Rome and who, meeting Browning, "kissed him in the street, mouth to mouth, a good deal to his surprise." Something profitable came of that encounter, however. Before leaving Florence Father Prout promised an introduction to the Grand Duke's librarian at the Pitti, a learned man who would give them access to the books they missed.

Florence, fair city of the lily, built on a field of flowers, Florence, heart of liberty, became "our Florence" to the poets. They knew every reflected sky-picture in the Arno as well as her historic canvases: the Cimabue *Madonna* that had long ago been carried in procession to such jubilation that from then on the quarter of the city where the artist lived was called the Borgo Allegri. They knew their Giotto and their Fra Angelico. In the Church of San Lorenzo they saw again and again Michelangelo's figures on the Medici tombs, the Night and Day, and Dawn and Twilight, those marble eternities couchant on the ashes of ephemeral glory. They looked up, on their walks, to Giotto's bell-tower, to Mrs. Browning

> like an unperplext
> Fine question heavenward, touching the things granted
> A noble people, who, being greatly vext
> In act, in aspiration kept undaunted.

They went often to the Loggia de' Lanzi to see

> Cellini's godlike Perseus, bronze or gold,
> (How name the metal, when the statue flings
> Its soul in your eyes?) . . .

Lines would come to Mrs. Browning which she later remembered for *Casa Guidi Windows*. Meanwhile her husband gathered impressions for his growing gallery of *Men and Women*.

They knew the city's traditions and thrilled to them. On the anniversary of Savonarola's death they too, with Florence's patriots, would strew with violets the few feet of ground where

> Savonarola's soul went out in fire.

That spring of 1848 the tribute of violets held special significance for the Florentines. The Grand Duke—"Our Good Grand Duke!" cried Ba clapping her hands—had given Tuscany a constitution, an excellent constitution with every religious distinction abolished at one sweep and many political freedoms permitted. All this, Ba asserted in her enthusiasm, by his free will and after long reflection.

The history books state the case quite differently. On February 15 the people of Tuscany had risen in righteous anger, following the example of Palermo, Messina, and Padua with their respective tyrants, and compelled the Grand Duke to listen. Far from being granted, the constitution had been won with difficulty by the awakened people. Everywhere in Italy, indeed, everywhere in Europe, liberty was leading the nations to such purpose that 1848 became known as the year of revolution. The Brownings cheered at the people's gains. Every morning when Robert went to the post and to look at the newspapers, Ba would call after him, "Bring me back news of a revolution!" Generously he would bring her back news of several. They shared the same views on many questions, except that Browning, with the Englishman's natural mistrust of violent political changes, lifted his brows at certain things. Ba would tease him by crying out when they disagreed: "*A bas les aristocrats!*"

They had never, for example, seen the Grand Duke through the same roseate spectacles. A shrewd judge of character, Browning quickly detected the weakness of the man. He had not been moved to tears by the Grand Duke's demagoguery when, on taking his patriotic oath, he had kissed his little sons before the clamorous people. How different with Ba!

> I saw the man among his little sons, . . .

she wrote of the event, after the Duke had proved his treachery,

> And I, because I am a woman, I
> Who felt my own child's coming life before

The prescience of my soul, and held faith high,—
I could not bear to think, whoever bore,
That lips so warmed could shape so cold a lie.

But shape that lie he did. Not only that, but soon the eyes of the hopeful were blinded by the dust of the Grand Duke's flying feet.

Browning bore his disillusionment calmly. But then, he had not expected as much as Ba from the ruler, nor, for that matter, from his comic opera civic guard, all shining helmets and epaulettes, who paraded endlessly in the piazza till he found himself asking: "Surely, after all this, they would use their muskets?"

In France liberty had led the people that year to greater effect. Mrs. Browning read the news avidly and her letters were staunchly libertarian. But perhaps because she had spent too much of her life in the calm level light of classical abstractions her thinking, if not her feeling, had a static quality that sometimes made it almost regressive. She found that her "heroic French" saw only half-truths. "Whatever, for instance, touches upon property," she wrote in a private letter, "is a wrong, and whatever tends to the production of social equality is absurd and iniquitous, and oppressive in its ultimate ends. Every man should have the right of climbing—but to say that every man should equally climb, (because the right is equal) is a wrong against the strong and industrious." Here, oddly, spoke the daughter of the West Indian plantation owner. "My idea of a republic" she wrote again, "is for every born man in it to have room for his faculties—which is perfectly different from swamping individuality in a mob."

At that very time the woman whom she respected above all women was working actively for the Republic. For George Sand to think an ideal was to help realize it. To her the people was never the mob. "I have seen the last barricades opening under my feet," she exulted at the great events. "I have seen the people, grand, sublime, sincere, largehearted—the people of France united in the heart of France, in the heart of the world!"

It was not enough for her to write to her friends; privately. In public brochures addressed to the middle class and to the rich, George Sand dealt courageously with public issues, warning against oppressive measures, recommending tolerance toward progressive ideas. "If the majority possesses the truth of the present, the minority holds the truths of the future. That is why you must respect and esteem the minorities, and give them freedom." Here was grandeur as well as practical common sense. But then George Sand had not had to wait till she was forty to break from her study to life and liberty.

This year, also in March, the Brownings' hope for a child was again frustrated when, soon after the Grand Duke's affectionate demonstration among his sons, Mrs. Browning had another miscarriage. She recovered with remarkable speed as before, but her husband thought it best to remove her to the little seaside town of Fano against the summer heat of Florence. There they found that they had exchanged bad for worse. Fano was so oppressively hot, in spite of the Adriatic, that they had enough of it after three days. In that short time, however, they had driven up to the monastery on the crest of Mount Giove, done their duty as tourists in the Cathedral of San Fortunato for Domenichino's frescoes, and visited the Church of Sant'Agostino for "The Guardian Angel" by Guercino.

Browning stood long before the picture of the sweet-faced angel teaching a little child to pray. The great white wings spread protectively over the naked babe whose folded hands are gently instructed by the angel's, whose rounded limbs have only just learned to kneel upon the tomb that is his pedestal. From a rift in the clouds three cherubs watch the lesson. Next day Browning returned to look at the painting with his wife, and once again before they left for Ancona.

The imaged lesson followed him there. The presence of his wife brought home his own felicity. The sea at Fano, at Ancona, spoke of distance, of dear ones far away. The complex of emotions found outlet in the eight stanzas of the poem, "The Guardian-Angel," which he wrote within sight and hearing of the sea-city's purple tides. A mood of quiet tenderness, of religious concentration, permeates the poem which time has made one of his best beloved—deservedly. There is also an undercurrent of a vague troubling of the soul.

> Dear and great Angel, wouldst thou only leave
>   That child, when thou hast done with him, for me! . . .

cries the Protestant brought up in the teachings of the Independent Chapel, and unaware of the Catholic belief that everyone has his guardian angel.

> If this was ever granted, I would rest
>   My head beneath thine, while thy healing hands
> Close-covered both my eyes beside thy breast,
>   Pressing the brain, which too much thought expands,

> Back to its proper size again, and smoothing
> Distortion down till every nerve had soothing,
>   And all lay quiet, happy and supprest.

But he had one who ministered to him as Guercino's "bird of God" might have done.

"My angel with me . . . My Love is here," he wrote of his wife in the last two stanzas of the poem which closed with the gentle resignation of an amen. In her own work in progress Mrs. Browning had paid him a similar tribute:

> And Vallombrosa, we two went to see
> Last June, beloved companion.

Leaving Ancona, they visited Loreto and then Ravenna. There they made a pilgrimage to Dante's bones which the city of his exile had refused to return to Florence that had cast him out. In the church of Santa Croce only an empty cenotaph memorialized him.

But the Florentines had not forgotten him, as the Brownings saw on their return. Nor had they relinquished their struggle despite the Grand Duke's playing at fast and loose with their demands. Near Santa Maria del Fiore there was a paving stone which tradition had known for many years as Dante's. On it, they said, he used to pull out his chair at twilight and unburden his laden spirit to the friends who passed by. Now, more often than ever before, the stone became the meeting-place of the Tuscan patriots planning the future of a united Italy.

Browning was not well. He had fallen ill in Fano and the malaise still lingered. He was also discouraged—as what true artist is not—about his poetry and how little the English public cared for it. Both factors may account for the hint of dejection in "The Guardian-Angel." At that very time, however, a group of artists and poets, boys still in their teens, were starting an artistic renaissance in London which, though they called it Pre-Raphaelite, included Browning as one of its animating spirits.

Dante Gabriel Rossetti, the leader of the movement, was already known to Browning by name, for in the autumn of 1847 he had received a letter from the youth asking whether he, Browning, had written the anonymous *Pauline* which he had read and copied out at the British Museum. It was not until 1848, however, that Dante Gabriel with his brother William and his sister Christina (not a member though a leading spirit), the painter John Everett Millais,

Holman Hunt and a few others, founded the Pre-Raphaelite Brother-
hood. Their aims were clear: to protest against the intellectual emptiness of their contemporaries and to bring back dignity and sincerity
to art. Besides planning an artistic revolution, they set out to storm
the bulwarks of the Philistines.

Rossetti exalted Browning as the spirit of modernity and rebellion,
the pharos of individuality, the clarion voice of the new renaissance,
and for proof he would read to the brethren hour-long passages
from *Paracelsus* and *Sordello* which he, at any rate, had no trouble
in understanding.

Mrs. Browning too the Pre-Raphaelites included in their orbit.
When they drew up their list of immortals—individuals who had
conferred immortality upon themselves by their achievement—they
found only two women worthy of mention. One was Joan of Arc, the
other Elizabeth Barrett Browning. It was with Browning, however,
that Rossetti felt more akin for his understanding of the medieval
and renaissance world which at that time was more real to Rossetti
than Victoria's. He also admired the vividness of Browning's imagery
and the richness of color and composition in his word pictures. One
of his earliest watercolors, "The Laboratory," Rossetti painted from
Browning's poem of a woman's devilish revenge upon her more
beautiful rival.

But the Brownings in Florence knew nothing of this resurgence
in England.

They had no sooner returned to Casa Guidi than their Old Man of
the Mountain, Father Prout, came calling and, once settled upon
them at his smoking post, refused to budge for hours at a time. Day
after day he came, till the Brownings thought it a decided gain if
they managed to finish their tea before his arrival. Then wine would
be rung for as a matter of course and "an apparatus for spitting"
brought in. In his poor state of health Browning found the whole
procedure detestable and there was a general burst of indignation
and a throwing open of doors the moment Father Prout's back was
turned. Still, both he and Ba liked the man and his jolly conversation
—and he did help Robert to regain his strength by a diet of eggs in
port wine, whipped up by his own capable hand the while their
man-servant watched malevolently, muttering, "This horrid *pretaccio*
wants to murder the master!"

Mrs. Browning was at that time—the end of November 1848—past
the fifth month of pregnancy, the longest period she had ever

succeeded in carrying a child. There was reason to hope that at last she would be rewarded. She had been very careful to do nothing to endanger her condition and had even left off the morphine entirely. Perhaps because of the auspicious auguries she and Browning began refurnishing her bedroom.

Early that year they had taken a six-room apartment at Casa Guidi and set about buying furniture for it. They had to be very careful of their finances since all the money they could count on came from Mrs. Browning's annual income, the proceeds from her poetry and Browning's negligible earnings from the same source. His father had given him a modest sum to start out with and he could always be depended upon to help. But Browning was proud and independent. Therefore when they began looking for the furniture for their palatial rooms it was to the curio shops that Browning went for it.

He did not do badly. With true antiquarian instinct he chose the very pieces that would best suit the height and spaciousness of their drawing room and anteroom where the piano had already been installed, in the place of honor. He bought rococo chairs, huge carved bookcases, tables and sofas. The only requirements Ba had suggested were a spring sofa to loll on and a supply of rain water for her complexion. Browning got her the first, and from the owners of Casa Guidi obtained an oil jar, large enough to hold the captain of the forty thieves, for the rain water which would fall from heaven. He bought satin from cardinals' beds, tapestries and hangings and other works of art. One day he came home with some paintings which he had found in a grain-shop on the outskirts of Florence. In his enthusiasm he was certain that they were Cimabues, Giottinos, and Ghirlandaios. At any rate they were hung in the drawing room in massive frames of black wood alternating with mirrors, wall hangings, and plaster casts.

There was another picture which Ba kept where she could look at it. Soon after she and Robert had taken their apartment she had asked for the picture of Henrietta: "Papa's I particularly want, and shall hang it up in my bedroom, opposite the bed. . . ."

Browning who had to have solitude for his writing, took over a small narrow room and made it look as much as possible like his Camberwell study. Ba, who could write anywhere, usually curled up in a vast green velvet easy-chair matching a vaster sofa of the same color in the drawing room and there, on scraps of paper resting on her knees, she put down the verses of *Casa Guidi Windows* as they came to her. They worked independently of each other and neither saw the other's work until it was finished.

Drawing room, study and anteroom all had their lares and guiding spirits. The death mask of Keats and an austere relief of Dante were in the salon. Medallions of Tennyson and Carlyle, for whom they reserved the Prophet's Chamber complete with bed and candlestick, hung in the dining room. Their most cherished possessions, their books, stood row on row in a tremendous case, carved with angels, infants and serpents, a treasure they discovered in a convent. No wonder people thought their salon "like a room in a novel."

Now they curtained Mrs. Browning's bed room anew in white muslin in a rather large pattern. They bought a chest of drawers of walnut inlaid with ivory in intricate designs. (Ba had always had a passion for chests of drawers even when they had had nothing to put into them. Browning, catering to her whim, presented her a few days later with a companion chest, also inlaid with ivory and furnished with gilt handles of Tritons holding masks. "My room will be something splendid when finished," she wrote Henrietta. Their nest decked and ready, they waited for what the new year would bring.

Before the old came to a close Browning was pulled back to the past on learning of the death of Sarah Flower. It was not so much her death as the memory of her sister's that grieved him, even though he felt genuinely afflicted. He had been in Italy when, almost exactly two years earlier, the funeral services for Eliza had been held by Mr. Fox in his South Place Chapel, before a gathering of her friends. Her own music was played and then Mr. Fox, struggling against his grief, stood up and uttered the one word, "God!" There was a long pause before he could go on with a brief and moving address to the Almighty. "Teach the heart to say," he prayed, "in filial submission and filial confidence, not our will but Thine be done!"

The news, read in cold print, made Browning relive his adolescent years, so much influenced by Eliza. He thought of *Pauline*. He thought of his letters, every one of which, together with copies of his immature poetry, Eliza had preserved. What would become of them now? Would those papers be discovered and published for a sensation-avid public, a public that would not read his poems but would relish any innuendo? In a panic he wrote to Mr. Horne, on the 3rd of December, to try to secure every scrap for him from the executors. "Poor Eliza Flower," he added, "has left us only her strange beautiful memory"—a memory which to the end could not be stirred in him without the deepest emotion.

As January of the new year went into February, Mrs. Browning drew near her term. The doctor was hopeful that all would go well even though Mrs. Browning was forty-three and had a long history of illness. She had taken every precaution this time, and prayed that at last the hypothetic claimant whom she and Browning had discussed before their marriage would come to crown their happiness.

It had been a humorous interchange of letters, three years ago, started by Browning's over-scrupulosity in not wanting to benefit by Ba's income. He had then insisted on her making out a will, leaving her "advantages" to her brothers and sisters, a suggestion that Ba with good common sense dismissed as monstrously unfair. Certain reasons for her refusal she made explicit enough for him to understand—which he did when he replied that, yes, "there may be even a *claimant* . . . of whatever either of us can bequeath—who knows?"

The claimant, "a fine, strong boy, like Harry Gill with the voice of three," a voice, indeed that made Browning aware of his existence through a thick wall and a double door, arrived at Casa Guidi on the 9th of March, 1849. Mrs. Browning bore her twenty-one hours' pain without one cry or tear, and recovered with extraordinary speed. Browning was so overwhelmed by this latest of Ba's achievements that he lapsed into ungrammar in one of his letters broadcasting the news. "Ba is going on perfectly good . . ." God, he went on, had rewarded that dearest, most precious of creatures for her patience, goodness, and self-denial. "That resolution of leaving off the morphine, for instance. Where is one among a thousand *strongmen* that would have thrown himself on the mercy of an angel, as she did on mine, quite another kind of being!"

She now appeared in her little front caps of net with a worsted edge—Wilson's handiwork—the picture of blissful motherhood. "You never saw such a fat, rosy, lively child," she boasted with a new pride. Henceforth her letters never failed to contain some allusion to the beauty, the intelligence, the wonder of her little Florentine.

Almost immediately the Brownings engaged a nurse whom they equipped in the Italian fashion, with the customary large, uncut Tuscan straw hat and long blue streamers—the color denoting the sex of her charge—a gown trimmed with blue ribbons, a white collar, a smart muslin apron, and a fine pocket handkerchief. This costume would carry her through the summer. In winter she would wear a beaver hat trimmed with black feathers and a habit to match.

As it happened Flush too had a new coat to honor the baby's
arrival, although it was really because of the Italian fleas that he
acquired it. In fact he had been so tormented by them that when,
some time earlier, the house trembled from a slight earthquake,
Robert had supposed it to be caused by Flush solacing himself by
a hearty scratch. For the poor dog's sake as well as for his own comfort, he had shaved the faithful follower to a hair's breadth of his
hide, except for a ruff that gave him the look of a lion. Now the
fur had grown back all glossy and brown. "If you were to see how
his eyes blaze!" Ba wrote her sisters. "But his insolence of vainglory
is incredible even for Flush." He now went out by himself, knowing
every street in Florence, and stayed away for hours together, making
friends with other dogs and with the venders in the market square
who gave special privileges to this *cane inglese*. No one worried over
his safety any more. He was as much at home in the city as at
Casa Guidi.

Hardly a week after the birth of Browning's son, and before she
could rejoice at the event, Browning's mother died. The shock threw
Browning into an abyss of grief even though Sarianna had tried to
soften the blow by carefully prepared letters which first told of grave
illness—actually after the mother's death—and then of the end itself.
There had always been a strong bond between mother and son, to the
extent of his suffering a sympathetic headache whenever she was
ailing. He blamed himself that during the three years he had been
away from England he had not once paid a visit home. Now he
could not. He told Ba that it would break his heart just to see his
mother's roses on the wall, or the place where she used to lay her
garden gloves and shears.

Ba, in her unfailing sympathy with her husband, suggested the
one thing which she knew would comfort him. They must call the
baby Wiedemann, thus keeping up the memory of the mother's
maiden name. Hence, when the child was three months old, they took
him to the French Evangelical Protestant Church, which was the
chapel of the Prussian Legation in Florence, and there had him
baptized Robert Wiedemann Barrett Browning. In this manner Mr.
Barrett who had not answered a single one of his daughter's letters,
not even the one announcing his grandson's birth, was also remembered.

Like all fairly well-to-do Florentines, the Brownings left the city
for the Bagni di Lucca for the summer. But not before an event that

convinced them never again to put their faith in princes. Not that Robert had ever believed in either duke or Pope. Ba, however, was much more trusting, possibly for a wished-for triumphant ending for her poem of liberation.

One May day, while her babe was sleeping, she heard the sound of tramping hoofs and looked up eagerly.

"Alas! Alas, Signora! These must be the Austrians!" cried the Tuscan nurse in dismay.

"No!—Do not wake the child," she said quickly, thinking that if such were the case the little one might as well sleep on through the world's baseness. When she looked out of the window there could be no mistake about it. From end to end the street was crowded with Austria's soldiers—ten thousand of them, and more coming, to reinstate with their bayonets the man who had fled the revolution. And so Grand Dukes come back!

"Wretched, infamous man!" she cried. "That ever I should have felt compassion for that man!"

Meanwhile, although the windows were crowded with faces and the streets bordered with people, not a sound came from them as in consternation they watched Austria's thousands trampling down their freedom.

At Lucca the Brownings celebrated their third wedding anniversary, their baby with them in a cap trimmed with pink ribbons and with cheeks to match. When Wilson brought him in he had a rose in his tiny fist, stretching it out for his mother to take; then by Wilson's contrivance, he held out another for his father. Wilson, as proud of the baby as if he were her own, insisted that he looked like the Barretts. Ba saw the resemblance but maintained that the mouth and chin were Robert's.

"Do you both of you thank God for me—I am not thankful enough!" she wrote to her sisters. "There is more love between us two at this moment than there ever has been. . . . We live heart to heart all day long and every day the same."

One morning, shortly after breakfast, while Browning was gazing out of the window facing a tall mimosa and a little church court, he heard Ba come in again a few moments after she had left. She stood behind him and slid something into the pocket of his coat.

"Do you know I once wrote some poems to you?" she said. And then, "There they are if you care to see them."

Then quickly she slipped out, leaving with him the manuscript of her sonnets.

Chapter XVII: Revolutions and Marvels

"YES, that was a strange, heavy crown, that wreath of Sonnets, put on me one morning unawares, three years after it had been twined . . ."[1] So Browning wrote to Julia Wedgwood in 1864. It was a heavy wreath because the laurel of immortality is perhaps the heaviest crown of all. Here the bays were triply woven, first because the sonnets carried their own immortality, then because Elizabeth Barrett Browning had written them and, finally, because Browning was the recipient.

What Browning thought or felt after reading the forty-four pages of his wife's manuscript remains in the silence of his private emotion. But when he could speak, he spoke out from the fullness of his heart and a sense of his unworthiness. For what mortal could be worthy of such tribute? Her letters had revealed the scope and range of her devotion. Their life together had proved with every passing moment the rightness of the union which for his sake she had at first been loth to consummate. The sonnets, while tracing the glory of their love, transcended it like all pure art and made it part of universal experience, so that there is no lover who does not hear his living heartbeat in the lyric pulsing of those passionate lines—the finest since Shakespeare, Browning pronounced them. Because he felt their greatness and because he found that greatness too much to bear alone, he urged his wife to publish them.

She would not hear of it at first, but Browning insisted. They need not be published under her name. The poems would thus speak for themselves with no hint of their very personal application. She weakened. Finally he suggested that she apply to them the name by which he sometimes called her, his "little Portuguese" from the Catarina of her poem. So the title *Sonnets from the Portuguese* evolved.

[1] This passage from the letters in *Robert Browning and Julia Wedgwood*, Frederick A. Stokes and Company, New York, 1937, corroborates the statement of Browning's son that the sonnets were given to his father at Bagni di Lucca and not at Pisa, as mistakenly believed, in 1846.)

They appeared in the second edition of Browning's two-volume collection, *Poems*, brought out under the imprint of Chapman and Hall, after Mr. Moxon withdrew out of timidity and care for his pocketbook. "Not minding the undue glory to me," Browning made it possible for the reader of 1850 to become acquainted with one of the cherished masterpieces of the literature of the heart.

The new volumes contained all his works except *Sordello, Pauline,* and *Strafford*. In April of the same year the fruits of his Italian harvest appeared in *Christmas-Eve and Easter-Day*, also under the imprint of Chapman and Hall.

The two poems, associated because of their mood and subject, form important chapters in Browning's quest for a personal religion between the Independent Chapel teachings of Camberwell and the broader aspects of the worship of God that, as a deeply religious man, he studied in the larger life about him. In a sense he had struck the keynote for the companion music of his *Christmas-Eve and Easter-Day* in the monochord of "The Guardian-Angel." In the new poems the music was more ambitious and the range covered heaven and earth as well as time and timelessness. Between the jogging rhythm of the opening of *Christmas-Eve* with the pathetically ludicrous faithful entering Zion Chapel, to the apocalyptic thunder of Judgment in *Easter-Day*, there is an aeon of spiritual development.

This time Browning did not speak through an imaginary character but in his own voice, as in the poem inspired by the angel at Fano, wherein he had at last obeyed the advice of his wife four years ago when she wrote him: "Yet I am conscious of wishing you to take the other crown besides—and after having made your own creatures speak in clear human voices, to speak yourself out of the personality which God made, and with the voice which he tuned into such power and sweetness of speech."

Certainly his power had never been greater even if the sweetness were wanting, at least in the opinion of the *Athenaeum* critic who praised him for beauties but deplored his lapses into doggerel. Yet to Browning's artistic conscience these lapses could have been justified as the most fitting for the matter dealt with, just as a musician would defend a dissonance.

None, however, could have felt anything but awe in this vision of Judgment when

> . . . I found
> Suddenly all the midnight round

One fire. The dome of heaven had stood
As made up of a multitude
Of handbreadth cloudlets, one vast rack
Of ripples infinite and black,
From sky to sky. Sudden there went,
Like horror and astonishment,
A fierce vindictive scribble of red
Quick flame across, as if one said
(The angry scribe of Judgment) "There—
Burn it!" And straight I was aware
That the whole ribwork round, minute
Cloud touching cloud beyond compute,
Was tinted, each with its own spot
Of burning at the core, till clot
Jammed against clot, and spilt in fire
Over all heaven. . . .

The message? some will ask. To struggle, and feel intensely alive
in the struggle in soul and body. To aspire

. . . And so I live, you see,
Go through the world, try, prove, reject,
Prefer, still struggling to effect
My warfare; happy that I can
Be crossed and thwarted as a man,
Not left in God's contempt apart,
With ghastly smooth life, dead at heart,
Tame in earth's paddock as her prize. . . .

The book sold two hundred copies within a fortnight and then
all sales ceased. But criticism and discussion kept it alive. In the
little magazine, the Germ, William Michael Rossetti kept Browning's light burning for the Pre-Raphaelites in a review of the new
work. A year passed before another of Browning's torchbearers, the
French critic Joseph Milsand, wrote an article on him in La Revue
des Deux Mondes and so initiated a lifelong friendship. However,
in England and in America Browning was still largely known as the
husband of Elizabeth Barrett Browning.

Mrs. Browning's reputation grew with everything she published.
She had the power to touch the heart, to speak directly to the
emotions, especially in her short lyrics whose unaffected simplicity
had universal appeal. In November of 1849 the infant daughter of one
of her friends, Sophia Cottrel, died. Her own child, just eight months

old, brought the mother's grief keenly to her, and she wrote "A Child's Grave in Florence" which the *Athenaeum* published. Like her son the child had been of English blood, of Tuscan birth.

> So, Lily, from those July hours,
>   No wonder we should call her;
> She looked such kinship to the flowers,
>   Was but a little taller . . .

> Too well my own heart understands,
>   At every word beats fuller—
> My little feet, my little hands,
>   And hair of Lily's color!

> But God gives patience; love learns strength,
>   And faith remembers promise . . .

From one mother's loss she made her appeal to all motherhood and with every reader she gained another admirer.

It was hardly to be wondered at, therefore, that when Wordsworth died in April of 1850, Henry Fothergill Chorley of the *Athenaeum* should suggest that the succession to the Laureateship should fall on Mrs. Browning, "as the equal to any living poet." Besides, there would be a certain appropriateness in choosing a woman to be Laureate to Queen Victoria. Mr. Chorley's suggestion found many adherents, not the least enthusiastic of them Browning himself.

"I am not likely to have it in any case," said Ba. "Oh, no!—notwithstanding the knight-errantry of the *Athenaeum*." She felt that Leigh Hunt should have the office despite his lack of delicacy and good taste. "But he is a great man and a good man."

The crown fell upon Rogers' denuded head. At eighty-seven, however, a man is more likely to think of joining the heavenly choir, so he wisely resigned the honor to Alfred Tennyson.

The year that ended had been full of vicissitudes not only for Florence but for the Brownings. Revolutions followed one another till one could scarcely keep up with them and "Grand-Duke out, Grand-Duke in" might have become a refrain in a children's game. The bells of San Felice more often rang an alarum than an office, while the square alternated between anger and rejoicing. One day the Brownings watched a tree of liberty being planted with great ceremony close to their door. The next they saw it ruthlessly uprooted as the winds of popular favor blew another way. They knew perilous moments, too. During one outbreak Browning barely managed to get home safely across the bridges. During another Dr. Harding, Ba's physician, had scarcely time to hide behind a stable door on the way to Casa Guidi when four men fell shot to death against it.

Mrs. Browning's political opinions had undergone considerable revision, not only concerning the Grand Duke—"that wonderful man"—but His Holiness as well, for Pio Nono had shown as much nimbleness at running as had Leopold when Liberty had become too uncomfortable an associate. "This new wonderful Pope" had now diminished to "the old serpent . . . wriggling his venom into free thought and action." It was impossible to keep up with political tergiversation. But calm always followed, if only briefly, and then the church of San Felice would echo to an air of Pergolese or some toccata of Galuppi's played on the organ by Robert while Ba sat by, listening.

Certain events in the immediate domestic circle had caused the impulsively forthgoing Ba to restrain her enthusiasm. Signor Righi, Wilson's betrothed, "with his most open, amiable, prepossessing countenance" had had an attack of cholera in the autumn. When he recovered from it he also recovered from his attachment. While he was convalescing at Prato he had not written Wilson as often as he might have done. Then, when he was quite well and Wilson expected him hourly to show his blooming six-foot handsomeness at the door of Casa Guidi, he never appeared. No one knew what to make of such negligence, but it soon became quite evident that Wilson would never become Signora Righi, for the gentleman resigned his post as a ducal bodyguard and became a haberdasher in Prato. By February of 1850 Wilson's heartache, according to her mistress, had been allayed. "She is over it completely. How could she continue to love such a man?" There, in his abysmal fall, we take our leave of Signor Righi.

Though Wilson did not marry that year, Henrietta did—in April —and so Captain Cook was rewarded for his five years of perseverance. But if Henrietta gained a husband she lost a father. Unlike her sister she had asked Mr. Barrett's permission, only to be told that if she dared to take the step he would never again hear her name mentioned.

Mrs. Browning was distressed by her father's unforgiving nature.

She believed that with the passing of time, however, his heart would soften, and she still had hope that some day she would have an answer to the letters she kept on writing to him. But she could not help dreading that Henrietta's marriage would revive his anger at her own, and she suffered because of it. Although she knew her father well, she did not know him wholly. When he made his will, exactly a year after Henrietta's marriage, there was no mention in it either of her, or of Elizabeth.

Still, news from home made the Brownings long for England, though not without pain, both because of Mr. Barrett's resentment, and the death of Browning's mother. Moreover they soon were filled with a general desire to travel—to Rome, to Naples, to Paris, even to New York.

"Robert! If I were to set my heart on going to live in New York! What then?"

"Why, then, we should go directly! But don't set your heart on it, Ba!"

They did not go to America, but America came to them. There was no visiting painter or writer who failed to call, armed with a letter of introduction. George Stillman Hillard, who had reviewed Mrs. Browning's poems, became rhapsodic before the visual presence. "I have never seen a human frame which seemed so nearly a transparent veil for a celestial and immortal spirit. She is a soul of fire enclosed in a shell of pearl. . . ." Was the language purple-tinged? It was not thought so in the middle of the past century, much less sophisticated than ours. Mrs. Browning herself could write without a blush and repeat *ad nauseam:* "My child is a little prince in his way, too . . . He runs about looking like a fairy born of a lily and a rose."

Hillard was not the most excessive in his praise. Christopher P. Cranch, the poet, and his wife, friends of Longfellow and Lowell, also turned ecstatic over that English pair whose union was the great romance of their day. The Greenoughs too came to worship, together with such a host of fellow Americans that many took it for granted that the Brownings were from across the ocean. Poe's praise of Mrs. Browning's poetry had done much toward spreading her fame in his country and had he ever gone to Italy Casa Guidi would have been for him a place of pilgrimage. But in 1849, from a Baltimore gutter at election time, he had taken the journey from which there is no return.

In the spring of 1850 the Brownings had a visit from Margaret Fuller who had secretly married the young Baron Ossoli two years earlier. Mrs. Browning admired the American, one of those women who like George Sand, were a glory to their sex. Browning respected her for her courage and intellect. "Dear, brave, noble Margaret Fuller," he described her, paying her the tribute of calling her by the name she had made famous. "He is a most true, cordial and noble man," she said of him. With Mrs. Browning she struck up a friendship which had as common ground their devotion to their little sons, both of the same age and born to them late in life. Angelino Ossoli, however, had not the beauty of the Browning child whom the Florentines would stop in the street, exclaiming: *"Che bel bambino."* Angelino was sickly, quiet and sad-eyed, a miniature of his young melancholy-looking father.

Sometimes with her husband, sometimes without, Margaret Fuller would call at Casa Guidi, or pick up Ba in a carriage to go driving.

After a few weeks of cordial intimacy, the Ossolis made ready to sail for America. Before leaving, Margaret Fuller called on the Brownings for the last time so that Angelino could give his farewell present to little Wiedemann. It was a small English Bible inscribed on the blank leaf: "Robert Wiedemann Barrett Browning, in memory of Angelo Eugene Philip Ossoli"—foreboding words from a child to a child.

The Ossolis were embarking on the *Elizabeth* at Leghorn. "I take the name as a good omen," said Margaret Fuller at parting. Then she remarked in her husband's presence that he had been warned never to make a voyage as the sea would be fatal to him.

"That does not much discompose you?" Browning asked Ossoli.

The baron only smiled and shook his head.

From Gibraltar Margaret Fuller sent a letter to her "dear, precious friends" begging them to write to her what should be "the first thing to meet her at home." Again, ominous words. She never reached home. Right off the Hamptons in Long Island, the brig which had weathered the ocean voyage was struck by a gale and went down in those wreck-filled waters after a struggle of more than eleven hours during which no help could reach her. Knowing her desperate situation, Margaret Fuller who could not swim, lashed little Angelino to an Italian woman and launched them from the sinking ship, hoping they would reach the shore.

She was drowned in the forecastle; Baron Ossoli's body was washed ashore. Thoreau, coming down from Concord to view the remains of his friend, leaned over her husband's corpse and ripped a button off his coat for a memento. Emerson, who had not had the heart to go, wrote in his journal: "To the last her country proves inhospitable to her; brave, eloquent, subtle, accomplished, devoted, constant soul!"

Two years later *The Memoirs of Margaret Fuller Ossoli* were issued in his care. Knowing the Brownings' intimacy with the Ossolis, Emerson asked them through Mrs. Story for their recollections. They wrote them down with painful emotions, reawakened whenever they read the note Browning had made in Angelino's Bible: "Florence, 1850. Second year of their lives. God keep them both, and lead them to fulness of love and wisdom. R.B."

The Storys remained the Brownings' closest American friends. Mr. Story, a poet as well as a sculptor, shared many tastes with Browning. His wife Emmeline went driving with Mrs. Browning, spoiled little Wiedemann who had begun to call himself more simply Penini, and gave and sought advice on household problems. Her daughter Edith and her little boy Joe became Penini's playmates. It was a pleasant relationship where each respected the others' creative privacy and where all enjoyed together their hours of relaxation.

Isa Blagden, however, who had already established herself as a central figure in expatriate Florentine society, early became Mrs. Browning's bosom friend—"Isa, perfect in companionship as in other things." Miss Blagden was just ten years younger than Mrs. Browning but of a human experience wide enough to bridge the difference. Browning soon adopted toward her a playful banter, the ripple and sparkle on the surface of a deep affection that was to subsist between them as long as she lived. In one of the earliest letters the Brownings sent Isa Blagden, Browning wrote at the close: "Good-bye, *t'abbraccio, ti streeeeeeeeeeeeeeeeeeeeeeeengo, as emphatic opera singers accent it.*"[2]

No one knew very much about Miss Blagden and she did nothing toward clearing the mystery. Small, well made, with a delicately articulated frame and an expressive large-eyed face set off by black hair, she had a hint of the East about her, even though she was accepted as English. Gossip began speculating about her from the moment she settled in Florence in 1849 or perhaps a little earlier. Some said she was born in India, the daughter of an English father and a native mother. Others inclined to consider her the illegitimate

[2] Holograph letter, Baylor Browning Collection.

offspring of a romantic liaison. No records have ever been unearthed. She had some culture, spoke well, and aspired to distinguish herself as a novelist. She also wrote verses.

She had means adequate enough for her to take one of the finest places in Bellosguardo, the Villa Bricchieri. From its terraces one overlooked the valley of the Arno, holding the jewel of Florence, brighter than the field of lilies from which it had arisen. The Brownings went often to the Villa Bricchieri. As time passed they were to know every flower along the garden wall, the floating gray of the olive-trees down the hillslope, and the line of cypresses that marked the way to and from Florence, whose cathedral, towers and palaces, silver river and golden domes, reflected every mood of the sky. Bellosguardo was ever to be associated for Browning with his happiest years. Mrs. Browning was to paint it in words in *Aurora Leigh*.

It was also associated with some of their pleasantest friendships which Isa Blagden made possible by her unfailing social magnetism. More important, the Brownings found in her a good neighbor, a ready help in an emergency, and a constant source of unselfish devotion. She was a general favorite and the name Isa became an open sesame to all hearts.

On the Piazza Indipendenza Thomas Adolphus Trollope had built himself a villa rivaling Miss Blagden's as a social center. But as they had many friends in common they shared, rather than disputed, them. Mr. Trollope had married Theodosia Garrow of whom Ba's doctor at Torquay had prognosticated a dire fate because she insisted on making rhymes, and so a new friendship was soon established. Landor, on his return from England, would recite his Alcaics from the terrace, or he would extemporize verses to Miss Blagden's young protégée, Kate Field, who had come to Florence to study music. Landor's own villa on the slopes of Fiesole served as a warehouse for his collection of paintings picked up at random, but all of which he declared to be treasures of great price by Giotto, da Vinci, Raphael, Ghirlandaio— unfortunately all unsigned. He had an embarrassing way of presenting them to his friends who did not know what to do with them. Later he looked upon them as a possible source of income, and would plague Browning with them.

"Poor, perverse Landor," Browning would complain, "has sent me the 'Sebastian del Piombo,' bless him! I shall be sure to offend him, whether I sell the picture for five pounds or buy it in for six."

Again, Landor saddled him with another art treasure to pay for his grave which, he said, he was certain he would be filling at any moment. Browning, watching the old lion at his morning meal, had his doubts about that eventuality. "May his shadow never be less!— as I judge it will not speedily be from the appetite he favored an omelette with . . . ! The plate was large, the eggs were four; he breakfasted, there was no more!"[3]

To the circle belonged Tennyson's elder brother Frederic, also a poet, but so overshadowed by the Laureate that his flowers wilted under the bays. A hypersensitive, shy man, he had married an Italian peasant girl and settled down in Florence with his growing family. Young Lytton—the later Owen Meredith—son of Sir Edward Bulwer-Lytton, soon joined the group. "As he is a seer of visions, a great supernaturalist, I shall comfort myself in his society," said Ba.

Besides his mystical qualities young Lytton held the practical post of attaché at the Embassy.

However, the resident expatriates did not lack their spiritualist and necromancer par excellence in Seymour Kirkup, whom long residence in Italy had made more Florentine than the Florentines. Like Leigh Hunt the venerable Kirkup had known Byron and Shelley, but unlike Hunt, he had not lost touch with them, for in his musty palace off the Ponte Vecchio he held constant communication with the spirits. Indeed, journeys backward through the centuries were nothing to him by virtue of his researches in necromancy. In the course of his conjurations the spirit of Dante, his predilected poet, materialized before him and soon was revealing astounding facts about his life on earth. Not only that, but through Regina, a peasant girl whom Kirkup employed as his medium, Dante informed him that under the coat of whitewash in the chapel of the Bargello was a portrait of him painted from life by his contemporary Giotto. What amazed the Florentines and indeed all Europe was the discovery of the fresco portrait exactly where, under spiritual direction, Kirkup had indicated.

He was to father a still more astounding miracle when Regina gave birth to a daughter. No one believed that a man of his advanced age could have accomplished the feat, nor did he believe it himself, except that on her deathbed, not long after the baby's birth Regina swore the child was his. That the spirits had had something to do with little Imogen's birth many began to credit when, almost as soon

[3] Holograph letter, Baylor Browning Collection.

They would have left for England the previous year had not Mrs. Browning had another miscarriage, in July, the fourth accident of the kind according to a letter of Browning's to John Kenyon. She had never been in worse danger, and Dr. Harding was in constant attendance. Slowly she began to recover, and as soon as she could travel they went to Siena for the more favorable climate. So far the hazards of motherhood had been a graver threat to her than her weakness of the chest.

Now in Venice, in June, Mrs. Browning exclaimed: "Never had I touched the skirts of so celestial a place. The beauty of the architecture, the silver trails of water up between all that gorgeous colour and carving, the enchanting silence, the moonlight, the music, the gondolas—I mix them all up together and maintain that nothing is like it." Robert shared her ecstasy; Penini and Wilson echoed it. But after a while Browning grew uncomfortable and unable to eat or sleep. Worse still, Wilson decided to emulate him and fell into a miserable condition of continual sickness and headache.

"Alas for these mortal Venices," Ba sighed, "so exquisite and so bilious!"

Nevertheless for a few days the Brownings led a true Venetian life, enjoying their coffee in the Piazza San Marco to the playing of music, gliding in gondolas to the Lido, and speculating on the one or two ex-kings and others of the more vulgar royalties who had decided to wrap themselves round in the beauty of the Queen of the Adriatic to forget their purple. "Or dream of it, as the case may be," said Ba, who also envied Taglioni for resting her feet from dancing by purchasing two of Venice's most beautiful palaces. Could they, as poets, ever own a palace in that magical city? As it was, they had been able to travel only because "that dearest, best friend to us," John Kenyon, who had been taking care of Ba's finances since her father washed his hands of them, had endowed them with an additional income on the birth of their child—an act of generosity which for its very delicacy they could not refuse. Robert, in his pride of independence had tried to. "All my life," he told his friend, "I have elected to be poor and perhaps the reason may be that I have a very particular capacity for being rich."

More tactful, Ba now thanked Kenyon for them both in one of those spontaneous passages that mark her genius as much as any poem: "I won't quite do like my Wiedemann, who every time he fires his gun (if it's twenty times in five minutes) says 'Papa, Papa,' because Robert gave him the gun, and the gratitude is reiterantly explosive. But one's thoughts may say what they please and as often as they please."

They could count on that one friend at least when they set foot in England. They still delayed, however, seizing on the convenient pretext of churches to visit, scenery to admire. As once before when they had made a pilgrimage on their wedding journey to Petrarch's "*chiare acque*" they now set out for Arqua to see the little room where the poet's great soul had exhaled itself. They made the journey alone in a calèche, leaving Wilson at the inn with Penini and Flush. The Brownings stood together in Petrarch's room looking out of the window at the green-peaked hills, unchanged through the centuries. Browning's eyes had tears in them when they met Ba's.

Through Brescia they galloped in the moonlight and the morning saw them all at Milan, with Mrs. Browning none the worse for the strenuous traveling. Of course, the cathedral had to be climbed to its topmost pinnacle. "How glorious," she exclaimed. "Worthy almost of standing face to face with the snowy Alps, and itself a sort of snow dream by an artist architect taken asleep in a glacier." Up the three hundred and fifty steps she followed Robert like a practiced climber when six years ago she had had to put as much effort into walking the few paces between her couch and the armchair.

Not a point of interest did they miss. At Parma they were especially delighted with Correggio's paintings which they found wonderful. Besides, had he not had the sense, commented Ba, to make his little angels the very likeness of their baby? Everywhere they went they were *eccellenza*'d and *signoria*'d like millionaires.

At Como the traveling diligence was left behind and they sailed to Lucerne through scenery that dwarfed man's works. A brief detour through Germany and then—Paris. What a change from Italy! There were beautiful cathedrals here too, but at the street corners enormous false teeth grinned at one from the dentists' shingles, disreputable prints flaunted their indecencies from bookstall and quay, fascinating hats caught the eye from shop windows. Then suddenly a terrifying clanking of hoofs made all heads turn toward the boulevard as M. le Président in a cocked hat rocketed past with a train of cavalry, to loud yells from an occasional Red. It was July, nearing the celebration of Bastille Day, the 14th.

Many changes had come over France during the past tempestuous decade. In 1848 Louis Philippe and his queen had fled the revolutionists who succeeded in proclaiming a Republic. As plain William Smith, the monarch found refuge in Claremont, the country-seat of King Leopold of Belgium, his son-in-law, leaving the field to a Republican provisional government led by such men as the poet Lamartine, the astronomer Arago, General Cavaignac and the astute and yet unrecognized Louis Blanc. Behind the scenes George Sand lent her pen to the republican cause, attended meetings of the provisional government disguised as a man since no woman was admitted to those precincts, and yearned for the time when the greatest good would be enjoyed by the greatest number.

Quiet as a shadow, but looming larger and larger, Louis Napoleon emerged as the chief aspirant to power. On his election to the Assembly he acted with becoming modesty. During his candidacy for President of the French Republic against Cavaignac and Lamartine, he swore that he would maintain the Republic and realize liberty, equality and fraternity for the people. He won the election on a majority of two million votes.

The republic flourished. In 1849, however, the Republicans began to have their doubts when to their dismay their President supported the Pope against Garibaldi's liberating forces. In vain Ledru-Rollin demanded the impeachment of the ministry after Oudinot started siege operations. Louis Napoleon reenforced the siege with troops. Garibaldi's men held out valiantly for a month, but outnumbered and then bombarded, they had finally to make way for the French who stormed the ramparts and entered the Holy City. The Pope's first act was to revive the Inquisition for the trial of the revolutionaries.

Anger boiled to fury among the Republicans in France and Louis Napoleon appeared less frequently among his people who felt their cause betrayed, especially after Venice, disheartened by the defeat of Rome, fell again to the Austrians. But time and his cunning worked for Louis Napoleon, ambitious for his uncle's imperial cloak embroidered with golden bees. Meanwhile Garibaldi, who had carried his fight to Venice, had a price on his head and was hunted from place to place.

To the Brownings, by this time attuned to political upheavals, the air of expectancy in Paris made them feel quite at home. Mrs. Browning became at once a partisan of Louis Napoleon, remembering him, perhaps, as the romantic prisoner of Ham who wrote humanitarian treatises on the extinction of pauperism. Moreover, to her as to

France the name of Napoleon still conjured up visions of glory, though in the Prince-President the claim to it came solely from his being the son of Napoleon's brother Louis and Hortense de Beauharnais, the daughter of Josephine. Also, even though Ba declared herself as hating and detesting masculine men, she admired strength, which could be turned to the good uses of humanity. In her generosity she failed to recognize that like a surgeon's knife it could, in the wrong hands, be used for murder.

Browning on the other hand, although keenly alive to men and events, was inclined to look upon them *sub specie aeternitatis*. He had no love for the name of Napoleon and roundly declared, "I hate all Buonapartes, past present or to come."

"You say that in your self-willed pettish way, as a manner of dismissing a subject you won't think about!" Ba taxed him. Why did Robert not react as she did, or like Penini who cried out with delight at the horses and cockades? Why did he not respond in poetry to living history instead of observing in silence, his clear grave eyes turned toward the unseen future? Except for the poem, "The Italian in England," a reminiscence of his Neapolitan visit of 1844, and his still unpublished "The Patriot," a six-stanza *Casa Guidi Windows*, written after the Florentine struggles of 1849, the contemporary political scene scarcely entered into his writing. When it did, as in this instance, it was focused on the drama of one individual, here a patriot, for whom but a year ago roses had been strewn in his way. Now

> I go in the rain, and, more than needs,
>   A rope cuts both my wrists behind . . .
> Thus I entered, and thus I go!

Browning's subtitle, "An old story," clearly expressed his personal view, not without a hint of bitterness, on the hero and fickle humanity.

The poem is like a vignette to Mrs. Browning's longer work which was just then being published as a book in England. "It will prevent everybody from speaking to me again," she wrote to Isa Blagden of *Casa Guidi Windows*. To Miss Mitford she voiced the same apprehensions. "Tell me how you like the poem—honestly, truly—which numbers of people will be sure to dislike profoundly and angrily perhaps."

Both the dislike and the anger had not the intensity she had anticipated, although the reviews pronounced on the whole unfavorably. Events, however thrilling when they occur, quickly become dated unless viewed with the eternity of a Browning. She had eloquence, but it did not suit her countrymen to listen when she invoked their aid toward peace, or bade England disband her captains and have no more "struggles and encroachment, no vile war!" The beauty of heart and word and image that shone like a sun of freedom over the poem, bat-eyed prejudice refused to see. What right had women to express opinions on things not of their concern? Mrs. Browning should continue writing her romantic poetry and leave politics alone. One man, the gentle William Howitt, later went so far as to declare in the *Spiritual Magazine* that in *Casa Guidi Windows* Mrs. Browning had been "biologized by infernal spirits" in the service of Moloch. The book, on the whole, received less disfavor than indifference. It might as well have remained unpublished for the little effect it had upon public opinion. In contrast her collected poems were selling better and better.

The Brownings had not much leisure to enjoy their Paris life, for London had to be faced, and soon. Tennyson who was traveling at the same time, came to call on them with his wife, and when he heard that they were about to leave for England, offered them his house at Twickenham. He would listen to no polite thanks but there and then insisted on writing his servants to give the Brownings possession immediately. "It is an autograph at once of genius and kindness," Ba remarked of the note. At parting she and Mrs. Tennyson—"a very sweet person"—kissed affectionately, while the young Laureate and Browning said good-by with cordial admiration for each other as men as well as poets.

At last there they were, in a fog, on English soil, early in August. Long before Mrs. Browning set foot ashore—in a puddle—she began to be assailed by fears that had all too real a foundation. She had not written to her father about their return, knowing that if the door of 50 Wimpole Street ever opened to her it would not be through his doing. Arabel was informed, however, and so was Henrietta who through her marriage found herself in the same situation. Her friend Mrs. Martin suggested a visit to Torquay. The very name only revived memories that lay too close to the surface of her consciousness as it was. "I had never but one brother who loved and comprehended me," she told Mrs. Martin, "and so that is just one thought that would be unbearable if I went into your neighborhood. . . . You know a little, if not entirely, how we loved one another . . . while God knows that death and separation have no power over such love."

Did she regret her marriage, Mrs. Martin asked her.

"It has made the happiness and honour of my life," she answered, "and every unkindness received from my house makes me press nearer to the tenderest and noblest of human hearts. . . . Husband, lover, nurse—not one of these has Robert been to me, but all three together. I neither regret the marriage . . . nor the manner of it."

She had never forgotten how, when they had been together scarcely a fortnight, Robert had said to her with earnest tenderness: "I kissed your feet, my Ba, before I married you. But now I would kiss the ground under your feet, I love you with so much greater love." That love, incredible as it had seemed to them, overwhelmed as they were by its tremendous impact, had continued growing like the living thing it was, searching profounder depths, expanding in spiritual light. As human beings they were fulfilled in a happiness that had no shadow. Shadow came only from without and the darkest was still cast by the house on Wimpole Street.

They found rooms, meager, dark, and unpleasant after Casa Guidi, at 26 Devonshire Street and there, uncomfortably, they had a *pied à terre* for the two months of their visit, in spite of Tennyson's offer and Mr. Kenyon's invitation. Mrs. Browning at last met Robert's father and sister, to whom she had written occasionally. Her comment was rather brief and general on Sarianna: "She is highly accomplished, with a heart to suit the head." When she learned to know Sarianna better, she had a constrained affection for her which had in it too much of her natural timidity to allow for expansion. She seemed overawed by Miss Browning's efficiency but was touched by her tenderness toward Mr. Browning who appeared to be the child of the child. Miss Browning, it seemed, had a speech defect that made it impossible for her to pronounce the letter r so that in her mouth her brother's name became Wobert.

The moment it was known that the Brownings were in London everyone came to call. Soon they could scarcely finish their tea for the intermittent ringing of the doorbell. Mrs. Fanny Kemble left them tickets for her reading of *Hamlet*. Mr. Arnould, now a Chancery barrister, begged them to accept the hospitality of his town house. Barry Cornwall (Bryan Procter) paid them daily visits and so did Mrs. Jameson, who left her newest work with them in defiance of the printers. They also went out a great deal. Forster gave them a

magnificent dinner at Thames Ditton where they could eat and enjoy
looking at the swans gliding on the water. They breakfasted with
Mr. Rogers and they passed an evening with Carlyle, one of the
great sights of England to Ba's mind. She was proud of the friendship
that crusty heart had for her Robert and it raised Carlyle the more
in her estimation. Leigh Hunt, that other old friend of Robert's and
a collector of gruesome mementos—at one time he had had Shelley's
heart in a little silken sack and a piece of jawbone rescued from the
pyre—gave them half of his lock of Milton's hair as a token of affection. Everywhere except at Wimpole Street and by everyone except
her father, they were overwhelmed with gifts and kindness, and the
kindest and most generous, as always, was John Kenyon.

From the first Mr. Kenyon had tried to soften for Ba the blow
from Mr. Barrett which he knew would come, and had advised her
not to write to him after all. But affection had been stronger than
his warning. Robert had also written to George Barrett who for
reasons of his own, had taken his father's part against his sister.
George called on them however, and was immediately won over by
the man whom Mr. Barrett considered a villain, and by his little
Florentine nephew. (Who would ever have dreamed of Ba as a
mother—and of such a child!) With Arabel there had been no
barrier to cross. She came to see them almost daily and could scarcely
be torn away from Penini. She was especially helpful during the
week that Wilson left for Sheffield to visit her family.

The London climate but more, the psychological effect of England
upon Ba, soon brought on the old symptoms. She coughed day and
night and looked so wretched that Robert took fright and would
have rushed her back to Paris at once. But Ba would not leave without some word from her father. He could not be so inhuman as to
refuse to answer her letter, nor Robert's manly, straightforward note,
so touching and so conciliatory that Ba would not believe it would
be read in vain.

Browning did hear from Mr. Barrett who sent a letter and a packet.
The missive, violent and unsparing, showed too clearly that Mr.
Barrett would carry his rancor to the grave. The packet contained
every letter his daughter had written him through the five years of
her absence. The letters were unopened, the seals unbroken. What
most shocked Mrs. Browning was the fact that even the letters that
she had sent in black-edged envelopes, and sealed with black wax,
had been left intact. Surely Mr. Barrett must have felt some fear

that her husband or her child might have died. Yet he had not even broken the seal to find out. How much farther could any human being go in hardening his heart?

"So there's an end!" Ba said bitterly.

Under the circumstances she could not plead with him to see her at least once before she left England, or to kiss his grandson who also bore his name. She resigned herself to the inevitable and in a disconsolate mood, she left England, holding closer to her heart her husband and her son, her whole world. Had it not been for some ties she would have said farewell forever to the country of her birth. "There's always an east wind with me in England!" she sighed.

On the voyage back to Paris they had Carlyle with them wrapped and invernessed in his philosophic tweeds. Robert showed the old prophet every consideration and Ba liked him better the more she saw him, concluding that the bitterness to which he treated the world was only melancholy and the scorn, sensibility. They were amused at his efforts to ingratiate their two-year-old son to whom they heard him say on one occasion: "Why, sir, you have as many aspirations as Napoleon!" Penini's answer, whether in Italian, English, or French, was not recorded though at that period of his "Babylonish education" he was perfectly capable of making one.

They found that the political situation had grown in intensity in France during their absence. At 138 Avenue des Champs Elysées they rented a suite of rooms on the sunny side of the tree-lined boulevard, as colorful as the Piazza Pitti with parading uniforms and cavalry. Besides a drawing room and dressing room they had a study for Robert, a small dining room and kitchen, two bedrooms and an additional one upstairs for the maid—all for two-hundred francs a month. They did not have to keep a carriage. A fiacre and coupé stand was close by for elegant drives, not to mention the convenience of the omnibuses that took one to the other end of Paris for a few sous. Considering the advantages, they decided to prolong their stay until the following summer.

Almost every day either the Prince-President or his retinue drove past the house to the joy of Penini who derived his politics from his mother and had learned to pipe "Vive Napoléon" in his shrill little voice. One day both Wilson and Penini came face to face with the great man when the Prince-President's carriage turned into a neighboring courtyard. In the exhilaration of the encounter Wilson found her tongue to describe the heap of petitions and nosegays which people had thrown in through the windows of the coach. Both petition and nosegay denoted the people's feeling toward Louis Napoleon, combining as it did a hope for betterment and a certain measure of approval.

As the autumn of 1851 drew on toward winter it was difficult to prophesy in the increasing political tension which way the Prince-President would go—whether in the direction of democratization or of a stronger centralizing of his power. So far no one could have acted with more exemplary modesty as the people's choice of man of the hour. Even after Louis Philippe's death in exile the previous year Louis Napoleon had given no indication that "The king is dead!" had as corollary "Long live the king!" To his ambition "Long live the emperor" had the pleasanter sound. But of that the people remained unaware, so skillfully did he mask his true face. Outwardly it might indeed have appeared as if he took to heart the counsel George Sand had given him: "The Napoleon needed today is the man who takes on the woes of the people." That little by little he was curtailing the privileges of suffrage and muzzling the press, only the radicals as yet fully realized. But the Prince-President's devoted chief of police, Maupas, discovered new plots by the hour against the sacred person, and boatloads of Reds found themselves heading toward Cayenne where their disaffection could do him no harm.

As the third anniversary of Louis Napoleon's inauguration was approaching, as well as the 2nd of December, memorable for the coronation of the first Napoleon, the Prince-President who knew the effect of such red-letter days upon the public decided that his hour of destiny had struck. It may be too that the spirit-rappings which he consulted gave him favorable augury. At any rate on the night of December 1, with the connivance of his bastard brother the Count de Morny who wore a tuft of hortensias in his buttonhole to denote his maternal descent, with Colonel Espinasse who received a hundred thousand francs and the promise of a general's rank for his part in the affair, and with the obsequious Maupas and others who could not resist a bribe, Louis Napoleon staged a coup d'état.

At the crack of dawn his troops occupied the government printing offices and forced the printers to set up the proclamations on which the Prince-President had exercised his literary art. At the same time agents in closed carriages dragged the leading members of the Assembly from their beds and placed them under arrest together with scores of Reds. By the time the Parisians opened their sleepy eyes they found their city plastered with the Prince-President's proclamation, further emphasized by a decree dissolving the National Assembly, declaring a state of siege, convoking the electoral districts, and doing away with the Council of State. To justify his actions the Prince-President denounced the Assembly as a hotbed of conspiracy and flattered the people by inviting them to judge between it and himself. Success was "in the bag" said the cynical de Morny—as indeed it was. What chance had the barricades hastily thrown up by the Reds against the armed troops? Who would heed the protest of the leaders behind prison bars? Louis Napoleon knew the effect of blood in quelling opposition and he commanded his troops to let it flow.

George Sand who had run to Paris to plead for her many radical friends caught in the political storm, found herself a witness to the coup d'état. Her generous heart bled for the tragedy of the nation, for those courageous men who had thrown themselves with only their ideals against ruthless armed ambition. "Here am I," she wrote in her journal, "alone by my fire, on the night of the 3rd and 4th (of December 1851) . . . How bitter it is to think that most of mankind dies deprived of everything! How have I deserved to sit quietly by my fire?" They were dark days, terrible days, those days in which liberty was slain.

It was surprising, therefore, to find Mrs. Browning writing to Mrs. Jameson on December 10: "We have suffered neither fear nor danger—and would not have missed the grand spectacle of the 2nd of December for anything in the world."

They had lived through so many revolutions that they took this one too with equanimity. On the day of the actual fighting the nurse took Penini out as usual, with the precaution to keep him in the immediate neighborhood, and on the very night that George Sand was feeling guilty at having the warmth of her fire amid the general suffering, Mrs. Browning in her dressing gown was sitting up with her husband, listening to the distant firing in the boulevards. Several days later they drove down to see the field of action of "the terrible Thursday," inspecting the holes in the walls made by the cannon and counting the smashed windows. The promenades swarmed with people as if nothing had happened. The shops, galleries, and theaters were open as usual. Penini whose one concern during the shooting had been that the soldiers would kill Punch, was shown to his satisfaction that all was well with the gentleman, who performed in the park as usual.

Robert and Ba had a few domestic émeutes, "Because he hates

some imperial names," said Ba. He looked darkly on the *coup d'état* and refused to give approval to such criminal seizure of power. But Ba had a weakness for strong men. Hadn't Mr. Kenyon taxed her for her "immoral sympathy with power?"

Ba justified herself vocally and in her correspondence. She admitted that she admired Louis Napoleon for what she called the consummate ability and courage of his political stroke, and though she granted that the purity of his patriotism was still to be proved, she held that a pure patriot might have taken the same steps. "He has broken certainly the husk of an oath," she conceded, "but fidelity to the intention of it seems to me reconcilable with the breach"—to all of which Robert gave a loud Carlylean Nay!

Ba then brought up as an argument in Louis Napoleon's favor the almost unanimous approval of their tradespeople. "*Il a bien fait! C'est le vrai neveu de son oncle!*"

When on the 21st of December Louis Napoleon made public the results of the popular plebiscite that won him a ten-year reelection it seemed as if according to the majority this true nephew of his uncle had indeed done well. His inauguration at Notre Dame on New Year's Day set a solemn seal of approval upon the people's choice. Not to imperil his gains, Louis Napoleon took the precaution of banishing eighty-three members of the Assembly and shipping off to the penal colonies some six-hundred opponents of his *coup d'état*.

Ba could see only the triumph of numbers in his election. "I'm no Napoleonist," she declared. "I am simply a democrat, and hold that the majority of a nation has the right of choice upon the question of its own government, even when it makes a mistake."

Meanwhile the latest political witticism was going the rounds— that for the effaced *liberté, égalité, fraternité* should be substituted *infanterie, cavallerie, artillerie*.

The name of George Sand was often on people's lips for her indefatigable efforts on behalf of her banished friends. The Republicans who noted her frequent visits to Louis Napoleon at the Elysée, while accepting the pardons she won from him, condemned her for having anything to do with him. Some broke their friendship with her altogether. But she continued doing what she thought right, sending money to the needy families of the exiles and writing to her comrades in Africa and Cayenne. After Louis Napoleon's coup she had no illusions left. She was tired. "I'm so thoroughly disgusted with everyone and everything in this world . . ." But disgusted or not, her conscience would not let her rest.

Mrs. Browning, on learning that George Sand was in Paris, had no peace until she obtained a letter of introduction from Mazzini. Everyone said to her, "She will never see you!" Why, George Sand had even assumed another name to escape from the plague of her notoriety. But the desire became an *idée fixe* with Ba, and she reproved Robert for being inclined to sit in his chair and be proud. "No, you *shan't* be proud," she teased, "and I *won't* be proud, and we *will* see her. I won't die, if I can help it, without seeing George Sand."

Obediently Robert signed the covering note that Ba penned for them both and the Mazzini letter was consigned to a friend for a friend who was to give it to still another friend who would deliver it to George Sand. To their amazement, they received a gracious note from her the following day, inviting them to visit her at No. 3 Rue Racine the coming Sunday—"*C'est le seul jour que je puisse passer chez moi, et encore je n'en suis pas absolument certaine—mais je ferai tellement mon possible, que ma bonne étoile m'y aidera. . . .*"

George Sand's star proved propitious in the business. So on the 14th of February, after a struggle with Robert who would have called off the appointment because the wind was too sharp, Ba put on her respirator, smothered herself in furs, and set out on the visit in a close carriage. Always a hero worshiper, Ba was "in ecstasies" at the prospect of meeting the one example among women whom she had admired and defended, envied a little and, in some respects, sought to emulate. How much George Sand had accomplished in a life of only two years' advantage over hers! Not only had she written novels that had spread her fame throughout the world, and plays which all Paris flocked to see, but she had lived to the full. The world of the Philistines was appalled by her open liaisons with the poet Alfred de Musset and later with Chopin, overlooking the immorality of a marriage law that condemned a woman to be bound till death to a husband unworthy of either love or respect. (George Sand had accomplished much toward the reform of the law by her separation suit.) A devoted mother, she had had almost the sole maintenance of her son and daughter, while their father stood firmly on his legal paternal rights. Though of a class that is not remarkable for undue concern over the rights of the poor, George Sand had thrown in her lot with her less privileged fellows, had spoken for the inarticulate and acted for the helpless, supporting meliorist causes and influencing opinion. In a man's world she had done a man's work with a courage and integrity that put many a hero to shame. (Some heroes, indeed, had been made through her.) As a reward she was reviled in some quarters, misunderstood in most, but blessed in many an obscure corner which her generous hand never failed to reach. Now, at forty-seven, she had wept over graves— Chopin's the nearest—and mourned over lost causes. But her spirit kept her in the fight.

She rose up as the Brownings entered and went to meet them with outstretched hand. Mrs. Browning, whose heart was beating fast, stooped and kissed it, but George Sand withdrew it quickly with, "*Mais non, je ne veux pas'* " and kissed her on the lips. She was not alone, they found, as they came into the room and saw several young men. They sat down among them, Ba the while missing no detail of George Sand's dress and appearance. She had expected to see a large, masculine woman, badly dressed and smoking a cigar. She found instead a person even smaller than herself though somewhat plump, dressed with the greatest nicety in a fashionable gray serge gown and jacket fastened up to the throat. "Her hair was uncovered," Ba described her to Miss Mitford, "divided on the forehead in black, glossy bandeaux, and twisted up behind. The eyes and brow are noble, and the nose is of a somewhat Jewish character. . . . There is no sweetness in the face, but great moral as well as intellectual capacities, only it never *could* have been a beautiful face, which a good deal surprised me." All the more because of the reputation of *femme fatale* that George Sand's candid relationships had attached to her.

Neither Ba nor Robert left any record of their conversation with George Sand. They had arrived in the midst of her activities for the release of her condemned Republican friends and therefore most of the time of their visit was taken up with her giving advice and various directions to her young helpers, showing her confidence in the Brownings by the freest use of names and unguarded allusions to facts. "She seemed to be, in fact, the *man* in the company," Ba shrewdly observed. She smiled only once and the brilliance lighted up her whole face. When they discussed her later Robert remarked that in all she said, even in her kindness and pity, lay an undercurrent of scorn. "A scorn of pleasing she evidently had," Ba agreed. "There never could have been . . . coquetry in that woman. I liked her. I did not love her, but I felt the burning soul through all that quietness, and was not disappointed in George Sand."

By what process of living had Aurore Dupin become George Sand?

Ba had the opportunity of trying to fathom her character on another visit, ten days later. That morning she and Robert found George Sand in a circle of eight or nine men. She was sitting by her fire, warming her feet quietly. There was a general silence, profoundly reverential on the part of the men as before an oracle. It was only through her splendid eyes that she spoke, as she sat in an aloofness almost akin to disdain. *She was George Sand; that was enough.* Ba admired her for that silent scorn as she sat there, so apart, so alone in her brooding. Robert was somewhat annoyed. "If any other mistress of a house had behaved so, I would have walked out of the room," he said.

Nonetheless he went to see her again three or four times when Ba could not go with him. Once he met her near the Tuileries and offered her his arm, with a touch of constraint on that occasion because she was "a little too much *endimanchée* in terrestrial lavenders and super-celestial blues," unlike her usual impeccable style. Her new play, *Les Vacances de Pandolphe*, was being put on and she offered her friends a loge. The Brownings could not attend, however.

As Browning saw more of the circle that surrounded her he went back to Ba with his vivid impressions of those crowds of ill-bred men who adored her on their knees, "between a puff of smoke and an ejection of saliva." His English respectability was affronted. Here a Greek in a Greek costume spoke to her familiarly and kissed her. There a vulgar actor went down on his knees before her and cried out, "*Sublime!*"

"*Caprice d'amitié,*" she apologized for the man, with quiet scorn.

"A noble woman under the mud, be certain," Ba defended her. "I would kneel down to her too, if she would leave it all, throw it off. But she would not care for my kneeling . . . Perhaps she does not care for anybody by this time—who knows?"

It was in a sense true. George Sand had turned from the one to the many, from self to humanity.

The meeting left a deep impression upon Mrs. Browning. Here was a woman who fulfilled herself as a person and as a creator, leaving her imprint upon her day—just such a woman as she had been dreaming of in her still unwritten novel in verse.[1]

---

[1] May I suggest a study on the influence of George Sand on *Aurora Leigh*?

who told her that by gazing into its depths one could divine one's future. A practical London optician, however, was now reproducing it by the hundreds.

Old friends like Mr. Fox came to call and new ones too, among them Dante Gabriel Rossetti and his brother, conducted thither by William Allingham. Mr. Fox's admiration for the poet he had discovered was unabated. He added to it admiration for his wife. "She talked lots of George Sand," he wrote to his daughter, "and so beautifully! And she silver-electroplated Louis Napoleon."

But Louis Napoleon was to do better than that for himself before the year had ended. On the anniversary of the *coup d'état* after holding another plebiscite, this time on the question of whether or not the empire should be reestablished, the Prince-President became Napoleon III, Emperor of the French. The title was officially made hereditary. Moreover, he lost no time in marrying to secure succession.

Chapter XIX: Men and Women

CASA GUIDI meant home, health, happiness and the joyous labor of their poetry to the Brownings. The cough that seemed to have come to stay when Mrs. Browning was in England, left her in the sunshine of Florence. Even Penini, pampered by his English relatives, sighed happily in the arms of his Italian nurse who cried, *"Dio mio, come è bellino!"* on seeing how very much prettier he had become. Their old friends welcomed them with undisguised affection; new ones came to worship. To old and new the Brownings recounted their adventures and told of the people they had met. George Sand occupied the most prominent place, her name recurring again and again in Mrs. Browning's conversation. She was obsessed with the Frenchwoman, so very unlike, and yet so like her in many respects. As she had talked to Mr. Fox, she talked to young Mr. Cassell who visited at Casa Guidi in February of 1853. There was no end to her enthusiastic accounts of George Sand's looks, of her activities, of her nobility of character, despite the "abomination of desolation" in which Browning thought she lived. Beside those paeans her feminist rejoicing over Mrs. Stowe and her phenomenally successful *Uncle Tom's Cabin* sounded feeble, though a Sandesque vigor energized her condemnation of slavery in the letter she sent to Mrs. Jameson in April. "I would not be an American for the world while she wears that shameful scar upon her brow."

Significantly, she informs her friend in the same letter of her progress on her novel in verse, at last begun—"the heroine, an artist woman—not a painter, mind. It is intensely modern, crammed from the times." Browning too had been hard at work, as he wrote to M. Milsand on the 24th of February. "I have not left the house one evening since our return. I am writing—a first step toward popularity for me—lyrics with more music and painting than before, so as to get people to hear and see."

This spirit of creativeness he had encouraged by a New Year's resolution while they were still in Paris—to write a poem a day as long as the mood lasted. On the first of the year he wrote "Women and Roses," a varied, Blake-like lyric, unique among his works for its mystical allusiveness and dreamy cadences. The previous day Ba had received a bunch of roses. The dream he had about them, he said, suggested the poem. Something of that dreamlike quality persisted through the following day when, incredibly, he wrote "Childe Roland," that disturbingly haunting picture of nature in desolation. With "Love among the Ruins," composed on the third day, inspiration abated, but did not cease. He now worked with more regularity than usual, and the poems grew in number as well as mastery, as Mrs. Browning saw with pride.

She had no uncertainty as to her husband's place in the temple of poetry. She put him as far above herself as her unerring judgment, uninfluenced by her love or by popular disfavor, could place him—and that was in the highest rank. As for herself, she knew her worth. She knew also her deficiencies and had her moments of doubt, soul strugglings which no honest artist can escape, as she revealed in the humbly confessional passage of *Aurora Leigh*:

> My own best poets, am I one with you,
> That thus I love you,—or but one through love?
> Does all this smell of thyme about my feet
> Conclude my visit to your holy hill
> In personal presence, or but testify
> The rustling of your vesture through my dreams? . . .

There was no questioning her estimate of Browning. He was one with the elect.

Meanwhile they worked independently of each other, neither discussing nor showing their poems until they were finished. They enjoyed their triumphs and comforted each other in the inevitable disappointments of a creative career. Browning, so far as the world was concerned, if indeed it showed any concern, had been silent since the scarcely noticed publication of *Christmas-Eve and Easter-Day*. Mrs. Browning, on the other hand, came constantly before the public through the magazines, where her poems were very much in demand. It came as most welcome news, therefore, when Helen Faucit, now Lady Martin, wrote Browning for permission to act in *Colombe's Birthday*.

"If there is a success," said Ba, for once practical, "it will be a good thing for us in a pecuniary point of view, and if not, there will be no harm done." The play had seven performances and a *succès*

d'estime at the Haymarket Theatre, with no considerable increment
to the household exchequer.

The Browning circle widened to include a young American sculptor, Harriet Hosmer, who had come to study under John Gibson in
Rome where, during their peregrinations in search of warmth or
coolness, the two poets met her. Browning adopted his usual banter-
ing manner toward the twenty-two-year-old girl no taller than a
child of twelve who jauntily wore her artist's beret and smock and
made the marble chips fly under her chisel. Later she was to have a
crew of Italian workmen to carve into marble her gigantic figures.
For the present she was content to work on less prodigious statues,
pretty mythological subjects which high society, including the young
Prince of Wales, bought for their pleasure. Hatty, as everyone called
her, was a hard worker and unusually competent, with a shrewd eye
even then for her rich and titled clientele whose tastes she knew to
perfection. She shared her studio apartment with a friend, a Miss
Hayes, who had translated George Sand and adopted in the process
a few of the Frenchwoman's discarded characteristics. Mrs. Browning was attracted and amused by the pair of emancipated women, as
she called them. Hatty she found very clever and very strange, but
she was somewhat disconcerted by Miss Hayes who dressed like a
man down to the waist in a gilet, collar, and neckcloth, and a jacket
made with a sort of wag-tail behind. They all had friends in common
in the Storys and Isa Blagden, not to mention almost everyone else
in the American and English sector. An Italian was included, the
scholar Pasquale Villari, later to distinguish himself for a masterpiece, his biography of Savonarola.

Everyone in the group had some claim to descent from the Muses
in greater or less degree, for all either wrote, painted, sang or played,
modeled in clay, hewed marble or, following the universal geniuses
of the Renaissance, did everything equally. It was a busy, gay, productive life, divided between work and play, all of it zestfully pursued. There was always good talk, especially when Browning or Mr.
Story held forth on favorite subjects. Sometimes Mrs. Browning contributed to the general conversation in her strange, soft, blurred voice.
But hers was the talent for the *tête-à-tête*, or better, for the epistolary
monologue. In company her reserve overcame her and she spoke
mostly with her large expressive eyes and the smile that gave a permanent lift to the corners of her mouth—"the little patient white
face that could smile so much more easily than speak," as her husband

said. But then she did not care to shine in society. It was enough
for her to listen to Browning and know him wholly hers.

"For the rest," she said, "if he is brilliant and I am dull, socially
speaking, love makes a level, which is my comfort."

Another member joined the Browning household soon after their
return to Casa Guidi, their new manservant, Ferdinando Romagnoli.
Penini adored him and the passion was mutual. During the summer
at Bagni di Lucca, the child, Ferdinando, and Wilson would go
down to the river every morning to make Flush swim, and wonderful
hours they had together. In the general gaiety Wilson would steal
a look now and then at Ferdinando. What she saw pleased her.
Besides being molto simpatico Ferdinando was quiet and gentle and
very considerate. At some point comparisons must have suggested
themselves in Wilson's mind between the majestic ducal guard and
this "good, tender-hearted man." Eventually the merits of Ferdinando
won out and again Wilson's Italian made seven-league strides, till
the two understood each other enough to talk of marriage.

The winter in Rome was one of the fullest the Brownings had ever
had. Everyone, it seemed, had converged from all corners of the
earth to the Eternal City, among whose pagan relics Mother Church
displayed her holy pageantries. The Storys at Piazza di Spagna engaged an apartment for the Brownings in Bocca di Leone not too
far away, lighting lamps and fires for their welcome. William Page,
who claimed he had discovered the secret of Titian's coloring, had
his studio just above them, and soon became an intimate with his
brushes in one hand and his palette in the other. He found a rewarding subject in Robert Browning. The portrait made Browning look
Italian, indeed, Venetian, and evoked rhapsodies from all who saw
it for the richness of its pigment, worthy, some said, of the brush of
a Renaissance master. Mrs. Browning admired it so much that the
artist gave it to her. It hung prominently first in Rome and then at
Casa Guidi waiting for time to give it the final mellowing. Alas,
where time had dealt kindly with the Venetian master, it showed
no such consideration for the work of Mr. Page which it mellowed
so thoroughly that finally the features merged indistinguishably with
the background. "It was indeed Browning," said a wit, "and has been
browning ever since."

An English artist, William Fisher, painted both Browning and
Penini to add to his collection which included Mr. Kenyon and
Walter Savage Landor. Mrs. Browning would have liked to keep

them, but "Oh, we couldn't afford to have such a luxury as a portrait done for us. . . ."

That winter they went through a period of agonized dread over Penini when little Joe Story, his constant playmate, contracted Roman fever. His sister caught it from him but recovered. The little boy died. Penini missed his little friend and asked innumerable questions. At last his parents had to tell him of Joe's death in such a way as not to shock his childish mind. The questions redoubled.

"Did Papa see the angels when they took Joe?" he asked his mother.

Mrs. Browning who had never deceived him by convenient fictions, was forced to answer, "No."

"Then did Joe *go up* by himself?"

At the thought that little Joe had had to make the journey alone he burst into sobs.

Several days later when he was given a medal of the Duke of Wellington, he suddenly asked his mother whether Joe had seen the "Dute of Wellyton" and was curious to know more about the hero. In a moment of national pride Browning explained that Wellington was the man who beat Napoleon. "Then I sint he a very naughty man. What! He beat Napoleon wiz a stit?"

At the picture of Wellington settling difficulties with a stick in a novel conception of history, Mrs. Browning laughed and Browning heartily joined her. They were happy in their child who made them hourly aware of their perfect happiness.

For that matter everyone who saw them was struck by their complete harmony. "They seem to be tremendously attached to one another, and exactly fitted for domestic happiness," Cassell noted after meeting them. Others expressed themselves in almost the same words. None, however, was more cognizant than Mrs. Browning of her felicity which she had tried to push away with both hands for fear of proving a burden to her husband. What if Browning had accepted her reiterated refusal out of weariness at being told of her illness, of her age?

She was still conscious of the difference in their years. Indeed, when Browning developed a grayness after shaving off his beard in a fit of impatience, she found that the argentine touch gave a character and elevation of thought to the whole physiognomy. To Mrs. Martin who had found George Barrett looking less young than formerly and philosophized that "We should all learn to hear and make such remarks with equanimity," Ba wrote an answer so impassioned that it left no doubt of her feelings on the encroaching years. "I never, if I live to be a hundred, should learn that learning. Death has the luminous side when we know how to look; but the rust of time, the touch of age, is hideous and revolting to me, and I never see it, by even a line's breadth, in the face of any I love, without pain and recoil of nature. I have a worse than womanly weakness about that class of subjects. Death is a face-to-face intimacy; age, a thickening of the mortal mask between souls. So I hate it, put it far from me. Why tell of age when it's just an appearance . . . when we are all young in soul and heart?"

Her husband saw only her soul and heart and the beauty that emanated from her eyes. Others might find her plain, a walking wraith. Like Frederick Locker who visited them in Paris, they might be struck by her physical shortcomings—"curls like the pendent ears of a water spaniel, and poor little hands, so thin that when she welcomed you she gave you something like the foot of a young bird." But even Locker had to pay tribute to her incomparable sweetness, the outward manifestation of the spirit within. As for Browning's dedication to that spirit, it surrounded her in a protective aura. Harriet Hosmer for all her youth had seen it and captured it by making a cast of their clasped right hands. The strong, manly fingers enclosing the delicate, trusting, emaciated hand seem to infuse it with their warmth and vigor, to lead it, as he had led her, from death to life. It was a testimony in bronze of their perfect union for which they never ceased thanking each other and God.

Not that they escaped minor disagreements, the passing clouds that make lovers all the more aware of the enduring sun. In politics, although mainly in accord, they differed in detail, Browning because of overcaution and she through headlong enthusiasm. They disagreed radically, however, on the subject of spiritualism.

At first Browning had humored her, going so far as to sit at a table with her and Lytton to get some obliging spirit to do a little rapping for them. Nothing happened because, insisted Lytton, Robert had been playing Mephistopheles. Browning shrugged skeptically; Ba was all for giving the spirits another chance under more favorable conditions. As time passed and interest in spiritualism assumed the proportions of a world-wide epidemic, Mrs. Browning became a more fervent believer, notwithstanding Robert's warning about the temptations it offered the charlatan. To her the manifestations represented the first glimmerings of a new spiritual dawn to which one had to attune both mind and vision. She felt also that strong compulsion to belief which sprang from her faith in the soul's immortality for which, since the unimaginative needed proof, proof was now being offered. There was certainly one death which such belief would have made more bearable. "I believe that love in its most human relations is an eternal thing," she declared. For love to be eternal the soul had perforce to survive death.

Browning was too much a man of his time to ignore what went on about him. He was amused with the rest to see in the neighborhood shop windows the picture of a spinning table, with Galileo's motto printed over it, "*E pur si muove.*" True, it moved. But who or what moved it? He was more inclined to think of the medium's hand or foot as the source of propulsion, while Ba cried "For shame!" at such incredulity. "If I am right, you will none of you be able to disbelieve much longer," she warned, citing as authority that the emperor of the French obtained oracles from the raps, and that both the Czar and the King of Holland were consulting the same source —not very compelling evidence, considering the state of Europe.

Still, things happened which admitted of no rational explanation. At one gathering a certain Count Giunasi who had psychic powers prevailed upon members of his audience to let him hold some personal article to stimulate the subliminal forces. Browning gave him his cuff links whereupon the count exclaimed, "There is something here which cries out in my ears, Murder! Murder!" Browning knew that the uncle from whom he had inherited them had been killed in St. Kitts', in fact that the links had been taken from his murdered body. The seance marked a triumph for the cause Ba espoused. She could see the humor as well as Robert, however, in Lamartine's experience with an American medium, "a very sweet girl" who summoned her compatriot Henry Clay from the spirit world for the express purpose of saying, "*J'aime Lamartine*"—doubtless a source of comfort to the poet-politician who had fallen into disfavor.

Penini, of course, participated in the psychic commotion, not altogether with the approval of his father who had qualms about the wisdom of introducing so young a child to such matters.

"I have no desire to mix up Penini in any of these phenomena," Mrs. Browning agreed. "Only I wish him to have right views as to the possible and probable influx of the spiritual world among us."

So Penini had the pleasure of hearing the spirit world inform him through the "raps" that he was four years old, a bit of knowledge which he relayed to all and sundry without the need of a seance. At the same time Harriet Hosmer followed the fashion by developing visionary powers and seeing a spirit some three feet high and exquisitely formed come dancing toward her.

"Wouldn't you like to have seen the little spirit?" Mrs. Browning asked Penini who had sat wide-eyed during the account.

"Oh, yes," said he, "velly much—a little pletty spillet like lat!" Then leaning his head to one side reflectively he added, "I sint if a velly large angel tame, I be lather aflaid."

With childhood's unquestioning acceptance he made room for spirits and angels in his small world in which he yearned for a little brother of his own. "I want you to buy a little carriage and a whip for me," he said to his father one day, "and a little brozer to go inside for a shentleman, and I be the toachman." Could not Ferdinando go out and catch a little boy for him to be his brother, he suggested. If only little brothers were so easily captured!

With all his winning ways which made his mother exclaim, "If not like a boy, yet so much like an angel!" he had something unreal, even disturbing, about him. He was too beautiful, too unusual, too precocious—qualities which his mother carefully tended. Browning would have given him a more robust education, starting with toy guns and going on to solid scales at the piano, under his guidance. Penini adored him, shot off his guns, and played his scales to please him with such proficiency that Browning too lost his sense of proportion and boasted that he could make an infant wonder of him in two years. The mother became a little jealous at Penini's partiality for his father, a trifle more possessive of this marvel among children, and felt hurt enough to note down his saying, when she asked for more kisses: "No —no more! All mine oller kisses are Papa's."

After Penini's fifth year his care except for his musical instruction and physical education was taken over almost wholly by Mrs. Browning. Not that Robert was excluded. Ba loved him too well to deprive him of the least pleasure in their son. But little by little Penini became his mother's boy, the ethereal creature she imagined him to be. She dressed him in velvets, laces, and plumes, flounced undergarments, and Renaissance hats. The blouses under his jacket were of silk, and embroidered. His boots, of the softest leather, were a marvel of Florentine art. He was her masterpiece and in many ways reflected her.

Like her he was considerably interested in the war. Didn't she dislike the Austrians very much, he asked her one day. "Yes, I dislike them in Florence," she answered him. "They have no business here."

Like her too he had definite opinions and delighted her by passing judgment on the nations with the succinctness of a statesman. "The Tedeschi are really velly naughty, I sint. The Flench are dood—the Russians—oh, hollid!"

By 1855, however, Penini had almost outgrown the babytalk which Mrs. Browning reproduced with such loving fidelity. Even more lovingly she recorded his utterances, finding portentous meanings in his words. Once, on coming back from a walk he said to her, "Dear Mama! I saw today the points of the trees of the place where they've put Joe's outside."

"A clairvoyant talking of the shell of us could not have spoken better of the burial of the body," she marveled.

In June the Brownings left for England, loitering only a week in Paris. They had work to do in London, as the sheaves of manuscript tucked away in their luggage indicated. Browning's *Men and Women* was complete, copied fair by the hand of a female admirer. Elizabeth's *Aurora Leigh* was nearly two-thirds done. While Robert was seeing his volumes through the press she would resume her novel-poem.

No sooner had they settled at 13 Dorset Street than they found to their dismay that Mrs. Browning's trunk had been misdirected. It was calamitous indeed! What would Penini do without his lovely wardrobe, the embroidered collars, the lace-edged breeches? Of course it was dreadful too that *Aurora Leigh* happened to be in the same trunk—but how could Ba replace Penini's finery, the setting for her living jewel? Fortunately the trunk arrived, and Penini escaped the indignity of dressing like other little boys.

The influx of visitors began anew in spite of the proof-sheets that soon began arriving from the printer. Arabel made daily visits. Henrietta, however, could not afford to come to London. Ba missed her, but she was more than ever grateful to Arabel who neglected her welfare work, more than ever demanding, for her sake. The previous year Arabel had helped to found a refuge for destitute girls for which she had enlisted Ba's aid and Robert's. They sent her a poem each, which she printed and sold as a pamphlet at a bazaar to help raise money. The *Two Poems* included in the title were Mrs. Browning's "A Plea for the Ragged Schools of London" and Browning's "The Twins." Even at the modest price of sixpence a copy the pamphlet sold so poorly that Arabel had a large stack on hand for many years.

That summer another Barrett incurred paternal anathema when Alfred had the temerity to marry his cousin Lizzie who had lived with the family at Wimpole Street. Mr. Barrett reacted to this latest disobedience which had taken place at a safe distance, at the Paris Embassy, by opening his will and disinheriting his son as he had done his daughters. The Brownings knew well by this time that they would have knocked at his door in vain.

But if Mr. Barrett remained his inexorable self—not unforgiving, for he allowed publicly that he had forgiven the daughters who had disgraced his family—there was always comfort in John Kenyon, who offered the Brownings his house at Devonshire Place. When they found it unavailable he insisted on their accepting a gift of fifty pounds toward their lodging expenses. Lord Lytton also invited the poets to Knebworth where his lordship was astounding his guests by pretending to be invisible. That invitation the Brownings were also obliged to refuse. The printers could not wait.

Not all the printers in the world, however, could keep Mrs. Browning at Dorset Street when Mr. and Mrs. Rymer, friends of hers and Robert's, invited them to meet the Scottish-American medium David Dunglass Home at their house in Ealing. The youth—he was only twenty-two—had been exercising his powers for five years or more in New York and Boston, violently rocking not only the cradle of American culture but the continent as well with his sensational phenomena. His fame had preceded him and it was with a sense of witnessing revelation that Mrs. Browning joined with her unwilling husband the seance that was held on that 23rd of July.

Before it began, the children of the house had gathered some flowers in the garden which the eldest daughter and Mr. Home twined into a wreath and left upon a table. Then the company formed a mystical circle at another, Browning, as the doubting one, being commissioned to investigate the phenomena as they occurred.

"We were touched by the invisible," Mrs. Browning recorded, "heard the music and raps, saw the table moved and had sight of the hands. Also, at the request of the medium, the spiritual hands took from the table a garland which lay there, and placed it upon my head. The particular hand which did this was of the largest human size, as white as snow and very beautiful. . . . I was perfectly calm! not troubled in any way."

In the 1872 edition of his *Incidents in my Life*, Home contributes his account. "During the seance this wreath was raised from the table by a supernatural power in the presence of us all, and whilst we were watching it, Mr. Browning, who was seated at the opposite side of the table, left his place and came and stood behind his wife, towards whom the wreath was being slowly carried, and upon whose head it was placed. . . . He expressed no disbelief . . . while Mrs. Browning was much moved, and she not only then but ever since expressed her entire belief and pleasure. . . ."

Between the seance and the writing of Mr. Home's recollections Browning's devastating "Mr. Sludge, the Medium" appeared. It left no one in doubt as to the original of the portrait, as honest as Browning's scorn and hate of all deceit could make it. Here the deceit was all the more reprehensible because it preyed on affliction. Mr. Home, in his account, now took revenge behind the shield of his hosts. "It was the remark of all the Rymer family, that Mr. Browning seemed much disappointed that the wreath was not put upon his own head instead of his wife's, and that his placing himself in the way of where it was being carried, was for the purpose of giving it an opportunity of being placed upon his own brow."

Far from expressing no disbelief in that evening's occurrences, as Home asserted, Browning demanded the opportunity of making further investigations to expose what he called the tricks of the father of lies. Moreover, when Home called at Dorset Street several days later, Browning would not shake hands with him. Indeed, for a few tense moments calculatedly insulting remarks flew from one to the other while Mrs. Browning, ready to faint at this treatment of a guest, took his hands as he was leaving and cried, "Dear Mr. Home, I am not to blame. Oh dear! Oh dear!"

This divergence between husband and wife persisted for a long time. "When you write me," Mrs. Browning warned Henrietta several weeks after the encounter, "don't say a word on the subject because it's a *tabooed* subject in this house—Robert and I taking completely different views."

The phenomenon of the ambulant wreath, however, gained currency. By the time it reached Mrs. Jameson through the *Court Journal* the story went that the spiritual hands of Dante had risen from the ground and crowned Mrs. Browning with an orange wreath under Mr. Home's influence. Mr. Browning, it seemed, was preserving the wreath "as a memorial of this honour." "Pray, never mention his name, though," Ba kept reminding her correspondents about the luckless medium.

An *entente cordiale* was eventually established on the psychic senior, while almost wholly ignoring him. As for the Laureate, he was so much engrossed in his poetry that he had no recollection whatsoever that besides the Brownings Rossetti, a considerable poet, had been among them. With Italian *cortesia* Rossetti gave his hosts the sketch of Tennyson,—not a very good one. That night Mrs. Browning copied on it the first line of "Maud":

I hate the dreadful hollow behind the little wood . . .

The poem was bitterly criticized when it appeared. What! The crowned poet of sweet cadences, the singer of the good and the beautiful, now writing of blood and passion? No! No! The Victorian dovecotes were one flurry of feathers. Delicate readers, both male and female, lifted up their voices in horror. Tennyson, deeply melancholy by nature, sank into another of his moods of depression into which he escaped from unpleasant reality.

In October the Brownings returned to Paris to await the publication of Robert's *Men and Women*. The proof-sheets were back at the printer's; the poems had been enthusiastically approved by Browning's literary godfather, Mr. Fox, to whom he had read them. Meanwhile Mrs. Browning had still to finish *Aurora Leigh* for which London life had allowed little leisure.

In the middle of November Chapman and Hall brought out *Men and Women* in two volumes like Mrs. Browning's *Poems* which had made her famous, and like them bound in green, the color of hope. Mrs. Browning who had read them in manuscript knew that here her husband had excelled himself. "Robert's poems are magnificent and will raise him higher than he stands," she declared. Her judgment about his work was as usual impeccable; her prophecy was to verify itself, if only at long range.

Browning too knew the quality of the fifty poems in which he had crystallized the thought and experience of his mature genius. He also knew that merit does not necessarily bring reward. Humanly, he wished the work to succeed, not alone for its own sake but because it was his justification to his wife that their love had made him what he now was. She had placed upon his brow the coronal of her *Sonnets from the Portuguese*. He now laid at her feet the tribute of his *Men and Women*, the fruit of the *vita nuova* to which they had been reborn with the birth of their love. "One Word More," his poem of dedication to E.B.B., which he added at the close, made the gift explicit to that "angel—borne, see, on my bosom!"

> Love, you saw me gather men and women,
> Live or dead or fashioned by my fancy,
> Enter each and all and use their service,
> Speak from every mouth . . .
> Let me speak this once in my true person,
> Not as Lippo, Roland or Andrea,
> Though the fruit of speech be just this sentence—
> Pray you, look on these my men and women,
> Take and keep my fifty poems finished;
> Where my heart lies, let my brain lie also!
> Poor the speech; be how I speak, for all things.

It was an England in the throes of the Crimean War, an England that had sustained grave losses since the previous year when it had joined France in declaring war against Russia, an England fearful of financial crisis that received Browning's *Men and Women*. Nevertheless, the first news that reached the Brownings on the fortunes of the book filled them with joy. Within the first three days the orders came in so rapidly that the publisher's expenses were entirely covered. Browning's Pre-Raphaelite admirers gave the poems an ecstatic reception. Not content with exulting in his immediate circle, Dante Gabriel Rossetti sang their praises to Ruskin at Denmark Hill, to his new disciples William Morris and Burne-Jones at Oxford. Morris, who had recently discovered that he could wield a pen as well as a brush, exercised his expansive talent in a review of *Men and Women* that fairly burst through the pages of the *Oxford and Cambridge Magazine*, child of Rossetti's extinct *Germ*.

Every important journal took notice of the new work. None gave it the perfervid response of the handful of youths who while the rest of England remained deaf heard in Browning a new voice, an individual music, a prophet, a teacher and a master. The future, Browning's true audience, recognized its own. As often before, the *Athenaeum*, spokesman for a literate John Bull, distinguished itself for obtuseness. "Who will not grieve," it apostrophized on *Men and Women*, "over energy wasted and power misspent,—over fancies . . . so overhung by the seven veils of obscurity? . . ."

The question found sympathetic response in extraordinary places. Ruskin, however, despite Rossetti's valiant exegesis on his admired Browning refused to understand and took it upon himself to instruct the poet on what poetry should be. Then the critical Mrs. Grundys took up arms for morality and charged Browning with advocating

illicit love in his poem of "The Statue and the Bust." The Church
in the person of the anonymous reviewer of the Catholic *Rambler*,
later identified as Cardinal Wiseman found "Bishop Blougram's
Apology" full of matter extremely offensive to Catholics, but concluded that "if Mr. Browning is a man of will and action, and not
a mere dreamer and talker, we should never feel surprise at his conversion."

The very variety of the sources of criticism argued Browning's far-
reaching interests. Nothing that concerned man, his mind, his past
and future, was alien to him. He had made that clear again and again,
as the function of the poet from the moment he had had to justify
himself. He had reiterated it in his essay written as an introduction
to the *Letters of Percy Bysshe Shelley* which Moxon had brought out
in 1852. Though the letters proved to be forgeries Browning's essay
remained as valid to the end of his life as when, in special-pleading
for his beloved Shelley, he also pleaded his case. "Genius is essentially
moral," he could have answered the detractors of *Men and Women*.
"In the face of any conspicuous achievement of genius, philosophy,
no less than sympathetic instinct, warrants our belief in a great moral
purpose having mainly inspired even where it does not look out of
the same . . . The whole poet's function [is one] of beholding with
an understanding and keenness the universe, nature and man, in their
actual state of perfection and imperfection. . . ."

Ruskin's didacticism he answered with a defiant letter from Paris.
"I look upon my own shortcomings too sorrowfully . . . But I shall
never feel other than disconcerted and apprehensive when the public,
critics and all, begin to understand and approve me . . . A poet's affair
is with God, to whom he is accountable, and of whom is his reward. . . ."

Still, he could not but feel dejected when the first flood of interest
in *Men and Women* stagnated to the usual indifference. He had
given England the very heart's blood of his genius. He had sung his
love in varied music, painted it in intimate glimpses of married bliss—

> . . . I will speak now
> No longer watch you as you sit
>   Reading by fire-light, that great brow
> And the spirit-small hand propping it,
>   Mutely . . .

> Oh, the little more, and how much it is!
> And the little less, and what worlds away!

He had given expression to the broken rhythms of modern man who was discovering psychology and could no longer tread the easy wellworn measures. He had wandered wide in lore and brought back treasures of learning. He had delved deep in philosophy and religion and transmuted his ore into poetry from which whole libraries grew. Verses from most of his poems were to become the familiar furniture of speech. But, except to the few, he remained alien and obscure. Besides, the public still heard ringing in its ears the stirring memorial to England's heroic dead in an episode of the war that was still in progress:

> Half a league, half a league,
> Half a league onward,
> All in the valley of Death
> Rode the six hundred . . .

In her private letters Mrs. Browning reiterated her faith in her husband's poems. "I am ready to die for them at the stake."

Chapter XX: "Beautiful!"

JOHN KENYON was ill, so very ill that in May of 1856 his only brother, Edward, was sent for from Vienna. When the Brownings heard of their friend's plight Robert immediately offered himself as nurse, but Kenyon was already under medical care. In June, therefore, they returned to London with Wilson, now Mrs. Ferdinando Romagnoli, and stayed at Mr. Kenyon's house in Devonshire Place. He himself had gone to the Isle of Wight. There the Brownings spent some time with him and left reluctantly, knowing that their generous friend, the lover of life, was lying on his deathbed. By an odd circumstance Edward Kenyon died suddenly, and so the dying man found his vast fortune increased by the considerable estate of his brother.

It had been painful to the Brownings to see the destruction that cancer had wrought upon their friend's shining mind and powerful frame. Mrs. Browning was also shocked by an accident to her father which left him permanently lame. Grieved by this knowledge of his affliction, once more that summer she endeavored to soften his heart. A stone would have been more responsive. Time had only aggravated his rancor which found relief in spiteful acts such as sending his family off to the country when he heard that his daughter was to be in London. Still Elizabeth never ceased writing her pathetic pleas to her sisters: "Always mention dearest Papa . . . Speak always of Papa . . . I dream of him and pray for him."

In John Kenyon's London house Mrs. Browning wrote the close of *Aurora Leigh* and prepared the book for the printer. She had not had time for it in Paris, what with Penini's lessons and the constant interruption of well-meaning visitors, when she would quickly thrust the manuscript under a cushion, not to be caught in the private act of creation. Before leaving for London she had shown Robert as much of the book as she had written, never having read him a line before.

"I wish, in one sense," he sighed, "that I had written, and she had read it, so."

His dejection over his own work deepened. He had not the heart

264

to begin anything new but put in futile months in the revision of *Sordello*. Meanwhile their expenses increased, while scarcely any money came in from his poetry. Surely it was of him, and of poets like him, that Mrs. Browning had her Aurora say:

> "The worthiest poets have remained uncrowned
> Till death has bleached their foreheads to the bone;
> And so with me it must be, unless I prove
> Unworthy of the great adversity."

Robert, certainly, seemed destined for that ultimate election.

Almost a year after the publication of *Men and Women*, Mrs. Browning's *Aurora Leigh*, which had long been talked about in literary circles, appeared before a public much relieved by the Treaty of Paris that terminated the Crimean War, and by a vast issue of paper notes which saved the Bank of England. Again the people had the peace of mind to enjoy their reading, and money enough to spend on books. Mrs. Browning's new work had much to recommend it. It was a novel, in itself a temptation to a novel-devouring public, and it had nothing, at any rate, little, to do with current politics. In her dedication to John Kenyon she wrote of the book as "the most mature of my works, and the one into which my highest convictions upon life and art have entered." The public always enjoys being uplifted if it is done in an entertaining manner. As before, the Brownings left England, this time for Florence, to give the book's fortunes the perspective of distance.

Despite the natural apprehension that always accompanies the throwing of one's brain-born Daniel to the critical lions, Mrs. Browning had faith in her book. She had put into it her thoughts, her emotions, her beliefs, her very soul, giving them objectivity through the person of her Aurora who combined the passion of a Florentine mother and the intellectual traits of an English father. By that device the author was able to draw upon her knowledge of English and Italian life, on a canvas already prepared by the vivid sketches in her letters. The subject of woman's personal dignity in the choice of her love and her art was very close to her.

Aurora Leigh had an immense success. The first edition sold out within a fortnight. A second followed. A third was required within a month. "The extravagances written to me about the book would make you laugh," Mrs. Browning wrote to a friend, "and the daily and weekly press upon which I calculated for furious abuse, has been

psychoanalytical research Mrs. Browning is completely vindicated.

Aurora Leigh was a remarkable work not because, as Barry Cornwall said, it was "the finest poem ever written by a woman," but rather because it expressed an enlightened modernity. Mrs. Browning had gone far since her volume of 1844. For eleven years her mind had been sharpened and refined by her husband's. Through his opening the door of her cage she had escaped from vicarious life to life itself. Together they had been living it fully—a life of the spirit, of solid scholarship and creativeness, as well as the simple diurnal living of a husband and wife who deeply loved not only each other but the world. Nothing that happened escaped their vigilant minds or failed to touch their hearts. In *Aurora Leigh* Mrs. Browning gave expression to her observation, her sympathy, her convictions on beauty and truth and the relations of the sexes. The book, for all its delving into depths of degradation that she could not have known except through her imagination, was personal enough to be selfportraiture. She admitted as much when she wrote to Mrs. Jameson: "I have put much of myself in it." The portrait did her credit and showed her to be as elevated in her moral character as in her poetic imagination. The story, like everything too close to its time, has dated, but the finest flights of her poetry endure in beauty as her moral values in their unchanging truth.

On the 3rd of December John Kenyon died. At the reading of the will his thoughtfulness manifested itself in death as in life. Among the bequests he left to his friends, the largest, of eleven thousand pounds, went to the Brownings. In a sense it was as much a tribute to poetry as to friendship as Elizabeth well knew when she read his last affectionate letter on her dedication to him of *Aurora Leigh*. Economic pressure no longer need worry Robert now. With the tact characteristic of him, Mr. Kenyon had apportioned the legacy in two unequal shares the larger of which went to Browning—possibly because unlike his wife, Browning had no income.

The bequest did not go unnoticed at Wimpole Street where Mr. Barrett fumed because his relative had not remembered him in the will. Elizabeth grieved at her father's vexation and found excuses for him. "If the principle of relationship had been recognized at all, which it was not," she said, "he had his undoubted claim."

But even if Mr. Barrett had entered his claim it would have been too late. In April of 1857 he too was dead, after a brief illness that neither he nor his family had taken too seriously. When Elizabeth learned of her father's death she was too stunned at first to accept it. Long since she had abandoned all hope of reconciliation, yet the finality of death left her so desolate that she hugged her grief and buried herself with it, away from Robert, away even from her child, in the same morbid death-in-life that had followed Edward's drowning. Again guilt and self-recrimination came to torment her. Had she not embittered her father's last years by her disobedience, her deception? Had she not justly incurred his unforgiving anger? The loving father of the Hope End days came to accuse her, the man who called her absurd pet names, the man who had made her a poet. If she had not disobeyed him . . .

For days she lay in bed, as incapable of action as a corpse but for her weeping. Robert hovered about her, tender and understanding. Penini gazed at her with great troubled eyes. What had happened to his happy Mamma who had watched him empty the stocking that Befana, the Fairy of Florence, had filled on Twelfth Night—filled full of oranges and bon-bons, a doll and a powder flask, and an accordion to make music on the carnival? Why was she crying, and why was Papa sad when they had all been so gay in their masks and dominos, Papa and Mamma in black, and he in beautiful blue, and everybody singing and dancing? And why did Mama not give him his lessons?

Gradually Mrs. Browning returned to life, but something of her died in the final sundering of that tie. Only now that her father was gone did she realize that although she had believed hope dead, she had never really accepted the brutal fact of remaining unforgiven, her husband unaccepted, her son unkissed by this most relentless of men. She clung more than ever to Robert and the boy. She took an interest once more in her friends who had been so considerate and understanding. But the corners of her mouth had something rueful in their smile. The little sieges of the old illness came more often now and lasted longer. But she obediently rested and took "cod's liver oil" and humored the doctors, assuring Robert in private: "This is only one of my old attacks. I know all about it and I shall get better." And invariably she would get better.

The visiting Americans that year included Mrs. Stowe. Because of the immense popularity of *Uncle Tom's Cabin* Ba had expected a vain, loud woman full of rampant Americanisms. She found instead a simple, gentle lady with a sweet voice. "Never did lion roar more softly," she commented. Here was a woman who exemplified in life her portrait of the dawning noble female, another Aurora Leigh. "Her books are not so much to me, I confess, as the fact is . . . that she has moved the world—and *for good*." The first visit pleased everyone so much that Mrs. Stowe called again the following morning, when Browning took her to see the *salvators* at the end of their street.

Interest in spiritualism had not subsided. At Isa Blagden's at Bellosguardo the mystic circles continued to form with Edward Robert Lytton, Ba, and as many others as wished to join, touching hands upon a table. "Seeing who will turn it least apparently!" Browning scoffed from a distance. Another medium, a Mr. Jarves, came from America to inquire at Casa Guidi whether it were true, as everyone said in Florence, that *Aurora Leigh* had been written by the spirits, Mrs. Browning only contributing her hand to hold the pen.

At the first fiery breath of summer the Brownings escaped to Bagni di Lucca with their friend Isa and young Lytton of the invisible father. The sessions round the table, while not productive of any sensational phenomena, had brought out a spiritual affinity between the twenty-six-year-old youth and the mature Isa. The walks among the chestnut trees, the excursions to the mountains, and the ever-present marital devotion of the Brownings drew them closer still. Then suddenly, not long after their arrival, Lytton succumbed to gastric fever and for nearly six weeks he could not leave his bed. Isa nursed him devotedly. Browning sat by his side at night. By the time Lytton was well enough to return to Florence Robert and Ba were certain that wedding bells would soon be ringing, especially since Isa and the young man planned to house together at her villa. "Unless Sir Edward comes down to catch up his son and change the plan," said Ba. No one knows whether His Lordship materialized for the snatching. But there was no marriage either then or later between Isa and Lytton, and only their poems preserved their summer love like a faded Victorian posy.

No sooner had Lytton left than Penini fell sick with the fever. For the first time in his life he was alarmingly ill and his mother was insane with anxiety during the two weeks that he lay in bed, his face flushed among his golden curls. "You pet! Don't be unhappy about me," he tried to cheer her. "Think it's only a boy in the street and be a little sorry, but not unhappy!"

No wonder she was prouder of him than of twenty *Auroras*, as she wrote to Leigh Hunt when he praised her poem.

Yet such sensibility was frightening in so young a boy. Hawthorne who saw him not long afterward at Casa Guidi confided his perturbation to his notebook. "I never saw such a boy as this before; so slender, fragile and spirit-like . . . as if he had nothing to do with human flesh and blood. His face is very pretty and most intelligent, and exceedingly like his mother's. He is nine years old, and seems at once less childlike and less manly than befit that age. I should not quite like to be the father of such a boy, and should fear to stake so much interest and affection on him as he cannot fail to inspire. I wonder what is to become of him,—whether he will grow to be a man,—whether it is desirable that he should."

Neither Robert nor Elizabeth was writing very much during the late fifties. The sustained effort of creating *Aurora Leigh* had been a drain upon Mrs. Browning's energy. The death of her father, bringing back the early years under his tutelage, dammed the poetic source. As for Browning, the cool reception of *Men and Women* aggravated the heartsickness of deferred hope. He knew well that apparent failure was only a stepping stone to ultimate triumph. He could console himself as the years passed, by his own verses:

> What's time? Leave Now for dogs and apes!
> Man has Forever.

Still, even the philosophical mind finds it hard to encompass Forever, while the heart humanly yearns for Now.

They traveled a great deal. But now the quest for sunshine and moderate winds became a necessity as Mrs. Browning's cough sounded more frequently over the animated conversation of the friends they had everywhere. During the summer of 1858 they went to Havre where they shared a house with old Mr. Browning and Sarianna. Winter took them to Rome. Then spring lured them back to Casa Guidi, the orange trees and camellias in the garden, and their balcony filled with blooms. But they did not stay long. The compulsion to move about seized them with the first change in the weather.

In July of 1859 Mrs. Browning had such a severe recurrence of the lung symptoms that Browning rushed her to Siena. The Storys and Landor—at war with his family and in disgrace with the world for a libelous article he had written against the Rev. Morris Yescombe— lived near the Villa Alberti where the Brownings were staying. They visited one another often, rode donkey-back, enjoyed lazy rambles over the gentle country in view of the purple hills and, in the evening, had music and conversation.

Penini, whose name was now shortened to Pen in deference to his maturity, had progressed sufficiently in his music to play duets with his father. He could also speak and read four languages, ride his own pony, and compose poetry which his mother esteemed far above her own. With the Story children, Edith, Julian, and Waldo, he watched the contadini at their work, sometimes helping them herd the sheep and drive the grape carts. Then his mother fondly converted him into a pastoral god. She could never get over his beauty.

In Rome, the previous winter, Munroe the sculptor had made a bust of him. "Really exquisite it is!" Mrs. Browning cried with delight. Now in Siena he was being painted on his pony by the Boston artist Hamilton Wild. His mother decked him in his most sumptuous finery even though he was not now, as in Rome, always in sight of the world—the excuse she gave for Pen's extravagant wardrobe of velvet blouses. Browning humored her, happy that she had less cough, that she got slowly but visibly stronger and could join him on short walks—a decided improvement over the first few weeks when in a letter to Isa Blagden he wrote words that must have resuscitated the early alarms of Wimpole Street: "She takes no solid food yet except a canary bird's allowance of toast at breakfast. She cannot walk alone from chair to sofa . . ."

That year the little domestic circle began breaking up. While at Siena, Browning had accepted the office of guardian for Landor who had been growing daily more fiery and irresponsible, despite his patriarchal beard. Between the raging old man and his irritating relatives Browning found it difficult to keep an equable course. He was fond of repeating a colloquy with Landor whom he went to visit on a Sunday morning. "Mrs. Landor called today," began Browning.

"Ha!" Landor snorted. "Why, you did not let her in? Never surely let her in?"

"Oh, I should let a dog in, even, bearing your name on the collar!"

"Ay, a dog—good; But a——?"

Before leaving for Florence Browning established the old lion in a pleasant little apartment, and Wilson, rather, Signora Romagnoli, was appointed his duenna on a salary of twenty-two pounds a year, "besides what is left of his rations." The pickings were not much, to judge by the poet's leonine appetite, not to mention his habit of throwing his plate out of the window or dashing it to the ground when he did not like his dinner.

Flush, too, at about this time, drops out of the letters and disappears from the scene. When did he die and how? Surely Ba mourned the faithful sharer of her London back bedroom, the only witness to her tears when, as she lay against her pillow

> . . . two golden-clear
> Great eyes astonished mine, a drooping ear
> Did flap me on either cheek to dry the spray.

There was no great poetry in the tribute but there had been great love. Love too was in the hands that laid Flush's little body in the vaults of Casa Guidi.

Political events in Italy were meanwhile reaching a crisis. For several years national feeling had been rising, fomented by revolutionaries of every party to bring about the wished-for unification. The great Venetian exile, Daniele Manin, declared as he lay dying in Paris: "Italy must be created! *Make Italy, and I am with you,* the republican party says to the House of Savoy!"

The House of Savoy was ready, with a willing king in Victor Emmanuel. Garibaldi, back from America, was waiting for action on the island of Caprera. Count Camillo di Cavour, who had earned the right to represent Italy at the Congress of Paris, soon won the majority of the people, eager to rally at the cry, "Italy and Victor Emmanuel!" Only Mazzini, brooding in London, clung to the revolutionary tenets of the Young Italy he had founded, and saw in Cavour an irreconcilable opponent. An indirect expression of Mazzini's disfavor came with Orsini's attempt on the life of Napoleon III who favored Cavour and the House of Savoy. Orsini, as a follower of Mazzini, of course incriminated his leader.

Mrs. Browning in Italy was as much shocked as the French nation by this attempt on the emperor's life. She had an unshaken faith in his friendship toward the Italian cause and broke out into a paean of rejoicing when in the spring of 1859 Napoleon III joined Italy after Austria had declared war. She did not know, as indeed she had no way of knowing, that before his noble intervention the emperor had made a secret pact with Cavour to receive Savoy and possibly Nice as the price of his support.

The stirring events awoke in her the desire to sing again. Even her epistolary prose became lyrical. "Louis Napoleon has acted—I was going to say—sublimely—and why should I not? . . . Italy stretches her arms to him as to the very angel of the resurrection. Emancipation was utterly impossible without foreign help, and he

no reason . . . To you I may say that the blindness, deafness and stupidity of the English public to Robert are amazing . . . Robert *is*. All England cannot prevent his existence . . . But nobody there except a small knot of Pre-Raphaelite men, pretends to do him justice . . . English people will come and stare at me sometimes, but physicians, dentists, who serve me and refuse their fees, artists who give me pictures, friends who give up their carriages and make other practical sacrifices, are not English—no. . . .".

It pleased her to know, however, that although Robert was no prophet in his own land he had a greater following than her own in America. There, as she said, he was a power, a poet. He was read. He lived in the heart of the people. They gave Browning readings and Browning evenings. But such appreciation from across the ocean did not suffice to make him sit at his desk like Tennyson in a productive routine of writing. Instead of immortal *Men and Women* Robert was making clay copies of "Psyche" and "Young Augustus."

Because she could not go out as often as before Ba insisted on Robert's visiting their friends without her. He would leave reluctantly, half-persuaded by her assurances that her coughing meant nothing, that she would soon be well again. Gone were the days when they mingled in the Florentine crowds, wandered through galleries for hours, went to masquerades, the theater, the opera. Now everything fatigued her. Last year in Rome she had been at death's door merely because she had ventured out in a closed carriage to the artist Castellani's shop to look at the presentation swords he had made— works of art worthy of his genius—for Napoleon III and Victor Emmanuel. The rain and the night air had been too much for her. Now even warmth and sunlight did not seem to help. She was also acutely distressed by the news from home of her sister Henrietta's illness. At her request Robert had been intercepting the letters, reading to her as much of the contents as she could bear to hear.

Casa Guidi no longer attracted them, Ba complaining that they were forced to go away in the winter, forced to go away in the summer. Except for the month of June, they spent a good part of 1860 in Rome in an apartment in Via Felice, easily accessible to the Storys and other friends. Burne-Jones and Val Prinsep, disciples of Dante Gabriel Rossetti, had called on them in Rome the previous winter when, after taking long walks with Browning, Prinsep found time to make a portrait sketch of Mrs. Browning. It is one of the most sensitive portraits ever drawn of a face whose subtleties baffled every artist —and they were many—who attempted to capture them. The eyes and brow have a grave, deep, spiritual calm. The whole face glows from an inner serenity made humanly beautiful by the resignation of the suffering lips.

As if to stay the passing moments the Brownings posed for Alessandri, the photographer. In one of his pictures Browning's thick dark hair, flowing mustache and short beard, his wide black hat and loose long coat give him an Italianate look. He might have been a Roman artist or musician in his vivid handsomeness. Ba sat for Alessandri with Pen who was then eleven years old. Her face between the black glossy wings of her hair is worn and ravaged. The eyes are sunken and shadowed, but the brave mouth still smiles. Pen in an elaborately braided jacket and white breeches is seated beside her in the better known of the two photographs. In the other he stands on her right, his left hand in hers, his feet in white socks and black dancing slippers poised as if he were about to take off in a ballet. Were it not for his breeches he might easily have been mistaken for a girl in his fancy broideries and hair as long as his mother's.

By one of those inexplicable circumstances the brief time the Brownings spent in Florence that year was of the utmost importance to Robert, the poet. At any rate he himself saw predestination in the walk he took one June day from Casa Guidi

> . . . when a Hand,
> Always above my shoulder, pushed me once . . .
> Across a square in Florence, crammed with booths,
> Buzzing and blaze, noontide and market-time;
> Toward Baccio's marble,—ay, the basement ledge
> O' the pedestal. . . .

There, in that corner of the Piazza San Lorenzo, amid an assortment of picture frames, angel heads, bits of worn tapestry, prints and odd volumes, he found a square book bound in yellowed vellum lying on a pile. He picked it up and at once knew that he must have it. He gave a *lira* for it—eightpence in English coin—and walked off with his prize.

He could not wait till he got home to examine the printed pamphlets and the sheets of manuscript that composed it, but then and there began to read it,

> . . . from the written title-page
> To written index, on, through street and street,
> At the Strozzi, at the Pillar, at the Bridge;
> Till by the time I stood at home again

In Casa Guidi by Felice Church . . .
I had mastered the contents. . . .

It was the court record, in Latin, of a triple murder that had shocked
all Rome in January of 1698.

The rest of the day Browning read on, most of the night also, resting the bulky tome on the cream-colored agate slab of the chest of
drawers and leaning his head on his elbow. He became so possessed
by the horror of the accounts that he had to step out on the terrace
to walk back and forth and find the world again in the chanting of
the cloistered nuns of San Felice. Here was an ingot of truth that
he had found. But he still had to fuse his "live soul and that inert
stuff" before attempting the smithcraft of art. Ba could not be drawn
to take any interest in the Roman murder story, not even so much
as to look through the old yellow book. The world of reality had
sorrow and anguish enough as it was.

When they closed Casa Guidi once more for Rome Browning,
still engrossed in the murder case, took the book along with him and
carried on further research of his own. They had hardly settled down
again in Via Felice when letters from England arrived which made
Robert anticipate the worst for Henrietta. He kept back the pur-
port of the communications from Ba as long as possible. But when
he realized that the end was inevitable he prepared her as gently as
he could. Nevertheless Henrietta's death from a lingering cancer
struck Ba a stunning blow, despite the suspense of weeks during
which she had been bracing herself against the news. "You know
Ba's ways," Robert wrote to Isa Blagden, "how she hides herself in
such trouble as this, and she has seen nobody as yet. . . . She will get
over this as other losses, in time: but she has endured and is still
enduring sorrow enough."

Just as when her father died some of her life went with him,
Henrietta's death depleted still further Ba's diminished forces. That
winter they did not return to Casa Guidi, as if from some vague fear
of the house they had loved so much. They spent a little time at
Arezzo for Robert's investigation of the Roman murder case, and in
the late spring of 1861, they again went to Rome. The coming summer they planned to spend with Browning's father and sister in Paris.

The national cause, nearing its accomplishment with the seizure
of the last stubborn strongholds by the patriots early in the year,
made the unification of Italy a question of months. Mrs. Browning
saw a dream fulfilled and was happy for the land that had meant

home, life, and liberty. Perhaps it was not altogether unfortunate that she could not take the long journey to Paris, although she felt guilty for keeping Robert from his father and Sarianna.

On the 4th of June they started off for Florence, stopping to rest for a few days in Siena. Casa Guidi had to be opened, but Isa Blagden, kindest of friends, would help. Dear Isa, to whom Ba dared to voice a premonitory feeling kept from Robert himself—the pain she had, these days, whenever she looked on the face of her little son.

The pleasant life of former times could not yet be reestablished. It was too far for Ba to walk to Bellosguardo. Robert went alone to see his difficult charge who had left Siena and was now staying with Isa. But what a transformed Landor! The great froth and bubblement of white beard had vanished together with every hair of his head. "To look younger," said some. "Cleaner," said others. Browning found enough reason to thank his stars at seeing him well and rationally disposed.

Everyone in Florence was looking forward hopefully to the great days ahead for the official recognition of the Italian nation when suddenly the country was thrown into mourning by the death of Cavour. The flags hung out for the triumph mingled with the funeral crepe. The joyful music became a dead march. "Italy is created—all is safe!" had been Cavour's last words.

"May God save Italy without his angels!" cried the grief-stricken Mrs. Browning.

For days she sat listless as if numbed by the calamity. "I have been beaten and bruised ever since," she wrote to the Storys. Robert, always afflicted by her suffering, stood by, helpless, as after the shocking peace of Villafranca, from which it had taken Ba a whole summer to recover. How like Pan's reed she was in that most beautiful of her lyrics, "A Musical Instrument"—the reed that makes music only when its pith is drawn out, like the heart of a man. For

> "This is the way," laughed the great god Pan,
>   (Laughed while he sat by the river,)
> "The only way, since gods began
>   To make sweet music, they could succeed. . . ."

Now Ba did not get better, and the intolerably hot weather oppressed her lungs. Clad only in her nightgown she would sit in the drawing room, the coolest in the house, and read the papers a little. To Robert's inquiries she would always answer that it was nothing—

she would get over this attack as before. But one day she admitted that although her cough had got well the weather was affecting her. Robert at once suggested their moving from Casa Guidi immediately.

"Ah, but I can't leave Florence, I like Florence!" she protested.

"No, there's Villa Niccolini," Robert suggested. "That would just suit."

"Yes, yes, that would suit. Try, inquire!" she agreed feverishly.

On the 20th of June toward evening Isa came while Robert was out and found Ba sitting in the doorway between cross-drafts of many windows. Isa remonstrated with her but Ba explained that the cushion back of her chair protected her. The following day she complained of a sore throat. All night long she coughed, sat up restlessly a great deal and seemed to suffer distressingly from congestion in the lungs. Robert left Ba with Annunziata and got Dr. Wilson, a chest specialist, out of bed. On examination Dr. Wilson told Browning that he found the right lung condensed and that he suspected an ulcer.

"It's the old story—they don't know my case!" said Ba. "This time it is said the right lung is affected. Dr. Chambers said just the contrary."

She followed the doctor's instructions, however, going to bed early and taking a little nourishment. "I feel rather better," she said cheerfully to Robert.

About a week later she was so weak that her voice was all but extinct. She dozed fitfully in the small bed that had been moved into the drawing room, but the coughing would awaken her. Then she began to complain of constant headache and confused thoughts. She told the doctor that she had been troubled because the windows seemed to be hung in the Hungarian colors. "Oh, I not only have asses' milk but asses' thoughts," she smiled while drinking the prescribed glass. "I am so troubled with silly politics and nonsense."

Everyone, however, including Dr. Wilson, thought that she was getting better. But Robert would not leave her, neither day nor night.

On the 29th her thoughts wandered whenever she awakened from her dozing. Robert, sitting by her, watched anxiously. Now and then he spoke to her. She would then open her eyes, smile at him, and relapse into semi-consciousness. He knew she would not outlive the night. Nevertheless with Annunziata's help he tried to preserve the flickering life. Toward three in the morning, when she opened her eyes, he asked softly, "You know me?"

"My Robert—my heavens, my beloved!" she said in her ghost of a voice, reaching up and kissing him. "Our lives are held by God."

Keeping her arms about him, she repeated, "God bless you"—till he laid her down gently to sleep, for the last time, as he knew. "How do you feel?" he asked her softly.

"Beautiful!" she sighed.

The following evening while her body was lying in the next room Browning, alone but for Annunziata and Pen, wrote to his sister, a long letter reliving those last weeks. All day, he told her, Pen had sat clasping him, saying things to him such as Ba would have said. "I shall now go and sit with herself—my Ba, forever . . . My life is fixed and sure now. I shall live out the remainder in her direct influence, endeavoring to complete mine, miserably imperfect now . . . I have our child about whom I shall exclusively employ myself, doing her part by him. I shall live in the presence of her, in every sense, I hope and believe—so that so far my loss is not *irreparable*—but the future is nothing to me now, except inasmuch as it confirms and realizes the past . . .

"How she looks now—how perfectly beautiful!"

There was a small gold ring on her finger made by Castellani in imitation of the Etruscan circlets found among the ruins. Browning wore it on his watch chain to the end of his life.

Chapter XXI: On the Stalwart Shoulders
of Youth

"DON'T fancy I am prostrated. I have enough to do for myself and the boy in carrying out her wishes," Browning wrote to Leighton not long after the first day of July 1861 when the rays of the dying sun fell for the last time on the mortal body of Elizabeth Barrett Browning. Amid the friends who had known and loved her, Browning stood in the shadow of the cypresses of the English Cemetery and watched each spadeful of earth as it fell, covering the dark narrow door that leads to eternal life.

Yet something more than his wife's frail body which had taken so little room in life as in death was buried under the sod of Florence. When Browning turned away from the grave he was on the surface the same man. But his heart was now only the efficient machine of his robust body. The heart that had known love lay buried with her.

To Macready, whom he wrote to congratulate on his second marriage—how soon some forget!—he repeated the same words as to Leighton. He would not permit himself to grieve. He had to fulfill his duty to her through their son. But Sarianna Browning, writing in August to an old friend, gave a truer picture. "The loss of my dear sister . . . was a sad blow and was followed by great anxiety on account of my poor brother . . . His bodily strength gave way and caused us great uneasiness. He has given up his residence in Italy and is now staying with my father and myself. The calmness and the sea have already done him great good."

Indeed, he could be seen in the morning sunlight running along the sands and leaping into the sea with Pen who was a changed boy, strong and bronzed. Browning noted with divided emotions that his son had a great capacity for suiting himself to circumstances. Some of the changes, however, were all to the good, though he looked back ruefully on what had been. "I seem hardly to remember the velvet tunic and short trowsers, the curls and hat and feathers of three months ago!" he wrote in September to Isa Blagden. "I have

more hopes than ever that he will take to what is good in English
life," he added.

Toward that end Isa had already preceded Browning as a sort of
advance guard to London. It was no empty compliment that Browning paid her when he said she was "perfect in friendship." She had
been at Casa Guidi just before Mrs. Browning's death. It was to Isa
the following dawn that Browning had sent a cabman with the
message, "*La Signora della Casa Guidi è morta.*" Isa it was who had
taken Pen and Edith Story whose parents had come from Leghorn
to be with Browning, to her own villa so that the children might be
spared the painful preparations of the funeral. Then, after Browning
returned to his empty house whose every object still bespoke *her*
presence—the chair in the drawing room drawn up close to the table
covered with *her* books and magazines; the bedroom curtained with
white where Pen was born; the chests of drawers for which *she* had
such partiality; *her* clothes lying about; *her* writing on the bits of
paper left scattered as if the pen had just dropped from her hand—
after the desolate man returned to a place so full, for all its emptiness,
it was Isa who gently led him up the hillslope to Bellosguardo and
kept him there till he was ready to leave the city of his greatest joy
and sorrow. Later, when Casa Guidi was dismantled, it was Isa who
went with Browning and Pen as far as Paris, where they parted—they
to go to St. Enogat, and Isa to find lodgings for Browning's eventual
return to England.

What, besides a natural kindness led Isa Blagden to befriend the
bereaved husband and his orphaned son? From the outset both
Browning and his wife had been drawn to Isa. The letters they exchanged were as unembarrassedly affectionate between Mrs. Browning and Isa as between Isa and Robert. Isa's villa was as much their
home as Casa Guidi. No invitations were necessary for the reciprocal
visits. In the course of the years during the intimacy of their close
living, Browning came to look upon Isa as almost another member
of the family, a sister like Sarianna, or Arabel, but fortunately nearly
always within reach. They built up their private *coteriesprache*, that
intimate language of banter and affection, of allusions to things done,
books read and discussed together, of sense and nonsense which, like
a firecracker, set off a series of delightful associations that remained
brilliant yet baffling to the uninitiate. More, they established a friendship that was neither afraid to use the word *love* nor to act upon it

—in tenderness in the common ways of life and in complete devotion in time of need.

The time of need had now come for Browning. Isa was ready to prove her love both for the departed friend and for the one who remained. They agreed to write to each other once a month wherever they might be, Isa Blagden on the 12th—the date of Browning's marriage—and he on the 19th. The letters were to be substitutes for conversations, easy, frank and intimate. They were also private. "Remember," he wrote to Isa, "I read your letters, twice, and then burn them: mine, I trust, earnestly conjure, you will never show: but you will not."

Isa Blagden never destroyed Browning's letters. They were found, carefully preserved, after her death in 1873.[1] It was another, a posthumous, token of devotion from "my nearly one, certainly best, woman friend," as Browning called her in a letter written the year after he had left Florence. Then he went on to make an outwardly puzzling reference which had its origin in their intimate language: "God bless you, we will be 'snakes' together yet if He pleases . . ." Again, in a subsequent letter, he said, "The years are going, Isa, and in three years I may begin to hope for a realization of the snake-metamorphosis . . . Take care of yourself for better reasons than the sake of your brother-snake that is to be."

There are at least half a dozen other allusions to their snake transformation at some future, idyllic time. To Browning who had no revulsion against snakes and who had made pets of them as a child, the reference held nothing sinister. On the contrary, when combined with the passage in Arnold's *Empedocles on Etna* which had given the colubrine creatures a place in Browning's intimate language with Isa Blagden, it puts their relationship in its true light and dispels the surmise some scholars have suggested that Miss Blagden aspired to become the second Mrs. Browning. In *Empedocles* occurs the song of Callicles:

> Far, far from here
> The Adriatic breaks in a warm bay

[1] These exceedingly important letters, invaluable for the light they shed on Browning's later years, are in the Baylor Browning Collection where they were generously put at the disposal of the author with other priceless Browning material. A major part of the letters were arranged for publication in 1923 by Dr. A. J. Armstrong as *Letters of Robert Browning to Miss Isa Blagden* and issued by Baylor University. A number of other letters exchanged by Browning and Isa Blagden appeared in *Letters of Robert Browning* edited by Thurman L. Hood, Yale University Press, in 1933.

> Among the green Illyrian hills . . .
> And there, they say, two bright and aged snakes,
> Who once were Cadmus and Harmonia,
> Bask in the glens or on the warm sea-shore,
> In breathless quiet, after all their ills. . . .

In another of Browning's letters the reference is still more direct: "Next time I may be three-parts 'the aged snake' and have house-room for you. Heart-room, meanwhile!" Clearly theirs was the purest friendship protected against ambiguity by Browning's calling himself Isa's "brother-snake." As for the expressions of love, they were of such long standing that their recurrence is merely the continuation of habit. In a note of 1857, added to one of Mrs. Browning's letters, he had written: "See what a little space is left me, dearest Isa! Shall I use it to tell you what you know already of my true love and constant remembrance of you? . . ." In another, from Havre, a year later, perhaps after some slight misunderstanding, he said: "Let us be very gracious to each other when we meet again. 'Love' each other we always did, I know, however portentous were the tokens of it." In April 1860, he wrote with somewhat heavy-handed levity: "Kiss and be friends, 'my own one' as the poet says, and how does he go on saying? Why, most appropriately. 'Now you are young, and when you are older, now you're coy, and when you're grown bolder, Now you're a maid, and when you're my wife, Till the end of this year, and the close of my life, I ever will love Thee!' Fact! . . ."

Not once after Mrs. Browning's death did he exceed such verbal demonstrativeness. Nevertheless, the love expressed in almost every one of the later letters is deeper and truer. The reason shines out in one of his earliest communications from St. Enogat, on the 31st of August, 1861. "I am indeed happy to get the letter from you . . . In all you say, dear, and in some respects, undue as your goodness is, I believe in it absolutely. And for me, it is just as true that no human being can give me one hand, with the feeling on my part that the other holds that of my own Ba, as you can do. . . ."

It was this bond of their love for Mrs. Browning that united them. Better than Mrs. Browning's sisters or Sarianna, Isa had known Ba the mother, the companion, and yes, the poet. As it happened, no one had been as intimately linked with the married life of the Brownings as Isa. Besides being their earliest Florentine friend, she had become as much part of the Browning household as their impeccable reserve permitted. They, for their part, had been privy to the romance between Isa and young Lytton. Indeed, after the parting Browning accounts, I look more favorably on than once would have been the case."

He spared nothing where the boy was concerned. For a number of years they spent their summers at Ste. Marie, near Pornic on the Brittany coast, living in the house of the Mayor. Often Sarianna and her father went with them. Of course Pen's pony too had to be transported since the boy could not do without his sport. All the complications of shipping the poor beast back and forth devolved upon the poet. He felt sufficiently compensated when, in London, people noticed his son. "Pen is increasingly fond of riding, figures every day in Rotten Row, and only yesterday somebody wrote to me saying how much his horsemanship was noticed."

He also told with unconcealed pride how at Ste. Marie Pen distinguished himself by applying the Humane Society Rules when a man sank and almost drowned. "So you see, he promises. He is drawing a good deal and reading Virgil with me." How anxious he was to have something favorable to say of Pen, almost, it seemed, as if to convince himself.

The boy, however, had much to overcome and very much to learn upon leaving the enchanted garden of his mother's protectiveness for the world of reality. The very contrasts would have affected even a less sensitive lad than the one Hawthorne had so feelingly described. On the one hand there was the London life which his father soon began to live, going out much and receiving fashionable and important people, at first in an effort to combat the recluse in him, and then for relaxation from the intense work into which Browning had plunged. On the other hand was the life at Ste. Marie, a very different sort of life. When Pen was only thirteen, he had heard the dying groans of the Mayor's wife in the room next to his. He had spent the following night with only a thin partition between his imagination and the corpse on the other side of it. Yet even such an experience could not have had the effect upon a growing lad as the influence of Ste. Marie itself which he sustained during the most impressionable period of his adolescence.

"The people here are good, stupid and dirty . . ." wrote Browning in 1865. "The Mayor, the master of this house is . . . abundantly rich, has houses and lands and other incomings, yet out of pure preference for piggishness, he sleeps in one room with his son and three daughters, the eldest being fifteen, and the (somewhat less ugly than usual) maid servant, of about nineteen or twenty, who is

entirely taken into service . . ." That same year Browning had exclaimed: "May it please you! Pen was sixteen . . . ! A great boy, or
rather young man. I took him to a party . . . and woe's me, he figured
in coat and white tie!"

Pen soon figured in other exploits in the headlong excitement of
living—exploits of which his father did not write in his letters, even
to his closest friends. It is hardly surprising, therefore, that Pen
failed of matriculation at Balliol, despite Browning's efforts and the
influence of Jowett.

At that time Browning had been suggested for the Poetry Professorship vacated by Arnold, and would have obtained it had he
also been conferred an honorary M.A. degree. The position involved
giving four lectures a year. He said, not without pathos, to Isa: "Had
they wished me to blacken their boots instead of polish their heads,
I should not have demurred, you understand, in the prospect of
possible advantage to Pen."

In January of 1869 Pen finally gained admission to Christ Church.
He remained desultorily for a year, distinguishing himself chiefly
in billiards and rowing. By that time Browning had begun to worry
about his son's future. "I have ten times the reason to lay up money
and do distasteful things," he confessed to Isa, "with a son who may
want no end of money." On realizing subsequently that Pen was
not intended for university life he made the best of his disappointment. "To a certain degree I am relieved . . . by knowing the very
worst of the poor boy, to wit that he won't work, or perhaps can't.
I shall go on now, as long as I am able, and do the best for us both,
taking the chances of this world."

Eventually, again through the help and influence of Browning with
such men as Millais and Leighton, Pen made himself a career as
painter and sculptor.

Long before feeling the pressure of Pen's financial requirements
Browning had set to work with the enviable regularity of Tennyson,
perhaps consciously obeying the wishes his wife had repeatedly expressed, especially during the time when he had tried to find solace
in Story's studio. In 1862 he had prepared Mrs. Browning's *Last
Poems* for the press, following them with a collection of her essays
on the Greek Christian and the English poets. In 1863 he assembled
a three-volume edition of his *Poetical Works*, edited by his friends
Forster and Barry Cornwall. He spent at least three hours every
morning working on new poems—new in every sense for the spirit in

Browning may have set out to expose a charlatan, which he succeeds in doing with devastating thoroughness. But both his faith that life does not cease with death and his godlike impartiality would not let him shut with finality the door to knowledge which man was perhaps in the initial stages of attaining. Not the least of the poem's marvels were the passages of extraordinary sublimity put into Sludge's unworthy mouth. For Sludge's original he maintained an abiding loathing, expressed in some of his least choice but always vigorous language. When he heard, while "Sludge" was going through the press, that Story had accepted Home as a pupil in his studio, Browning exclaimed: "It is Story's business! He chooses to take this dung-ball into his hand for a minute, and he will get more and more smeared."

Although "Mr. Sludge, the Medium" created a great deal of discussion, the monologues "Abt Vogler" and "Rabbi Ben Ezra" found most favor with the critics and the public alike. Posterity has sustained the choice, despite one of the most awkward juxtapositions of words that the English language ever suffered, in Rabbi Ben Ezra's questions:

> Irks care the crop-full bird? Frets doubt the maw-
> crammed beast?

The monologues, which follow each other, are two expressions in a different key, of Browning's view of life. Abt Vogler's is a muted, musical extemporizing on the metaphysical theme of man in his relation to the world and God, in achievement perhaps the peak of Browning's poetry in that genre. Rabbi Ben Ezra's vigorously assertive paean chants man's triumphant struggle in the light of eternity against the hedonism of the momentary pleasure. The drum beat is heard here against the organ majesty of Abt Vogler. Both found responsive listeners in the youths of the universities who took Browning for their own and his gospel for theirs.

Dramatis Personae sold well. Wonder of wonders, a new edition was called for in a few months. The collected poems too had a brisk sale. Chapman wrote Browning in elation: "The orders come from Oxford and Cambridge."

And so Browning was borne to triumph on the stalwart shoulders of youth.

Chapter XXII: The Ring and the Book

O N THE 19th of August 1864 Robert Browning, at Cambo near
Bayonne in the Pyrenees, was writing letters to Isa Blagden and
to another female correspondent. Isa had evidently been piqued
about something, enough not to mention Browning's new book. "I
dare say you have seen it," he wrote, "and like the proud puss you
are, you won't speak about it. Just as if there were one person in the
world whose opinion I care more about, I mean, whose sympathy I
wanted more! Goodbye with that sweet word, and God bless you,
my dearest friend."

What was it that had annoyed Miss Blagden? Recently officious
gossip had linked Browning's name with this or that eligible lady
and Isa had taken umbrage. Was it another such rumor? If so, Isa
might have had some justification for her jealous fears. On the 2nd
of August, before leaving England, Browning had sent to another
woman a note which opened, "Goodbye, dearest friend."

This correspondence had been going on since May 14, when
Miss Julia Wedgwood, whose family Browning had known for some
time, initiated it with a letter to the poet, to inform him of the
health of her brother James. The young man, a friend of Browning's,
was dying. "You have shown so much interest in us," began Miss
Wedgwood, "that I am glad to tell you that my Brother, though not
any better, and never to be so in this world . . . seems now a little
further removed from the end than I thought when I saw you
last. . . ."

So far Miss Wedgwood's might have been the usual polite note
called forth by the circumstances. Her next paragraph, however, gave
it extraordinary significance to Browning. "Your own unparalleled loss
must dwarf in comparison every other separation, but I believe it is
just those who have experienced that terrible wrench, who can also
feel the most for those who undergo a lighter form of it. You were
an old friend to me long before I saw you, so that it does not seem
unnatural for me to express the deep sympathy which I long have had
for such a loss as yours. . . ."

She went on to say that she wanted no response to her note, yet followed the declaration with the blunt notice that she would be at home from one to half-past two the following day.

Browning called and continued calling. When next Miss Wedgwood wrote him on the 25th of June he had already become her "Dear and kindest friend." This time she informed Browning of her brother's death and did more than full justice to the relative importance of his loss and hers.

It would seem intrusive for such a comparatively recent friend to reawaken a grief of three years' standing. But it was this very insistence on the part of Miss Wedgwood, who lost no occasion to dwell upon the subject, which made its strongest appeal to Browning, especially since, well read as she was in his work and his wife's, she knew their view on death. How could he resist total agreement when she wrote: "While I have shivered in this cold darkness without a glimmer of hope . . . I have felt with you in the presence of one who could bear a loss so much greater than mine because the remnant of life was an insignificant break in the intercourse not more secure in the Past than in the Future."

He answered her the very same day with, for him, such unreserve on the hallowed subject that it demonstrated the force of her appeal: "Three years ago, in this very week, I lost my own soul's companion . . . If I can retain and rightly reason upon the rare flashes of momentary conviction that come and go in the habitual dusk and doubt of one's life . . . I dare believe that you and I shall recover what we have lost."

In that linking of her bereavement and his Browning accepted Miss Wedgwood's friendship. More, he delicately made her feel his need of her, perhaps in the future. "In the meeting of our hands, mine has seemed somewhat to lift, rather than be lifted by, yours. But that has been only a chance—and any day you would help me as much."

But Miss Wedgwood desired "the little more." She was thirty-one when she began writing to the fifty-two-year-old Browning. A descendant of Josiah Wedgwood the potter, and a niece of Charles Darwin, she had the advantages of wealth and erudition. She was, perhaps, a little too much the intellectual woman, dangerously bordering on the bluestocking, a condition somewhat forced upon her by her being so hard of hearing as to be almost deaf.

Already she had published two novels and a number of learned articles, one of them on her uncle's *Origin of Species.* Her plain, strong-featured, intellectual face was redeemed by fine eyes and lips which, however, tended to fall open. She wore her hair parted in the middle and drawn back severely with no wave or curl. But she compromised with feminine coquetry by a locket on a black ribbon, and dresses edged with lace at the throat and bosom. There all coquetry ended. In her behavior toward Browning she made much, too much even, of her masculine directness and honesty, virtues which o'erleapt themselves and, alas! were to have another effect than the one intended. She was, moreover, straitlaced while believing herself to be emancipated; a good critic but opinionated, with too high an estimate of her mental powers, and arrogant and imperious in the guise of humility. Her way of requesting Browning to call on her was typical: "I shall very soon wish to see you again and perhaps you will let me summon you."

It may be she had loved before. Her letters seem to imply some unfortunate early disillusionment. At any rate she knew herself well enough to lay whatever blame there was at the right door. "I dread myself, for I know there is in me an exacting spirit that dries up all the love and kindness which it needs so terribly."

She was aware of her breach of decorum in writing to Browning instead of her waiting for him to make the first move, but she could not let her fault rest in silence. She also wished their friendship to mature to a more intimate relation, yet she expressed her desire as a fear: "Your being a man and my being a woman is inimical to its long existence in this personal form."

Browning was too experienced a reader of the human heart, however, not to perceive the true meaning behind the words, and that meaning he had as yet no desire to understand. He would be happy to have her confidence and her friendship, but as for Miss Wedgwood's dread of what might be inimical to their relationship, he set her right at once in the plainest terms: "When you talk of . . . the chances which are natural, I can only remind you that circumstances guard me against many of these—that the veriest weathercock may rust and hardly turn again—and that I see a plain line to the end of my life on which I shall walk, unless an accident stop all walking,—I shall not diverge, at least."

A less intelligent but more intuitive woman would have been warned that certain sanctities were best let alone. Miss Wedgwood on the contrary reverted to them again and again, summoning up Mrs.

Browning, her *Sonnets from the Portuguese*, her qualities both as woman and poet, as if to make the memory of the wife plead for her with the living husband. "Oh, if we women knew when to hold our tongues!" she cried without making personal application of such wisdom.

By the time Browning left for his vacation in the Pyrenees with his father, his sister, and his son, a tone of weariness had begun to enter into his letters, despite the "dearest friend" in his note of farewell. Certainly his journal-like communications during his two-months' travels could not have been more impersonal.

Miss Wedgwood sensed the change. She became clumsily coquettish, then more reserved on his return, and, finally, overcautious when he resumed his visits. By the end of February 1865, the situation became untenable, at least for Miss Wedgwood. People were beginning to talk about Mr. Browning's visits—something to be avoided if those attentions did not have the proper culmination. When Miss Wedgwood realized that their friendship would never go beyond itself, she decided to extricate herself from an ambiguous position. On March 1, after two vain attempts at wording the proper letter, she gave Browning his congé. "I have reason to know," she wrote, "that my pleasure in your company has had an interpretation put upon it that I ought not to allow." Therefore she wished never to see him again much as she would suffer from the parting. "You are to me the friend of years, I only of months to you."

Manlike, Browning accepted his dismissal as gracefully as possible, but advised a little less decisiveness. "Two persons who suddenly unclasp arms and start off in opposite directions look terribly intimate," he said. But Miss Wedgwood had made up her mind if not her heart.

Florence, meanwhile, received repercussions of the rumors. They soon reached Isa who did not hesitate to write Browning about them. He denied them by indirection. Sarianna, he said, had told him that a Mrs. Carmichael would come to condole with her regularly about Pen's impending change of circumstances under a new "mother-in-law."

Miss Wedgwood did not see Browning again except twice, when she met him accidentally in the street but did not speak to him. They resumed their correspondence on the publication of *The Ring and the Book* which she did not like because of its unpleasant subject, though she gave Browning some excellent criticism mixed with acerbity and not a little arrogance. What precipitated the final break, however, occurred in 1870 when, with inconceivable callousness in discussing Pompilia's character in *The Ring and the Book* Miss Wedgwood wrote: "I look for something from you that I can more fully enter into. You know you owe us an adequate translation of what your wife was to you."

This was indeed seizing the Holy Grail with desecrating hands. Browning spoke out and then he said no more. ". . . Why or how do I owe you—or whomsoever is included in us—any *adequate translation of what my wife was to me?*—except in saying, as I devoutly do on other occasions than sitting down at meals, *For these and all other mercies God be praised? Let us show forth that praise not in our lips but in our lives.* . . ." The italics are Browning's.

She wrote him once more. He sent no answer for her to tie up with the rest of his letters, to keep as her life's secret in a drawer until nearly a quarter of a century after her death[1] when both the packet and its secret came to light.

But to go back to Cambo in the summer and autumn of 1864, and the impersonality which Browning's letters there assumed. A reason that had little to do with Julia Wedgwood and a great deal to do with his poetry accounted, more than anything else, for the altered tone. One of those accidental flashes of revelation that open wide the windows of the creative mind had come to him soon after his arrival, changing his whole outlook.

In the sketchbook which the Brownings had taken along and which all of them used for jotting down their impressions, are found several drawings of a mountain pass, *Le Pas de Roland.* The best and most finished of them was titled and dated August 27 in the handwriting of Sarianna. For that reason it has been assumed that the revelation occurred on that day, as Browning was almost invariably accompanied by his sister on his walks. Since his letter of August 19 to Isa Blagden made no mention of the *pas*, and since another letter to Mrs. Story, published without date in Henry James's *William Wetmore Story and his Friends*, specified seeing the mountain pass "two days ago," the date of that momentous event has remained largely conjectural.

However, in his journal-letter to Julia Wedgwood, begun on August 19, he has under the date of the 20th the clear and precise account which establishes beyond a doubt the day, almost the hour,

[1] Julia Wedgwood died unmarried in 1913.

of the kindling flash that was to prove so important to English literature. "I went this morning," he wrote, "to see the mountain-pass called *Le pas de Roland*—the tradition being that he opened a way through a rock that effectually blocks it up, by one kick of his boot, and so let Charlemagne's army pass. . . . It is a striking little bit of scenery . . . but I think I liked best of all a great white-breasted hawk sunning himself on a ledge, with his wings ready."

Even Browning could scarcely have devised a more effective bit of symbolism for his long-obstructed imagination than that great window of light kicked through the impeding rock, and the white-breasted hawk with wings ready.

It was immediately after this sight that the plan of *The Ring and the Book,* for years gestating in the poet's mind, sprang to birth. That Browning visited and revisited the liberating view is sufficiently evidenced by the various drawings of Roland's pass in the sketchbook, culminating in the one of the 27th of August, so carefully detailed by Sarianna. The experience had been of such moment that nearly four years later—on the 15th of March, 1868—Browning gave as vivid an account of it to William Michael Rossetti as if he had just relived it. Rossetti noted the conversation in his diary. "Browning's forthcoming poem exceeds 20,000 lines. . . . He began it in October '64. Was staying at Bayonne, and walked out to the mountain gorge . . . and there laid out the full plan of his twelve cantos, accurately carried out in the execution . . . Often stores up a subject long before he writes it . . . He has written his forthcoming work all consecutively."

If, as Browning told William Rossetti, he had begun *The Ring and the Book* in October of 1864, he must have worked with tremendous impetus since on the 17th of the month he was writing to Leighton in Rome to go into the church of St. Lorenzo in Lucina— the scene of Pompilia's marriage and of the exposure of the murdered bodies of her foster parents—"and look attentively at it, so as to describe it to me on your return . . . if with a nave—pillars or not— the number of altars . . . I don't care about the *outside.*"

The particulars Browning wrought into the opening of the second book:

> Lorenzo in Lucina—here's a church
> To hold a crowd at need, accommodate
> All comers from the Corso! If this crush
> Make not its priests ashamed of what they show
> For temple-room, don't prick them to draw purse
> And down with bricks and mortar, eke us out

> The beggarly transept with its bit of apse
> Into a decent space for Christian ease,
> Why, to-day's lucky pearl is cast to swine . . .
> From dawn till now that it is growing dusk . . .
> People climbed up the columns, fought for spikes
> O' the chapel-rail to perch themselves upon,
> Jumped over and so broke the wooden work
> Painted like porphyry to deceive the eye:
> Serve the priests right!

If Browning derived the details from Leighton, the painter indeed had served him well. The vividness and excitement he owed to himself alone, however. Again, if between the releasing experience of August 20 and the 17th of October he had written the whole of the first canto of *The Ring and the Book*, nearly fifteen hundred lines, then Julia Wedgwood had met another rival, as powerful as Mrs. Browning, in the poetry which with Browning always included her. Indeed, the closing passage of that first canto, besides being a dedication to Elizabeth Barrett Browning:

> O Lyric Love, half-angel and half-bird
> And all a wonder and a wild desire—

avers Browning's debt of inspiration to her, in life as in death, in terms of such sublime humility as he was never again to reach in writing of her.

> Hail then, and hearken from the realms of help!
> Never may I commence my song, my due
> To God who best taught song by gift of thee,
> Except with bent head and beseeching hand—
> That still, despite the distance and the dark,
> What was, again may be; some interchange
> Of grace, some splendour once thy very thought,
> Some benediction anciently thy smile:
> —Never conclude, but raising hand and head
> Thither where eyes, that cannot reach, yet yearn
> For all hope, all sustainment, all reward,
> Their utmost up and on,—so blessing back
> In those thy realms of help, that heaven thy home,
> Some whiteness which, I judge, thy face makes proud,
> Some wanness where, I think, thy foot may fall!

The importance of the decisive effect of *Le Pas de Roland* may best be gauged when one realizes how very close Browning had been to not writing his masterpiece, despite the fascination exerted by the

Old Yellow Book from the moment he rescued it from among the litter of a street stall. At first his wife's lack of interest in the Roman criminal trial may have deterred him. But his admitted penchant for morbid cases of the soul made him read and reread the yellowed documents. (He read them over eight times before completing his poem.) Also, he never tired of seeking out other sources to clarify the story. On the 19th of September, 1862, he wrote to Isa from Pornic, asking her to remind their friend, Mrs. Baker, of her promise to lend him a manuscript which he believed concerned the protagonist of his trial. Mrs. Baker had shown it to Trollope thinking it might interest him but—fortunately!—Trollope had found nothing in the subject to his purpose. Yet at that time Browning would not have taken it to heart had Trollope made something of the murder story. As it was, Browning had already offered it both to Miss Ogle, the novelist, and to W. C. Cartwright, almost as if he wished to relieve himself of an incubus.

The Baker manuscript, however, revived his interest. It did concern his Count Guido, and although it was incorrect in some respects, it contained a few notices of his execution subsequent to the accounts he had. "I am going to make a regular poem of it . . . a strong thing if I can manage it." This he wrote to Isa from London on the 18th of October. A month later he reverted once more to the subject: "Early in the spring I print . . . a new edition of all my old things corrected: then begin on my murder-case." So time passed in work accomplished, but with nothing but good intentions on Count Guido until Roland's propulsive kick to Browning's imagination. He was still feeling its tremendous force when he wrote to Miss Wedgwood from Biarritz on October 3, 1864: "I've got the whole of that poem . . . well in my head, shall write the Twelve books of it in six months, and then take breath again."

He had the overoptimism of the man inspired. It took him four years to compose *The Ring and the Book*, a time of accumulating honors, of intense application and equally intense living, a time of change also, and of loss.

Landor's death occurred first, in 1864, after the old man had sent him another of his letters in which he spoke of dying in a few weeks or days. This time he had meant his cry of "Wolf!" Browning heard later of the funeral. The grand old solitary who had alienated so many people was followed to the grave by two of his sons and nobody else. "The elephant is devoured by ants in his inaccessible solitudes . . ."

Browning pondered Landor's words, the many irritations of his life, the havoc he had caused when at the goading of those who should have loved him, he ran amok, not caring what he destroyed. But Browning remembered also that Landor had written passages that few could rival.

With the death of Landor Wilson gradually fades out of the picture, to reemerge for a last glimpse in 1897 when she was living, a venerable widow, in Pen's Venetian palace.

Then, in June of 1866, Browning's father died in Paris. Browning was at his bedside. The mind of the old scholar retained its faculties to the end. "What do you think death is?" he asked his son. "Is it a fainting or is it a pang?" To Sarianna he confided that he had no doubt as to his future state, "having the promise of One who cannot lie." At the very moment of expiring Robert, who could not bear that final struggle, asked him, to relieve him: "Shall I fan you?"

"If you please, dear," he answered on his last breath. "I'm only afraid of tiring you."

To Robert such considerateness brought to mind the hardness of another. "He was worthy of being Ba's father," he wrote to Isa of his parent. "She loved him,—and he said, very recently, while gazing at her portrait, that only that picture had put into his head that there might be such a thing as the worship of the images of saints."

Mr. Browning was buried in Paris. Soon afterward Sarianna Browning went to live with her brother at Warwick Crescent and continued with him to the end.

Two years later, almost to the day, Browning stood by another deathbed. On Thursday, the 11th of June, he wrote to Lady Carmichael: "I have a very sad task to fulfill—you must imagine already what it is. Bear the news well, for the sake of those dearest to you. My own beloved sister Arabel is with God as I am assured. She passed away just now in my arms as her sister did seven years ago . . .²" When he wrote to Isa Blagden as usual on the 19th of the month, he advised her of Arabel's death and copied out for her a note which he had made on the 21st of July 1863 after Arabel had recounted to him a dream she had had the night before. In the dream Elizabeth had appeared to her, and when Arabel asked, "When shall I be with you?" Elizabeth had answered: "Dearest, in five years." It lacked but a month to their completion.

² Holograph letter, Baylor Browning Collection.

"Only a coincidence, but noticeable," commented the author of "Mr. Sludge, the Medium."

As soon as he could after attending to "every sort of sad business that seems duty" he crossed the Channel with Sarianna, leaving Pen in charge of Mr. Jowett for the studies that were to prove so fruitless. Brother and sister traveled for a few weeks in France, then settled down at Audierne, an unspoiled little fishing village in the most westerly part of Brittany, with the ocean infinite in front and woods, hills, dales, and lanes behind and around. The two would walk for hours enjoying the landscape, with Sarianna now and then setting down an impression in her sketchbook. For Browning it was a time for drawing deep breaths. The work on his great poem was over but for the final details before it went to press.

When the first of the four volumes of The Ring and the Book came out in November of 1868, the author's name was qualified with the addition of "M.A. and Honorary Fellow of Balliol College, Oxford." Both honors had come to him the previous year, too late for the Poetry Professorship but early enough for him to crow over the M.A. by diploma: "A very rare distinction, said to have only happened in Dr. Johnson's case." With the increase of fame he was to receive many more such distinctions and not alone from Oxford.

The publishers were no longer Chapman and Hall but Smith, Elder and Company. Browning had severed relations with Chapman —"poor fellow!"—out of loyalty to Isa Blagden who felt that her Nora and Archibald Lee, published in the spring of 1867, had been poorly paid for and insufficiently advertised. For that matter, like most dissatisfied authors, Isa had had the same complaints to make of the three novels that had preceded it. But now, besides suffering in her purse, she was hurt in her pride, and chided Browning for lack of appreciation of her novels. Her reproaches he patiently and lengthily denied, laboring to say gracious things, offering suggestions of a constructive sort and pointing out stylistic flaws for her to avoid in the future. For all his kindness his true opinion was evident enough. Fundamentally he did not like her work. But then, he had lived too long with genius to be easily pleased.

He could offer Isa comfort of a practical nature, however. "I part from Chapman pursuant to my resolution taken when you were last in England, and go to Smith and Elder," he wrote her in November, 1867, following the letter in January of the new year with more specific particulars as to the causes of the severance. "He [Chapman]

scarcely advertised it [her novel] at all. It consequently passed
unnoticed . . . I conclude he was determined to spend not a farthing more than he paid yourself, and *that* was just fifty pounds more
than he gave me for an edition of my poems in three volumes . . .
Oh, dear Isa, you don't think *I* am the man to judge the worth of a
book by the money it brings!" By that time the *entente cordiale*
had been sufficiently reestablished between them for Browning to
close his letter with: "What love have I to send,—have I not given
you all by this time?"

The publication of the second volume of *The Ring and the Book*
followed in December and of the third and fourth in January and
February of 1869. That it catapulted Browning to the height of the
fame which had long been his due was evidenced by his almost
immediate recognition by Queen Victoria who till then had scarcely
been aware of his existence. On the 13th of March *The Court Circu-
lar* recorded that on the preceding Thursday "Her Majesty had the
pleasure of becoming personally acquainted with two of the most distinguished writers of the age—Mr. Carlyle and Mr. Browning. These
eminent men," the article went on, ". . . so far as intellect is concerned, stand head and shoulders above their contemporaries." A
tactless remark and unintentionally rude to the two other notables,
George Grote, the historian, and Sir Charles Lyell, the geologist,
who had also taken tea and conversed with Her Majesty for an hour
and twenty minutes. Browning's popularity took a leap. Where the
Queen led the rest of society made haste to follow.

If Browning had been grieved in the past by the grudging
acknowledgments of reviewers he had only cause for rejoicing in the
praise that poured from the critical great on the work that had
occupied nearly ten years of his life. With the subliminal awareness
of the creator, he knew that from the "mere oozings from the mine"
of the *Old Yellow Book,* he had fashioned "the rondure brave, the
lilied loveliness" of his life's achievement. He had taken for his theme
a sordid murder plot that others had shuddered away from, and
transmuted it to an enthralling human story wherein good and evil
fused for the ultimate clarification of the ways of God to man.

Carlyle put it in his inimitable homely way: "It is . . . one of the
most wonderful poems ever written. I re-read it all through—all made
out of an Old Bailey story that might have been told in ten lines, and
only wants forgetting."

Like him and Miss Wedgwood a number of other readers disapproved of the theme. But to see only the sordidness is to be blind to the great light of which it is the shadow. Certainly there is nothing edifying in the story of Count Guido Franceschini of Arezzo who with the help of his bravos murders his estranged wife and her foster parents, then at the trial seeks to defend his deed by accusing her, Pompilia, of illicit love for the priest who rescued her from his brutality. It is even less pleasing to realize that the underlying motive for the murders is sordid profit. But between the dim dark seed deep underground and the sky-reaching tree there is all of Browning's genius.

Why did Browning choose Franceschini's story? Because, he admitted, he was struck by its depths of wickedness and the incidental evolution of good from all that evil. "The curious depth below depth of depravity here," he wrote to Miss Wedgwood, "—in this chance lump taken as a sample of the soil—might well have warned another from spreading it out—but I thought that, since I could do it, and even liked to do it, my affair it was rather than another's."

The form he gave his poem was superbly suited to his hand—the dramatic monologue, here carried to its utmost use and perfection both as an instrument of psychological probing and as a means of presenting every aspect and interpretation of the deed. Browning always maintained that he adhered to historic fact. But he was undervaluing his art, as the most cursory reading of the Old Yellow Book in its masterly translation by Charles W. Hodell reveals, and as further research into the other sources conclusively proves.

Browning used the image of the making of the Etruscan ring worn by his wife to show what he had done with the raw material of history and the alloy of his imagination. His process, however, was allied rather to the making of the faceted diamond from the mined lump. The core of light was there, yes, latent in the dull, rough mass: the facets were implicit. But it took imagination and wisdom, a sapient cunning as well, to make that drab inertness come alive, to turn that lump of matter to spiritual light. Each of Browning's monologues—his own, in the first book and the last; the three of the varying opinions of the people of Rome; Count Guido's; Caponsacchi's; the touching purity of Pompilia's; the two of the "buffoon lawyers" as Browning called them elsewhere; the count's final intellectualized justification and the Pope's lofty but anachronistic theological excursion—contributes, just as does each facet of the diamond, toward bringing forth every ray of light and truth.

The *Athenaeum*, once so blind, perceived at last what Browning had sought to accomplish and summed it up for public opinion to adopt: "We must record . . . not merely that *The Ring and the Book* is beyond all parallel the supremest poetical achievement of our time, but that it is the most precious and profound spiritual treasure. . . ."

Like all unqualified praise it had its truth and its exaggeration. The popular bard, Tennyson, was unceremoniously cast out by that "supremest poetical achievement." But if in the word *poetical* one included the making of music, then Browning, least musical of poets, received unearned laurels. For a skilled performer and musicologist, he carried over very little of the art into his verses except in the short lyric, and there but rarely with the infallible ear of a Shelley, a Byron, or a Swinburne. Like that other poet, the prophet through whom a divinity declared itself, he must ejaculate, cry out, roar and bellow his convulsive words. It was a deep perception indeed that qualified the prophetic Whitman by a "barbaric yawp." Browning's utterance, too intellectually refined for such qualification, resembled rather a chaotic extemporizing on an organ with all its stops pulled. But it was the extemporizing of a Bach.

A precious and profound spiritual treasure *The Ring and the Book* was indeed. Into it Browning had put a lifetime of learning and observation, of restless speculation and vast psychological research. He had reaffirmed his faith in the validity of good, of great human passion, of courage and nobility of action and, not the least of all, faith in life and a brave acceptance of its challenges. He had also enshrined in it his *donna beata*, his Pompilia-Elizabeth, his Lyric Love as a beginning and an end.

> If the rough ore be rounded to a ring . . .
> Might mine but lie outside thine, Lyric Love,
> Thy rare gold ring of verse. . . .

Posterity has made other disposition. Still, Browning's *Ring* is her lasting monument.

The poet enjoyed his success. Everyone invited him and he made as many visits as the hours allowed. There was scarcely a fashionable house in England that was not the healthier for his bracing presence, his loud, assertive, stimulating talk. "Will you honour the University by accepting a D.C.L. degree?" sped the flattering offers from the learned institutions. From his friend, the solemn scholar Benjamin Jowett, came a dubious accolade on *The Ring and the Book*. "I have read it through very hurriedly—indeed I could hardly lay the book down . . . I was wholly taken up with the poem . . . It shows the highest dramatic power and is full of noble thoughts, of wisdom and humour and knowledge of the world—also that it is a curious work of art and (with the exception of a very few lines) perfectly intelligible."[3]

Then, in January of 1869, at the Queen's Concert Rooms, Hanover Square, Robert Buchanan gave the first of what later became a plague of Browning readings. Somewhat belatedly the parodists discovered the poet too, and added their thistle to his crown of bays. Calverley led them all with *The Cock and the Bull*, of obvious origin.

> Do you see this pebble-stone? It's a thing I bought
> Of a bit of a chit of a boy i' the mid o' the day.—
> I like to dock the smaller parts o' speech,
> As we curtail the already cur-tailed cur,
> (You catch the paranomasia, play o' words)—
> Did, rather , i' the pre-Landseerian days.
> Well, to my muttons. . . .

[3] Holograph letter, Baylor Browning Collection.

Chapter XXIII: One Who Never Turned His Back

"I DINED last week with Lord Lytton . . . He gets agreeable people, too," wrote Browning to Isa Blagden on the 21st of May 1871. "The town is full and I can't help keep half the engagements . . . But I do sometimes a little more than I otherwise would when I stimulate myself by the reflection that it stings such vermin as little Austin to the quick that I 'haunt gilded salons. . . .'"

Here is the diner-out, the society man, speaking. Also the Browning of violent, inveterate passions when touched to the quick. Alfred Austin, the five-foot homunculus and poetaster, had been acting as a gadfly toward Browning since the publication of *The Ring and the Book*, in one of those inexplicable antipathies that nothing can heal. Among other blandishments Austin had charged in print and in private that Browning was striving hard to be an original poet, "a thing which for the life of him could not be." His chosen king of poets was Tennyson whom he feared Browning was beginning to rival in fame if not also in popularity. Moreover, in his aspiring imagination he saw the crown of the Laureateship descending from Tennyson's lofty brow onto his own head. Any threat to such a consummation he dealt with in critical squibs fired behind the shoulders of his betters. As it happened, by one of those sardonic tricks of fate, Austin did become Laureate after Tennyson. But by then Browning was no more.

While he was still in the world, however, he had his faults, like all mortality. He had his pride, easily hurt. He had his vanity and a pugnacity quick to stir to verbal if not physical violence. In Austin's case he gave vent to his annoyance in his letters and in quips at dinner parties. Then in 1876 he settled old scores not only with Austin but with his critics in general in his volume *Of Pacchiarotto and How He Worked in Distemper*. It had given him a roguish satisfaction to call his two pet geese Edinburgh and Quarterly after the two magazines that had hissed and cackled at him most. But he wanted a public vindication as well as his private joke and thus he made the mistake of Byron before him, though without Byron's cleverness.

G. K. Chesterton used to enjoy telling how a lady of his acquaintance understood the title of Browning's volume to imply the story of a dog, Pacchiarotto, and of his faithful service even while suffering from distemper. As far as the general public was concerned it labored under a like misapprehension. But the critics understood and they did not take their chastisement lightly. As for the pun, it had pertinence, alas, to the poet who in telling off his detractors allowed his own distemper to spatter his canvas of griefs with vulgar hues.

Musically *Pacchiarotto* is a charivari banged on the most discordant of household utensils not excluding the untranslated *skoramis* in the hands of Pacchiarotto's maid—

> If once on your pate she a souse made
> With what, pan or pot, bowl or *skoramis*,
> First comes to her hand,—things were more amiss!
> I would not for worlds be your place in—
> Recipient of slops from her basin!

The rhymes were Browning's most grotesque. The taste, as in the *skoramis* passage, was execrable. His revenge on the minikin poet resembled that of the elephant on the flea.

> While as for Quilp-Hop-o'-my thumb, there,
> Banjo-Byron that twangs the strum strum there—
> He'll think as the pickle he curses,
> I've discharged on his pate his own verses!
> "Dwarfs are saucy," says Dickens; so, sauced in
> Your own sauce ****

It took no ingenuity to supply the proper name for the missing rhyme.

In May of 1871, however, Browning was haunting the gilded salons of such social arbiters as Countess Cowper, listening to music at the houses of other friends who invited the best performers of the day, worrying about his son's incapacity to work and earn, and turning over in his mind a proposal of marriage to another queen of fashion, Lady Ashburton rich, beautiful, his admirer, and a widow. He was also writing with an intensity extraordinary even for him, the poem of *Balaustion's Adventure*, undertaken at the request of Countess Cowper, but given impetus by his great love Euripides and his greater love, E.B.B., as he now referred to his wife in his letters.

Browning had met Louisa, Lady Ashburton before her husband's death in 1864, but it was not until 1869 that he joined the coterie of rich and talented women like Lady Marian Alford, Lady Ashburton's friend, and others of the circle who threw open to him their town and country houses. Lady Marian's Belton House in Surrey received the poet as often as Lady Ashburton's Loch Luichart Lodge in Scotland. But whereas Browning would write without concealment to Isa of Lady Marian and her hospitality, he maintained a suspicious reticence about Scotland and Lady Ashburton, contenting himself with such innocuous information as, "Here, at an old friend's . . ." Was he afraid of rousing Isa's jealousy?

At this time Lady Ashburton was forty-two years old, radiant, healthy, vivacious and the center of a life of cultivation and ease. Both her father, the Rt. Hon. James Alexander Stuart Mackenzie and her late husband, William Bingham, Baron Ashburton, were reckoned as very rich men. Lady Ashburton's lands alone brought her an income of six thousand pounds a year. As for Browning, at fifty-seven, at the height of his success, he was nevertheless physically and mentally exhausted from the long effort of his masterpiece. He had, besides, the care of a household on his mind as well as the future of his son, with, mostly, the uncertain income from his work to count upon. Mrs. Browning's poetry, issued over and over under his supervision, was still much in demand, however. There were also a few wise investments that brought in money.

In the summer of 1869 Browning felt the need of a holiday and went to Scotland with Pen and Sarianna and the Storys. For a while they stayed at a little inn near Garve. Later they were to be found more often at Lady Ashburton's than at home, except in September when they were the guests of the Earl of Carlisle at Naworth Castle, Cumberland. There Browning would read for the company from *The Ring and the Book*, his face absorbed and intense, his body impelled toward the volume held nearsightedly close, his right elbow propped on his knee and the whole posture indicative of physical energy held in check by intellectual force. It was at such a moment that the Earl of Carlisle captured him in a very lifelike drawing showing the man still vigorous and handsome, less Italianate than on his return to England, yet sufficiently romantic to create a stir in any salon.

Harriet Hosmer, who had met Lady Ashburton in Rome, has left a description of her, exaggerated in its adulation and not a little cal-

culating, yet something of the woman's physical power is evident
through the cotton-wool of words. "I have a distinct recollection of
stonily gazing at the lady . . . and so remaining, gazing . . . It seemed
to my bewildered senses that the Ludovisi Goddess in person, weary,
perhaps of the long imprisonment of Art, had assumed the stature
and the state of mortals and stood before me. There were the same
square-cut and grandiose features, whose classic beauty was humanized
by a pair of keen, dark eyes, lovely smile, and then a rich, musical
voice of inquiry. . . . Did no wave of the Fortunate Isles bear to me
a prophetic whisper of this beautiful woman?"

If such a wave failed of prophecy Hatty's common sense was quick
to tell her that here was a woman to cultivate, and cultivate her she
did, so that when Browning was staying at Loch Luichart Lodge
Hatty's absence was felt. At the request of the hostess the poet sent
Hatty a poetic round-robin, a stanza for each guest there, the whole
effervescing with Browning's revived spirits.

> Dear Hosmer; or still dearer Hatty—
> Mixture of *miele* and of *latte*,
> So good and sweet and—somewhat fatty—
>
> Why linger still in Rome's old glory
> While Scotland lies so cool before ye?
> Make haste and come!—quoth Mr. Story . . .
>
> Say not (in Scotch) "in troth it canna be"—
> But honey, milk and, indeed, manna be!
> Forgive a stranger!—Sarianna B.
>
> Don't set an old acquaintance frowning,
> But come and quickly! quoth R. Browning.
> For since prodigious fault is found with you,
> I—that is, Robin—must be Round with you. . . .

The easy intimacy established that summer was renewed at intervals during the next two years. Meanwhile, though Browning was
writing, he had printed nothing since *The Ring and the Book* except
"Hervé Riel" in the *Cornhill Magazine* for March 1871, overcoming
his antipathy to publication in a periodical because on that occasion
he was enabled to perform an act that Mrs. Browning would have
commended. The Parisians were under the heel of the Prussians during the Franco-Prussian war. The people were enduring untold hard-
ship. When the *Cornhill* offered a hundred guineas for the ballad of

the humble hero of Croisic, Browning accepted and sent the money
to a fund for the French. His own resources, however, were being
drained by a son who had left college and was now trying to find
himself in the field of art. Browning's letters at this period often reflect a mind much distressed by financial worry. Perhaps because of it
he is met with more frequently than ever at the great houses.

Mary Gladstone, the statesman's daughter, then a girl of twenty-
four, was often house-guest at the same time with Browning at
Lady Alford's, when they would be the sole occupants of the little
gallery of the Belton chapel at morning prayers. Miss Gladstone had
not liked Browning then as she had not yet discovered the poet in the
man who "talked so loud and breathed into one's face and grasped
one's arm." But she was shrewd enough to see that something was
afoot at the time between Browning and that other guest, Lady Ashburton. "We all supposed he was proposing to Lady Ashburton . . ."
she reminisced years later. "At least she let it be thought so." A feline
comment but not unperceptive.

Browning did propose finally on the 2nd of October, 1871. Lady
Ashburton rejected him. Browning never forgave either her[1] or himself though he had little to reproach himself with except his absolute
honesty, unpardonable, however, to the woman who had to listen to
the truths which he felt must be told.

"I suppose," he wrote to Edith Story from Lady Marian's six
months later when the group had split into enemy camps, "that Lady
A. did not suppress what she considered the capital point of her
quarrel with me when she foamed out into the couple of letters she
bespattered me with,—yet the worst she charged me with was,—having said that my heart was buried in Florence, and the attractiveness
of a marriage with her lay in its advantage to Pen—two simple facts—
as I told her,—which I had never left her in ignorance about. . . ."

Alas, they were the two facts that only a superior woman over-
whelmingly in love and capable of understanding such candor could
have accepted. Lady Ashburton was neither superior nor in love. To
her the simple facts, without full knowledge of the person who so
declared himself, could not but have been odious. Besides, for a
reigning beauty to be told that she could not expect love from the
man who was asking her to marry him because his heart was buried
in Florence, must have been profoundly humiliating.

As it was, besides being ever present in her husband's poetry Mrs.

[1] For her reappearance as the "bold she-shape" in his later poetry see Prof.
W. C. DeVane's study, *Browning's Parleyings*, 1927.

Browning had been constantly in his thoughts, quite understandably, during the time that he had been contemplating a marriage of convenience. It was therefore no mere coincidence that when he wrote to Isa Blagden on August 19, a week after the publication of *Balaustion's Adventure* and six weeks before the proposal, he dwelt upon Mrs. Browning's poetry and put himself in a humbler place. The mood of the letter hardly betokens the would-be suitor. "At this place, I and Pen are alone at a shooting lodge . . . He goes away early to sport, and I am blessedly alone . . . I have even a piano, books of course, and I find an impulse to write: if I were let alone I should *do* far better than I have done. But no, dearest Isa, the simple truth is that she was the poet and I the clever person by comparison." He also wrote in a more personal connection: "All is best as it is, for her, and me too. I shall wash my hands clean in a minute, before I see her, as I trust to do."

He believed then, as he was to believe to the end, that one day he would realize Dante's prophecy which he, Browning, had recorded in his wife's copy of the Testament at her death: "Thus I believe, thus I affirm, thus I am certain it is, that from this life I shall pass to another better, there where that lady lives of whom my soul is enamoured." What chance had a mere Lady Ashburton against the eternally beloved?

It is significant too that *Balaustion's Adventure* for all that it celebrated an event in Athenian history, was still another projection of Elizabeth Barrett Browning. Who was Balaustion, "the lyric girl" not found in any classical dictionary, but Browning's "Lyric Love" here given by him a name that means "wild pomegranate flower"?

It was through *Bells and Pomegranates* that Elizabeth Barrett had known Browning before she met him. In her first poetic reference to him she very aptly chose the pomegranate "which if cut deep down the middle, shows a heart within blood-tinctured . . ." A personal symbol now, Persephone's fruit with its blood-red grains appears and reappears in their poetry. It is found in the "O Lyric Love" passage of *The Ring and the Book* where Browning combines it with Elizabeth's first tribute to him and describes her as "human at the red-ripe of the heart." The link between Mrs. Browning and Balaustion is further strengthened by the verses from her "Wine of Cyprus" which Browning printed as a keynote to his poem:

> Our Euripides, the Human,
> With his droppings of warm tears,

> And his touchings of things common
> Till they rose to touch the spheres.

Yet more than all these, it is the patriotic fervor of Balaustion who saves her captive comrades through song when she recites *Alkestis* to the Euripides-loving Sicilians, that evokes the Mrs. Browning of the poems of liberation.

Browning's choice of *Alkestis* from the great dramatist's works has also its significance in the restoration of the pure and noble wife from the realm of death. Then, too, Leighton's painting of Heracles wrestling with Death for the Body of Alkestis, finished just before Browning had begun his poem, no doubt contributed to the amalgam of creation by the association Browning necessarily made between the painter of Alkestis and the designer of his wife's monument. The two are certainly linked in *Balaustion's Adventure* wherein Leighton's canvas is vividly described.

> There lies Alkestis dead, beneath the sun
> She longed to look her last upon, beside
> The sea . . .
>   There strains
> The might o' the hero 'gainst his more than match,
> —Death, dreadful not in thew and bone, but like
> The envenomed substance that exudes some dew
> Whereby the merely honest flesh and blood
> Will fester up and run to ruin straight,
> Ere they can close with, clasp and overcome
> The poisonous impalpability
> That simulates a form beneath the flow
> Of those gray garments. . . .

Indirectly the words expressed Browning's gratitude for the Florence memorial: one monument for another. Leighton in a graceful letter understood them so. "Last night," he wrote on the 16th of August, 1871, "I finished (the poem) and saw in the last lines what, if vanity does not deceive me is a description of my poor picture . . . I know the value of the pen which has painted over again, and bettered in painting, my insufficient work, and of the page in which you have given it a lasting home and added dignity."[2]

With the exception of *La Saisiaz* of 1878, *Balaustion's Adventure* is the last utterance of Browning the poet. He was to produce fourteen more volumes during the next two decades, but after 1871 his

[2] Holograph letter. Baylor Browning Collection.

best work lay behind him. Not that he failed in power and, some-times, beauty. Passages here and there, in the two volumes of the *Dramatic Idyls, Ferishtah's Fancies, Parleyings with Certain People of Importance, Aristophanes' Apology* and his transcription of the *Agamemnon* of Aeschylus were fitfully illuminated by the beacon of his inspiration. But alas, it was inspiration itself that was running low. He was still at his best in such revealing portraits as *Prince Hohen-stiel-Schwangau*, on Napoleon III, in the manner of "Mr. Sludge, the Medium," and of "Bishop Blougram's Apology," but the colors are cruder here, and the brushstrokes of satire heavy-handed.

He is still absorbed in morbid cases of the soul. However, his study of suicide, *Red Cotton Night-Cap Country*, unlike *The Ring and the Book*, holds more of alloy than of art. The title itself, suggested by Anne Thackeray, is wholly inappropriate. In *The Inn Album* which had the distinction of being serialized in the *New York Times* on the last three Sundays of November, 1875, though it was hardly literature for the Lord's Day, the morbidity of soul involves a Balzacian plot of cupidity, seduction, gambling, intrigue and murder. According to Browning's note it was suggested by an incident in the life of Lord de Ros, a friend of Wellington's who had been the central figure in a scandal some years earlier. But the melodramatic coincidences, the character of the noble maligned female who dies conveniently in the end, the wayward youth who wins redemption, smell too powerfully of the fumes of the footlights for the odor of Apollo's thyme to assert itself.

The sensation created by *The Inn Album* in a public that had once ignored *Paracelsus* should have warned Browning. He was making money. The lures of American publishers no longer astounded him by their fabulousness. Time was when he had thought a two-hundred pound offer for *The Ring and the Book* flattering enough for him to crow over to all his correspondents. Now he could get as much for a single short poem.

In spite of his productivity people complained: "Browning has dinnered himself away." To those who saw him in the latter part of his life, an unfailing guest at dinner parties and musicales, at the open-ing of exhibitions and at the theater, it seemed a wonder that he produced at all, and the story went round that he had a spirit working at home while he enjoyed the busy life of the London season. He kept a horse and brougham on continual hire to take him to his en-gagements, except when he walked with Sir Frederick Leighton, now

President of the Royal Academy. The two became familiar figures, the tall lean Leighton taking long strides and the stocky Browning, his head on a level with his companion's shoulder, walking briskly beside him, holding aloft a rolled umbrella like a folded standard in his left hand.

He was sought after by many ladies but now his manner toward them assumed something of the patriarchal. He would kiss them on their arrival and when they went away. According to his valet who wrote an anonymous article about the poet, "Miss Browning said to the master, 'Wobert, why don't you mawwy one of these ladies who are so fond of you?' He looked up at the big picture of Mrs. Browning which hung on the wall opposite him . . . and he said, 'Never.'"

There is something authentic about the article in spite of a touch of vulgarity. The curious in personality might be interested in this intimate glimpse of Browning *sans pantoufles:* "He took no early tea but only fruit before breakfast . . . Then he went into his bath, an old-fashioned bath with a tank on top. He would . . . splash violently, singing at the top of his voice in Italian and French the airs he had heard at the opera the night before . . . There was a bookcase in the bathroom of very old books. . . ."

The rumors of Browning's marrying this or that lady nevertheless persisted, exasperating him to violent utterance. "It is funny," he exploded when his name had been linked with Jean Ingelow's whom he had seen only once at a musical party, "it is funny people think I am likely to do nothing naughty in the world, neither rob nor kill, seduce, nor ravish—only honestly marry—which I should consider the two last—and perhaps two first—naughtiness united, together with the grace of perjury."

Had he ever joined his life with another's, it would most likely have been with Isa Blagden's even though all was not untroubled harmony between them. "But what are the differences we ever differed about by the side of the great agreement in all that is essentially worth agreeing upon?" he inquired. "Yet we are so made that I suppose we should tease each other again if the seas and lands did not separate us. . . ." One letter is of especial note considering that Browning wrote it to Isa the day before his proposal to Lady Ashburton: "I repeat to my darling 'bright and aged (to become) snake' that, if I could dispose properly of Pen, see him advantageously disengaged from me, I would go to live and die in Italy tomorrow. . . ." O complexities of the human heart!

There was never to be any refuge in Illyria for them. Fifteen months later Isa Blagden died in Florence, at the age of fifty-five. "Since poor Isa left off writing, I have no means of getting informed about friends there," was Browning's reference to her death.

He was addressing Miss Annie Egerton Smith, part owner of the *Liverpool Mercury*, an old friend of his and of his sister. She was a woman of great refinement, with a love of literature and music that made its appeal to Browning. Often in London it was with Miss Smith that Browning would be seen at concerts. She was as much of a traveler as the Brownings, too, and they would often take their holidays together. No breath of gossip ever touched this friendship, as abstract as a fugue of Bach's and, spiritually, as solidly constructed. In her special way Miss Smith substituted for the loss of Isa.

During the summer of 1877 the three—Browning, Sarianna and Miss Smith—went to Switzerland, taking the chalet La Saisiaz in the Savoyard mountains, some five miles from Geneva. It was not the first time that they had occupied the tall, red-roofed house in its setting of poplars through which, from a balcony on the top floor, they could see the blue shimmer of the lake. They knew the walks around it; they had even done some mountain climbing. They were planning an excursion to the top of Mt. Salève for the 14th of September, and the night before, they parted full of anticipation. The following morning Browning and his sister waited for Miss Smith to join them for coffee on the terrace, but she did not come. Perhaps she was saving herself for the journey, Browning said to Sarianna. But as the hours passed they were alarmed and Sarianna went to Miss Smith's room. She found her lying on the floor, unconscious. By the time the doctor arrived Miss Smith was dead.

From the suddenness of this death came Browning's *La Saisiaz*, published the following year together with *The Two Poets of Croisic*. The poems form a diptych like *Christmas-Eve* and *Easter-Day*, the one on the transitoriness of human life, comforted by a faith in immortality, the other on the still briefer span of mortal fame. Browning dedicated the volume to Mrs. Sutherland Orr, Leighton's sister and his future biographer.

La Saisiaz took hold of the British public for the hopeful answer it provided to the ageless questioning of the spirit. To the critics it offered a welcome return to the Browning of *Balaustion's Adventure* and helped to dissipate the unpleasantness of *Pacchiarotto* and the earlier *Fifine at the Fair*, that cynical probing into amorality. This book lost him the friendship of Dante Gabriel Rossetti who felt himself attacked in it. Perhaps because he knew that Rossetti had grounds for feeling as he did, Browning did nothing to heal the rift. At that time, however, Rossetti had sunk too deep into an inferno of his own to think of Browning's attack as more than another flame lick of the consuming fire.

The fact was that Browning had never really liked either Pre-Raphaelite painting or pre-Raphaelite verse. He thought that the whole school was tainted with effeminacy and when, one day, he was invited to look at some of the work of the poet-painter Simeon Solomon, he broke out with, "One great picture show at the Academy, the old masters' exhibition, ought to act as a tonic to these girlish boys and boyish girls, with their heavenly bridegrooms and such like . . ." Again, "How I hate Love," he exploded, "as a lubberly naked young man putting his arms here and his wings there, about a pair of lovers,—a fellow they would kick away, in the reality!" He had just been reading Rossetti's poetry.

If Browning lost old friends, he had no lack of new ones. His address book read like an Almanach de Gotha crossed with the register of the great in all the arts. Some, like Milsand, the Storys and, until the death of the prophet, Carlyle, he cherished with an abiding affection. He also had the satisfaction of renewing his youthful friendship with Domett who returned to England.

Pen at last began to show results from his study with Heyermans and Rodin. Browning was delighted and sent out joyful bulletins of a sold canvas to his friends. They rejoiced with him. "The first sale is an unforgettable event in a young artist's life not for the money's sake but because it lifts his work at once into a new category," Leighton wrote to Browning.

The statue of Dryope held spellbound by Apollo in the form of a serpent was not so fortunate as Pen's canvas, however. The lifesize figure, which cost a thousand pounds to cast in bronze, was found too coarse for the taste of the Royal Academicians who, in spite of Leighton's pleas, would not accept it. Browning was indignant. How could the Academy be so blind? He pulled every string to have the statue shown, but Dryope remained in the studio. Not long since, Sir Coutts Lindsay had founded the more liberal Grosvenor Gallery. Browning applied to the director on behalf of his son's work. The man could not withstand the tears rolling down the poet's cheeks. The statue was exhibited, but Dryope found no buyer, either then or later.

As time wrought its changes on the poet, Pen chose to record them in paint and marble. One of his best portraits shows Browning in his Oxford gown, seated in a carved chair, holding in his hands the "square old yellow book." Browning presented the painting to Oxford which had bestowed so many honors upon him. Jowett received it in March of 1886 and wrote to thank Browning. "I think it is a noble work which has an additional interest because it is painted by [your son]. He has made you a trifle too stern and serious but this, if it be an error, is on the right side . . . We have been lately promised a portrait of Southey who is an old member of the college. I hope that you will not mislike his company,"[3] Jowett added, remembering, perhaps, that before entering the sacred precincts of Balliol Southey had been marked with the revolutionary stigma, like Coleridge and Wordsworth. But time can bring about extraordinary changes in the malleable stuff of character.

Now and then Pen managed to sell a painting, an event which Browning would always signalize by broadcasting the news. It was with undisguised relief that he finally announced the marriage of his son in October of 1887, to the rich Miss Fannie Coddington of New York. Pen was thirty-eight years old, but still dependent on his father, as is all too evident in the letter Browning had sent him after the engagement. "Miss Coddington has spoken to me with the greatest frankness and generosity of the means she will have of contributing to your support—for my part, I can engage to give you £300 a year: this, with the results of your work—if you can manage to sell but a single picture in the year—will amply suffice. Of course, at my death you will have whatever I possess: and meantime if any good fortune comes to me—well, it will be, as it has ever been, your good fortune also."

That year, perhaps because of Pen's marriage, Browning left Warwick Crescent for his last London home at 29 De Vere Gardens. But the traveler did not allow himself to sink deep roots there. His books were very much in demand, a fact which pleased him although in later years he was fond of saying, half in jest, that it was all due to Furnivall's Browning Society, kept up with the religiousness of a church. Certainly the little volume, *Jocoseria*, whose curious poems derived from such divergent sources as Talmudic lore and the hopeless love of Mary Wollstonecraft for Fuseli, astonished both him and the publisher by an unprecedented sale. *Ferishtah's Fancies*, next

[3] Holograph letter. Baylor Browning Collection.

year, did equally well. Royalties were also coming in from earlier editions.

He was disappointed, however, by the reception of *Parleyings with Certain People of Importance in their Day* with which he had heralded the year of Pen's marriage. But it was not entirely the public's fault. The characters with whom he parleyed in his verses were for the most part strangers to his contemporaries, however much Gerald de Lairesse, Daniel Bartoli, Francis Furini and the rest had contributed to Browning's intellectual development. If, in his old age, he was writing autobiography in verse, he was the only one who knew it. The critics certainly did not. They reviewed the book as if it were the utterance of the Sphinx, but unlike Oedipus, they remained perplexed.

Just as he harked back to the intellectual influences of his youth, Browning yearned again for the places that had touched his imagination on his Italian journeys. Florence, too closely associated with the heart of his life, he kept as a sanctuary in his memory, but he and Sarianna were often the guests of Mrs. Arthur Bronson in Venice. An American woman of wealth, charm, and a talent for writing deft little comedies, Mrs. Bronson had established herself with her young daughter Edith in the Casa Alvisi, on the Grand Canal. But though Browning enjoyed the palace life and his roamings with Edith through the Venetian calles, he loved best to stay at La Mura, Mrs. Bronson's villa at Asolo. It was exactly the sort of place to appeal to him—a lofty eyrie, half built into one of the towers of Asolo's ancient walls, with one side completely open to the landscape and the sky.

Soon after his marriage Pen talked of having a house in Venice. Browning looked about for one to buy and had settled upon a palace that he liked. While negotiating for it, he was amazed and a trifle discomfited to learn that Pen had bought the Palazzo Rezzonico. The vast eighteenth century marble edifice was one of the grandest in Venice, though not one of the most beautiful. The façade with its rococo ornaments, arches, columns and balustrades cut up the surfaces too much for beauty. It had magnificence and a square solidity, however, and it could not have occupied a better site on the Grand Canal. Pen set to work having the necessary repairs made in the interior before inviting his father and his aunt to visit in the fall of 1889.

It had been a busy year for Browning. In March he had begun to revise for the press another collected edition of his works. He was

also planning a new volume to follow *Parleyings*. The rereading of
his past work revived many an association of joy and pain. His son's
marriage made those associations more poignant still. Perhaps it was
at this time that he wrote the most touching stanzas in *Asolando* referring to his love and his loss:

> Others may need new life in Heaven—
> 　Man, Nature, Art—made new, assume!
> Man with new mind old sense to leaven,
> 　Nature,—new light to clear old gloom,
> Art that breaks bounds, gets soaring-room.
>
> I shall pray: "Fugitive as precious—
> 　Minutes which passed,—return, remain!
> Let earth's old life once more enmesh us,
> 　You with old pleasure, me—old pain,
> So we but meet nor part again!"

Considering the abiding presence in Browning's life and thoughts,
one can understand the distress with which one day in July, while he
was turning over the pages of the *New Letters of Edward FitzGerald*
at his club, he came upon the words: "Mrs. Browning's death is
rather a relief to me, I must say. No more Aurora Leighs, thank God!
A woman of real genius, I know; but what is the upshot of it all? She
and her sex had better mind the kitchen and the children; and perhaps the poor. Except in such things as little novels, they only devote
themselves to what men do much better. . . ."

In the reading, Browning was blinded to everything in FitzGerald's
misogynistic diatribe except the opening words where the great tragedy of his life was spoken of as "rather a relief" to the writer. Browning did not care that FitzGerald had been dead for six years, nor that
his words had been penned more than a quarter of a century earlier.
They wounded as if they had been spoken within his hearing at the
peak of his grief.

In pain and anger he dashed off a sonnet and sent it at once to the
Athenaeum. His misquoting of FitzGerald clearly revealed what had
most pained him—

> That you, FitzGerald, whom by ear and eye
> 　She never knew, "thanked God my wife was dead."
> Ay, dead! and were yourself alive, good Fitz,
> How to return you thanks would task my wits:
> 　Kicking you seems the common lot of curs—

While more appropriate greeting lends you grace:
Surely to spit there glorifies your face—
   Spitting—from lips once sanctified by Hers.

Browning regretted his haste in making his hurt public, but the telegram he sent to Norman Mac Coll of the *Athenaeum* was so delayed—some say intentionally by the editor himself—that he did not succeed in stopping publication. The sonnet appeared over Browning's signature in the issue of the 13th of July, starting off a wave of feeling for and against him. He defended his action in innumerable letters but nothing he could say or do made the hurt less painful.

His health was affected. When Pen and his wife invited him to the Rezzonico, Browning's response on the 16th of August had little of the old cheeriness. He spoke of having benefited by a rest of three weeks from dining out, quoted a very friendly letter he had received from Tennyson and then reverted to the subject that still preyed upon his mind: "I want you to know that Tennyson is not the man to sympathize with a poor creature like FitzGerald, whom I punished no more than he deserved—heartily wishing he were alive in the body —not, for the first time, alive in his words. . . ."

Sarianna's note in the same letter betrays her concern. "You need not be told I am glad your papa resolves on Asolo and Venice . . . I wish he would start at once before waiting till he falls ill. . . ."

They went to Asolo in September while the Rezzonico was still undergoing repairs, and stayed at La Mura with Mrs. Bronson. In the congenial atmosphere of the picturesque little town Browning's impulse to work returned and under Mrs. Bronson's roof he put together the poems for his next volume, adding a number of new lyrics. Next month he sent the finished manuscript to his publisher. He called the volume *Asolando*, borrowing the title from Cardinal Bembo's invented verb, *asolare*, "to disport in the open air." It was, however, his tribute to Pippa's town which he was seriously thinking of making his own. High up on its crowning point, like a watchtower commanding the surrounding view, the townsfolk had begun to build a schoolhouse, then abandoned it. This shell of four stone walls it was that the aged snake, alone now, chose for his Illyrian hibernation. Before Pen came to conduct him to the refurbished Rezzonico on the last day of October, Browning had entered his bid with the township for the purchase of the abandoned school.

There were guests at the Rezzonico when Browning and Sarianna arrived, among them a young Scotchwoman, Miss Evelyn Barclay.

Mr. G. D. Giles, whom she later married, had gone with Pen to fetch the poet. Miss Barclay was still young enough for hero worship and from the moment of Browning's arrival kept a sort of irregular diary.[4] She remarked that he was in great spirits, delighting in the palace and everything in it, and complimenting Pen at every turn with a marveling: "I never thought it was in him." She also noted that he seemed to feel the long stairs which made him very breathless.

This did not keep him from his usual active life. For the first few days he spent his mornings at the Lido and the afternoons with Mrs. Bronson who had left Asolo for Casa Alvisi. But soon all Venice came to call on him at the Rezzonico—Sir Henry and Lady Layard, his old friends the Ralph Curtises, the Cornell professor on Sabbatical leave, Dr. Hiram Corson, one of the best explicators of Browning's poetry, Miss Eden, Count Moncenigo, Princess Montenegro, Miss Montalba, M. Michele, a French artist, and Mr. Allan, a young Greek student. He had time for all and delighted in all.

He had been given a grand sala for himself but he preferred to sit in the Pope's Chamber, a little sitting room where Jacko the parrot had his perch. Perhaps the bird reminded him of Bob, his pet owl in London that used to nestle in the crook of his arm while he fed it bits of meat and read at the same time from the open book on the table before him. Miss Barclay was amused at his affection for "the beast" to which he would take fruit and cake from every meal.

The poet spent the early mornings working and reading. He had proofs to correct and his eager mind had to be nurtured. One afternoon—the 19th of November—he gave an informal reading of the *Asolando* poems at the Curtises' before a large gathering.

"He began to read at 4.30," wrote Miss Barclay, "and read standing with one short interval till 6.30. He began with the short poems in the beginning of the volume which were very light, he said, as people accused him of being obscure."

He had read about half the volume, judging by the poems Miss Barclay notes, and then—the inevitable happened as always, alas, when people are exposed to a long session of poetry, even if read by a Browning. They began to leave. Browning then turned to Mr. Allan, the Greek student, and said, "By the way, I will read you this and see if any of you will guess my meaning." What poem it was Miss Barclay does not say. But she is specific about the outcome. "Everyone had to confess they had not caught it."

[4] Presented by her to Dr. A. J. Armstrong in 1932 and now in the Baylor Browning Collection.

On an earlier evening Browning had been reading aloud from the proofs for Sarianna and his daughter-in-law when he came to the third stanza of "Epilogue," that strangely premonitory poem:

> One who never turned his back but marched breast forward,
>   Never doubted clouds would break,
> Never dreamed, though right were worsted, wrong would
>   triumph,
> Held we fall to rise, are baffled to fight better,
>   Sleep to wake.

"It almost looks like bragging to say this," he interrupted himself, "and as if I ought to cancel it. But it's the simple truth," his honesty assured him, "and as it's truth, it shall stand."[5]

The last week in November the weather turned foggy and cold, but nothing would keep Browning from going to the Lido in the morning, sirocco or no sirocco. He began to cough much, ate very little and scarcely spoke at meals. Pen was alarmed and insisted on wrapping him up warm when he would not forego his engagements. "My dear boy, I never catch cold," Browning assured him. He would not have a doctor called and was most obstinate in his refusal. "No, they are all fools," he said. Ill as he was, he would not miss a performance of *Carmen* although when he returned from the opera that evening he was close to collapse.

In spite of his objections, Mrs. Browning had Pen call a doctor. Browning had bronchitis. "The danger would be his heart," said the doctor.

Now Browning was moved to Mrs. Browning's room, the sunniest in the palace, and had physicians and nurses in constant attendance. No more going to the Lido now, nor to the opera, not even to the court of the palace, the perfect setting for Pen's Dryope which he so much admired, nor to the little white-and-gold alcove where Pen had had the inscription reproduced that the proud people of Florence had set in the wall of Casa Guidi to tell the world: "*Qui scrisse e morì Elisabetta Barrett Browning che in cuore di donna conciliava scienza di dotta e spirito di poeta. . . .*"

Visitors still came and went, now drawn there by the news of his illness. In London the papers began carrying bulletins on his progress and an avalanche of telegrams followed. Browning at first did not seem aware of the gravity of his condition. When Mr. Giles went to say good-by to him on the 7th of December, Browning assured him that he would see him later in London. Not long since, Mr. Giles at his request had made a pencil sketch of him on a plain card. Browning wrote on it:

> Here I'm gazing, wide awake
> Robert Browning, no mistake.

"Now you have an unpublished work of mine," he said jocularly to the artist. As it was, Mr. Giles' sketch was the last made of him while he lived.[6]

On the 10th Browning had a heart attack and everyone thought it was the end. Sarianna was now constantly beside him, as well as the hospital nurse who had been sent for from Rome. After a delirious night he seemed better the following day. Pen, however, hesitated to give him the copy of *Asolando* which had arrived from England, for fear of exciting him, but on the morning of the 12th he showed it to him. "What a pretty color the binding is," he said. Then he turned to his daughter-in-law and gave her the book. Toward evening a telegram arrived from George Murray Smith to inform the poet that the first edition of *Asolando* was nearly exhausted. Pen bent over his father and read it to him.

"More than satisfied," Browning said feebly. "I am dying . . . my dear boy . . . my dear boy."

Did he, at the news of this final triumph, think of what he had recently told Mrs. Bronson, of that son in whose face he always saw the image of his mother: "I would renounce all personal ambition and would destroy every line I ever wrote if by so doing I could see fame and honors heaped upon my Robert's head."

With the telegram from the publisher came also the decision of Asolo to sell to the poet the pile of stones that he had chosen for his final refuge. But he had no further need for earthly habitation. That night, just as the clock of San Marco was striking ten, Browning went on from life to immortality.

He was not buried in Florence beside his wife as he had always hoped. On the 14th of December another telegram arrived from Mr. Smith. "Authorized by Dean to offer burial in the Abbey—advise acceptance."

The following day, Sunday, in the presence of the English Consul and other dignitaries, the plain polished wood coffin was sealed. But not before Pen had placed a crown of laurel on his father's head. At

---

[6] The sketch is in the Baylor Browning Collection.

noon the bier was carried down to the great hall on the first floor of
the Rezzonico and covered with a mauve silk pall. The many wreaths
and flowers that had arrived were displayed around it on the ground.
Upon it lay only a coronal of bays tied with a wide white ribbon. "In
front, in the place of honor," noted the *Gazzetta di Venezia*, "the
wreath of our Municipality, of willow leaves in wrought metal and
porcelain flowers, was indeed notable."

Venice had wished to give the poet a public funeral, but since the
burial was not to be in Italy, it honored the dead by a solemn cortege
to the Cemetery of San Michele. A brief service was read by an English clergyman over the body, and then it was conveyed out of the
palace to the waiting barge, funereally majestic in black and gold, with
its gondoliers also in gold and black velvet. Between the carved angel
of the prow and the lion at the stern, the bier was laid amid flowers
under the canopy, and then the barge was taken in tow by a launch.
Along the lagoon the funeral boat wound in the light and reflections
of a setting sun, to the chapel on the island of Murano.

Two days later Browning's body started on its last voyage home.
But Italy also claimed him. On the walls of the palace where he died,
Venice inscribed his verses attesting his love of the Italy he had seen
come to birth. But Florence it was that held his heart, even though
all that remained of his mortal self was entombed among England's
great dead on the final day of the year.

Acknowledgments

No book ever springs full-panoplied like Minerva from the brow of Jove. Even works of the rarest imagination owe their being to the sum of their authors' experience. It is with a sense of the deepest gratitude, therefore, that I wish to express my thanks to those who have made this book possible. First of all, to Dr. A. Joseph Armstrong of Baylor University I am deeply obliged for his placing at my disposal the Browning Collection which is making of Waco, Texas, the Mecca of all Browning scholars. The result of decades of dedication on the part of Dr. Armstrong, the collection of Browning manuscripts, books, paintings, busts and personalia is perhaps the most important in the world today. My obligation, however, extends beyond the Collection itself to the storehouse of Dr. Armstrong's knowledge of the Brownings—a knowledge generously imparted in our talks during my stay at Waco. My thanks go also to Miss Sue Moore, custodian of the Browning Collection, for her many kindnesses.

To my publishers, Harper & Brothers, I am indebted for their permission to quote freely from *The Letters of Robert Browning and Elizabeth Barrett Barrett, 1845-1846.* For similar generosity I am beholden to the Macmillan Company for quotations from *The Letters of Elizabeth Barrett Browning,* edited by Frederick G. Kenyon; to John Murray of London for the use of *Letters of Elizabeth Barrett Browning to her Sister,* edited by Leonard Huxley, and for quotations from the letters *From Browning and Elizabeth Browning,* edited by William Rose Benét; to the Yale University Press and to Dr. Thurman L. Hood for extracts from *Letters of Robert Browning,* collected by Thomas J. Wise; to Stokes and Company and my old friend Richard Curle for permission to quote from *Robert Browning and Julia Wedgwood: a Broken Friendship as Revealed by their Letters;* to Chapman and Hall of London for quotations from *The Diaries of William Charles Macready,* edited by William Toynbee, and, finally, to Moffatt and Yard for several extracts from *Harriet Hosmer, Letters and Memories,* edited by Cornelia Carr.

My indebtedness would be incomplete without mention of the unfailing help and courtesy of the attendants at the New York Public Library, the Morgan Library and the British Museum whenever it has been my good fortune to avail myself of their rich stores.

Bibliography

ABBOTT, EVELYN and LEWIS CAMPBELL. *Life and Letters of Benjamin Jowett*. London, 1897.

AGRESTI, ALBERTO. "Il pensiero sociale nella poesia di Roberto Browning." *Nuova Antologia*. Rome, November, 1911.

ALLINGHAM, WILLIAM. *A Diary*. Edited by H. Allingham and D. Radford. London, 1907.

ARMSTRONG, A. JOSEPH. *Browning the World Over—A Bibliography of Foreign Browningiana*. Baylor University, Waco, Texas, 1933.

———. *Browning's Testament of Hope*. Waco, Texas, 1935.

——— (editor). *Letters of Robert Browning to Miss Isa Blagden*. Waco, Texas, 1923.

———. *Robert Browning through French Eyes*. Waco, Texas, 1932.

AUSTIN, ALFRED. *The Poetry of the Period*. London, 1870.

BARCLAY, EVELYN. *Diary*. Baylor University, Waco, Texas. No date.

Baylor's Old Yellow Manuscripts. Translated from the original Italian by Dr. Beatrice Corrigan, with an introductory essay by William O. Raymond. Baylor University, Waco, Texas, 1941.

BAYNES, DOROTHY JULIA (Dormer Creston). *Andromeda in Wimpole Street*. New York, 1930.

BENEDETTI, ANNA. "Impressioni d'Italia nella poesia di Roberto Browning." *Nuova Antologia*. Rome, October, 1930.

BENÉT, WILLIAM ROSE (editor). *From Browning and Elizabeth Browning*. London, 1936.

BERDOE, EDWARD. *The Browning Cyclopaedia*. London and New York, 1892.

BERGER, PIERRE. *Robert Browning*. Paris, 1912.

BERLIN-LIEBERMAN, JUDITH. *Robert Browning and Hebraism*. Jerusalem, 1934.

BESIER, RUDOLF. *The Barretts of Wimpole Street*. Boston, 1931.

BLAGDEN, ISA. *Poems*. Posthumously published, with a memoir by Alfred Austin. Edinburgh, 1873.

———. *The Cost of a Secret*. Three volumes. London, 1863.

———. *The Woman I loved and the Woman Who loved Me*. Tauchnitz: Collection of British authors, 1872.

BLANC, LOUIS. *History of Ten Years*. Two volumes. London, 1844-1845.

BOAS, LOUISE SCHUTZ. *Elizabeth Barrett Browning.* London and New York, 1930.

Boston Browning Society Papers, 1886-1897. New York, 1897.

BREWER, LUTHER A. (editor) *Some Lamb and Browning Letters to Leigh Hunt.* Privately printed, Cedar Rapids, Iowa, 1924.

BROCHER, HENRI. *La Jeunesse de Browning et le Poème de Sordello.* Genève, 1930.

BRONSON, KATHERINE. "Browning in Asolo." *Century Magazine.* Volume 29, 1900.

BROOKS, A. E. *Browningiana in Baylor University.* Waco, Texas, 1921.

BROWNING, ELIZABETH BARRETT. *Essays on the Greek Christian Poets and the English Poets.* New York, 1863.

———. *Hitherto Unpublished Poems and Stories.* Bibliophile Society. Two volumes. Boston, 1914.

———. *Last Poems.* London, 1862.

———. *Letters addressed to Richard Hengist Horne.* Edited by S. R. Townshend Mayer. Two volumes. London, 1877.

———. *Letters from Elizabeth Barrett to B. R. Haydon.* Edited by Martha Hale Shackford. New York and London, 1939.

———. *Letters of Elizabeth Barrett Browning.* Edited by Frederic G. Kenyon. Two volumes. London, 1897.

———. *Letters to her Sister, 1846-1859.* Edited by Leonard Huxley. London, 1929.

———. *Poetical Works.* Eight volumes. London, 1906.

———. *The Poets' Enchiridion; a hitherto Unpublished Poem.* Bibliophile Society. Boston, 1914.

———. *Psyche Apocalypté, a Lyrical Drama projected by Elizabeth Barrett and R. H. Horne.* London, 1876.

———. *Stanzas, a Fragment, March 1845.* Stanford University, California, 1943.

———. *Twenty-two Unpublished Letters by E. B. Browning and Robert Browning.* The United Features Syndicate, New York, 1935.

BROWNING, MRS. FANNIE BARRETT. *Some Memories of Robert Browning.* Boston, 1928.

BROWNING, ROBERT. *Complete Poetical Works, with additional Poems first published in 1914.* Fifteen volumes. New York, 1937.

———. "Correspondence between Carlyle and Browning." *Cornhill Magazine.* Number 227. London, 1915.

———. "Deux lettres inédites de Robert Browning à Joseph Milsand." *Revue Germanique.* Année 12, Paris, 1921.

———. *Letters of Robert Browning, collected by Thomas J. Wise.* Edited with introduction and notes by Thurman L. Hood. Yale University Press, New Haven, 1933.

————. Works of Robert Browning. Edited by F. G. Kenyon. (Centenary Edition.) Ten volumes. London, 1912.

———— and ELIZABETH BARRETT. *Letters of Robert Browning and Elizabeth Barrett, 1845-1846*. Two volumes. New York and London, 1898.

BROWNING, R. WIEDEMANN BARRETT. *The Browning Collections*. Catalogue. J. Tregaskis, London, 1913.

Browning Society's Papers. London, 1881-1891.

BURDETT, OSBERT. *The Brownings*. London, 1928.

BURTON, JEAN. *Heyday of a Wizard, Daniel Home*. New York, 1944.

CARLYLE, THOMAS. *Letters of Thomas Carlyle to Mill, Sterling and Browning*. Edited by Alexander Carlyle. London, 1923.

CARR, CORNELIA (editor). *Harriet Hosmer, Letters and Memories*. New York, 1912.

CARY, ELIZABETH L. *Browning, Poet and Man*. New York and London, 1899.

CHARLTON, H. B. "Browning's Ethical Poetry." *John Ryland's Library*. Volume 27, Manchester, 1942.

CHESTERTON, G. K. *Robert Browning*. (English Men of Letters.) London, 1904.

CHUBB, EDWIN W. *Masters of English Literature*. Chicago, 1917.

CLARKE, ISABEL C. *Elizabeth Barrett Browning: a Portrait*. London, 1929.

COHEN, MARY M. "Browning's Hebraic Sympathies." *Poet-Lore*. Volume 3. Philadelphia, 1891.

CORSON, HIRAM. *An Introduction to the Study of Robert Browning's Poetry*. Third edition. Boston, 1898.

CRAMER, MAURICE M. "Browning's Friendships and Fame before Marriage." *Publications of the Modern Language Association*. Volume 55. Menasha, 1940.

CROSS, J. W. (editor). *George Eliot's Life as related in her Letters and Journal*. New York, 1884.

CUNLIFFE, JOHN W. "Elizabeth Barrett's Influence on Browning's Poetry." *Publications of the Modern Language Association*. Volume 23. Cambridge, 1908.

CURLE, RICHARD (editor). *Robert Browning and Julia Wedgwood; a Broken Friendship as Revealed by their Letters*. New York, 1937.

DARMESTETER, MARY J. "Ménage de Poètes." *Revue de Paris*. Volume 5. Paris, 1899.

DE VANE, WILLIAM C. *A Browning Handbook*. New York, 1935.

————. *Browning's Parleyings: the Autobiography of a Mind*. Yale University Press, New Haven, 1927.

————. "The Harlot and the Thoughtful Young Man." *Studies in Philology*. Volume 29. University of North Carolina, Chapel Hill, 1932.

————. "Sordello's Story Retold." *Studies in Philology*. Volume 27. University of North Carolina, Chapel Hill, 1930.

DICKSON, ARTHUR. "Browning's Source for 'The Pied Piper of Hamelin.'" *Studies in Philology*. Volume 23. University of North Carolina, Chapel Hill, 1926.

DOBELL, BERTRAM. *Browning Memorials*. Catalogue. London, 1913.

————. "The Earliest Poems of Robert Browning." *Cornhill Magazine*. Volume 36. London, 1914.

DOMINIQUE, I. "Le Poète Browning à Sainte-Marie de Pornic." *Revue de Bretagne de Vendée et d'Anjou*. Volume 22. Paris, 1899.

DOWDEN, EDWARD. *Robert Browning*. London and New York, 1904.

————. *Transcripts and Studies*. London, 1896.

DRINKWATER, JOHN. "Some Letters from Matthew Arnold to Robert Browning." *Cornhill Magazine*. Volume 55. London, 1923.

DUCKWORTH, FRANCIS R. G. *Browning: Background and Conflict*. New York and London, 1931.

DUFF, DAVID. *An Exposition of Browning's "Sordello."* Edinburgh and London, 1906.

ELLIOTT, G. R. "Browning's Whitmanism." *Sewanee Review*. Volume 37. Sewanee, Tennessee, 1929.

EMERSON, R. W., W. H. CHANNING and J. F. CLARKE. *Memoirs of Margaret Fuller Ossoli*. Two volumes. 1852.

FIGGIS, DARRELL. *Studies and Appreciations*. London, 1912.

FISCHER, CHARLES. "The Idea of Evolution in Browning's Poetry." *Temple Bar*. Volume 118. London, 1899.

FORSTER, JOHN. *Walter Savage Landor; a Biography*. London, 1876.

FROUDE, J. A. *Thomas Carlyle: a History of his Life in London*. Two volumes. New York, 1904.

FURNIVALL, F. J. *A Bibliography of Robert Browning from 1833 to 1881*. Browning Society's Papers. No. 2. London.

————. *How the Browning Society came into Being*. London, 1884.

GAYLORD, HARRIET. *Pompilia and her Poet*. New York, 1931.

GIRAUDEAU, FERNAND. *Napoléon III intime*. Paris, 1895.

GOODRICH, FREER A. "Robert Browning the Musician." *Nineteenth Century*. Volume 49. London, 1901.

GOSSE, E. W. *Robert Browning; Personalia*. Boston, 1890.

GRIFFIN, W. HALL. "Early Friends of Robert Browning." *Contemporary Review*. Volume 87. London, 1905.

————. *Life of Robert Browning*. Completed and edited by Harry Christopher Minchin. London, 1910.

HARROD, HAZEL. *Correspondence of Harriet Beecher Stowe and Elizabeth Barrett Browning*. Texas University Studies in English. Austin, June, 1948.

HAWTHORNE, JULIAN. *Hawthorne and his Circle.* New York and London, 1903.

HAWTHORNE, NATHANIEL. *English Notebooks.* London, 1841.

———. *Passages from his French and Italian Notebooks.* Two volumes. Boston, 1871.

HEARN, LAFCADIO. *Pre-Raphaelite and other Poets.* New York, 1922.

HERFORD, C. H. *Robert Browning.* New York, 1905.

HEWLETT, HENRY G. (compiler and editor). *Autobiography, Memoir and Letters of Henry F. Chorley.* Two volumes. London, 1873.

HODELL, CHARLES W. "A Literary Mosaic." *Publications of the Modern Language Association.* Volume 23. Cambridge, 1908.

——— (editor and translator). *The Old Yellow Book.* Carnegie Institute, Washington, 1908.

HOLMES, STEWART W. "The Sources of Browning's Sordello." *Studies in Philology.* Volume 34, University of North Carolina, Baltimore, 1937.

HOME, DANIEL DUNGLASS. *Incidents in my Life.* Series 1-2. New York, 1872.

———. *Lights and Shadows of Spiritualism.* New York, 1879.

HOOD, THURMAN L. "Browning and Lady Ashburton." *Yale Review.* Volume 22, New Haven, 1932.

HORNE, R. H. *The New Spirit of the Age.* London, 1844.

HOVELAQUE, HENRI LÉON. *La Jeunesse de Robert Browning.* Paris, 1932.

HUNT, LEIGH. *Correspondence.* Edited by Thornton Leigh Hunt. Two volumes. London, 1862.

HUXLEY, LEONARD (editor). "A Visitor to the Brownings." *Yale Review.* Volume 13. New Haven, 1924.

INGRAM, J. H. *Edgar Allan Poe: his life, Letters and Opinions.* London, 1880.

———. *Elizabeth Barrett Browning.* Boston, 1893.

JAMES, HENRY. "Browning in Venice . . . recollections of the late Katherine de Kay Bronson." *Cornhill Magazine.* Volume 12. London, 1902.

———. *Essays in London and Elsewhere.* New York, 1893.

———. "The Novel in *The Ring and the Book.*" *Quarterly Review.* Volume 217. London, 1912.

———. *Views and Reviews.* Boston, 1908.

———. *William Wetmore Story and his Friends.* Two volumes. Boston, 1904.

KENYON, SIR F. G. (editor). *New Poems by Robert Browning and Elizabeth Barrett Browning.* London, 1914.

——— (editor). *Robert Browning and Alfred Domett.* (Letters.) New York, 1906.

KESSEL, ELIZABETH. *Elizabeth Barrett Browning: die Geschichte einer grossen Liebe*. Berlin, 1939.

KING, BOLTON. *A History of Italian Unity*. Two volumes. London, 1912.

KING, ROMA A. *Robert Browning's Finances from his own Account Book*. Edited by A. J. Armstrong. Baylor University, Waco, Texas, 1947.

KINGSLAND, WILLIAM G. *Robert Browning, Chief Poet of the Age*. London, 1887.

KOEPPEL, EMIL. *Robert Browning*. (Literarhistorische Forschungen.) Berlin, 1911.

L'ESTRANGE, REV. A. G. *The Life of Mary Russell Mitford . . . Revealed in a Selection from her Letters to her Friends*. London, 1870.

LOCKWOOD, FRANCIS C. *Robert Browning*. Cincinnati, 1906.

LOLIÉE, FRÉDÉRIC. *Le Duc de Morny et la Société du Second Empire*. Paris, 1909.

LOTH, DAVID G. *The Brownings; a Victorian Idyll*. New York, 1929.

LOUNSBURY, THOMAS R. *The Early Literary Career of Robert Browning*. Barbour-Page Foundation Lectures. University of Virginia. New York, 1911.

LYTTON, EDWARD. *Letters from Owen Meredith to Robert and Elizabeth Barrett Browning*. Edited by Aurelia Brooks Harlan and J. Lee Harlan, Jr. Baylor University, Waco, Texas, 1937.

MARKS, JEANNETTE A. *The Family of the Barretts, a Colonial Romance*. New York, 1938.

MARRARO, HOWARD E. *American Opinion of the Unification of Italy*. Columbia University Press. New York, 1932.

MERLETTE, GERMAINE M. *Le Vive et l'Oeuvre d'Elizabeth Barrett Browning*. Paris, 1905.

MILSAND, JOSEPH. "Robert Browning." *Revue des Deux Mondes*. Volume 11. Paris, August 15, 1851.

————. "Elizabeth Browning, J. E. Reade et Henri Taylor." *Revue des Deux Mondes*. Volume 13. January, 1852.

MINCHIN, H. C. *Walter Savage Landor; last Days, Letters and Conversations*. London, 1934.

MOLMENTI, POMPEO. "Elisabetta Barrett Browning." *Nuova Antologia*. Volume 157. Rome, 1898.

MONTI, GIULIO. "Elisabetta Barrett Browning." *Emporium*. May, 1896.

NETTLESHIP, JOHN T. *Essays on Robert Browning's Poetry*. London, 1868.

NEW YORK BROWNING SOCIETY. *Addresses Commemorating the Birth of Robert Browning*. New York, 1912.

ORR, MRS. SUTHERLAND. *Life and Letters of Robert Browning*. London, 1891. Also a new and revised edition, in part rewritten by F. G. Kenyon. Boston and New York, 1908.

Ossoli, Margaret Fuller. *Art, Literature and the Drama*. Edited by Arthur B. Fuller. Boston, 1860.

Palmer, G. H. "The Monologue of Browning." *Harvard Theological Review*. April, 1918.

Paxeco, Elza. "Camoëns e Elizabeth Barrett." *Revista Faculdade de Letras*. Lisbon Universidade. Volume 9. Lisbon, 1943.

Pellegrini, Lino. "Robert Browning a Venezia e ad Asolo." *Ateneo Veneto*. Venice, February, 1938.

Phelps, William Lyon. "Browning and Alfred Austin." *Yale Review*. April, 1918.

——. "Notes on Browning's *Pauline*." *Modern Language Notes*. Volume 47. Baltimore, 1932.

——. "Notes on *The Ring and the Book*." *Yale Review*. Volume 18. Brattleboro, 1928.

——. *Robert Browning*. Indianapolis, 1932.

——. "Robert Browning on Spiritualism." *Yale Review*. Volume 23. 1933.

Pottle, Frederick A. *Shelley and Browning: a Myth and some Facts*. Chicago, 1923.

Raymond, W. O. "Browning and Higher Criticism." *Publications of the Modern Language Association*. June, 1929.

——. *Browning's Roman Murder Story as recorded in a hitherto unknown Italian contemporary Manuscript*. Baylor University, Waco, Texas, 1939.

——. "Our Lady of Bellosguardo: a pastel Portrait." *University of Toronto Quarterly*. Volume 12. Toronto, 1943.

Rebora, Piero. "Robert Browning nel Cinquantenario della Morte." *Studi Inglesi. Bollettino dell'Istituto britannico di Firenze*. Florence, 1939.

Renton, Richard. *John Forster and his Friendships*. London, 1912.

Reul, Paul De. *L'Art et la Pensée de Robert Browning*. Bruxelles, 1929.

Rhys, Ernest. *Frederic Lord Leighton*. London, 1898.

Ritchie, Anne Isabella Thackeray. *Records of Tennyson, Ruskin, Browning*. New York, 1892.

Rossetti, Dante Gabriel. *His Family Letters, with a Memoir*. Edited by William Michael Rossetti. Two volumes. Boston, 1895.

Rossetti, William Michael (editor). *Pre-Raphaelite Diaries and Letters, 1835-1853*. London, 1900.

——. *Ruskin: Rossetti: Pre-Raphaelitism*. New York, 1899.

Russell, Mrs. F. T. *One Word More on Browning*. Stanford University, California, 1927.

Saintsbury, George. *Corrected Impressions*. New York, 1895.

Santayana, George. *Interpretations of Poetry and Religion*. New York, 1900.

SARRAZIN, GABRIEL. *La Renaissance de la Poésie Anglaise.* Paris, 1889.

SCHELLING, F. E. *Two Essays on Robert Browning.* Philadelphia, 1890.

SCHMIDT, KARL. *Robert Brownings Verhaltnis zu Frankreich.* Berlin, 1909.

SHACKFORD, MARTHA HALE. *Elizabeth Barrett Browning: R. H. Horne: Two Studies.* Wellesley, Mass., 1935 .

————. *The Brownings and Leighton.* Wellesley, Mass., 1942.

SHANKS, EDWARD. "Robert Browning." *London Mercury.* Volume 12. London, 1925.

SHARP, WILLIAM. *Life of Robert Browning.* London, 1890.

SILVESTRI-FALCONIERI FRANCESCO DI. "Robert Browning e il suo Capolavoro." *Roma Letteraria.* Volume 12. Rome, 1910.

SIM, FRANCES M. *Robert Browning: the Poet and the Man.* New York, 1923.

SMALLEY, DONALD. *Browning's Essay on Chatterton.* Cambridge, 1948.

SOMERVELL, D. C. *The Reputation of Robert Browning.* Essays and Studies by Members of the English Association. Volume 15. 1929.

STEPHEN, LESLIE. "Browning's Casuistry." *Eclectic Magazine.* Volume 140. Boston, 1903.

STORY, WILLIAM WETMORE. *Conversations in a Studio.* Two volumes. Boston and New York, 1890.

————. *Roba di Roma.* Two volumes. London, 1864.

————. *The American Question.* London, 1862.

SWISHER, WALTER S. "A Psychoanalysis of Browning's Pauline." *Psychoanalytic Review.* Volume 7. Lancaster, Pa., 1920.

SYMONS, ARTHUR. *An Introduction to the Study of Browning.* London, 1890.

THOMAS, W. "Deux Lettres inédites de Robert Browning à Joseph Milsand." *Revue Germanique.* July and September, 1921.

THOMPSON, ELBERT. "The Interest of English Poets in Italian Freedom." *Philological Quarterly.* July, 1924.

THOMSON, JAMES. *Biographical and Critical Studies.* London, 1896.

TISDEL, FREDERICK. "Balaustion's Adventure as an Interpretation of the Alcestis of Euripides." *Publications of the Modern Language Association.* Volume 25. Boston, 1917.

TOYNBEE, WILLIAM. *The Diaries of William Charles Macready.* London, 1912.

TRIGGS, OSCAR LOVELL. *Browning and Whitman: a Study in Democracy.* London, 1893.

VIEL-CASTEL, COMTE HORACE DE. *Mémoires sur le Règne de Napoléon III.* Three volumes. Paris, 1883.

WATKIN, RALPH G. *Robert Browning and the English Pre-Raphaelites.* Breslau, 1905.

WAUGH, A. *Robert Browning.* Boston, 1900.

WENGER, CHRISTIAN N. *The Aesthetics of Robert Browning.* Ann Arbor, Michigan, 1924.

WHITE, H. "The Theology of Robert Browning." *Poet-Lore.* Volume 4. Boston, 1900.

WHITING, LILIAN. *The Brownings: Their Life and Art.* Boston, 1911.

WINWAR, FRANCES. *Poor Splendid Wings: the Rossettis and their Circle.* Boston, 1933.

————. *The Life of the Heart: George Sand and her Times.* New York, 1945.

WISE, THOMAS J. *A Bibliography of the Writings in Prose and Verse of Elizabeth Barrett Browning.* London, 1918.

————. *A Browning Library: a Catalogue of Printed Books, Manuscripts etc. of Robert Browning and Elizabeth Barrett Browning.* London, 1929.

WOOLF, VIRGINIA. *Flush: a Biography.* New York, 1933.

WRIGHT, ALDIS (editor). *Life and Letters of Edward FitzGerald.* London, 1889.

WYNDHAM, HORACE. *Mr. Sludge, the Medium: Being the Life and Adventures of Daniel Dunglass Home.* London, 1937.

ZAMPINI-SALAZAR, FANNY. *Roberto ed Elisabetta Browning.* Naples, 1896.

INDEX